Turtle Geometry

The MIT Press Series in Artificial Intelligence

Turtle Geometry

The Computer as a Medium for Exploring Mathematics

Harold Abelson
Andrea A. diSessa

The MIT Press
Cambridge, Massachusetts
London, England

Third printing, February 1982
Second printing, September 1981

This book was set using the TEX typesetting system by Michael Sannella and printed and bound by Halliday Lithograph in the United States of America.

Library of Congress Cataloging in Publication Data

Abelson, Harold.
    Turtle geometry.
    (The MIT Press series in artificial intelligence)
    Includes index.
    1. Geometry—Study and teaching. 2. Computer-assisted instruction. I. DiSessa, Andrea, joint author.
II. Title. III. Series: MIT Press series in artificial intelligence.
QA462.A23 1981   516'.007'8   80-25620
ISBN 0-262-01063-1

85285

Contents

Series Foreword

Artificial intelligence is the study of intelligence using the ideas and methods of computation. Unfortunately, a definition of intelligence seems impossible at the moment because intelligence appears to be an amalgam of so many information-processing and information-representation abilities.

Of course psychology, philosophy, linguistics, and related disciplines offer various perspectives and methodologies for studying intelligence. For the most part, however, the theories proposed in these fields are too incomplete and too vaguely stated to be realized in computational terms. Something more is needed, even though valuable ideas, relationships, and constraints can be gleaned from traditional studies of what are, after all, impressive existence proofs that intelligence is possible.

Artificial intelligence offers a new perspective and a new methodology. Its central goal is to make computers intelligent, both to make them more useful and to understand the principles that make intelligence possible. That intelligent computers will be extremely useful is obvious. The more profound point is that artificial intelligence aims to understand intelligence using the ideas and methods of computation, thus offering a radically new and different basis for theory formation. Most of the people working in artificial intelligence believe that these theories will apply to any intelligent information processor, whether biological or solid state.

There are side effects that deserve attention, too. Any program that will successfully model even a small part of intelligence will be inherently massive and complex. Consequently, artificial intelligence continually confronts the limits of computer technology. The problems encountered have been hard enough and interesting enough to seduce artificial intelligence people into working on them with enthusiasm. It is natural, then, that there has been a steady flow of ideas from artificial intelligence to computer science, and the flow shows no signs of abating.

The purpose of this MIT Press Series in Artificial Intelligence is to provide people in many areas, both professionals and students, with timely, detailed information about what is happening on the frontiers in research centers all over the world.

Patrick Henry Winston
Mike Brady

Preface

> Some mathematician, I believe, has said that true
> pleasure lies not in the discovery of truth, but in
> the search for it.
>
> Tolstoy, *Anna Karenina*

Five centuries ago the printing press sparked a radical reshaping of
the nature of education. By bringing a master's words to those who
could not hear a master's voice, the technology of printing dissolved
the notion that education must be reserved for those with the means
to hire personal tutors. Today we are approaching a new technological
revolution, one whose impact on education may be as far-reaching as
that of the printing press: the emergence of powerful computers that
are sufficiently inexpensive to be used by students for learning, play,
and exploration. It is our hope that these powerful but simple tools for
creating and exploring richly interactive environments will dissolve the
barriers to the production of knowledge as the printing press dissolved
barriers to its transmission.

This hope is more than our wish for students to experience the joy of
discovery and the give and take between investigator and investigation
that typifies scientific research. Like Piaget, Dewey, and Montessori, we
are convinced that personal involvement and agency are essential to truly
effective education. Yet much of almost any mathematics curriculum is
devoted to practicing rote algorithms and rehashing ancient theorems.
It is the rare student who gets the chance to approach mathematics
by doing it rather than only learning about it, by investigating new
phenomena, by formulating original hypotheses, or by proving original
theorems. Computation—especially the activity of programing—can
offer many opportunities for students to engage in such activities without
first having to master a formidable apparatus. We hope to demonstrate
how a computational approach can change the relation between the
students and the mathematical knowledge.

Experience is an important ingredient in discovery. The abundance
of the phenomena students can investigate on their own with the aid
of computer models shows that computers can foster a style of education where "learning through discovery" becomes more than just a well-
intentioned phrase. Computers can bring to learning the essential element of surprise, for despite the popular belief that a computer can
never surprise its programer since it does only what it was programed to

do, even very simple algorithms can and often do produce unexpected and striking results. Encountering one of these results, studying it, and understanding how it comes about can be an open-ended adventure very different from most of the "discovery methods" in teaching, in which the teacher knows beforehand precisely what is supposed to be "discovered."

This book is a computer-based introduction to geometry and advanced mathematics at the high school or undergraduate level. Besides altering the form of a student's encounter with mathematics, we wish to emphasize the role of computation in changing the nature of the content that is taught under the rubric of mathematics. We wish to demonstrate a curriculum that shows the computational influence in its choice of ideas as well as in its choice of activities. Some of the major themes of the book illustrate the point: representation, local-global dichotomy, linearity, state and state-change operators. Most important in this endeavor is the expression of mathematical concepts in terms of constructive, process-oriented formulations, which can often be more assimilable and more in tune with intuitive modes of thought than the axiomatic-deductive formalisms in which these concepts are usually couched. As a consequence we are able to help students attain a working knowledge of concepts such as topological invariance and intrinsic curvature, which are usually reserved for much more advanced courses.

Chapter 1 shows how to regard plane-geometric figures not as static entities but as tracings made on a display screen by a computer-controlled "turtle" whose movements can be described by suitable computer programs. Even very simple programs produce geometric designs whose surprising symmetry and regularity provoke investigations in geometry and number theory. Chapter 2 illustrates how endowing the turtle with senses of "sight" and "smell" or modeling patterns of growth in shells and trees can serve as a springboard for forays into mathematical biology. Chapter 3 compares turtle methods and coordinate methods for drawing on the display screen, both for two-dimensional figures and for three-dimensional figures shown in perspective. This not only explains how to implement turtle graphics using traditional programing languages, but also illustrates the clarifying power of linearity and vector representations. Chapter 4 discusses the topology of curves in the plane and applies topological principles to the design of an algorithm that enables the turtle to escape from any maze.

Chapter 5 frees the turtle from confinement to the flat plane and presents a turtle's-eye view of the geometry of curved surfaces. This perspective is applied in chapters 6, 7, and 8, where extending the two-dimensional computer display to simulate drawing on the surface of a cube, a sphere, and beyond highlights the importance of some of the central ideas in modern mathematics: linearity, symmetry groups, and invariance. As a bonus these surfaces disclose rich new worlds of "nonflat" geometric phenomena to explore. In chapter 9 this computational exploration of curved surfaces provides a conceptual framework for studying Einstein's General Theory of Relativity and for developing a computer program that simulates the motion of particles in a gravitational field as predicted by the theory.

This material was created during the past ten years at the Massachusetts Institute of Technology, and has been used by MIT undergraduates in courses and seminars in the Department of Mathematics and the Division for Study and Research in Education, and by high school juniors in summer institutes sponsored by the MIT Artificial Intelligence Laboratory and the National Science Foundation. The projects can serve as the basis for a computer mathematics laboratory, introduce the geometry and topology of curves and surfaces, and, most important, provide an opportunity for students at the high school or undergraduate level to engage in genuine and significant mathematical discovery. Many parts of the book can be used by students equipped with only paper and pencil, but the contents will be most useful to those who have access to interactive computer graphics.

Although our book is addressed to students, we would also like to reach two other audiences: those mathematics educators who are considering using computers in their teaching but are unsatisfied with the superficial computer-directed instruction and the "insert parameter, see result" simulations that have been predominant modes of computer use in education, and those educators and shapers of educational policy who are trying to find more productive images of the role of computation in reforming both the style and the content of curriculum. The computer will have a profound impact on our educational system, but whether it will enrich the lives of students will depend upon our insight and our imagination.

Acknowledgments

Turtle geometry has grown out of work with the many students, from preschool to postdoctoral, who have worked with the materials developed by the Logo Group of the MIT Artificial Intelligence Laboratory since 1970. Anyone familiar with this work will recognize the enormous debt we owe to Seymour Papert, director of the Logo Group, who not only initiated work on turtle geometry, but also authored a broad vision of the use of computers in education that nurtured its growth.

This book was written under the aegis of the MIT Division for Study and Research in Education, an organization that is almost unique in viewing education research as, at once, an enterprise in teaching, cognitive studies, science, mathematics, and technological innovation. This kind of perspective is, we believe, a prerequisite to the development of any educational technology that will be more than old wine in new bottles. We also owe a great deal to the Artificial Intelligence Laboratory as a whole, for without its computational support this work would have been impossible. More than that, its spirit of playful innovation along with serious concern for the way people think and learn was the rich soil in which these ideas germinated.

We thank the following people for their comments on drafts: John Berlow, Alfred Bork, Mike Brady, Gerhard Fischer, Ken Kahn, Seymour Papert, Howard Peelle, Radia Perlman, Neil Rowe, Bertrand Schwartz, and our students. For suggesting approaches, examples, and exercises we thank Bonnie Dalzell, Paul Goldenburg, Ira Goldstein, Nat Goodman, Andrew Gratz, Ellen Hildreth, Doug Hill, Glenn Iba, Kenneth Kahn, Henry Lieberman, Seymour Papert, David Roberts, and Neil Rowe.

Preliminary Notes

This is a book about exploring mathematics, and the most important thing about exploring mathematics is for you to do it rather than just passively read what we've written. Many of the sections (in particular chapter 2, the latter part of chapter 3, and chapters 6 through 9) contain extended descriptions of computer projects for you to implement and investigate. Additional open-ended projects, indicated with a [P], are listed with the exercises at the end of each section. In the text and exercises we have taken pains to show both the breadth and the depth of possible work with turtle geometry. What is most encouraging to us, however, is that we are certain that we have only scratched the surface. So do not hesitate to depart from the problems and projects we've included in order to follow your own ideas.

The computer used to undertake these projects must be capable of producing drawings in response to "turtle graphics" commands. Fortunately, most computer graphics systems can be readily adapted to execute turtle commands. A detailed explanation of how to do this is given in chapter 3, and appendix B includes a typical implementation of turtle commands in BASIC. In addition, there are (as of January 1981) a few commercially available computer systems that have turtle graphics built in. The most widespread of these is the Pascal system for the Apple II. (See appendix B for others.)

In writing a book about computer graphics projects we had to select a notation in which to describe the algorithms. Using a standard programing language such as BASIC would have forced us to specify numerous implementation-dependent "computerish" details, which would have obscured the simplicity of the programs. Our response was to choose a notation in which turtle algorithms can be expressed simply, and yet which is close enough to real programing languages so that you should have little troubling translating our programs into the language of your choice. In fact, our notation is quite similar to the programing language Pascal (if one ignores details about declaring variables and data types), and even closer to Logo, a language developed at MIT especially for this kind of educational use. Appendix A provides details on our "computer language" notation, and appendix B illustrates sample turtle programs translated into standard programing languages.

Besides computer projects, we've included numerous exercises to test understanding, suggest inquiry, or just pique the imagination. These range in scope from simple problems to extended research topics. The more difficult ones are indicated with a [D]. There are also a few problems marked [DD]. If you tackle one of them, be prepared for a real challenge. We've provided two separate answer sections, one of hints and one of more complete answers; exercises are marked with [H], [A], or [HA], depending on whether we've furnished a hint, an answer, or both. If you get stuck on an [HA] exercise, try working with the hint before looking up the answer.

You should not feel constrained to read this book straight through. Indeed, we hope even casual readers will sample various sections, digging into what they find most interesting. The closest things to prerequisites for later chapters are as follows: The first few sections of chapter 1 introduce the basics of turtles and turtle geometry. Chapter 3 contains the most essential technical material, vectors and coordinate methods, which we use freely in explanations and programs in later chapters. Chapter 5 broaches the new area of nonflat geometries, which will occupy the rest of the book, but even here only the most general notions are necessary to proceed. By and large we have placed the most important material toward the beginnings of chapters and sections.

The tradition of calling our display creatures "turtles" started with Grey Walter, a neurophysiologist who experimented in Britain during the early 1960s with tiny robot creatures he called "tortoises." These inspired the first turtles designed at MIT—computer-controlled robots that moved around on the floor in response to the commands FORWARD and RIGHT. Work in the present mathematical and computer-graphics context followed directly and inherited the turtle terminology.

Turtle Geometry

1

Introduction to Turtle Geometry

We start with the simplest vocabulary of images,
with "left" and "right" and "one, two, three," and
before we know how it happened the words and
numbers have conspired to make a match with
nature: we catch in them the pattern of mind and
matter as one.

Jacob Bronowski, *The Reach of Imagination*

This chapter is an introduction on three levels. First, we introduce you
to a new kind of geometry called turtle geometry. The most important
thing to remember about turtle geometry is that it is a mathematics
designed for exploration, not just for presenting theorems and proofs.
When we do state and prove theorems, we are trying to help you to
generate new ideas and to think about and understand the phenomena
you discover.

The technical language of this geometry is our second priority. This
may look as if we're describing a computer language, but our real aim is
to establish a notation for the range of complicated things a turtle can
do in terms of the simplest things it knows. If you wish to actually program a computer-controlled turtle using one of the standard programing
languages, you will need to know more details than are presented here;
see appendixes A and B.

Finally, this chapter will introduce some of the important themes
to be elaborated in later chapters. These themes permeate not only
geometry but all of mathematics, and we aim to give you rich and varied
experiences with them.

1.1 Turtle Graphics

Imagine that you have control of a little creature called a turtle that
exists in a mathematical plane or, better yet, on a computer display
screen. The turtle can respond to a few simple *commands*: FORWARD
moves the turtle, in the direction it is facing, some number of units.
RIGHT rotates it in place, clockwise, some number of degrees. BACK
and LEFT cause the opposite movements. The number that goes with a
command to specify how much to move is called the command's *input*.

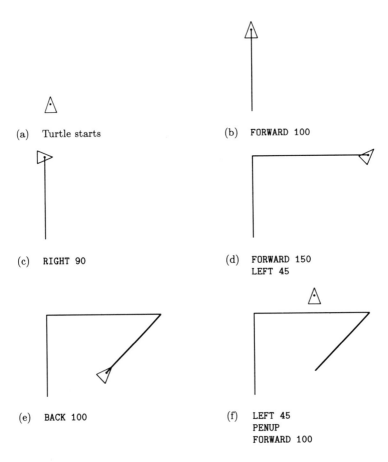

Figure 1.1
A sequence of turtle commands.

In describing the effects of these operations, we say that FORWARD and
BACK change the turtle's *position* (the point on the plane where the turtle
is located); RIGHT and LEFT change the turtle's *heading* (the direction in
which the turtle is facing).

The turtle can leave a trace of the places it has been: The position-
changing commands can cause lines to appear on the screen. This is
controlled by the commands PENUP and PENDOWN. When the pen is down,
the turtle draws lines. Figure 1.1 illustrates how you can draw on the
display screen by steering the turtle with FORWARD, BACK, RIGHT, and
LEFT.

1.1.1 Procedures

Turtle geometry would be rather dull if it did not allow us to teach the turtle new commands. But luckily all we have to do to teach the turtle a new trick is to give it a list of commands it already knows. For example, here's how to draw a square with sides 100 units long:

```
TO SQUARE
    FORWARD 100
    RIGHT 90
    FORWARD 100
    RIGHT 90
    FORWARD 100
    RIGHT 90
    FORWARD 100
```

This is an example of a *procedure*. (Such definitions are also commonly referred to as programs or functions.) The first line of the procedure (the *title line*) specifies the procedure's name. We've chosen to name this procedure SQUARE, but we could have named it anything at all. The rest of the procedure (the *body*) specifies a list of instructions the turtle is to carry out in response to the SQUARE command.

There are a few useful tricks for writing procedures. One of them is called *iteration*, meaning repetition—doing something over and over. Here's a more concise way of telling the turtle to draw a square, using iteration:

```
TO SQUARE
    REPEAT 4
        FORWARD 100
        RIGHT 90
```

This procedure will repeat the indented commands FORWARD 100 and RIGHT 90 four times.

Another trick is to create a SQUARE procedure that takes an input for the size of the square. To do this, specify a name for the input in the title line of the procedure, and use the name in the procedure body:

```
TO SQUARE SIZE
    REPEAT 4
        FORWARD SIZE
        RIGHT 90
```

Now, when you use the command, you must specify the value to be used for the input, so you say SQUARE 100, just like FORWARD 100.

The chunk FORWARD SIZE, RIGHT 90 might be useful in other contexts, which is a good reason to make it a procedure in its own right:

```
TO SQUAREPIECE SIZE
    FORWARD SIZE
    RIGHT 90
```

Now we can rewrite SQUARE using SQUAREPIECE as

```
TO SQUARE SIZE
    REPEAT 4
        SQUAREPIECE SIZE
```

Notice that the input to SQUARE, also called SIZE, is passed in turn as an input to SQUAREPIECE. SQUAREPIECE can be used as a *subprocedure* in other places as well—for example, in drawing a rectangle:

```
TO RECTANGLE SIDE1 SIDE2
    REPEAT 2
        SQUAREPIECE SIDE1
        SQUAREPIECE SIDE2
```

To use the RECTANGLE procedure you must specify its two inputs, for example, RECTANGLE 100 50.

When programs become more complex this kind of input notation can be a bit hard to read, especially when there are procedures such as RECTANGLE that take more than one input. Sometimes it helps to use parentheses and commas to separate inputs to procedures. For example, the RECTANGLE procedure can be written as

```
TO RECTANGLE (SIDE1, SIDE2)
    REPEAT 2
        SQUAREPIECE (SIDE1)
        SQUAREPIECE (SIDE2)
```

If you like, you can regard this notation as a computer language that has been designed to make it easy to interact with turtles. Appendix A gives some of the details of this language. It should not be difficult to rewrite these procedures in any language that has access to the basic turtle commands FORWARD, BACK, RIGHT, LEFT, PENUP, and PENDOWN.

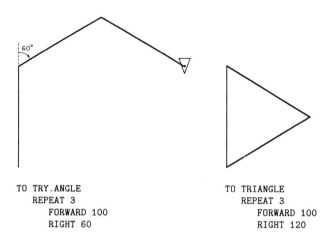

```
TO TRY.ANGLE                    TO TRIANGLE
    REPEAT 3                        REPEAT 3
        FORWARD 100                     FORWARD 100
        RIGHT 60                        RIGHT 120
```

Figure 1.2
Attempt to draw a triangle.

Appendix B gives some tips on how to implement these commands in some of the more common computer languages, and includes sample translations of turtle procedures.

1.1.2 Drawing with the Turtle

Let's draw a figure that doesn't use 90° angles—an equilateral triangle. Since the triangle has 60° angles, a natural first guess at a triangle procedure is

```
TO TRY.ANGLE SIZE
    REPEAT 3
        FORWARD SIZE
        RIGHT 60
```

But TRY.ANGLE doesn't work, as shown in figure 1.2. In fact, running this "triangle" procedure draws half of a regular hexagon. The bug in the procedure is that, whereas we normally measure geometric figures by their interior angles, turtle turning corresponds to the exterior angle at the vertex. So if we want to draw a triangle we should have the turtle turn 120°. You might practice "playing turtle" on a few geometric figures until it becomes natural for you to think of measuring a vertex by how much the turtle must turn in drawing the vertex, rather than by

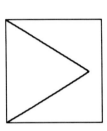

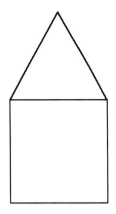

```
TO HOUSE SIDE            TO HOUSE SIDE
   SQUARE SIDE              SQUARE SIDE
   TRIANGLE SIDE            FORWARD SIDE
                           RIGHT 30
                           TRIANGLE SIDE
```

Figure 1.3
(a) Initial attempt to draw a house fails. (b) Interface steps are needed.

the usual interior angle. Turtle angle has many advantages over interior angle, as you will see.

Now that we have a triangle and a square, we can use them as building blocks in more complex drawings—a house, for example. But figure 1.3 shows that simply running SQUARE followed by TRIANGLE doesn't quite work. The reason is that after SQUARE, the turtle is at neither the correct position nor the correct heading to begin drawing the roof. To fix this bug, we must add steps to the procedure that will move and rotate the turtle before the TRIANGLE procedure is run. In terms of designing programs to draw things, these extra steps serve as an interface between the part of the program that draws the walls of the house (the SQUARE procedure) and the part that draws the roof (the TRIANGLE procedure). In general, thinking of procedures as a number of main steps separated by interfaces is a useful strategy for planning complex drawings.

Using procedures and subprocedures is also a good way to create abstract designs. Figure 1.4 shows how to create elaborate patterns by rotating a simple "doodle."

After all these straight line drawings, it is natural to ask whether the turtle can also draw curves—circles, for example. One easy way to do

```
TO THING
    FORWARD 100
    RIGHT 90
    FORWARD 100
    RIGHT 90
    FORWARD 50
    RIGHT 90
    FORWARD 50
    RIGHT 90
    FORWARD 100
    RIGHT 90
    FORWARD 25
    RIGHT 90
    FORWARD 25
    RIGHT 90
    FORWARD 50
```

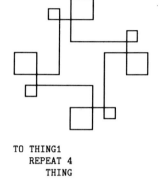

```
TO THING1
    REPEAT 4
        THING
```

```
TO THING2
    REPEAT FOREVER
        THING
        RIGHT 10
        FORWARD 50
```

```
TO THING3
    REPEAT FOREVER
        THING
        LEFT 45
        FORWARD 100
```

Figure 1.4
Designs made by rotating a simple doodle.

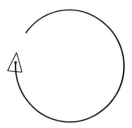

Figure 1.5
FORWARD 1, RIGHT 1, repeated draws a circular arc.

this is to make the turtle go FORWARD a little bit and then turn RIGHT a
little bit, and repeat this over and over:

```
TO CIRCLE
    REPEAT FOREVER
        FORWARD 1
        RIGHT 1
```

This draws a circular arc, as shown in figure 1.5. Since this program
goes on "forever" (until you press the stop button on your computer), it
is not very useful as a subprocedure in creating more complex figures.
More useful would be a version of the CIRCLE procedure that would
draw the figure once and then stop. When we study the mathematics of
turtle geometry, we'll see that the turtle circle closes precisely when the
turtle has through $360°$. So if we generate the circle in chunks
of FORWARD 1, RIGHT 1, the circle will close after precisely 360 chunks:

```
TO CIRCLE
    REPEAT 360
        FORWARD 1
        RIGHT 1
```

If we repeat the basic chunk fewer than 360 times, we get circular arcs.
For instance, 180 repetitions give a semicircle, and 60 repetitions give a
$60°$ arc. The following procedures draw left and right arcs of DEG degrees
on a circle of size R:

```
TO ARCR R DEG
    REPEAT DEG
        FORWARD R
        RIGHT 1
```

```
TO ARCL R DEG
   REPEAT DEG
      FORWARD R
      LEFT 1
```

(See figure 1.6 and exercise 3 for more on making drawings with arcs.)

The circle program above actually draws regular 360gons, of course, rather than "real" circles, but for the purpose of making drawings on the display screen this difference is irrelevant. (See exercises 1 and 2.)

1.1.3 Turtle Geometry versus Coordinate Geometry

We can think of turtle commands as a way to draw geometric figures on a computer display. But we can also regard them as a way to describe figures. Let's compare turtle descriptions with a more familiar system for representing geometric figures—the Cartesian coordinate system, in which points are specified by two numbers, the x and y coordinates relative to a pair of axes drawn in the plane. To put Cartesian coordinates into our computer framework, imagine a "Cartesian turtle" whose moves are directed by a command called SETXY. SETXY takes two numbers as inputs. These numbers are interpreted as x and y coordinates, and the turtle moves to the corresponding point. We could draw a rectangle with SETXY using

```
TO CARTESIAN.RECTANGLE (WIDTH, HEIGHT)
   SETXY (WIDTH, 0)
   SETXY (WIDTH, HEIGHT)
   SETXY (0, HEIGHT)
   SETXY (0, 0)
```

You are probably familiar with the uses of coordinates in geometry: studying geometric figures via equations, plotting graphs of numerical relationships, and so on. Indeed, Descartes' marriage of algebra and geometry is one of the fundamental insights in the development of mathematics. Nevertheless, these kinds of coordinate systems—Cartesian, polar, or what have you—are not the only ways to relate numbers to geometry. The turtle FORWARD and RIGHT commands give an alternative way of measuring figures in the plane, a way that complements the coordinate viewpoint. The geometry of coordinates is called *coordinate geometry*; we shall refer to the geometry of FORWARD and RIGHT as *turtle geometry*. And even though we will be making use of coordinates later

TO CIRCLES
    REPEAT 9
        ARCR 1 360
        RIGHT 40

TO PETAL SIZE
    ARCR SIZE 60
    RIGHT 120
    ARCR SIZE 60
    RIGHT 120

TO FLOWER SIZE
    REPEAT 6
        PETAL SIZE
        RIGHT 60

TO RAY R
    REPEAT 2
        ARCL R 90
        ARCR R 90

TO SUN SIZE
    REPEAT 9
        RAY SIZE
        RIGHT 160

MONSTER

Figure 1.6
Some shapes that can be made using arcs.

on, let us begin by studying turtle geometry as a system in its own right. Whereas studying coordinate geometry leads to graphs and algebraic equations, turtle geometry will introduce some less familiar, but no less important, mathematical ideas.

Intrinsic versus Extrinsic

One major difference between turtle geometry and coordinate geometry rests on the notion of the *intrinsic* properties of geometric figures. An intrinsic property is one which depends only on the figure in question, not on the figure's relation to a frame of reference. The fact that a rectangle has four equal angles is intrinsic to the rectangle. But the fact that a particular rectangle has two vertical sides is *extrinsic*, for an external reference frame is required to determine which direction is "vertical." Turtles prefer intrinsic descriptions of figures. For example, the turtle program to draw a rectangle can draw the rectangle in any orientation (depending on the turtle's initial heading), but the program CARTESIAN.RECTANGLE shown above would have to be modified if we did not want the sides of the rectangle drawn parallel to the coordinate axes, or one vertex at $(0, 0)$.

Another intrinsic property is illustrated by the turtle program for drawing a circle: Go FORWARD a little bit, turn RIGHT a little bit, and repeat this over and over. Contrast this with the Cartesian coordinate representation for a circle, $x^2 + y^2 = r^2$. The turtle representation makes it evident that the curve is everywhere the same, since the process that draws it does the same thing over and over. This property of the circle, however, is not at all evident from the Cartesian representation. Compare the modified program

```
TO CIRCLE
    REPEAT FOREVER
        FORWARD 2
        RIGHT 1
```

with the modified equation $x^2 + 2y^2 = r^2$. (See figure 1.7.) The drawing produced by the modified program is still everywhere the same, that is, a circle. In fact, it doesn't matter what inputs we use to FORWARD or RIGHT (as long as they are small). We still get a circle. The modified equation, however, no longer describes a circle, but rather an ellipse whose sides look different from its top and bottom. A turtle drawing an ellipse would have to turn more per distance traveled to get around its "pointy" sides

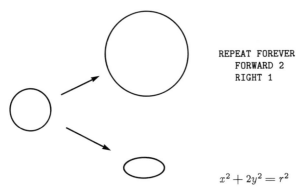

REPEAT FOREVER
FORWARD 2
RIGHT 1

$$x^2 + 2y^2 = r^2$$

Figure 1.7
Modifying the turtle program still produces a circle. Modifying the equation gives
an ellipse.

than to get around its flatter top and bottom. This notion of "how
pointy something is," expressed as the ratio of angle turned to distance
traveled, is the intrinsic quantity that mathematicians call *curvature*.
(See exercises 2 and 4.)

Local versus Global
The turtle representation of a circle is not only more intrinsic than the
Cartesian coordinate description. It is also more *local;* that is, it deals
with geometry a little piece at a time. The turtle can forget about the
rest of the plane when drawing a circle and deal only with the small part
of the plane that surrounds its current position. By contrast, $x^2 + y^2 = r^2$ relies on a large-scale, *global* coordinate system to define its properties.
And defining a circle to be the set of points equidistant from some fixed
point is just as global as using $x^2 + y^2 = r^2$. The turtle representation
does not need to make reference to that "faraway" special point, the
center. In later chapters we will see how the fact that the turtle does its
geometry by feeling a little locality of the world at a time allows turtle
geometry to extend easily out of the plane to curved surfaces.

Procedures versus Equations
A final important difference between turtle geometry and coordinate
geometry is that turtle geometry characteristically describes geometric
objects in terms of procedures rather than in terms of equations. In formulating turtle-geometric descriptions we have access to an entire range
of procedural mechanisms (such as iteration) that are hard to capture in

the traditional algebraic formalism. Moreover, the procedural descriptions used in turtle geometry are readily modified in many ways. This makes turtle geometry a fruitful arena for mathematical exploration. Let's enter that arena now.

1.1.4 Some Simple Turtle Programs

If we were setting out to explore coordinate geometry we might begin by examining the graphs of some simple algebraic equations. Our investigation of turtle geometry begins instead by examining the geometric figures associated with simple procedures. Here's one of the simplest: Go FORWARD some fixed amount, turn RIGHT some fixed amount, and repeat this sequence over and over. This procedure is called POLY.

```
TO POLY SIDE ANGLE
    REPEAT FOREVER
        FORWARD SIDE
        RIGHT ANGLE
```

It draws shapes like those in figure 1.8.

POLY is a generalization of some procedures we've already seen. Setting the angle inputs equal to 90, 120, and 60, we get, respectively, squares, equilateral triangles, and regular hexagons. Setting the angle input equal to 1 gives a circle. Spend some time exploring POLY, examining how the figures vary as you change the inputs. Observe that rather than drawing each figure only once, POLY makes the turtle retrace the same path over and over. (Later on we'll worry about how to make a version of POLY that draws a figure once and then stops.)

Another way to explore with POLY is to modify not only the inputs, but also the program; for example (see figure 1.9),

```
TO NEWPOLY SIDE ANGLE
    REPEAT FOREVER
        FORWARD SIDE
        RIGHT ANGLE
        FORWARD SIDE
        RIGHT (2 * ANGLE)
```

(The symbol "*" denotes multiplication.) You should have no difficulty inventing many variations along these lines, particularly if you use such procedures as SQUARE and TRIANGLE as subprocedures to replace or supplement FORWARD and RIGHT.

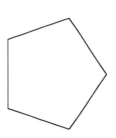

ANGLE = 72

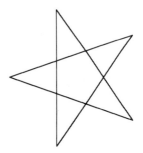

ANGLE = 144

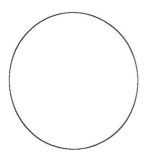

ANGLE = 1

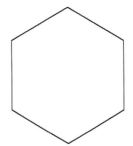

ANGLE = 60

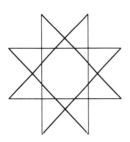

ANGLE = 135

ANGLE = 108

Figure 1.8
Shapes drawn by POLY.

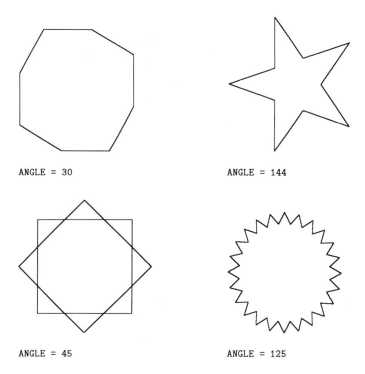

ANGLE = 30   ANGLE = 144

ANGLE = 45   ANGLE = 125

Figure 1.9
Shapes drawn by NEWPOLY.

Recursion

One particularly important way to make new procedures and vary old ones is to employ a program control structure called *recursion;* that is, to have a procedure use itself as a subprocedure, as in

```
TO POLY SIDE ANGLE
    FORWARD SIDE
    RIGHT ANGLE
    POLY SIDE ANGLE
```

The final line keeps the process going over and over by including "do POLY again" as part of the definition of POLY.

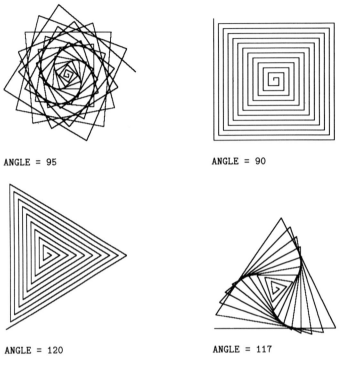

ANGLE = 95   ANGLE = 90

ANGLE = 120   ANGLE = 117

Figure 1.10
Shapes drawn by POLYSPI.

One advantage of this slightly different way of representing POLY is
that it suggests some further modifications to the basic program. For
instance, when it comes time to do POLY again, call it with different
inputs:

```
TO POLYSPI SIDE ANGLE
    FORWARD SIDE
    RIGHT ANGLE
    POLYSPI (SIDE + 1, ANGLE)
```

Figure 1.10 shows some sample POLYSPI figures. Look carefully at how
the program generates these figures: Each time the turtle goes FORWARD
it goes one unit farther than the previous time.

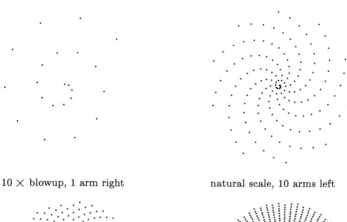

10 × blowup, 1 arm right   natural scale, 10 arms left

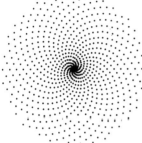
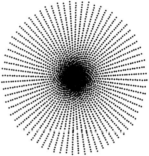

$\frac{1}{4}$ reduction, 31 arms right, 41 left $\frac{1}{10}$ reduction, 72 arms straight

Figure 1.11
The vertices of a POLYSPI.

A more general form of POLYSPI uses a third input (INC, for increment) to allow us to vary how quickly the sides grow:

```
TO POLYSPI (SIDE, ANGLE, INC)
    FORWARD SIDE
    RIGHT ANGLE
    POLYSPI (SIDE + INC, ANGLE, INC)
```

In addition to trying POLYSPI with various inputs, make up some of your own variations. For example, subtract a bit from the side each time, which will produce an inward spiral. Or double the side each time, or divide it by two. Figure 1.11 illustrates a pattern made drawing only the vertices of POLYSPI, shown at four scales of magnification (see exercise 13).

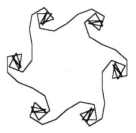

ANGLE = 0
INCREMENT = 7

ANGLE = 40
INCREMENT = 30

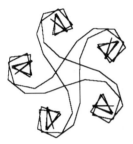

ANGLE = 2
INCREMENT = 20

Figure 1.12
Examples of INSPI.

Another way to produce an inward spiral (curve of increasing curvature) is to increment the angle each time:

```
TO INSPI (SIDE, ANGLE, INC)
   FORWARD SIDE
   RIGHT ANGLE
   INSPI (SIDE, ANGLE + INC, INC)
```

Run INSPI and watch how it works. The turtle begins spiraling inward as expected. But eventually the path begins to unwind as the angle is incremented past 180°. Letting INSPI continue, we find that it eventually produces a symmetrical closed figure which the turtle retraces over and over as shown in figure 1.12. You should find this surprising. Why should this succession of FORWARDs and RIGHTs bring the turtle back precisely to its starting point, so that it will then retrace its own path? We will see in the next section that this closing phenomenon reflects the elegant mathematics underlying turtle geometry.

Exercises for Section 1.1

1. We said in the text that when the inputs to the POLY procedure are small, the resulting figure will be indistinguishable from a circle. Do some experiments to see how large you can make the inputs and still have the figure look like a circle. For example, is an angle of 20° small enough to draw acceptable circles?

2. The sequence of figures POLY(2,2), POLY(1,1), POLY(.5,.5), ... all with the same curvature (turning divided by distance traveled), approaches "in the limit" a true mathematical circle. What is the radius of the circle? [HA]

3. [P] Write a procedure that draws circular arcs. Inputs should specify the number of degrees in the arc as well as the size of the circle. Can you use the result of exercise 2 so that the size input is the radius of the circle? [A]

4. Although the radius of a circle is not "locally observable" to a turtle who is drawing the circle, that length is intimately related to a local quantity called the "radius of curvature," defined to be equal to 1 ÷ curvature, or equivalently, to distance divided by angle. What is the relation between radius and radius of curvature for a POLY with small inputs as above? Do this when angle is measured in radians as well as in degrees. [A]

5. [P] Construct some drawings using squares, rectangles, triangles, circles, and circular arc programs.

6. [P] Invent your own variations on the model of POLYSPI and INSPI.

7. How many different 9-sided figures can POLY draw (not counting differences in size or orientation)? What angle inputs to POLY produce these figures? How about 10-sided figures? [A]

8. [PD] A rectangle is a square with two different side lengths. More generally, what happens to a POLY that uses two different side lengths as in the following program?

```
TO DOUBLEPOLY (SIDE1, SIDE2, ANGLE)
    REPEAT FOREVER
        POLYSTEP SIDE1 ANGLE
        POLYSTEP SIDE2 ANGLE
```

In particular, how does the symmetry of DOUBLEPOLY relate to that of POLY with the same ANGLE input? [HA]

9. [D] Which encloses the larger area—POLY(5,5) or POLY(6,6)? [HA]

10. [P] Find inputs to INSPI that give a nonclosed figure. Can you give a convincing argument that the figure is really nonclosed rather than, say, a closed figure too big to fit on the display screen? [A]

11. [P] If the display system you are using allows "wraparound," you can get some interesting effects by trying POLYs with very large sides. Explore these figures. [H]

12. There are three kinds of "interchanges" we can perform on turtle programs: interchanging RIGHT and LEFT, interchanging FORWARD and BACK, and (for programs that terminate) reversing the sequence of instructions. Describe in geometric terms the effect of each of these operations, both by itself and in combination with the others. Start with the class of programs that close (return the turtle to its initial position and heading). [HA]

13. [P] The pattern made by the vertices of POLYSPI can be an interesting object of study. The dots seem to group into various "arms," either straight or curving left or right. To draw these patterns, you can use the procedures

```
TO SPIDOT ANGLE
   SUBSPIDOT 0 ANGLE

TO SUBSPIDOT SIDE ANGLE
   FORWARD SIDE
   DOT
   RIGHT ANGLE
   SUBSPIDOT (SIDE + 1, ANGLE)

TO DOT
   PENDOWN
   FORWARD 1
   BACK 1
   PENUP
```

For example, predict what you will see between SPIDOT 90, which has four arms, and SPIDOT 120, which has three. Can you explain the sequence of figures you actually do see? Figure 1.11 shows how the figure drawn by the same SPIDOT program seems to have different numbers of spiral arms when viewed at different scales of magnification, which can be accomplished by changing the increment to SIDE in SUBSPIDOT. Study this phenomenon. [H]

14. [P] Suppose we have a function called RANDOM that outputs a random digit (0 through 9). Play around with the procedure

```
TO RANDPOLY SIDE ANGLE
   REPEAT FOREVER
      IF RANDOM = 0 THEN PENDOWN
               ELSE PENUP
      FORWARD SIDE
      RIGHT ANGLE
```

Use this program as the basis for some psychology experiments. For instance, what is the average number of sides that must be drawn before people can recognize which POLY it is?

15. [D] Find some local and intrinsic way to describe an ellipse. Write a program that makes the turtle draw ellipses, where the inputs specify the size and eccentricity of the ellipse. [A]

1.2 POLYs and Other Closed Paths

This section develops some general theorems about turtle programs by studying one of the simplest of them, POLY—which, when it closes, exhibits clearly some properties shared by all closed paths, no matter how complicated. Even when POLY doesn't close, it can serve as a model that clarifies symmetry and other important properties of a very general class of programs. Careful and patient study of such a simple program will be richly rewarded.

1.2.1 The Closed-Path Theorem and the Simple-Closed-Path Theorem

You have probably already noticed that POLY with an angle input of $360/n$ draws a regular n-sided polygon. But it is not always true that (number of sides)$\times$(angle) $= 360$. If you try running POLY with an angle of 144 you will see that it draws a five-pointed star, and $5 \times 144 = 720$, not 360. Noticing that 720 is exactly twice 360 might lead us to guess the following formula:

(number of sides) $\times$ (angle) $= 360 \times$ (an integer).

It's not hard to see why this formula is true. The number of sides times the angle is precisely the *total turning* done by the turtle in walking once around the figure—the net change in heading. If the path is to close legitimately, and not just cross itself, then the turtle must end its trip with the same heading it started out with. Thus, the total turning must be some multiple of 360°.

Total turning is the central concept here. It certainly need not be restricted to POLY. One can imagine any turtle program keeping a running count of its turning, adding in RIGHTs and subtracting LEFTs. Because only RIGHTs and LEFTs change heading, this total turning is always exactly the total change in heading. In particular, if the path is a *closed path* (one which restores the turtle's initial position and heading), we can be confident that the net turning (= change of heading) is a multiple of 360°. This gives us our first turtle-geometric theorem:

Closed-Path Theorem The total turning along any closed path is an integer multiple of 360°.

Total turning is an intrinsic property of a path. It does not depend on where the path starts, or how it is oriented with respect to "vertical." The total turning of a closed path is frequently summarized simply by the particular integer that multiplies 360. That integer is called the *rotation number* of the path. As an exercise, follow the turtle around the sample paths in figure 1.13 and compute the rotation numbers.

Does your experience with POLY suggest an improvement to the closed-path theorem? A little experimentation should convince you that there are two essentially different classes of POLY paths: simple polygons (such as squares, triangles, and hexagons); and star polygons (such as five-pointed stars), which are characterized by the fact that the paths cross themselves. The simple polygons always appear to have total turning equal to +360° or −360°, depending upon the direction in which the turtle traverses the path. The star polygons, however, always have total turning different from ±360°.

One wonders if this experimental correlation has general significance. It is not hard to prove its validity for POLYs (see exercise 11 below). But the more important conjecture involves generalizing from POLYs to any *simple closed path* (a closed path that does not cross itself):

Simple-Closed-Path Theorem The total turning in a simple closed path is 360° (to the right or to the left). That is to say, the rotation number of any simple closed path is ±1.

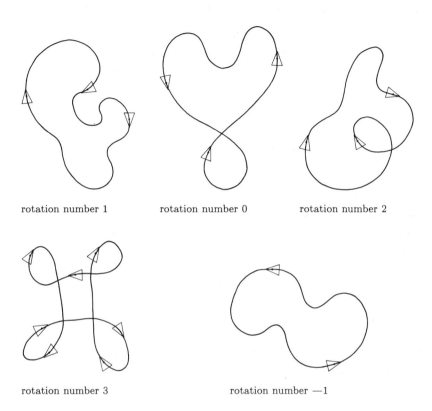

rotation number 1   rotation number 0   rotation number 2

rotation number 3   rotation number −1

Figure 1.13
Rotation numbers of closed paths.

Take a look at some examples of simple closed paths to convince
yourself of the plausibility of this theorem, which is difficult to prove
rigorously. We will return to it later, in chapter 4. For now you should
note that this theorem says that there is a relation between two very
different aspects of a closed path—the turning and the crossing points.
That makes it considerably less obvious than the closed-path theorem,
but also much more powerful. We give one example of the power here
and several more in the exercises.

The simple-closed-path theorem says that the sum of the exterior
angles of any simple polygon is 360°. For triangles, we can rewrite this
in terms of the three interior angles A, B, and C to get

$$(180 - A) + (180 - B) + (180 - C) = 360,$$

and thus

$(A + B + C)$ = the sum of interior angles = $3 \times 180 - 360 = 180$.

So, as a corollary of the simple-closed-path theorem, we have derived the familiar result that the interior angles of a triangle must sum to 180°. (Exercises 6–9 detail some other applications of the simple-closed-path theorem.)

1.2.2 The POLY Closing Theorem

The POLY procedures we've written so far, iterative and recursive, have one fault: They never stop. That makes it generally impossible to use them as subprocedures in more complicated programs. Moreover, the "inefficiency" of a drawing program that doesn't know when it is done may simply offend one's sensibilities. The problem of making a POLY program that stops is a mathematical one with two fundamentally different approaches.

The *global approach* is as follows: Sit back and look ahead. Given an ANGLE input, compute how many times the turtle must run the basic POLY step, FORWARD SIDE, RIGHT ANGLE, before the path closes and starts again. Then you need only repeat the POLY step that many times. The *local approach* revolves around questions like the following: How can the turtle know, as it is walking along, when it is done? What clue can the turtle be watching for? We will take the second approach here, as it turns out to be simpler. The first approach, however, is mathematically rich and is pursued in section 1.4.

Consider: How could a turtle, while walking along drawing a POLY, know when the figure has been completed? (A computer turtle cannot see the lines it is drawing.) Thinking locally, the turtle knows only two things, position and heading. Neither of these is truly local, for to measure them usually involves a coordinate system. But the one locally computable quantity we know about—total turning—can do the trick. The closed-path theorem says that if the path closes, then total turning must be a multiple of 360°. How about the converse: If the total turning reaches a multiple of 360°, will the path be closed? This is not true for turtle paths in general, but it is true for POLY:

POLY Closing Theorem A path drawn by the POLY procedure will close precisely when the total turning reaches a multiple of 360°.

There is one bug in this theorem, one exceptional case: If the angle of the POLY is equal to 0 then the turtle just walks off along a straight line. The path never closes, even though at every point the total

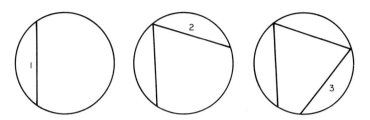

Figure 1.14
POLY lays down a sequence of equal chords.

turning is 0, a perfectly good multiple of 360. But this exceptional case, FORWARD SIDE, RIGHT 0, is transparent enough so that we can just leave it out of consideration in most instances. Any multiple of 360° will, of course, have the same effect as a turn of 0.

We'll outline two different proofs of the POLY closing theorem.

Sketch of Proof 1 Have you noticed the important fact that the vertices of POLY lie on a circle? (Everything about POLY seems to be circular!) We leave the proof of this geometric fact to you in exercise 2. Using this fact, one can redescribe POLY as the sequential laying down of fixed-length chords on a fixed circle as shown in figure 1.14. The point is that there is only one chord of the required length that can be produced by the turtle starting at any given heading. (Actually there are two, but one of them has the wrong sense—the turtle would turn off the circle after traversing the chord.) Thus, whenever the turtle returns to its initial heading (total turning = any multiple of 360°) it will be about to retrace the first chord and so should stop. Notice how this proof breaks down for the exceptional case FORWARD SIDE, RIGHT 0. The turtle must do some turning or else the vertices will lie on a straight line rather than on a circle.

An alternative proof is inspired less by geometry and more by ideas from the theory of computation. It proceeds as follows.

Sketch of Proof 2 Assume that we have a turtle following a POLY procedure, and that at some time the turtle returns to its initial heading (heading change = a multiple of 360°) but not to its initial position. We will show that this assumption leads to a contradiction. (The trick of the proof is to show that the turtle must walk off to infinity in some

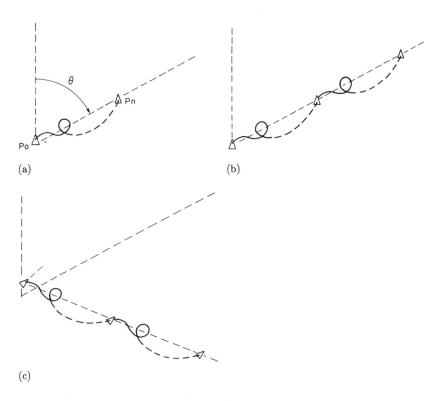

Figure 1.15
The POLY closing theorem. (a) Suppose the turtle returns to his initial heading, but
not his initial position. (b) n more steps must do the same thing again. (c) From a
new heading (after one POLY step), chunks of n steps carry the turtle away on a new
line.

direction. Then, by regrouping the sequence of commands, we'll show
that the turtle runs off to infinity in a different direction.)

By assumption, the turtle returns to its initial heading after some
number (say, n) repetitions of the POLY step. (Notice that n cannot
be 1 if we neglect the exceptional case ANGLE = 0.) Draw a dotted
line connecting the turtle's initial position p_0 to its position p_n after n
repetitions. This line makes some angle θ with the turtle's initial heading
(figure 1.15a).

Now let the turtle continue for n more repetitions of the POLY step.
Since the turtle starts out from p_n with the same heading it had when
it started at p_0, the effect of n more POLY steps will be to do the same

thing again, moving the turtle farther out along the same line, and again bring it back to the initial heading (figure 1.15b). Continuing with n more repetitions, and n more, and so on, we see that the turtle must run off infinitely far in the direction of the dotted line. Moreover, at no point can the turtle's path stray very far from the line, since the turtle must get back to it at the end of every n POLY steps.

Now let's return the turtle to the initial state and run the POLY step for one iteration. We will now see the turtle at a new position p_1 with a different heading. If we continue with n repetitions from here, the turtle will end up on a new dotted line that lies at angle θ to this new heading. (figure 1.15c).

But the problem is obvious now. Running another sequence of n, then another and another, forces the turtle off infinitely far along this new line. But the turtle cannot remain close to both dotted lines as it marches off to infinity. This contradiction means that our assumption that the turtle does not come back to the initial position must have been wrong. This completes the proof.

This second proof demonstrates an important computational strategy: Divide a process into meaningful chunks (for example, the parts of the POLY between equal headings), then pay close attention to the net action of the chunks. Structuring a complex program as a group of subprocedures illustrates the same strategy.

Here finally is our POLY with stop rule:

```
TO POLYSTOP SIDE ANGLE
    TURN ← 0
    REPEAT
        FORWARD SIDE
        RIGHT ANGLE
        TURN ← (TURN + ANGLE)
    UNTIL REMAINDER (TURN, 360) = 0
```

Note the use of the new symbol ←, which means "assign to the variable on the left the value given on the right." The procedure REMAINDER is a function that computes the value of its first input modulo its second input. The program also makes use of the iteration construct "REPEAT ... UNTIL ⟨some condition⟩", which keeps repeating the indented portion until the condition is true (and always does the indented part at least once).

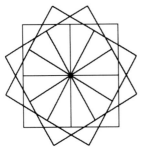

POLYROLL 100 90 30   POLYROLL 100 60 45

Figure 1.16
Examples of POLYROLL.

This program allows us to use POLYs as building blocks in more complex figures; for example (see figure 1.16),

```
TO POLYROLL SIDE ANGLE1 ANGLE2
    REPEAT FOREVER
        POLYSTOP SIDE ANGLE1
        RIGHT ANGLE2
```

Exercises for Section 1.2

1. The simple-closed-path theorem has a serious bug as it stands. It pur-
ports to give the precise multiple of 360 that describes the total turning
for a set of paths. Unfortunately, one can insert a step, RIGHT 360,
that does not change the path at all, yet changes the multiple of 360
given by total turning. These gratuitous 360s must be pruned from
the program before the theorem can hold. However, the pruning can
be somewhat complicated if the gratuitous 360s are hidden—as, for example, LEFT 160 followed by RIGHT 360 being written as RIGHT 200.
Give general rules for pruning. (Think of writing a procedure that takes
the text of a turtle procedure as input and returns the pruned version.)
Try your method on the following program:

```
TO PRUNE.ME
    FORWARD 5
    RIGHT 360
    FORWARD 5
    LEFT 240
```

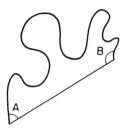

Figure 1.17
Relate the angles A and B to the total turning over the arc.

```
FORWARD 10
LEFT 120
FORWARD 0
LEFT 120
FORWARD 10
RIGHT 120
```

Can you give some motivation for pruning other than that it makes the simple-closed-path theorem true? [A]

2. Fill in the details in the first proof of the POLY closing theorem (see "sketch of proof 1"), including a proof that the vertices of POLY lie on a circle. [H]

3. Prove that if the angle input to POLY is an irrational number, the turtle never returns to its initial position, and yet always remains within a finite distance from it. [A]

4. [P] Invent some variations on the POLYROLL program, perhaps modeled after POLYSPI and INSPI.

5. Rewrite the POLYSTOP program recursively, so that it doesn't use the REPEAT command. [A]

6. What is the sum of the interior angles of an n-gon? What is the interior angle of a regular n-gon? Show how these formulas can be easily derived by using the simple-closed-path theorem. [HA]

7. Suppose we have a simple arc (an arc that does not cross itself) and that we join the endpoints of the arc by a straight line. Suppose further that the line and the arc do not intersect except at the endpoints (figure 1.17). Use the simple-closed-path theorem to give a formula relating the

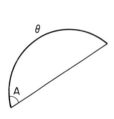
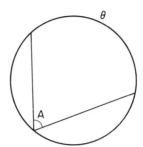

Figure 1.18
Solve for A in terms of θ.

total turning over the arc to the (interior) angles that the arc makes with the line. [HA]

8. Apply the result of the previous exercise to find the angle between a chord of a circle and the arc that it subtends (figure 1.18a). [A]

9. Use the previous exercise to compute the arc of a circle subtended by an inscribed angle (figure 1.18b). [HA]

10. Proof 1 of the POLY closing theorem was based on the fact that the vertices of a POLY all lie on a circle. Use the simple-closed-path theorem to show that the amount of arc on the circumscribed POLY circle from one vertex to the next is just the angle input to the POLY procedure. [H]

11. We said that we would delay giving a proof of the simple-closed-path theorem until chapter 4. Give a proof of the theorem in the special case where the simple closed path is a POLY figure. [H]

12. If you take a bicycle and lock the front wheel at angle θ from straight ahead (where θ is rather small), the bicycle will turn in a circle. What is the radius of the circle, given that the length between wheel centers of the bicycle is D? [HA]

1.3 Looping Programs

We said that the turtle approach allows us to take concepts that are useful in thinking about computation and apply them to the study of geometry. One such concept is that of *state*. Of course the idea of state is not unique to computer science. It is important in physics, chemistry, and any other field involving configurations that are subject to change. But we do not generally look upon geometry in this way; geometric figures are usually regarded as static objects. Turtle geometry provides a more dynamic perspective—the geometry is tied to movements.

The state of the turtle is given by specifying its position and its heading. From the state point of view, the basic turtle commands— FORWARD, BACK, LEFT, and RIGHT—are *state-change operators*: They cause the turtle to change state. In this section we will look at a sequence of turtle commands purely in terms of its net effect in changing the initial state to the final state, ignoring what comes between. Thus, a sequence of turtle commands can be summarized as a single state-change operator. At this level of abstraction all programs that generate a closed path are the same—they are all *state-change-equivalent*. They correspond to the simplest of all state-change operators, the one that does nothing and leaves the initial state *invariant*.

1.3.1 The Looping Lemma

There is something striking about the paths drawn by the modifications to POLY discussed at the end of section 1.1. It is as if their descent from POLY cannot be suppressed! You should have noticed the same phenomenon in many of your own programs. Figure 1.19 shows a POLY skeleton in dotted lines underlying the elaborate surface structures of NEWPOLY and INSPI. Can we understand this phenomenon?

The key observation is this: Between successive vertices of the POLY skeleton, the program does the same thing. We might say that the program is just a decorated version of the underlying POLY. That the paths of NEWPOLY and INSPI consist of a collection of identical pieces is evident from the pictures they draw. In the case of NEWPOLY the repetitive or looping behavior is clear in the program structure. INSPI's program structure will require a second look. For now we proceed on the basis of the visual evidence of the paths and consider the class of programs that do the same thing over and over, regardless of the complexity of the *basic loop* (the thing that is repeated).

We can peel away the decoration by focusing on the net result of the basic loop. What is the difference between the initial state and the final state of the turtle? By the nature of the turtle only two things can

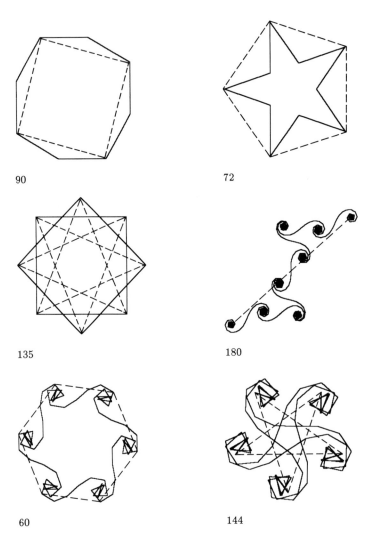

90

72

135

180

60

144

Figure 1.19
NEWPOLYs and INSPIs with "POLY skeletons" indicated by dashed lines. (Numbers are
skeleton angles.)

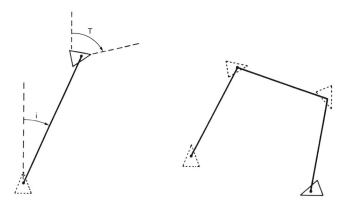

Figure 1.20
(a) The net result (state change) of some basic loop. (b) Repeating the net result lays down the POLY skeleton.

happen: a net change of position and a net change of heading. Figure 1.20a shows the general case. Notice that we cannot assume that the change of position is in the same direction as the turtle's original heading; hence, we must include an angle i between the initial heading and the change-of-position line.

When the basic loop is repeated, the same change of state must occur, but now relative to the new heading and hence rotated by the heading change which the turtle underwent in the first loop. We will call this change of heading T (for total turn). The next loop must follow the same pattern, and so on. Figure 1.20b shows the repeated process laying down the skeleton POLY. The angle i is *irrelevant* to the intrinsic properties of the underlying POLY—it just determines the relative orientation of the POLY with respect to the initial heading of the turtle. The important quantity is the heading change from beginning to end of the basic loop, the total turning T in the basic loop. This is the angle of turning from one segment of the POLY to the next, and it determines the figure's properties. We can state this result more formally:

Looping Lemma Any program that is just a repetition of some basic loop of turtle instructions has precisely the structure of POLY with an angle input equal to T, the total turning in the loop.

You should be able to say what "has the structure of POLY" means in detail. It includes such things as repeatedly touching base with a circle if total turning is not equal to a multiple of 360°, and touching base with a line if it is. It also includes the fact that the symmetry type of the figure is the same as that of the underlying POLY. For instance, if the total turning of the basic loop is 90°, the repeated loop will have the fourfold symmetry of a square, necessarily closing in four iterations of the loop.

1.3.2 Examples of Looping Programs

Let's analyze some simple looping programs. In NEWPOLY the total turning is $3 \times$ ANGLE. If ANGLE is 144, then $T = 3 \times 144 = 432$, which is equivalent to $72 = 360/5$. Hence, the five-pointed star NEWPOLY actually has the structure of a pentagon (not a POLY with ANGLE 144)—something that might not have been apparent from just looking at the path. (The fact that the path is simple is a clue. Also, observe that the program visits the vertices of the underlying pentagon in sequence, as does POLY with an ANGLE of 72, rather than skipping between vertices, as does POLY with ANGLE 144.)

Let's take a look at INSPI—in particular INSPI with ANGLE equal to 2 and INCREMENT equal to 20, which draws the decorated five-pointed star shown in figure 1.12. The program simply alternates FORWARD SIDE with turning RIGHT an ever-increasing angle which is tabulated in the following:

```
RIGHT 2
RIGHT 2 + 20
RIGHT 2 + 2*20
RIGHT 2 + 3*20
     .

     .
RIGHT 2 + 17*20
RIGHT 2 + 18*20 = 2 + 360
```

The last command has the same effect as the first, and the one to follow, RIGHT 2 + 19 $\times$ 20 = RIGHT 2 + 20 + 360, is the same as the second. The program is clearly staging a repeat performance of the first 18 steps. Computing the total turning, we find

$$2 + (2 + 20) + (2 + 2 \times 20) + \cdots + (2 + 17 \times 20)$$
$$= 18 \times 2 + (1 + 2 + \cdots + 17) \times 20 = 3,096,$$

which is equal to 216, or -144, modulo 360. (When computing the

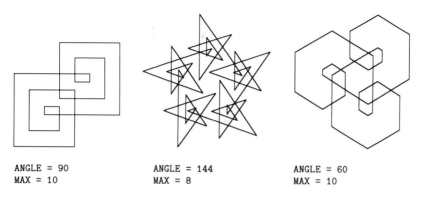

ANGLE = 90   ANGLE = 144   ANGLE = 60
MAX = 10   MAX = 8   MAX = 10

Figure 1.21
Spirolaterals.

heading change, we need only consider the turning modulo 360°.) We
now see the origin of the five-pointed star POLY skeleton. INSPI is typical
of the way in which, because of the modulo-360 effect, many seemingly
ever-changing programs actually form repeating loops.

Another interesting repeating-loop program draws the family of figures
called spirolaterals shown in figure 1.21:

```
TO SPIRO (SIDE, ANGLE, MAX)
    REPEAT FOREVER
        SUBSPIRO (SIDE, ANGLE, MAX)

TO SUBSPIRO (SIDE, ANGLE, MAX)
    COUNT ← 1
    REPEAT
        FORWARD (SIDE * COUNT)
        RIGHT ANGLE
        COUNT ← (COUNT + 1)
    UNTIL COUNT > MAX
```

If you study this procedure you will see that it amounts to having the
turtle draw an initial chunk of a POLYSPI (in fact, the first MAX lines of
a POLYSPI) and repeat this over and over. It is easy to see that the basic
loop in SPIRO has total turning ANGLE × MAX.

We will refer to the figures drawn by SPIRO as *simple spirolaterals*. A
more general kind of spirolateral (shown in figure 1.22) maintains a basic
loop in which each vertex has the same amount of turning, but allows the
turtle to turn left rather than right at some of the vertices. To specify

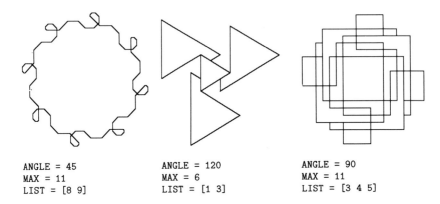

ANGLE = 45   ANGLE = 120   ANGLE = 90
MAX = 11   MAX = 6   MAX = 11
LIST = [8 9]   LIST = [1 3]   LIST = [3 4 5]

Figure 1.22
Generalized spirolaterals.

these figures we need to indicate the direction of the turtle's turning at each vertex. The corresponding GSPIRO procedure takes four inputs: a side length (the length of the shortest side in the figure), an angle through which the turtle turns left or right at each vertex, a number MAX telling how many steps are in the basic loop, and a list of numbers specifying the vertices at which the turtle should turn left. If the vertex number is a member of the list, then the turtle turns left at the vertex; otherwise the turtle turns right. (The MEMBER command is used to tell whether or not something is a member of a list.) Thus, the GSPIRO procedure is

```
TO GSPIRO (SIDE, ANGLE, MAX, LIST)
    REPEAT FOREVER
        SUBGSPIRO (SIDE, ANGLE, MAX, LIST)

TO SUBGSPIRO (SIDE, ANGLE, MAX, LIST)
    COUNT ← 1
    REPEAT
        FORWARD SIDE * COUNT
        IF MEMBER (COUNT, LIST)
            THEN LEFT ANGLE
            ELSE RIGHT ANGLE
        COUNT ← COUNT + 1
    UNTIL COUNT > MAX
```

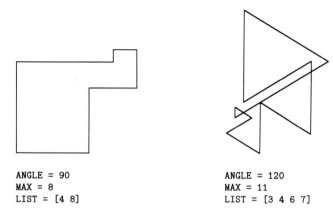

ANGLE = 90   ANGLE = 120
MAX = 8   MAX = 11
LIST = [4 8]   LIST = [3 4 6 7]

Figure 1.23
Unexpectedly closed spirolaterals.

The basic loop SUBGSPIRO makes MAX − L right turns and L left turns where L is the number of elements in LIST, making a total turning of

$$(\text{MAX} - L) \times \text{ANGLE} - L \times \text{ANGLE} = (\text{MAX} - 2L) \times \text{ANGLE}.$$

One intriguing property of spirolaterals is that they may be closed even when the heading change is a multiple of 360°. Total turning a multiple of 360° would lead you to expect a POLY substrate that would march off on a straight line to infinity. But, by a remarkable coincidence, the sidelength of the underlying POLY (which we did not bother to compute for any of these other programs) might turn out to be 0 as well! This corresponds to having a looping program in which the basic loop closes all by itself. This phenomenon deserves a name: *unexpectedly closed*. Figure 1.23 gives some examples of unexpectedly closed spirolaterals.

1.3.3 More on the Looping Lemma

We end the body of this section with two remarks about the looping lemma—one about its implications beyond predicting the symmetry of looping programs, the other about increasing the strength of the lemma.

First, the looping lemma constrains the behavior of any looping program. Under many circumstances, it may be possible to exclude simple looping as a way of generating a class of paths. For example, any infinite spiral neither touches base on a fixed circle nor marches off to infinity around a line as POLY does, so it cannot be drawn by any looping program.

Second, it can be very valuable to know how to identify which programs are looping programs without a detailed look at each particular case. We can give a purely program-structural criterion that serves to identify such programs: A program must loop (or terminate) if it consists of any combination of

- fixed and finite sequences of turtle commands FORWARD, BACK, LEFT, and RIGHT with specified numeric inputs (these are called *fixed instruction sequences*),

- repeats, and

- calls to programs that satisfy these properties.

Notice that this criterion is recursive in form.

1.3.4 Technical Summary

The following is a technical recap of results stated or implied in this section. The detailed proofs of these facts are left as exercises.

The Canonical Form of a Turtle State-Change Operator
Any fixed instruction sequence of turtle commands is state-change-equivalent to a POLY step sandwiched between a RIGHT I and LEFT I for some angle I:

```
RIGHT I
FORWARD D
RIGHT T
LEFT I
```

The angle T is precisely the total turning of the fixed instruction sequence.

Looping Lemma and Classification of Looping Programs
Any program that repeats a fixed instruction sequence (or the equivalent, as in INSPI) has the behavior of a POLY with angle T and side D in the following senses (the angle T may be simply determined as the total turning in the basic loop):

Boundedness If $T \neq 0$ then the figure drawn by the program will lie within a fixed distance from some circle, and hence will be bounded. In the exceptional case, $T = 0$, the figure will lie within a fixed distance from some line (figure 1.24).

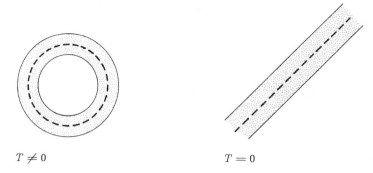

$T \neq 0$ $T = 0$

Figure 1.24
Any looping program is confined to a region (a) near a circle ($T \neq 0$) or (b) in the exceptional case ($T = 0$) near a line.

Closing If T is a rational multiple of 360°, the program will always draw a closed path, with the usual exception, $T = 0$, which causes the program to walk off to infinity. The exception to the exception is when D is also zero, the equivalent of POLY 0 0, in which case the program is "unexpectedly" closed. If T is irrational the program will never close.

Symmetry The program must have the same rotational symmetry as POLY D T. In particular, if $T = 360s/r$ where s/r is a fraction in lowest terms, then the program will have r-fold symmetry. (We have not yet discussed symmetry in detail. This topic will form the basis of section 1.4.)

1.3.5 Nontechnical Summary
Doing the same thing over and over is either circular, straight-linish, or very dull.

Exercises for Section 1.3

1. [P] Draw at least three distinct (ignoring size) INSPI figures with sixfold symmetry.

2. Give a proof of the looping lemma and the classification of looping programs given in the technical summary. This may be done using the form of a general state-change operator (given above) or by modifying

Proof 2 of the POLY closing theorem of subsection 1.2.2. Give bounds for the "fixed distances" specified in the boundedness part in terms of the instructions in the basic loop.

3. [P] Figure 1.23 shows some unexpectedly closed spirolaterals. Find some more.

4. What is the heading change for INSPI with an ANGLE of A and an INCREMENT of 10? [A]

5. [D] What is the heading change for INSPI with an ANGLE of A and an INCREMENT of $360/n$, where n is an integer? [HA]

6. [DP] Compute the total turning, T, of the basic loop in the following looping program in terms of the angle inputs BOTTOM and TOP. Use your formula to draw at least three different (ignoring size) figures with threefold symmetry; fourfold, fivefold. [HA]

```
TO POLYARC (SIDE, BOTTOM, TOP)
    REPEAT FOREVER
        INSPI.STOP (SIDE, BOTTOM, TOP, 1)
        INSPI.STOP (SIDE, TOP, BOTTOM, -1)

TO INSPI.STOP (SIDE, START.ANG, END.ANG, INC)
    REPEAT
        FORWARD SIDE
        LEFT START.ANG
        START.ANG ← START.ANG + INC
    UNTIL START.ANG = END.ANG
```

7. [P] Make "even more general" spirolaterals by allowing the turtle to move BACK at certain of the vertices. Analyze this program. Find some unexpectedly closed figures.

8. [DD] Show that a simple spirolateral can never be unexpectedly closed. [H]

9. [DD] Can INSPI produce unexpectedly closed figures?

10. [P] Invent some disguised looping programs like INSPI. Give a formula for the total turning of the basic loop in terms of the inputs to the procedure. Find inputs that draw figures with simple symmetry. Find inputs that draw unbounded figures. Determine whether any of these figures are unexpectedly closed.

11. When we summarize turtle paths as state-change operators, the closed paths are precisely those operators that leave the turtle's state unchanged. This suggests the generalization of studying operators that, when run twice (or three times, and so on), leave the state unchanged. Describe the paths corresponding to these operators. [A]

12. [P] Can you characterize "looping programs" in terms of the commands used in writing them? In particular, consider the following program structures, where X and Y are variables and n is some fixed number:

- do loops

- goto statements

- assignment statements of the form X ← n

- assignments of the form X ← Y + n

- conditional statements of the form IF X = n ...

For each kind of structure, say whether a program that repeats a block of instructions consisting of basic turtle commands together with that particular structure must necessarily be equivalent to a program which repeats a fixed instruction sequence. Are there bad combinations, in the sense that two structures which separately lead to looping may not loop when combined in a single program?

1.4 Symmetry of Looping Programs

Section 1.3 showed how the symmetry of any looping program is determined by the symmetry of an underlying POLY skeleton. But what determines the symmetry of the POLY? To begin with, it is clear that the SIDE input in POLY SIDE ANGLE does not affect the shape of the figure at all but only determines the size. The real question is: How does the ANGLE input affect the symmetry of POLY? To be more precise, we can break this question into two questions:

For a given ANGLE input, how many vertices will the resulting POLY have?

Conversely, if we want to produce a POLY with a specified number of vertices, what number(s) can we use for the ANGLE input?

The purpose of this section is to answer these questions, and in doing so to provide a taste of the mathematics of number theory.

1.4.1 The Symmetry of POLY

We want to relate the number of vertices, n, to the input ANGLE, which we'll call A for short. The POLY closing theorem of 1.2.2 gives us a very good start. It says POLY is done when the turtle has turned a multiple of $360°$, that is, when n turns of A each is some multiple of 360:

$$nA = 360R.$$

We've given the multiple the name R for a good reason: It is the rotation number of the figure, as defined in subsection 1.2.1.

But the above equation, which defines a common multiple of A and 360, doesn't tell the whole story. R and n aren't just any integers satisfying the equation; they are the smallest (positive) that do so, corresponding to the first time heading change reaches a multiple of 360. That is why the number $nA = 360R$ is called the *least common multiple* of A and 360, denoted $\mathrm{LCM}(A, 360)$. The answer to our first question is:

For an ANGLE input of A, the number of vertices of the resulting POLY is $n = \mathrm{LCM}(A, 360)/A$ and the rotation number is $R = \mathrm{LCM}(A, 360)/360$.

What we've done so far is little more than giving the answer a name. How does one go about computing the least common multiple? One way, which assumes that A is an integer, is to express A and 360 as products of primes. Then each of the expressions nA and $360R$ will give a partial view of the factorization of $\mathrm{LCM}(A, 360)$. For example, if $A = 144$ then we have $A = 2^4 \times 3^2$, $360 = 2^3 \times 3^2 \times 5$. Using this decomposition, we can deduce that

$$\mathrm{LCM}(144, 360) = n \times 2^4 \times 3^2 = R \times 2^3 \times 3^2 \times 5$$
$$= 2^4 \times 3^2 \times 5 = 720,$$

for it is easy to see that the LCM must contain at least four factors of 2 (from A), one factor of 5 (from 360), and two factors of 3 (from either A or 360), and from this we derive that $n = 5$ and $R = 2$. So POLY 100 144 has fivefold symmetry (it consists of $n = 5$ identical pieces identically hooked together) and rotation number 2.

Another way to compute the least common multiple is to solve the equation $nA = 360R$ exactly as the procedure POLY solves it: by running until it closes! Make a list of $n \times A$ for $n = 1, 2, 3, \ldots$ and see when $n \times A$ is a multiple of 360. Applying this method to our example $A = 144$ gives

n	nA	multiple of 360?
1	144	no
2	288	no
3	432	no
4	576	no
5	720	yes

We can formulate this method as a procedure for computing the least common multiple:

```
TO LCM A B
    N ← 0
    REPEAT
        N ← N + 1
        MULTIPLE ← N * A
    UNTIL REMAINDER (MULTIPLE, B) = 0
    RETURN MULTIPLE
```

Such "brute force" methods of computation can be very useful. We will see in the next subsection the utility of a simple modification of this process, called Euclid's algorithm. The LCM procedure uses RETURN—a command we haven't seen before. Since the procedure is supposed to be computing some value, we need to have some method for "getting the value out of the procedure." This is what RETURN does. In practice the returned value will be used as an input to another operation, for example, PRINT LCM(144,360).

Let's turn to our second question about the symmetry of POLY figures. Suppose we want to produce figures of a given symmetry; what ANGLE can we use? To answer this question, let's start again with the basic symmetry equation $nA = 360R$. Since we want to find values for A that will produce a given value for n, we should be able to use any A that satisfies $A = 360R/n$. The question is: What value(s) can we choose for R? For instance, we can take $R = 1, A = 360/n$, which always works—it makes a regular n-sided polygon. But $R = 2, A = 2 \times 360/n$ may not work. Here's an example: Suppose we want tenfold symmetry, $n = 10$. If we take $R = 2$, then A will be 72. This makes a pentagon, not a figure with tenfold symmetry.

We've been fooled. $A = 360R/n$ doesn't always give n-fold symmetry. Let's look more carefully at the above guess, $R = 2, n = 10$.

Not only does the resulting pentagon not have tenfold symmetry, but it has rotation number 1, not 2. We clearly are not justified in naming our guesses 10 by n and 2 by R, so let's give them new names, n' and R'. How do these relate to the real n and R?

Let's compute the real n and R that correspond to $A = 360R'/n'$. We want the smallest positive integers n and R that satisfy $nA = 360R$. But this equation is satisfied by all pairs of integers R and n with the property that $R/n = R'/n'$. Since we want R and n to be the smallest pair with this property, we should take them to be the numerator and denominator of the fraction R'/n' reduced to lowest terms. In our example we had $R'/n' = 2/10 = 1/5$, so $n = 5$ and $R = 1$. To put this another way, $A = 360R'/n'$ will give n'-fold symmetry only when R'/n' cannot be reduced, that is to say, when R' and n' have no factors in common. Thus, the answer to the second question above is the following:

To generate a POLY with n-fold symmetry, take the ANGLE input to be $A = 360R/n$, where R is any positive integer that has no factors in common with n.

1.4.2 Common Divisors

We've answered our questions about the symmetry of POLY in terms of such concepts as common multiples and common factors. Let's take a detour from turtle geometry and turn this process around to see what knowing about POLY can tell us about these number-theoretic concepts.

To begin with, the previous subsection led us to consider pairs of integers n and R that have no common factors. Such pairs are called *relatively prime*. We saw that $A = 360R/n$ draws an n-sided POLY precisely when R is relatively prime to n. We'll reinterpret this fact in terms of a new way of looking at the POLY process.

Think of the n vertices of POLY lying on a circle and numbered from 0 through $n - 1$. To construct the various n-sided POLYs we can connect the vertices in sequence using the following sorts of rules: (1) Connect each vertex to the very next one; (2) connect the vertices, skipping one in between; (3) connect the vertices, skipping 2 in between; and so on. Figure 1.25 illustrates the various patterns for $n = 8$. There are $n - 1$ possibilities, which correspond to $R = 1, 2, \ldots, n - 1$ in the formula $A = 360R/n$. For any choice of R, if we start at the vertex numbered 0, then that is connected to the vertex numbered R, which is connected to the vertex numbered $2R$, and so on. Since we're counting these ver-

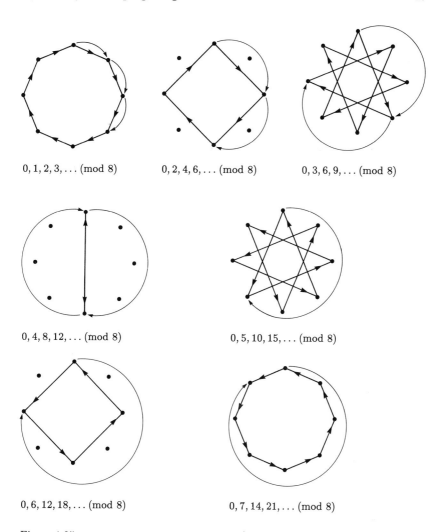

0, 1, 2, 3, ... (mod 8)   0, 2, 4, 6, ... (mod 8)   0, 3, 6, 9, ... (mod 8)

0, 4, 8, 12, ... (mod 8)   0, 5, 10, 15, ... (mod 8)

0, 6, 12, 18, ... (mod 8)   0, 7, 14, 21, ... (mod 8)

Figure 1.25
Patterns of connecting eight points, $n = 8$.

tices modulo n, we see that the sequence of vertices hit are precisely the multiples $0, R, 2R, \ldots, (n-1)R$ taken modulo n.

Now we saw in the previous subsection that, if R and n are relatively prime, then the resulting POLY figure will have n vertices. In terms of the circle picture this means that all vertices on the circle $0, 1, 2, \ldots, n-1$ are reached. Consequently, if R and n are relatively prime, then the multiples of R taken modulo n must include all the numbers between 0 and $n-1$. In other words, if s is any integer between 0 and $n-1$, then there is some multiple of R, say pR, with $pR = s$ (mod n). Moreover, if R and n are not relatively prime, then at least one of the n vertices will not be touched by the POLY process, and so there will be some number s which is not equal to pR (mod n) for any p. Restating the equality modulo n in terms of precise equality, we have the following:

Two integers R and n are relatively prime if and only if, for any integer s, we can find integers p and q such that $pR - qn = s$.

This condition can be written in an equivalent form (exercise 10) that reflects the fact that, if the vertex labeled 1 is hit, then all vertices must be:

Two integers R and n are relatively prime if and only if there exist integers p and q such that $pR + qs = 1$.

In summary: We have shown how to translate a condition about the relative primality of two integers into a rather different condition which has to do with representing integers as sums.

What exactly happens when R and n are not relatively prime? Figure 1.25 includes some examples: Taking $n = 8$ and $R = 2$ hits all the even vertices (the multiples of 2); $n = 8$ and $R = 4$ hits only 0 and 4 (multiples of 4); $n = 8$ and $R = 6$ hits all the multiples of 2. In general, the vertices which are hit—numbered $0, R, 2R, \ldots, (n-1)R$, taken modulo n—give precisely the multiples of some integer d. This integer d is called the *greatest common divisor* of n and R, and it can be defined by stating that $d = \mathrm{GCD}(n, R)$ is the largest integer that divides both n and R. The fact that the vertices which are hit are precisely the multiples of d follows from the fact that $\mathrm{GCD}(n, R)$ can alternatively be defined as the smallest positive integer that can be represented as $pR + qn$, where p and q also integers. We leave it to you (exercise 11) to verify these claims. You can see that the GCD of n and R is an important quantity. When it is 1, n and R are relatively prime and the POLY has n-fold symmetry. When the GCD is not 1, it gives d, the integer whose multiples are the vertices actually hit.

Neither definition of GCD—as the largest common divisor, or as the smallest positive $pR + qn$—seems very helpful in actually computing the GCD of two given integers. One method for doing so is Euclid's algorithm. The idea of the algorithm is very simple: The common factors of n and R are the same as the common factors of $n - R$ and R. (Prove this.) And so the problem of finding the GCD of n and R can be reduced to finding the GCD of $n - R$ and R:

Euclid's Algorithm Start with two numbers. (1) If the two numbers are equal, then stop; the GCD is their common value. (2) Subtract the smaller number from the larger and throw away the larger. (3) Repeat the entire process using, as the two numbers, the smaller number and the difference computed in step 2.

The process produces ever smaller numbers and stops with two equal numbers. Take as an example 360 and 144. The sequence of pairs generated is

$$(360, 144) \rightarrow (216, 144) \rightarrow (72, 144) \rightarrow (72, 72) \rightarrow \text{done: GCD} = 72$$

Finding the GCD of 360 and 144 can be interpreted as follows: Any POLY with an integer angle will touch some subset of the vertices of a regular 360-gon. If the angle is 144, the vertices touched will be the multiples of 72.

We can translate Euclid's algorithm into a recursive computer procedure:

```
TO EUCLID (N, R)
    IF N = R THEN RETURN N
    IF N > R THEN RETURN EUCLID (N - R, R)
    IF N < R THEN RETURN EUCLID (N, R - N)
```

There's an obvious way to speed up the algorithm: Subtract multiple copies of the smaller number from the larger in a single step. Even better, we can divide the smaller number into the larger, taking the smaller number and the remainder to start the next step. This has an additional advantage—we will know automatically that the remainder is smaller

than the original smaller number, so it will not be necessary to test to
see which of the two inputs is smaller:

```
TO FAST.EUCLID (N, R)
    IF N = R THEN RETURN N
        ELSE RETURN FAST.EUCLID (R, REMAINDER (N, R))
```

Note that Euclid's algorithm is very nearly the reverse of the "brute
force" method for finding the least common multiple given in subsection
1.4.1. In fact the algorithm gives us a new way of computing the LCM
of two numbers because of the formula

$$\text{LCM}(p, q) \times \text{GCD}(p, q) = p \times q,$$

which is true for any integers p and q. (See exercise 16.)

As a final remark we point out that, whereas the REMAINDER function
used in FAST.EUCLID is defined only for integers, the operations in the
original EUCLID procedure make sense for any numbers. So we can define
the GCD for any two numbers (not just integers) to be the value returned
by the EUCLID procedure. (Exercises 15–17 invite you to investigate the
properties of this generalized GCD.) We see here how the procedural
formulation of a concept can suggest new insights and directions for
exploring. Further explorations suggested by the EUCLID procedure are
illustrated in exercises 18–25.

Exercises for Section 1.4

1. Determine the symmetry of POLY with $A = 350, 35, 37, 12\frac{1}{2}, 26\frac{2}{3}$. For
each value of A, find p and q such that $A = 360p/q$ where p/q is a
fraction reduced to lowest terms. [A]

2. Using only integer angles, what are all the possible values of n for
which POLY can draw an n-sided figure? [HA]

3. [D] Show that the POLY symmetry determined by ANGLE $= 360 - A$
is the same as the symmetry of ANGLE $= A$. What about the symmetry
of ANGLE $= 180 - A$? [HA]

4. Consider the process of finding the least common multiple of A and
B. Show that the "brute force" method will find the same minimal
number n such that $nA = RB$ as it will for $n(Ax) = R(Bx)$ where x is
any number, and hence that $\text{LCM}(Ax, Bx) = x \times \text{LCM}(A, B)$. Use this
idea to show how to compute least common multiples of (noninteger)

rational numbers. If $A = p/q$ and $B = r/s$, both fractions in lowest terms, show how to pick x so that one can use the prime factorization method to compute LCM(A, B). [A]

5. We saw that $A = 360R/n$ will produce an n-pointed figure for any integer R relatively prime to n. But how many of these Rs actually produce POLYs that look different? How many different POLYs are there with $n = 10, 36, 37$? How many in general? [A]

6. In solving the previous problem you may want to make use of the Euler ϕ function, which is defined for positive integers n to be the number of integers less than n and relatively prime to it. Euler gave a formula for $\phi(n)$, which works as follows: Suppose that $p_1, p_2, \ldots$ are the distinct prime factors of n, that is $n = p_1^a p_2^b \ldots$. (For example, $3960 = 2^3 \times 3^2 \times 5 \times 11$.) Then

$$\phi(n) = n\left(1 - \frac{1}{p_1}\right)\left(1 - \frac{1}{p_2}\right)\cdots.$$

Use this formula to compute $\phi(1,000,000)$. [A]

7. [D] Use the fact that, for R relatively prime to n, the multiples of R include all the integers $1, 2, \ldots, n - 1$ (mod n) to prove Fermat's Little Theorem: If p is a prime and R is any positive integer less than p, then $R^{p-1} = 1$ (mod p). [HA]

8. [P] Fermat's Little Theorem lies behind a recently discovered way to test by computer whether large numbers are prime. The idea is to start with a number p, pick a random number a less than p, and compute a^{p-1} (mod p). If the answer is not 1, then p is not prime. Conversely, it is known that, in general, if p is not prime, then most of the numbers a less than p will not satisfy $a^{p-1} = 1$ (mod p). So if we test, say, 10 different choices for a and they all satisfy Fermat's equation, then we can be virtually certain that p is prime. Implement this method in a computer program and use it to find, say, the ten largest primes less than one billion. (There are choices for p, called "Carmichael numbers," that will fool this test. They are nonprime, and yet satisfy the condition $a^{p-1} = 1$ (mod p) for every a. But they are few and far between.)

9. [P] Write a procedure that, given a number n, returns a list of all the primes dividing n. Use this together with Euler's formula of exercise 6 to produce a procedure that calculates the Euler ϕ function.

10. Given integers R and n, show that there exist integers p and q such that $pR + qn = 1$ if and only if, for any integer s, there exist integers p_s and q_s such that $p_s R - q_s n = s$. [A]

11. [D] Prove that if we define the greatest common divisor $d = \text{GCD}(n, R)$ as the largest integer that divides both n and R, then d is the smallest positive integer that can be expressed as $\langle\text{integer}\rangle R + \langle\text{integer}\rangle n$. Show also that the multiples of R taken modulo n are precisely the multiples of d. [H]

12. [D] Show that the EUCLID procedure works when its inputs are positive integers. That is, show that it will always terminate and that what it returns is in fact the GCD of its inputs.

13. [P] In subsection 1.2.2 we discussed the problem of writing a POLY procedure that draws the figure once and then stops. We implemented POLYSTOP using the "local" strategy of having the turtle count total turning. Write a version of POLYSTOP which uses the "global" strategy of taking the ANGLE input and computing in advance how many times to run the basic loop. Can you design the program so that it works not only for integer angles but for (noninteger) rational angles as well?

14. Show directly that if Euclid's algorithm returns d given R and n as inputs, then there exist integers p and q such that $pR + qn = d$. [H]

15. [D] Show that the EUCLID procedure terminates whenever its inputs are positive rational numbers, and thus allows us to extend the definition of greatest common divisor to all positive rational numbers. What is the "GCD" of $\frac{1}{2}$ and $\frac{2}{3}$? of a/b and c/d where a, b, c and d are integers? What can you say about the behavior of the algorithm when the inputs are not both rational? [A]

16. [D] Prove for integers p and q that $\text{GCD}(p, q) \times \text{LCM}(p, q) = p \times q$. Does this formula hold as well for rational numbers (with GCD defined as the result of the EUCLID procedure and LCM defined as indicated in exercise 4)?

17. [D] What can you say about the $\langle\text{integer}\rangle R + \langle\text{integer}\rangle n$ definition of GCD as it relates to the GCD for rational numbers (defined as the result of the EUCLID procedure)?

18. [D] Modify the EUCLID procedure to define a procedure DIO which not only computes $d = \text{GCD}(n, R)$ but also returns integers p and q

such that $pR + qn = d$. The DIO procedure should take two inputs and return a list of three numbers p, q, d. [HA]

19. [D] Show how to speed up the DIO procedure by using the reduction method of the FAST.EUCLID procedure. Write the corresponding FAST.DIO program. [HA]

20. The name DIO comes from "Diophantine equations." These are equations which are to be solved for integer values of the unknowns. Use your DIO or FAST.DIO procedures to find integers x and y which satisfy the equation $17x + 117y = 1$; the equation $1234567x + 7654321y = 1$. [A]

21. Let T denote the transformation $(n, r) \to (r, n - r)$ which is used by the EUCLID program. Show that the transformation S defined by $(x, y) \to (x + y, x)$ is inverse to T in the sense that, for any pair (a, b), $T(S(a, b)) = S(T(a, b)) = (a, b)$. If we start with the pair $(1, 0)$ and repeatedly apply S we obtain

$$(1, 0) \to (1, 1) \to (2, 1) \to (3, 2) \to (5, 3) \to (8, 5) \to (13, 8) \to \cdots.$$

The sequence of numbers formed by this operation is called the Fibonacci numbers; that is,

$$F(0) = 0, F(1) = 1, F(2) = 1, F(3) = 2, F(4) = 3, F(5) = 5, F(6) = 8,$$

and so on. Use the fact that S and T are inverse to show that for any integer n, $F(n)$ and $F(n - 1)$ are relatively prime. [A]

22. [P] Show that $F(n) = F(n - 1) + F(n - 2)$ and hence that the Fibonacci numbers can be generated by the procedure

```
TO FIB N
    IF N = 0 RETURN 1
    IF N = 1 RETURN 1
    RETURN FIB (N-1) + FIB (N-2)
```

Why does this procedure run so slowly? Can you find a faster method of computing the Fibonacci numbers? [A]

23. [DD] Expanding on the result of exercise 21, investigate the greatest common divisor of $F(n)$ and $F(n + k)$. State and prove a theorem about $GCD(F(a), F(b))$. [HA]

24. [D] Use the `DIO` or `FAST.DIO` procedures (exercises 18,19) to solve Diophantine equations of the form $xF(n) + yF(n-1) = 1$ for integers x and y. What is the solution in general? [HA]

25. [P] For any pair of numbers p, q we can define a new sequence of numbers $F(p, q; n)$ by applying the transformation S of exercise 21 beginning with (p, q) rather than $(1, 0)$. Write a program to generate these sequences and investigate their properties. Can you express $F(p, q; n)$ in terms of the usual Fibonacci numbers? [A]

2

Feedback, Growth, and Form

> We watch an ant make his laborious way across a
> wind- and wave-molded beach. He moves ahead,
> angles to the right to ease his climb up a steep
> dunelet, detours around a pebble, stops for a mo-
> ment to exchange information with a compatriot.
> Thus he makes his weaving, halting way back home.
> ... His horizons are very close, so that he deals with
> each obstacle as he comes to it; he probes for ways
> around or over it, without much thought for future
> obstacles. It is easy to trap him into deep detours.
>
> Herbert Simon, *The Sciences of the Artificial*

Chapter 1 presented the rudiments of a computational view of geometry
and introduced some themes—local versus global, intrinsic versus extrinsic, state, and fixed instruction programs—that will be important in
chapters to come. The most important theme of all, however, is that
turtle geometry is a mathematics designed for exploring. Now it's time
to explore. This chapter presents some ideas for using turtle graphics to
investigate mathematics in an experimental and phenomenon-oriented
way. Randomness, feedback systems, growth, differential games, and
designs based on recursion are all fruitful areas. With the initiation
provided here, we hope you will take the time to investigate some of
these topics in depth.

2.1 The Turtle as Animal

We introduced the turtle as a mathematical "animal"; let's pursue that
point of view by thinking of the turtle's motion as a behavior pattern
and the turtle programs as models of simple animal behavior. Turtle
geometry is particularly well suited to such modeling because of the
local and intrinsic ways we specify the turtle's movements. Expressing
motions in terms of FORWARDs and RIGHTs is a much more direct way of
dealing with an animal's behavior than, say, describing movements in
response to stimuli as changes in x and y coordinates.

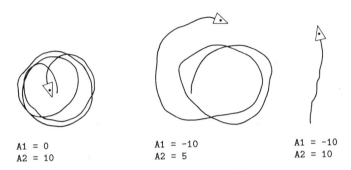

A1 = 0   A1 = -10   A1 = -10
A2 = 10   A2 = 5   A2 = 10

Figure 2.1
Sample paths generated by RANDOM.MOVE

2.1.1 Random Motion

Perhaps the simplest kind of motion to model with the turtle is random
motion (repeatedly going forward and turning random amounts). To
implement this in a procedure, let's assume that our computer language
has a random-number generator RAND(LOW,HIGH) that outputs a random
number between LOW and HIGH. Using this we can write a procedure that
takes four inputs specifying the ranges from which to select the inputs
to FORWARD and LEFT:

```
TO RANDOM.MOVE (D1, D2, A1, A2)
    REPEAT FOREVER
        LEFT RAND (A1, A2)
        FORWARD RAND (D1, D2)
```

Even with this simple program, there is much to investigate. How do
the bounds on the FORWARDs or the turns affect the path? For instance,
unless you make A1 negative, the turtle will always turn left and the
path will look roughly like a circle. In fact, except when A1 is chosen to
be the negative of A2, the turtle's turning will be biased in one direction
or the other and this will be reflected in the shape of the path. Figure
2.1 shows some examples. How about the case where the turning is
unbiased? Would you expect the turtle to go off "to infinity"? Or will
it instead travel in a very large circle? More generally, can you say
anything about the radius of the "average path" as a function of the
bounds on the turns? One way to investigate these random motions is to
write a record-keeping procedure that repeatedly runs, say, 100 rounds
of the RANDOM.MOVE loop and automatically records such statistics as
the turtle's heading and distance from the origin after those 100 rounds.

Can you say anything about the average values of these quantities? (See exercises 2 and 3.)

Random-motion procedures such as this will often run the turtle off the edge of the display screen. Forcing the turtle to stay on the screen suggests modifying the random motion to model the behavior of an animal crawling in a box. To enable the turtle to do this, we'll supply two new procedures: CHECK.FORWARD, which is just like FORWARD except that it won't allow the turtle to move if the result would take it outside of some fixed square box around the origin, and STUCK, which tells whether or not the last move tried to place the turtle outside of the box.

The CHECK.FORWARD program works by moving the turtle "invisibly" to the new position, then using a subprocedure OUT.OF.BOUNDS? to check whether the new position is within bounds, and finally redoing the move visibly only if it is within bounds. This procedure makes use of some new operations in our turtle graphics system. HIDETURTLE causes the turtle indicator not to be displayed; SHOWTURTLE restores the indicator; XCOR and YCOR output, respectively, the x and y coordinates of the turtle; TURTLE.STATE outputs (as a list) the position and heading of the turtle; and SETTURTLE takes as input a list such as is produced by TURTLE.STATE and restores the turtle to that state:

```
TO CHECK.FORWARD DISTANCE
    OLD.POSITION ← TURTLE.STATE
    PENUP
    HIDETURTLE
    FORWARD DISTANCE
    FORWARD.FAILED ← OUT.OF.BOUNDS?
    SETTURTLE OLD.POSITION
    PENDOWN
    SHOWTURTLE
    IF NOT FORWARD.FAILED THEN FORWARD DISTANCE

TO STUCK
    RETURN FORWARD.FAILED

TO OUT.OF.BOUNDS?
    IF EITHER
            ABS(XCOR) > BOXSIZE
            ABS(YCOR) > BOXSIZE
        THEN RETURN "TRUE"
        ELSE RETURN "FALSE"
```

(ABS is the absolute value function.)

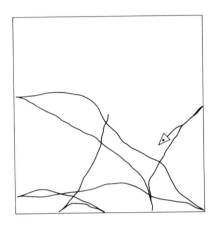 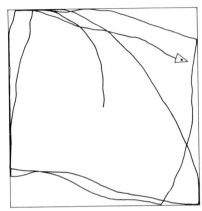

Figure 2.2
(a) Edge "reflection" generated by IF STUCK THEN RIGHT 180. (b) Edge-following
behavior generated by IF STUCK THEN WRIGGLE.

We can use these procedures to model appropriate behaviors that
will keep the turtle in the box. Here, for example, is a version of
RANDOM.MOVE that has the turtle turn 180° whenever it runs into an
edge:

```
TO RANDOM.MOVE (D1, D2, A1, A2)
    REPEAT FOREVER
        LEFT RAND (A1, A2)
        CHECK.FORWARD RAND (D1, D2)
        IF STUCK THEN RIGHT 180
```

Figure 2.2a shows a sample path. A second possibility for edge behavior
is to have the turtle turn a little at a time, until it can go forward again.
To do this, change the last line in the above procedure to

IF STUCK THEN WRIGGLE

where WRIGGLE is defined as

```
TO WRIGGLE
    REPEAT
        RIGHT 1
        CHECK.FORWARD 1
    UNTIL NOT STUCK
```

Figure 2.2b shows how this variation, incorporated into a random-motion procedure, causes the turtle to spend most of its time wandering along the edges of the box. You may have observed the similar behavior of a real insect trapped in a box. Of course, with a real insect, this behavior is often interpreted as the insect trying to get out of the box by following the walls. The turtle program calls into question the validity of such anthropomorphizing. If edge-following behavior can be produced by a simple combination of random motion plus wall avoidance, are we really justified in saying that the insect is "trying" to follow the edge? Could we legitimately make this claim about the turtle?

2.1.2 Directed Motion: Modeling Smell

We can make our simulation more elaborate by allowing the turtle's behavior to be affected by some stimulus. For example, we could imagine that there is some food located in the box with the turtle and design mechanisms that allow the turtle to find the food "by sense of smell." There are many different ways we could provide turtles with information corresponding to an ability to smell. For example, the "amount of smell" could be a value that depends on how far the turtle is from the food (the larger the distance, the weaker the smell); or the turtle might not sense any particular level of smell, but at each move be able to detect whether the smell is getting stronger or weaker.

We'll begin with the second possibility. This "stronger-weaker" kind of smell can be modeled by

```
TO SMELL
    IF DISTANCE.TO.FOOD > DISTANCE.LAST.TIME
        THEN RESULT ← "WEAKER"
        ELSE RESULT ← "STRONGER"
    DISTANCE.LAST.TIME ← DISTANCE.TO.FOOD
        ; save the current distance to use in the next comparison
    RETURN RESULT
```

How can the turtle use this information to locate the food? One possibility is this: If the turtle finds that the smell is getting stronger, it keeps going in the same direction; otherwise it turns:

```
TO FIND.BY.SMELL1
    REPEAT FOREVER
        FORWARD 1
        IF SMELL = "WEAKER" THEN RIGHT 1
```

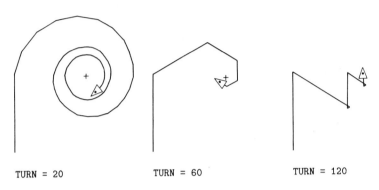

TURN = 20   TURN = 60   TURN = 120

Figure 2.3
Paths generated by FIND.BY.SMELL2.

Experimenting further, we can add a parameter to adjust the size of the turtle's turns. This leads to an interesting study of how the geometry of the path varies with the turn angle. (See figure 2.3.)

```
TO FIND.BY.SMELL2 (TURN)
    REPEAT FOREVER
        FORWARD 1
        IF SMELL = "WEAKER" THEN RIGHT TURN
```

A more realistic simulation would also include some of the random motion of section 2.1.1:

```
TO FIND.BY.SMELL3 (D1, D2, SMELL.TURN, RAND.TURN)
    REPEAT FOREVER
        FORWARD RAND (D1, D2)
        LEFT RAND ( - RAND.TURN, RAND.TURN )
        IF SMELL = "WEAKER" THEN RIGHT SMELL.TURN
```

In this procedure the turtle's motion is governed by two opposing tendencies: a "random motion" scaled by RAND.TURN and a "directed motion" scaled by SMELL.TURN. This can be highlighted by adjusting the relative sizes of the two parameters. As an experiment, see how large RAND.TURN must be with respect to SMELL.TURN before the random motion dominates completely and the turtle makes no discernible progress towards the food. (See figure 2.4.)

A different possibility for sensing "smell" is to have the turtle respond to an intensity directly, rather than to a change in intensity. Biologists have suggested various simple mechanisms by which animals can use

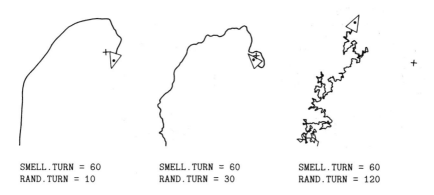

SMELL.TURN = 60   SMELL.TURN = 60   SMELL.TURN = 60
RAND.TURN = 10   RAND.TURN = 30   RAND.TURN = 120

Figure 2.4
FIND.BY.SMELL3 illustrates degeneration of the algorithm under increasing randomness.

such intensity information to approach or avoid stimuli. Wood lice, for example, are observed to aggregate in moist places and avoid dry places. It is believed that they move in random directions, but that the moisture level governs their speed—they move more slowly when it is damp and hence spend most of their time in moist regions. This mechanism for aggregation is called *orthokinesis*. A different mechanism, *klinokinesis*, is claimed to govern the behavior of paramecia in aggregating in dark areas. In klinokinesis, the animal's speed is constant, but the rate of turning varies with the intensity of the stimulus. (For more information on these and other orientation mechanisms, see G. Fraenkel and D. Gunn, *Orientation in Animals* [New York: Dover, 1961].) Try writing procedures embodying these mechanisms, and then try inventing new mechanisms. Good questions to guide your exploration are: How "efficient" is your method (how long does it take the turtle to reach the stimulus point)? How does the turtle's path change as you vary the initial position and heading, or as you vary the parameters to the program? How does the mechanism degenerate as you incorporate some randomness into the turtle's motion (for example, as in the FIND.BY.SMELL3 procedure above)? Will even a slight amount of randomness destroy the turtle's ability to reach the goal, or is your mechanism relatively stable with respect to random distortions?

In a more abstract vein, investigate the mathematical properties of simple POLYlike programs, but think of some aspect of the turtle's motion as governed by the distance from some chosen point. Try, for example,

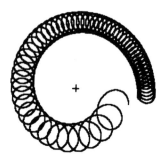

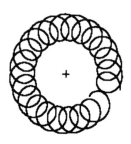

VARY.STEP 1500 10   VARY.TURN 10 2000

Figure 2.5
Samples of paths generated by VARY.STEP and VARY.TURN.

having the turtle turn a constant angle while going forward a distance
that depends on the distance from the point:

```
TO VARY.STEP (SIDE, ANGLE)
    REPEAT FOREVER
        FORWARD (FACTOR * SIDE)
        LEFT ANGLE
```

Or take a constant FORWARD step and vary the turn:

```
TO VARY.TURN (SIDE, ANGLE)
    REPEAT FOREVER
        FORWARD SIDE
        LEFT (FACTOR * ANGLE)
```

FACTOR here can be something like

```
TO FACTOR
    RETURN (1 / DISTANCE.TO.CHOSEN.POINT)
```

Figure 2.5 shows some sample paths. As you can see, the procedures
seem to do different sorts of things. VARY.STEP tends to draw spirals,
whereas VARY.TURN tends to draw bounded figures. Investigate these
programs and come up with some conjectures about their behavior. Can
you prove your conjectures?

2.1.3 Modeling Sight

As with smell, the first step in providing turtle with simulated sight is to
decide what information the "eye" should receive from the environment.

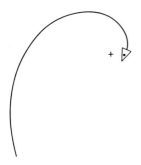

Figure 2.6
`KEEP.A.BEARING: ANGLE = 60.`

We could hardly begin to model the complexity of human vision. A much simpler model ignores color, shape, and texture and registers merely the intensity of light reaching the eye. This kind of "sight" is not so different from the "smell" discussed above. Each sense receives some kind of intensity information from the environment. The major difference is that sight is directional; it depends on how the turtle is facing with respect to the stimulus. Algorithms for locating an object by sight are therefore different from "smelling something out."

Facing a Stimulus
The first model for sight assumes that any creature able to see a light is able to turn to face that light. (See exercise 10.) Investigate what new things the turtle can do when given the ability to FACE a named point. For example, getting to the point is easy: Simply face the point and go forward. (But how does the turtle know when to stop?) Another use for the FACE command is to have the turtle move while keeping some point at a fixed bearing. The following procedure makes the turtle walk with a fixed bearing of ANGLE with respect to a fixed POINT:

```
TO KEEP.A.BEARING POINT ANGLE
    REPEAT FOREVER
        FACE POINT
        LEFT ANGLE
        FORWARD 1
```

If you try this procedure (figure 2.6) you will find that it causes the turtle to spiral about the point. Does this remind you of anything? How about a moth getting trapped by a light? Can you think of a reason why a moth would be trying to keep a light at a fixed bearing? Some

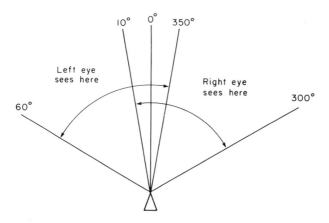

Figure 2.7
Fields of vision for two-eye model.

people believe that moths and other night-flying insects have learned to
fly along straight paths by keeping the moon at a constant bearing as
they fly. Keeping a very distant light like the moon at a fixed bearing
would indeed make the insects fly straight. When they confuse the moon
with a nearby light, the fixed-bearing mechanism causes them to spiral.

A Two-Eye Model
The next model focuses on how a creature might use vision in order to
face a point. Assume that the turtle has two eyes, each with its own
field of vision, as shown in figure 2.7. We give the turtle the ability to
tell whether a point is within each eye's field of vision:

```
TO RIGHT.EYE.SEES POINT
    IF BEARING(POINT) > 300 THEN RETURN "TRUE"
    IF BEARING(POINT) < 10 THEN RETURN "TRUE"
    RETURN "FALSE"

TO LEFT.EYE.SEES POINT
    IF BEARING(POINT) > 350 THEN RETURN "TRUE"
    IF BEARING(POINT) < 60 THEN RETURN "TRUE"
    RETURN "FALSE"
```

(These procedures use a subprocedure called BEARING that outputs the
angle that the turtle would need to turn left in order to face a given
point. Exercise 10 outlines how BEARING can be implemented.)

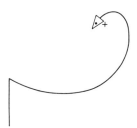

Figure 2.8
Behavior of HEAD.FOR.

The turtle will know that it is facing roughly in the direction of a named point when the point lies in the field of vision on at least one side. So, as the turtle moves, it should keep checking that it can still see the point. Otherwise it turns until it can see the point:

```
TO HEAD.FOR POINT
    REPEAT FOREVER
        IF EITHER
            LEFT.EYE.SEES(POINT),
            RIGHT.EYE.SEES(POINT)
        THEN FORWARD 10
        ELSE LEFT 10
```

It may seem amazing that a turtle following this procedure manages to reach the specified point despite the fact that its way of heading for the point is so inaccurate. (See figure 2.8.) This illustrates the effectiveness of a *feedback mechanism*—constant adjustment can often compensate for lack of accuracy. You might try combining this mechanism with some of the random-motion procedures of subsection 2.1.1.

A Two-Eye Model With Intensity
A more elaborate model for vision registers not only the presence of a light source in the visual field, but also the intensity that each eye receives from the source. This intensity depends on the strength of the source, the distance of the source from the eye, and the angle at which the light strikes the eye. The intensity is greatest when the light hits the eye straight on and tapers off to zero as the light source moves toward the edge of the visual field.

Suppose we have procedures INTENSITY.LEFT and INTENSITY.RIGHT that output the intensity each eye receives from a light source. (We'll

Figure 2.9
Path generated by FIND.BY.SIGHT.

worry about how to design these INTENSITY procedures later.) There is
a simple yet effective way to incorporate such intensity information in a
feedback mechanism to make the turtle approach the light source:

```
TO FIND.BY.SIGHT SOURCE
   REPEAT FOREVER
      FORWARD 1
      IF INTENSITY.LEFT(SOURCE) > INTENSITY.RIGHT(SOURCE)
         THEN LEFT 10
         ELSE RIGHT 10
```

The turtle walks forward while trying to keep the amount of light
received at both eyes in balance. If the turtle sees more light to its
right, it turns slightly to the right. If it sees more light to its left, it
turns slightly to the left. (See figure 2.9.)

Some animals may actually use this mechanism for approaching light
sources. Biologists have obtained experimental evidence for this conclusion by taking an animal and masking one of its eyes. What happens
when the animal tries to approach the light? You can simulate this experiment by modifying INTENSITY.LEFT to always return 0 and have
the turtle follow the FIND.BY.SIGHT procedure. Now the turtle will always turn right, and will therefore travel in a circle. Biologists call this
behavior "circus movement." It has been observed in experiments with
numerous species of insects.

A variation of this experiment is to modify INTENSITY.LEFT to output
half its normal value. (This corresponds to an animal with weak vision
in one eye.) What kind of path does FIND.BY.SIGHT produce now? Does
the animal still reach the light? How does the path degenerate to a circus
movement as the eye becomes weaker and weaker?

Finally, consider what happens when there are two or more light sources. The intensity for each eye can be found by adding together the intensities from the individual sources:

```
TO FIND.BY.SIGHT2 (SOURCE1, SOURCE2)
    REPEAT FOREVER
        FORWARD 1
        TOTAL.LEFT ← INTENSITY.LEFT(SOURCE1)
                            + INTENSITY.LEFT(SOURCE2)
        TOTAL.RIGHT ← INTENSITY.RIGHT(SOURCE1)
                            + INTENSITY.RIGHT(SOURCE2)
        IF TOTAL.LEFT > TOTAL.RIGHT
            THEN LEFT 10
            ELSE RIGHT 10
```

How does the turtle behave? Does it go to the stronger light? Between the lights? Keep records of what happens for sources with different strengths and for different initial positions of turtle and sources. This "two-light experiment" is often performed with real insects.

The intensity procedures used in these projects can be designed according to a model given in the book by Fraenkel and Gunn mentioned above. They compute the intensity of light falling on the eye as $(S/D^2)\cos A$ where S is the strength of the source, D is the distance from the source, and A is the angle at which light from the source strikes the eye. (See figure 2.10.) The turtle procedure based on this would be

```
TO INTENSITY.LEFT SOURCE
    IF NOT LEFT.EYE.SEES(SOURCE) THEN RETURN 0
    FACTOR ← STRENGTH / (DIST(SOURCE) ↑ 2)
    ANGLE ← BEARING (SOURCE) - 45
    RETURN (FACTOR * COS(ANGLE))
```

STRENGTH here is a parameter you supply to indicate the intensity of the source. Note the computation of ANGLE, which reflects the fact that the left eye is offset 45° from the turtle's heading. INTENSITY.RIGHT is implemented in a similar fashion.

Exercises for Section 2.1

1. [P] In the RANDOM.MOVE procedure of 2.1.1, how does the turtle's path change if the turning is generated by LEFT RAND(0,50) followed by RIGHT RAND(0,50) rather than LEFT RAND(-50,50)? How is the

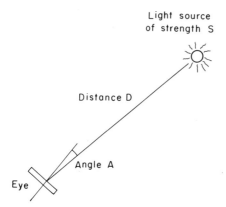

Figure 2.10
Intensity of light seen by eye is $(S/D^2)\cos A$.

distribution of numbers produced by RAND(-50,50) different from that of RAND(0,50) - RAND(0,50)? [A]

2. [PD] Starting with the turtle facing straight up, run the RANDOM.MOVE procedure until the turtle exceeds distance n from the start, that is, crosses a circle of radius n centered at the starting point. At what point did the turtle intersect the circle? Repeat this process over and over and study the distribution of intersection points on the circle. What is its "average value"? How does the distribution change as n varies? Answer the same sort of questions about the number of steps taken before crossing the circle. [H]

3. [PDD] If the turtle follows RANDOM.MOVE with the turn angle evenly distributed between −10 and 10, will you expect it to go off to infinity, or to travel in a large circle? Make some studies of this phenomenon. For example, graph the turtle's distance from the origin after n steps. Is there an average graph for many tries of this experiment? Alternatively, if the angle is not evenly distributed, the program will cause the turtle to tend to walk in circles. But do the circles wander off to infinity? How fast?

4. [P] Investigate randomized POLY procedures such as

```
TO RANDOM.POLY (SIDE, ANGLE)
    REPEAT FOREVER
        FORWARD SIDE
        LEFT (ANGLE * RAND(LOW, HIGH))
```

5. [P] In the FIND.BY.SMELL2 procedure of 2.1.2, how does the time required to reach the food vary with the angle the turtle turns? In the randomized FIND.BY.SMELL3 procedure, what is the average time as a function of the SMELL.TURN and RAND.TURN? (Do some experiments and take statistics.)

6. [P] Implement procedures for orthokinesis and klinokinesis. Which is more efficient? Which is more stable under adding a bit of randomness? Does the stability depend on the kind of randomness?

7. [P] Play around with the VARY.STEP procedure of 2.1.2. Does the turtle always spiral inwards or outwards? Does this depend on the initial position or heading with respect to the fixed point? Try also taking different values for FACTOR, such as making it directly proportional to the distance from the point or inversely proportional to the distance squared.

8. [P] What can you say about the VARY.TURN procedure? Does the turtle always stay within a bounded distance from the fixed point? Try this also with the variations on FACTOR, as in exercise 7.

9. [P] Try procedures like VARY.STEP and VARY.TURN, only this time where FACTOR depends on the change in distance (as with the SMELL procedure of 2.1.1). For instance, suppose FACTOR is equal to DISTANCE—DISTANCE.LAST.TIME. Consider the procedure

```
REPEAT FOREVER
    FORWARD SIDE
    LEFT FACTOR
```

Prove that this can never draw a simple closed figure. [HA]

10. [P] Implement the FACE and BEARING procedures used in the sight programs of 2.1.3. BEARING should return the amount the turtle needs to turn left in order to face the point. Then FACE can be immediately implemented as LEFT(BEARING(POINT)). BEARING, in turn, can be implemented in terms of the turtle's heading and another function, TOWARDS, which outputs the heading of the line directed from the turtle to the point. This can be computed using an arctangent function. [A]

11. [P] Make a careful investigation of the two- (or more) light experiment. How does the turtle's path vary with the relative intensities of the light?

12. [P] Suppose the turtle lives in a square room with a light at each corner. Instead of using a rectangular coordinate system, the turtle can "get its bearings" by measuring the observed angles between the lights. Suppose the turtle starts at some point P and records the observed angles. Now move the turtle to a different point. Design a simple feedback algorithm that enables the turtle to return to P by moving and watching how the angles change.

2.2 Turtles Interacting

One natural extension of the previous section's "turtle biology" is to consider multiple turtles and the interactions produced by simple algorithms. As we shall see, even simple algorithms may lead to complex phenomena, and a study of these phenomena can be an invitation to the theory of "differential games."

2.2.1 Predator and Prey

Consider how the FIND.BY.SMELL mechanism of subsection 2.1.2 would behave if the food were also moving, as in the case of a predator trying to catch dinner. There are many possible variations to try. Suppose, for example, that the hunted creature, unaware of the predator's intentions, moves round and round in a circle and that the predator follows the prey according to the FIND.BY.SMELL2 procedure of 2.1.2. One way to implement this interaction is to write separate procedures for predator and prey that describe how each creature generates a single forward step:

```
TO PREY.STEP (SPEED, TURN)
   FORWARD SPEED
   RIGHT TURN

TO PREDATOR.STEP (SPEED, TURN)
   FORWARD SPEED
   IF SMELL = "WEAKER" THEN RIGHT TURN
```

Now supply a monitor procedure called EXECUTE.TOGETHER that executes these two procedures alternately, over and over:

```
TO EXECUTE.TOGETHER (PREDATOR.PROCESS, PREY.PROCESS)
   REPEAT FOREVER
           ; set the turtle at the predator state and
           ; execute the predator's procedure
       EXECUTE.STEP (PREDATOR.PROCESS, PREDATOR.STATE)
```

```
        ; save the predator state for next time
    PREDATOR.STATE ← TURTLE.STATE
        ; execute the prey's procedure
    EXECUTE.STEP (PREY.PROCESS, PREY.STATE)
        ;save the prey state
    PREY.STATE ← TURTLE.STATE
```

The inputs to this procedure are to be the STEPs above, with their inputs. For instance,

```
EXECUTE.TOGETHER ("PREY.STEP (1,1)","PREDATOR.STEP (2,90)")
```

makes the prey and predator execute simultaneously.

The EXECUTE.STEP procedure is responsible for executing the process in the right place. It makes the turtle follow a given process starting from a given state.

```
TO EXECUTE.STEP (PROCESS, STATE)
        ; with the pen up move the turtle to the starting state
    PENUP
    SETTURTLE STATE
        ; put the pen down and execute the process
    PENDOWN
    EXECUTE PROCESS
```

At any point during the process, the variables PREDATOR.STATE and PREY.STATE specify the position and heading of the creatures. Set these to their initial values before starting the EXECUTE.TOGETHER procedure. (Note: Some computer languages have built-in facilities for parallel processing, which eliminate the need for such a EXECUTE.TOGETHER procedure. But since these languages are not yet widespread, we show how to implement this in a more conventional language. Also, see appendix A for details about the EXECUTE command.)

Figure 2.11 shows the result of the two procedures with the predator's TURN equal to 90° and with predator moving twice as fast as prey. As you can see, the FIND.BY.SMELL mechanism, which works so well with a fixed food source, does very poorly when the food is moving. The geometry of the path, however, is interesting. Notice that, after an initial segment, the predator's path is closed. Can you see why? Investigate this phenomenon for different TURN angles in the PREDATOR.STEP procedure and also for varying relative speeds of predator and prey.

Now conduct a similar investigation with some of the other animal-orientation mechanisms of section 2.1. Do they all do so poorly when

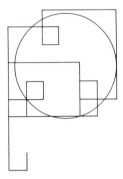

Figure 2.11
Closed-path phenomenon. Predator uses `FIND.BY.SMELL` with `TURN = 90`; prey moves
in circle. Predator speed is twice prey speed.

the food is moving? Or consider the use of these simple algorithms
as avoidance mechanisms. For example, set up a situation in which
a predator uses one of the sight algorithms of 2.1.3 to chase another
creature that is using an `AVOID.BY.SMELL` procedure. (Note: To convert
`FIND.BY.SMELL` to `AVOID.BY.SMELL`, simply modify the procedure so
that the creature will turn whenever the smell is getting stronger.) Any
such combination of the behaviors illustrated in section 2.1 can serve as
the basis for a project.

2.2.2 Following and Chasing

In a slightly different framework, we can consider "chase and evade"
strategies for two turtles. The simplest strategy is for the chasing turtle
to run directly towards the evader, and for the evader to run directly
away from the chaser. More interesting is the situation when both
creatures are constrained to stay within a square box. There are lots
of possibilities for projects here. Begin by programing simple strategies
using the `EXECUTE.TOGETHER` framework of 2.2.1. Now make the chaser
a bit smarter so that he can generally catch the evader—for example, by
driving him into a corner. Now make the evader smarter, so that he can
avoid the trap. Now make the chaser smarter still, and so on. When you
get some really clever programs, modify the setup so that you control
one of the creatures by hand and the computer controls the other. Are
your clever procedures more skilled at the chase-evade game than you
are? As a test of skill and strategy, try varying the relative speeds of
chaser and evader. If they both move at the same speed, can the evader
always avoid being caught?

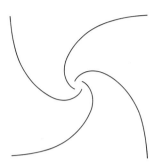

Figure 2.12
Spiral paths generated by four "bugs" starting at vertices of square.

It's also interesting to examine the paths generated by interacting creatures. One example is the widely known mathematical problem of the four "bugs" who start at the vertices of a square and move at the same speed, each one following the bug to its right. Set this up using the EXECUTE.TOGETHER procedure (suitably modified to handle four creatures) and the FOLLOW mechanism:

```
TO FOLLOW THAT.BUG
    FACE THAT.BUG
    FORWARD 1
```

Now make bug 1 follow bug 2, bug 2 follow bug 3, bug 3 follow bug 4, and bug 4 follow bug 1:

```
EXECUTE.TOGETHER "FOLLOW BUG2" "FOLLOW BUG3"
                 "FOLLOW BUG4" "FOLLOW BUG1"
```

Figure 2.12 shows the paths generated by the four bugs. As you can see, they all meet at a single point. One notable property of the "four bugs" situation is that the length of the path traveled by each bug is equal to the side of the original square. See if you can prove that. Modify FOLLOW to keep track of how far each bug moves, and compare the computed value with the theoretical value.

Here is another interesting chase phenomenon with two creatures, the chaser and the evader. The chaser heads directly towards the evader:

```
TO CHASE
    FACE EVADER
    FORWARD CHASE.SPEED
```

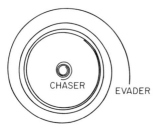

Figure 2.13
Stable configuration generated by interaction of CHASE and EVADE.

But the evader, instead of running directly away, heads at a constant
90° bearing from the chaser:

```
TO EVADE
   FACE CHASER
   RIGHT 90
   FORWARD EVADE.SPEED
```

When the two creatures move at the same speed, the chaser always
catches up, as you might expect. But when the evader's speed is increased, both chaser and evader begin to spiral in towards each other.
The spirals eventually degenerate into closed circles (see figure 2.13),
which are stable configurations for the chaser-evader situation. Even
though the algorithm seems "directed," the creatures end up retracing
their paths over and over.

A multiple-turtle setup can also be used to investigate some of the
phenomena in the area of "differential games," which has to do with
finding optimal strategies in situations similar to "chase and evade." An
example is provided by a "target defending" game consisting of two
players and a target. The attacker's object is to get as close to the
target as possible; the defender's object is to intercept the first player as
far from the target as possible. Assume that both players have the same
speed and that the defender starts out closer to the target. It turns out
that this situation has a simple optimal strategy, which is the same for
both players: Each time you move, head for the point that is closest to
the target and that lies on the perpendicular bisector of the line joining
your position to your opponent's (see exercise 11). Of course, if both
players are computerized and move with optimal strategy (figure 2.14a)
the resulting paths aren't very interesting—a better idea might be to
arrange things so that you control one player and the computer controls

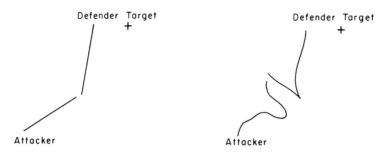

Figure 2.14
Target-defending game. (a) Both players following optimal strategy. (b) Attacker manually controlled; defender computer-controlled following optimal strategy.

the other (see figure 2.14b). Try playing against the computer both on attack and on defense. How well can you do in comparison with the theoretical optimum?

Books on differential games suggest many more situations that can be made into games between a person and a computer. In general these are very difficult to analyze for optimal strategies; the target-defending game explained above is unusually straightforward. There is a way to simplify the situation: Restrict all creatures to move on a square grid; that is, only allow turns that are multiples of 90° and distances that are multiples of some fixed length, or, alternatively, specify that at each step a creature can move only to an adjacent square in the grid.

Exercises for Section 2.2

1. [PD] Can you verify, as asserted in subsection 2.2.1, that a predator using FIND.BY.SMELL to chase a creature moving in a circle will eventually travel in a closed path? How does this depend on the angle turned? On the relative speeds of predator and prey? On the initial positions?

2. [P] Set up a predator using FIND.BY.SIGHT (subsection 2.1.3) to chase a prey using AVOID.BY.SMELL. Does he catch him if the two creatures have equal speeds? Does this depend on the angles that the creatures turn? What happens as the speeds vary?

3. [P] Implement a general EXECUTE.TOGETHER facility that can handle, say, two, three, or four creatures simultaneously. Notice that the procedure given in the text draws only the creatures' paths and not the creatures themselves. Maybe you'd like to improve upon this.

4. [P] Implement a general "chase-evade" system that allows you to specify procedures to guide both chaser and evader, or to control either creature by hand.

5. [PD] Set up the "four bugs" simulation. Have the system calculate the distance traveled by each bug. Does your result agree with the claim in the text that this distance is equal to the side of the original square? Can you prove this claim?

6. [PDD] Suppose that, instead of four bugs, we have three bugs starting in the vertices of an equilateral triangle. How far does each bug travel now? Generalize this to consider n bugs starting at the vertices of a regular n-gon. Given a formula for the distance traveled by each bug in terms of the side of the n-gon, and check your formula by doing some computer simulations. [A]

7. [P] Make up and investigate some variations on the "four bugs" problem. For example: Suppose the bugs start on a figure that is not so symmetric. (How about a rectangle?) Suppose one bug goes faster than the other. Suppose instead of each bug following the one to its left, they follow each other in some other order.

8. [P] What kinds of initial conditions, speeds, and following mechanisms will ensure that all bugs eventually meet at one point?

9. [PD] Investigate the modified chase-evade simulation that yields the stable circles of 2.2.2, assuming that the evader movers faster than the chaser. Why does the process stabilize? When it does stabilize, what is the approximate distance of chaser from evader? How does this distance depend on the speeds of chaser and evader? Give a formula for the distance. [HA]

10. [P] Find other chase-evade pairs that produce stable configurations.

11. In the "target-defending" game, give a formula for the coordinates of the point to head for when following the optimal strategy, and use this to implement the strategy on the computer. [HA]

12. [D] Analyze the target-defending game in the case where the two players have different speeds. What is the optimal strategy for each player? [HA]

13. [P] Carry out a detailed study of chase-evade for creatures moving on a grid. Invent strategies and counterstrategies. Can the evader always avoid getting caught if the two creatures move at equal speeds? If they move at different speeds?

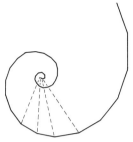

Figure 2.15
Equiangular spiral formed by EQSPI with ANGLE = 20, SCALE = 1.1.

2.3 Growth

Besides simulating animal behavior, another good source of turtle biology projects is modeling patterns of growth. In this section we'll examine
two models: the equiangular spiral, which emerges in the shapes of shells
and horns; and models for branching in the growth of trees.

2.3.1 Equiangular Spirals

We've already seen in section 1.1 how to transform the POLY program

```
TO POLY SIDE ANGLE
    FORWARD SIDE
    LEFT ANGLE
    POLY SIDE ANGLE
```

into a program for drawing spirals:

```
TO POLYSPI (SIDE, ANGLE, INCREMENT)
    FORWARD SIDE
    LEFT ANGLE
    POLYSPI (SIDE + INCREMENT, ANGLE, INCREMENT)
```

Here is another way to make a spiral: Rather than increasing the side by
adding a fixed increment, multiply the side by a constant scale factor:

```
TO EQSPI (SIDE, ANGLE, SCALE)
    FORWARD SIDE
    LEFT ANGLE
    EQSPI (SIDE * SCALE, ANGLE, SCALE)
```

This spiral (shown in figure 2.15) is called an *equiangular spiral* (also
sometimes called a *logarithmic spiral*). Connecting the vertices of the
spiral to a central point shows that the spiral can be generated by suc-

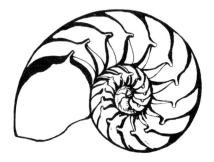

Figure 2.16
The shell of the chambered nautilus clearly exhibits the spiral-growth phenomenon.

cessions of similar triangles, each one built upon the previous. This principle of constructing a pattern through the accumulation of similar shapes lies behind the spiral's appearance in many biological forms, especially in shells and horns. The nautilus shell, shown in figure 2.16, gives a clear illustration. The entire shell is constructed as a sequence of "chambers," each chamber built on the previous chamber and similar to it. (The chambers are similar because the creature doesn't change shape as it moves from chamber to chamber; it just grows.) The result is that corresponding points of successive chambers lie on equiangular spirals.

We'll exhibit a turtle program that mimics this kind of equiangular growth, using quadrilateral chambers. Each quadrilateral, as indicated in figure 2.17a, will be specified to the program by three sides and two angles. If the turtle starts in the lower left corner, the base and sides of the quadrilateral can be drawn by

```
TO CHAMBER (BASE, S1, S2, A1, A2)
        ; save the position of the lower left vertex
    LOWER.LEFT ← TURTLE.STATE
        ; draw the base and right side and save the
        ; position of the upper right vertex (see below)
    FORWARD BASE
    LEFT A2
    FORWARD S2
    UPPER.RIGHT ← TURTLE.STATE
        ; return to the lower left vertex and draw the left side
    PENUP
    SETTURTLE LOWER.LEFT
    PENDOWN
    LEFT A1
    FORWARD S1
```

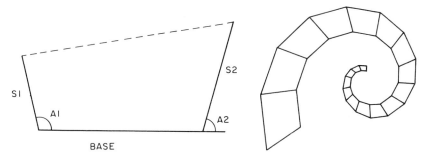

Specifying a quadrilateral for the   SPIRAL.GROWTH (10,10,15,90,90)
CHAMBER procedure.

Figure 2.17
The SPIRAL.GROWTH procedure.

At the end of this procedure the turtle is sitting at the upper left corner
of the chamber, which is the same as the lower left vertex of the next
chamber. To prepare for drawing the next chamber we must point the
turtle along the base of the next chamber, that is, point the turtle
towards the upper right vertex of the chamber just drawn. We can do
this using the FACE procedure of section 2.1, whose implementation is
outlined in exercise 10 of that section. Having done this, we are ready
to draw the next chamber. The angles of the next chamber are the same
as before. The base of the next chamber is the top edge of the previous
chamber, and the size of the next chamber is determined by the ratio
of the old base to the new base. All together, the program for spiral
growth is

```
TO SPIRAL.GROWTH (BASE, S1, S2, A1, A2)
      ; draw one chamber and face along the edge of the new chamber
   CHAMBER (BASE, S1, S2, A1, A2)
   FACE UPPER.RIGHT
      ; the length of the next chamber's base is the distance
      ; from the current location to the upper right corner of
      ; the chamber just drawn
   NEXT.BASE ← DISTANCE (UPPER.RIGHT)
      ; compute the ratio of the sides of the new chamber to the
      ; sides of the previous chamber
   R ← NEXT.BASE/BASE
      ; now repeat the process, using as inputs
      ; the sides and angles of the new chamber
   SPIRAL.GROWTH (NEXT.BASE, S1 * R, S2 * R, A1, A2)
```

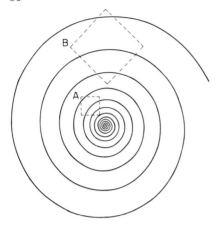

Figure 2.18
Demonstration that curves of equiangular spiral are everywhere the same. Chunk *B*
is the same as chunk *A* blown up by a factor of 3.

The recursive structure of the program implies that each chamber generates
a new chamber. There is no stop rule and the program goes on forever.
Whether the chambers increase or decrease in size depends on the initial
sides and angles. A sample "shell" drawn by this program is illustrated in
figure 2.17.

Growing Turtle Geometry
Equiangular spirals underlie uniform growth such as the SPIRAL.GROWTH
shown above in the same way that a circle underlies any turtle program
that does the same thing over and over. The reason for both of these
facts becomes clearer when one describes the equiangular spiral and the
circle as curves that are "everywhere the same." In the case of a circle,
that means any chunk of the circle can match any other chunk of the
circle if you are allowed to move and turn the first chunk. In the case
of the spiral, one must allow changing scale (making a bigger or smaller
model of a piece), in addition to moving and turning, to show that one
piece matches another. See figure 2.18.

One can augment turtle geometry to make scale changes by introducing a new "scaled forward" command and a GROW command to change
scale:

```
TO S.FORWARD DISTANCE
    FORWARD (SCALE * DISTANCE)

TO GROW FACTOR
    SCALE ← (SCALE * FACTOR)
```

SCALE should now be considered a part of the turtle state—it's a kind of "size" of the turtle that determines the size of the next step just as heading determines the direction of the next step. (SCALE should start equal to 1.)

The analog to POLY is precisely EQSPI:

```
TO EQSPI (SIZE, ANGLE, FACTOR)
    REPEAT FOREVER
        S.FORWARD SIZE
        RIGHT ANGLE
        GROW FACTOR
```

You should be able to show that any looping program which involves only S.FORWARD, RIGHT, and GROW will have an EQSPI skeleton, just as POLY is the skeleton for looping programs without GROW (see exercise 10). Incidentally, a circle is an "equiangular spiral with no growth" in the same way a line is "a circle with no turning." Finally, notice that the chambered growth shown in figure 2.17 ensures that the growth is uniform by having the bottom edge of one chamber be related to the bottom edge of the preceding precisely as the ratio of top to bottom edge of the previous chamber. Because the chambers are constructed to be similar, that ratio never changes.

2.3.2 Branching Processes: A Lesson in Recursion

A different kind of growth pattern we can mimic with turtle graphics is the branching process that characterizes the growth of trees. We'll start by drawing a very regular binary tree, that is, a tree in which each branch sprouts two more branches. We'll make the length of each sprouted branch half that of the parent. Conceptually, each branch consists of a straight line, with two more branches at its end. Notice the fundamentally recursive nature of this description—a branch consists of something (the stem) plus sub-branches (things with the same structure as the branch). In a program, that structure will appear in the standard recursive way, as a procedure calling itself as a subprocedure.

If we assume that the branching angle is 45°, then a first try at a program might be

```
TO BRANCH LENGTH
      ; draw the main branch
   FORWARD LENGTH
      ; turn to point along the left
      ; secondary branch and draw it
   LEFT 45
   BRANCH LENGTH/2
      ; now draw the right secondary branch
   RIGHT 90
   BRANCH LENGTH/2
```

But if we try this procedure, we'll find that it has a bug: The turtle starts drawing a branch, then its left secondary branch, then that branch's left secondary branch, and so on and so on. No right branches ever get drawn. At some point, we must make the process stop generating new left branches and come back to do the right branches. We'll accomplish this by giving the BRANCH process a second input called LEVEL, which counts down as the program moves from each branch to its secondary. We can think of LEVEL as labeling the type (complexity) of the branch: A level 1 branch is a tip (a branch with no secondaries); a level 2 branch will sprout two level 1 secondaries; a level 3 branch will sprout level 2 secondaries, and so on. The program should stop generating secondary branches whenever the level reaches 0:

```
TO BRANCH (LENGTH, LEVEL)
   IF LEVEL = 0 THEN RETURN
   FORWARD LENGTH
   LEFT 45
   BRANCH (LENGTH/2, LEVEL - 1)
   RIGHT 90
   BRANCH (LENGTH/2, LEVEL - 1)
```

Unfortunately, as shown in figure 2.19a, there is still a bug in the program. This bug, which is tricky to find, comes up often in such recursive descriptions: We must ensure that after drawing the left secondary branch the turtle returns to the base of that branch, or else the RIGHT 90 instruction will not align the turtle correctly for drawing the right secondary branch. In other words, we must ensure that the process that draws the left secondary branch restores the state of the turtle to what the

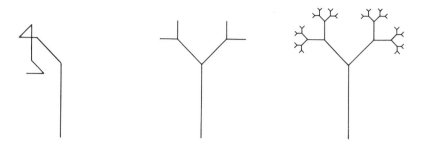

Figure 2.19
The BRANCH procedure. (a) Version with state bug, LEVEL = 3. (b) Debugged version,
LEVEL = 3. (c) Debugged version, LEVEL = 6.

state was before the process began. The technical term for a process that leaves the turtle in the same state in which it found it is *state-transparent*.

BRANCH will work only if its sub-branches are state-transparent. But since the sub-branches as programs are just copies of BRANCH itself, BRANCH must be made state-transparent. (In a recursive society all you must do to make sure your offspring have some property is have it yourself.) Here is the debugged program:

```
TO BRANCH (LENGTH, LEVEL)
    IF LEVEL = 0 THEN RETURN
    FORWARD LENGTH
    LEFT 45
    BRANCH (LENGTH/2, LEVEL - 1)
    RIGHT 90
    BRANCH (LENGTH/2, LEVEL - 1)
        ; turn and back up to make the
        ; procedure state-transparent
    LEFT 45
    BACK LENGTH
```

Using this simple binary tree as a model, we can go on to construct figures that look more like real trees. For example, we might add inputs to the program to allow some other variation of the size of the secondary branches besides "divide by 2." Another possibility is to make the length of stem depend not on the level, but on whether the stem belongs to a left or a right sub-branch.

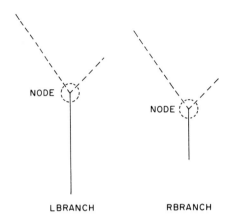

Figure 2.20
LBRANCH and RBRANCH have NODE in common.

The cleanest way to implement this idea is to have separate left and
right procedures that produce stems of different lengths. As the dashed
lines in figure 2.20 indicate, each of these must prepare for the next-level
branch. Though the preparation is not hard, it is more than half the
procedure, and both left and right branch procedures must do it. So
it makes sense to make it a subprocedure called NODE. We can also
make NODE responsible for the stop rule, which is common to the two
procedures.

```
TO LBRANCH (LENGTH, ANGLE, LEVEL)
     ; draw a long stem
   FORWARD (2 * LENGTH)
     ; do next level
   NODE (LENGTH, ANGLE, LEVEL)
     ; make LBRANCH state-transparent
   BACK (2 * LENGTH)

TO RBRANCH (LENGTH, ANGLE, LEVEL)
     ; draw a short stem
   FORWARD LENGTH
     ; do next level
   NODE (LENGTH, ANGLE, LEVEL)
     ; make RBRANCH state-transparent
   BACK LENGTH
```

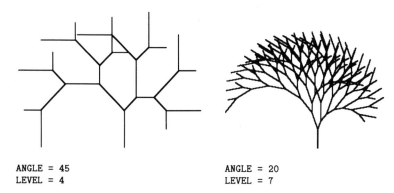

ANGLE = 45   ANGLE = 20
LEVEL = 4   LEVEL = 7

Figure 2.21
Branching figures drawn by LBRANCH.

```
TO NODE (LENGTH, ANGLE, LEVEL)
    IF LEVEL = 0 THEN RETURN
        ; point along left branch and draw it
    LEFT ANGLE
    LBRANCH (LENGTH, ANGLE, LEVEL -1)
        ; draw right branch
    RIGHT (2 * ANGLE)
    RBRANCH (LENGTH, ANGLE, LEVEL - 1)
        ; make NODE state-transparent
    LEFT ANGLE
```

You can start the process with either LBRANCH or RBRANCH. Figure 2.21 shows some of these trees. Notice that at first sight the growth pattern looks random, even though it is actually very regular.

More information on the spiral shapes of shells, horns, claws, and teeth can be found in *On Growth and Form* by D'Arcy Thompson (abridged edition; Cambridge University Press, 1961). The branch procedure is adapted from a model discussed in *Patterns in Nature,* by Peter S. Stevens (Boston: Atlantic Monthly Press, 1974). Both of these books are well worth having a look at if you are interested in mathematical models in biology.

Exercises for Section 2.3

1. [P] Figure 2.22 shows some animal horns. Can you find inputs to the SPIRAL.GROWTH program that produce horns shaped like these?

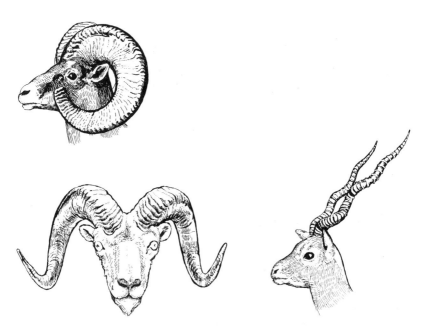

Figure 2.22
Examples of animal horns that can be modeled by SPIRAL.GROWTH.

2. [P] Invent variants of the SPIRAL.GROWTH procedure in which the chambers are not quadrilaterals.

3. [P] Efficiency experts may object that our SPIRAL.GROWTH procedure is inefficient in that the ratio of one chamber to the next should be computed only once, rather than each time a new chamber is drawn. But our version is easy to modify so that this ratio (and hence the shape of the chambers) can be varied from one chamber to the next. We might let the left and right sides grow more slowly (with a different ratio) than the tops and bottoms, and so get a figure which becomes stubbier as it grows. Experiment with possibilities like these. What kinds of shapes arise if the change in growth is periodic (seasonal)? If the rate of growth is random?

4. What is the total length of all the lines drawn by the BRANCH procedure for a given length and level? [HA]

5. [P] Modify NODE so that the choice of whether the left or the right sub-branch is to be the long one is made randomly at each level.

6. Make a branching model in which each left sub-branch is twice as long as each right sub-branch and sprouts two left-right branches. What is the total length of all the branches drawn for a given length and level? [HA]

7. [P] Create some variations that introduce randomness into the model given in the previous exercise. For instance, the left branch may sprout either one or two branches at each level.

8. [D] Does EQSPI $(2, 2, 2)$, EQSPI $(1, 1, 1)$, EQSPI $(.5, .5, .5)$, ... approach a limiting spiral the way POLY (n, n) does, as n goes to 0? Explain why or why not. How about EQSPI $(n, n, n + 1)$? How about EQSPI (n, n, k^n), k constant? [A]

9. What parameters describe equiangular spirals the way radius or curvature describes a circle? Relate these to the inputs of EQSPI. [HA]

10. [D] Prove the assertion that any looping program which uses only S.FORWARD, RIGHT, and GROW has an EQSPI skeleton, paralleling the results of section 1.3. What are the angle and the growth factor for the steps of the skeleton? [H]

2.4 Recursive Designs

The branching models of section 2.3 could be described as *recursive designs,* because these figures contain subparts which are in some sense equivalent to the entire figure (for example, a branch is made up of branches). We've already run into two important considerations for writing turtle procedures to generate such designs: We need to include some kind of stop rule so that the process eventually stops generating more and more subfigures, and we need to keep track of the state of the turtle in designing the interface between part and subpart. In particular, it helps to make each part state-transparent.

2.4.1 Nested Triangles

The nested triangle design shown in figure 2.23 illustrates these principles. The central observation is that the figure consists of a triangle plus a smaller copy of itself at each corner, just as the trees of the last section were forks plus smaller copies of themselves on each prong. Thus, we imagine the turtle drawing our figure as follows: At each of

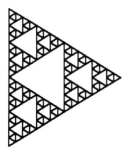

Figure 2.23
Figure drawn by `NESTED.TRIANGLE`.

the vertices of the largest triangle, pause and construct a smaller figure
of half the size, in the corner. The smaller triangles should follow the
same rules, drawing a still smaller triangle at each of their corners, and
so on, and so on. Finally, we'll stop generating subtriangles when the
sides get very small. All together, the procedure is

```
TO NESTED.TRIANGLE SIZE
    IF SIZE < 10 THEN RETURN
    REPEAT 3
        NESTED.TRIANGLE SIZE/2
        FORWARD SIZE
        RIGHT 120
```

Notice that each `NESTED.TRIANGLE(SIZE)` will be state-transparent as
long as each `NESTED.TRIANGLE(SIZE/2)` drawn in its corners satisfies
that property. In turn, that state transparency depends on the state
transparency of smaller and smaller `NESTED.TRIANGLE`s until, when `SIZE`
is less than 10, the program stops, ensuring state transparency all the
way back up the line. A simple variation on this program draws smaller
figures outward from the corners:

```
TO CORNER.TRI SIZE
    IF SIZE < 10 THEN RETURN
    REPEAT 3
        FORWARD SIZE
        CORNER.TRI SIZE/2
        RIGHT 120
```

Yet another way to interface a triangle to a recursive call to itself is to stop halfway through a side and put the recursive call there:

```
TO OUTWARD.TRI SIZE
   IF SIZE < 10 THEN RETURN
   REPEAT 3
      FORWARD SIZE/2
      INSERT SIZE
      FORWARD SIZE/2
      RIGHT 120

TO INSERT SIZE
   LEFT 120
   OUTWARD.TRI SIZE/2
      ; ensure state transparency of INSERT
   RIGHT 120
```

These triangle procedures can be generalized to arbitrary POLY figures. The only tricky part is to make sure we know how many sides to draw, say, as a function of the POLY's angle. As we saw in chapter 1, this can be done by accumulating total turning and stopping when the total turning is a multiple of 360°:

```
TO CORNERPOLY (SIZE, ANGLE, TOTALTURN)
   IF SIZE < 10 THEN RETURN
   REPEAT
      CORNERPOLYSTEP (SIZE, ANGLE)
      TOTALTURN ← TOTALTURN + ANGLE
   UNTIL REMAINDER (TOTALTURN, 360) = 0

TO CORNERPOLYSTEP (SIZE, ANGLE)
   FORWARD SIZE
   CORNERPOLY (SIZE/2, - ANGLE, 0)
      ; using - ANGLE "symmetrizes" the figure
   RIGHT ANGLE
```

The CORNERPOLY procedure is invoked with the third input, TOTALTURN, equal to zero. Figure 2.24 shows some samples drawn by this program.

Although we've been using the side length as a stop rule for these designs, you might prefer to stop at a particular level of recursion. For example,

ANGLE = 90

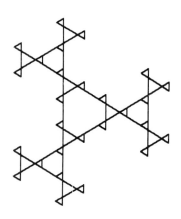

ANGLE = 120

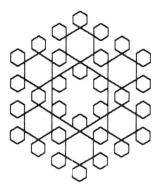

ANGLE = 60

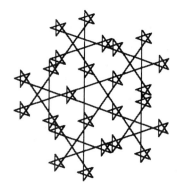

ANGLE = 144

Figure 2.24
Shapes drawn by CORNERPOLY.

```
TO NESTEDTRIANGLE (SIZE, LEVEL)
   IF LEVEL = 0 THEN RETURN
   REPEAT 3
      NESTEDTRIANGLE (SIZE/2, LEVEL - 1)
      FORWARD SIZE
      RIGHT 120
```

2.4.2 Snowflakes and Other Curves

In some instances the effect of state transparency can be achieved although there is not true state transparency. In such cases, each procedure knows the state change of its subprocedures and hence knows
what to do to compensate (if necessary). If the state change of the subprocedure is simple there are few disadvantages to this method, and if
the state change is exactly what the main procedure needs to prepare
for a next step this method can be advantageous.

This strategy is illustrated by a program to draw the snowflake curve
shown in figure 2.25. Think of this curve as a triangle in which each side
is made up of four subsides, each subside is made up of four sub-subsides,
etc. Rather than making the procedure state-transparent, we'll design
each side to move the turtle forward a certain distance without changing
the heading:

```
TO SNOWFLAKE (SIZE, LEVEL)
   REPEAT 3
      SIDE (SIZE, LEVEL)
      RIGHT 120

TO SIDE (SIZE, LEVEL)
   IF LEVEL = 0 THEN
      FORWARD SIZE
      RETURN
   SIDE (SIZE/3, LEVEL - 1)
   LEFT 60
   SIDE (SIZE/3, LEVEL - 1)
   RIGHT 120
   SIDE (SIZE/3, LEVEL - 1)
   LEFT 60
   SIDE (SIZE/3, LEVEL - 1)
```

Until now the LEVEL = 0 process has been trivial, and has been state-
transparent by virtue of doing nothing at all. Here the LEVEL = 0 action
is crucial so that the LEVEL = 1 process gets the state change expected,
FORWARD(SIZE). In fact, in the snowflake procedure no FORWARD commands will be issued except when LEVEL = 0.

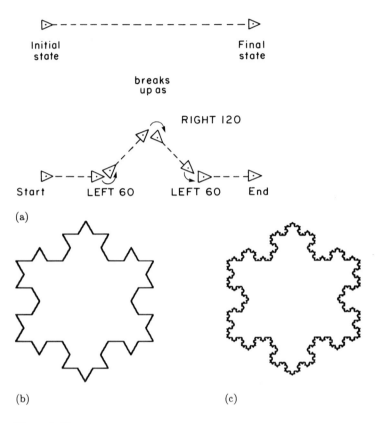

(a)

(b)   (c)

Figure 2.25
The snowflake curve. (a) Recursive decomposition of a "side." (b) Snowflake,
LEVEL = 2. (c) Snowflake, LEVEL = 4.

Another related curve is the "C curve" shown in figure 2.26a. A level
0 C curve is just a line; a level n C curve consists of two level $n-1$ C
curves at right angles to each other, followed by a 90° turn to restore
the heading:

```
TO C (SIZE, LEVEL)
   IF LEVEL = 0 THEN
      FORWARD SIZE
      RETURN
   C (SIZE, LEVEL - 1)
   RIGHT 90
   C (SIZE, LEVEL - 1)
   LEFT 90
```

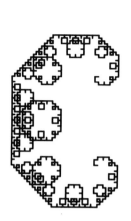

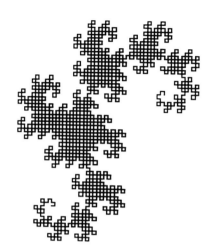

Figure 2.26
(a) C curve, LEVEL = 10. (b) Dragon curve, LEVEL = 11.

The "dragon curve" shown in figure 2.26b is similar to the C curve; however, there is only one 90° turn, and its direction changes from level to level. We can think of it as generated by a pair of procedures LDRAGON and RDRAGON specified as follows: A level n LDRAGON is made up of a level $n-1$ LDRAGON and a level $n-1$ RDRAGON with a left turn in between; a level n RDRAGON is made up of a level $n-1$ LDRAGON and a level $n-1$ RDRAGON with a right turn in between; a level 0 dragon is a line:

```
TO LDRAGON (SIZE, LEVEL)
   IF LEVEL = 0 THEN
      FORWARD SIZE
      RETURN
   LDRAGON (SIZE, LEVEL - 1)
   LEFT 90
   RDRAGON (SIZE, LEVEL - 1)

TO RDRAGON (SIZE, LEVEL)
   IF LEVEL = 0 THEN
      FORWARD SIZE
      RETURN
   LDRAGON (SIZE, LEVEL - 1)
   RIGHT 90
   RDRAGON (SIZE, LEVEL - 1)
```

2.4.3 Space-Filling Designs

Suppose we write a program that draws something inside a square. For the moment, we won't care what the program does, but we will insist that the initial and final states of the turtle are related to the square as shown in figure 2.27a. Consider a new square that consists of nine smaller squares. We can use our simple program in each smaller square to produce a more complicated program winding through the new square (figure 2.27b). All we need is appropriate interfacing between subsquares.

This more complicated program relates to the new square in exactly the same way that the simple program related to the first square, so we can continue this process. In the end we will have a square, consisting of nine smaller squares, each of which consists of still smaller squares, and so on. The process is recursive, and can be implemented in the usual way (by writing the higher-level procedure in terms of the lower-level one). The interfaces between the various subfigures are shown in figure 2.27b. For a level 0 process, we can use the simplest possible way of entering and leaving a square, as assumed—FORWARD(SIZE). This gives the following procedure:

```
TO FILL (SIZE, LEVEL)
    IF LEVEL = 0 THEN
        FORWARD SIZE
        RETURN
        ; side of small square is 1/3 side of large square
    FILL (SIZE/3, LEVEL - 1)
        ; interface to next subfigure is LEFT 90
    LEFT 90
    FILL (SIZE/3, LEVEL - 1)
        ; next three subfigures have RIGHT 90 as interface
    REPEAT 3
        RIGHT 90
        FILL (SIZE/3, LEVEL - 1)
        ; next three have LEFT 90 as interface
    REPEAT 3
        LEFT 90
        FILL (SIZE/3, LEVEL - 1)
        ; final subfigure has RIGHT 90 interface
    RIGHT 90
    FILL (SIZE/3, LEVEL - 1)
```

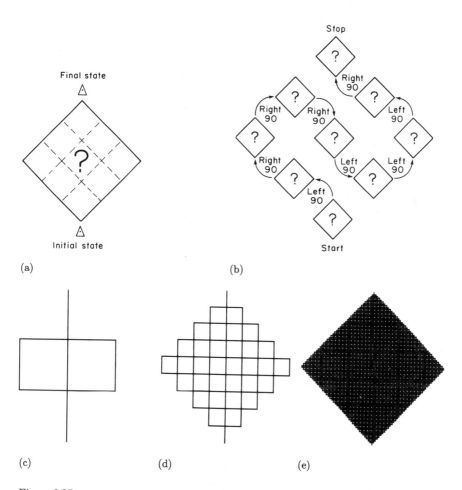

Figure 2.27
The FILL procedure. (a) Initial and final states for traversing a square. (b) Traversing
the square, decomposed into traversing nine subsquares plus left-right interfacing.
(c–e) The pattern drawn by FILL at LEVEL = 1, 2, and 4.

This FILL procedure is an example of a *space-filling design*. If we make LEVEL greater and greater, then the FILL curve winds through the square in finer and finer subdivisions. For LEVEL very large, we could imagine FILL as passing through every point of the square. FILL, as written, draws a curve that intersects itself; however, it is possible to separate the nine subsquares with small interfaces to avoid intersection. (See exercise 5.) If done properly, this will not affect the space-filling property of the design.

Perhaps the most famous space-filling design is the curve (shown in figure 2.28) invented by the German mathematician David Hilbert. As indicated in figure 2.28e, we can think of the level n Hilbert curve as made up of four level $n - 1$ Hilbert curves, joined by interfaces which are straight line segments. Another way to picture this is to imagine the square as divided into four subsquares. The Hilbert curve traverses the square by visiting each of the subsquares and placing the interfaces in between. (See figure 2.28d.)

In designing a program to draw the Hilbert curve we must be careful to keep track of how each level of the curve affects the state of the turtle. Assume that the turtle begins facing along the edge of the square that it traverses, and ends in the same direction. Then pasting together four level $n - 1$ curves to form the level n curve requires interface turns as shown in figure 2.28f. A second tricky point is that there are really two different level $n - 1$ Hilbert curves—one that traverses its square to the left and one that traverses to the right—and that the level n curve is made up of two of each parity. Finally, notice that the interfaces alone provide the state change assumed at each level, so we can let the level 0 curve be simply a point; then the interfaces in level 1 will provide the state change assumed by higher levels. The complete program consists of two procedures, LHILBERT and RHILBERT:

```
TO LHILBERT (SIZE, LEVEL)
    IF LEVEL = 0 THEN RETURN
        ; rotate and draw first subcurve
        ; with opposite parity to big curve
    LEFT 90
    RHILBERT (SIZE, LEVEL - 1)
        ; interface to and draw second subcurve
        ; with same parity as big curve
    FORWARD SIZE
    RIGHT 90
    LHILBERT (SIZE, LEVEL - 1)
```

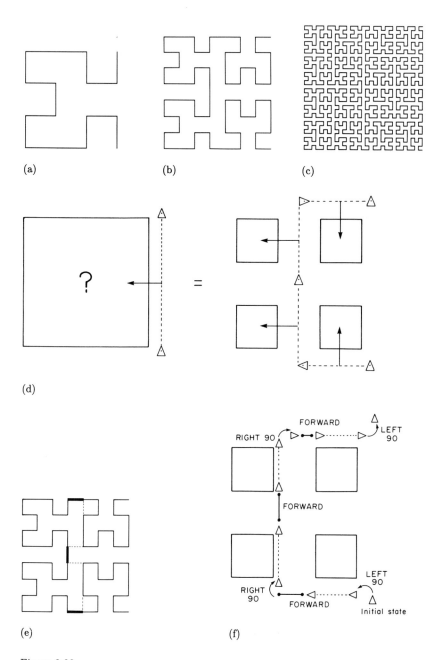

Figure 2.28
The Hilbert curve. (a) LEVEL = 2 (b) LEVEL = 3 (c) LEVEL = 5 (d) Turtle "traverses" square by traversing each subsquare. (e) Decomposition of level n Hilbert curve into four level $n-1$ curves together with interfaces. (f) Details of interfacing.

```
   ; third subcurve
FORWARD SIZE
LHILBERT (SIZE, LEVEL - 1)
   ; fourth subcurve
RIGHT 90 FORWARD SIZE
RHILBERT (SIZE, LEVEL - 1)
   ; a final turn is needed to make the turtle
   ; end up facing outward from the large square
LEFT 90
```

The RHILBERT procedure is the same, but with all the turns reversed:

```
TO RHILBERT (SIZE, LEVEL)
   IF LEVEL = 0 THEN RETURN
   RIGHT 90
   LHILBERT (SIZE, LEVEL - 1)
   FORWARD SIZE
   LEFT 90
   RHILBERT (SIZE, LEVEL - 1)
   FORWARD SIZE
   RHILBERT (SIZE, LEVEL - 1)
   LEFT 90
   FORWARD SIZE
   LHILBERT (SIZE, LEVEL - 1)
   RIGHT 90
```

We can combine LHILBERT and RHILBERT into a single procedure by providing a third input, equal to $+1$ or -1, whose sign is reversed to convert left turns to right turns:

```
TO HILBERT (SIZE, LEVEL, PARITY)
   IF LEVEL = 0 THEN RETURN
   LEFT (PARITY * 90)
   HILBERT (SIZE, LEVEL - 1, - PARITY)
   FORWARD SIZE
   RIGHT (PARITY * 90)
   HILBERT (SIZE, LEVEL - 1, PARITY)
   FORWARD SIZE
   HILBERT (SIZE, LEVEL - 1, PARITY)
   RIGHT (PARITY * 90)
   FORWARD SIZE
   HILBERT (SIZE, LEVEL - 1, - PARITY)
   LEFT (PARITY * 90)
```

Exercises for Section 2.4

1. [P] Try the following variant of the nested-triangle procedure, which adds only one smaller triangle at each level connecting the midpoints of the larger triangle:

```
TO NEST (SIZE, LEVEL)
    IF LEVEL = 0 THEN STOP
    FORWARD SIZE/2
    SUBNEST (SIZE, LEVEL)
    FORWARD SIZE/2
    RIGHT 120
    FORWARD SIZE
    RIGHT 120
    FORWARD SIZE
    RIGHT 120

TO SUBNEST (SIZE, LEVEL)
    RIGHT 60
    NEST (SIZE/2, LEVEL - 1)
    LEFT 60
```

Generalize this procedure to produce designs based on nested POLYs. [HA]

2. What is the length of the level n snowflake curve? How much area does it enclose? [HA]

3. [P] Write a procedure that generalizes the (triangular) snowflake curve to produce arbitrary "polysnowflakes."

4. [D] What is the length of the level n Hilbert curve? [HA]

5. [P] The FILL curve is not as elegant as it might be because it intersects itself. Add interfaces, in the same way that HILBERT has them, to separate the squares a bit. (See figure 2.29.) Note that the net effect of the interfaces by themselves (including turning to set up for diagonals) is the state change assumed for each level of FILL. This is the same as with the interfaces to HILBERT, and makes it possible to allow the level 0 curve to be simply RETURN. Try this possibility for FILL as well.

6. [P] The Hilbert curve is constructed on the following model: (1) Walk along the side of a square, and imagine filling the square. (2) Divide the square into four subsquares. Construct a similar space-filling curve based on dividing a triangle into four subtriangles.

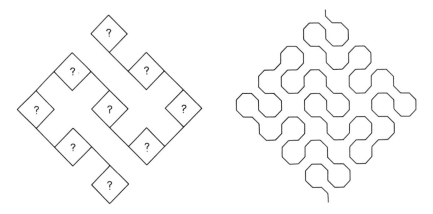

Figure 2.29
Interfaces to FILL and resulting (level 2) design.

7. [P] Construct a space-filling curve on the Hilbert model, but based on dividing a square into nine subsquares.

8. [PD] Write a procedure to draw the space-filling curve shown in figure 2.30. (This curve was invented by the Polish mathematician Wraclaw Sierpinski.) [HA]

9. [P] Invent some new space-filling designs.

10. [P] Can you build a recursive design like FILL or HILBERT, but based on entering the middle of the side of the square rather than the corner?

11. [P] How much does the FILL curve depend on the particular level 0 step used? Does FILL change its character if you use some more complicated level 0 step than FORWARD(SIZE)?

12. [P] Notice that in none of our recursive designs does the turtle have any representation of the curve except the program itself. On the other hand, by encoding turtle commands as letters, one can construct an explicit representation in the following way: Let F stand for FORWARD SIZE, L for LEFT 60, and R for RIGHT 120; then construct a string representing the side of a snowflake curve with the rules

$$S_0 = F,$$
$$S_n = S_{n-1}LS_{n-1}RS_{n-1}LS_{n-1}.$$

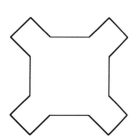

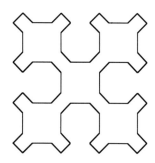

LEVEL = 1   LEVEL = 2

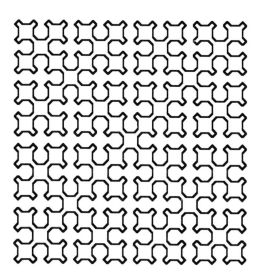

LEVEL = 4

Figure 2.30
The Sierpinski curve

In fact a program to draw the side could be enacted as follows: Initialize $S \leftarrow F$; apply the recursive step $S \leftarrow SLSRSLS$ (juxtaposition denotes concatenation) n times; have the turtle interpret the resulting string. Try this with several known recursive designs, such as HILBERT and SNOWFLAKE. Now explore the possibilities of this "word generation" method by varying level 0, the recursive step, and the interpretation of letters. You may wish to add more variable symbols to the process, for example, $T \leftarrow SRSLSRS$.

13. [PD] All our recursive designs have maintained the constraint that turtle must not lift the pen. Thus, the recursive step in FILL consisted of taking a certain walk through a square and then using that walk nine times in sequence to make a more complex walk through a square. But we could just as easily imagine taking any design whatsoever in a square (not necessarily a walk through it) and gluing nine copies to make a larger square (without making sure the designs hook up simply). (See figure 2.31a.) Of course the overall design will appear more impressive if some lines do "accidentally" hook up. This is like tiling a floor with more and more complex tiles. Varying the design on the level 0 tile together with the orientations for the tiles in the recursive step makes a fascinating artistic and mathematical exploration. To aid the exploration you may wish to implement the recursive gluing-together steps as programs that can take arbitrary design-drawing programs, including glued-together designs, as inputs. That way a level 3 recursive tile will look like GLUE1(GLUE2(GLUE3(SHAPE1))). Figure 2.31b–e shows designs that can be made in this way. See if you can find the level 0 design in each.

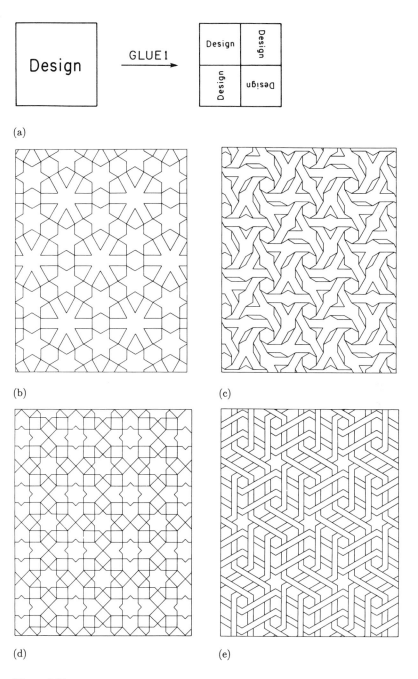

Figure 2.31
(a) Recursive decomposition of tiling designs. (b–e) Four tiling designs.

3

Vector Methods in Turtle Geometry

> I am sorry that I had to torture you with these
> elements of analytic geometry. The purpose of this
> invention of Descartes' is nothing but to give *names*
> to the points X in a plane by which we can distin-
> guish and recognize them. This has to be done in a
> systematic way because there are infinitely many of
> them; and it is the more necessary as points, unlike
> persons, are all completely alike, and hence we can
> distinquish them only by attaching labels to them.
>
> Hermann Weyl, *Symmetry*

In chapter 1 we emphasized how turtle geometry provides an alternative to Cartesian coordinates for exploring geometry with a computer display screen. This chapter introduces a third way to represent
geometric phenomena: vector representation. Vectors methods are, in
many ways, intermediate between pure turtle methods and coordinate
methods. We will be making use of vectors as a mode of representing
geometric phenomena that is sufficiently intrinsic and local to capture
simply some essential features of turtle geometry but also shares the algebraic nature that makes analytic geometry so generally useful. More
than that, the algebra of vectors is easily reduced to simple arithmetic
operations through the introduction of vector coordinates. Since they
link well with geometry on one side and with numerical calculation on the
other, vectors are an ideal representation to use in computer programs
dealing with geometry. Using this fact, we will show how to implement
turtle geometry from scratch on almost any computer graphics system,
how to extend turtle geometry into three dimensions, and (in later chapters) how to design exotic turtles that walk on cubes, on spheres, and
even in Einstein's curved spacetime.

Despite this great power and the detailed work necessary to harness
it, we encourage you not to lose sight of the most important reason
for a combined look at turtles and vectors: Turtle geometry and vector
geometry are two different representations for geometric phenomena,
and whenever we have two different representations of the same thing
we can learn a great deal by comparing representations and translating
descriptions from one representation into the other. Shifting descriptions
back and forth between representations can often lead to insights that
are not inherent in either of the representations alone.

We will start this chapter by looking at some of the familiar turtle phenomena—POLYs, closed paths, and so on—in terms of vectors. After dealing with vectors as conceptual entities, we will reduce vectors to coordinates and thus gain the ability to manipulate vectors on the computer.

3.1 Vector Analysis of Turtle Programs

The turtle commands FORWARD, BACK, LEFT, and RIGHT describe changes relative to the turtle's current state. For example, the pair of commands RIGHT 90, FORWARD 100 results in a motion of 100 steps from the turtle's current position and at 90° from the current heading. This relativity is exactly what allows turtle programs to be simple intrinsic descriptions of shapes such as circles and POLYs. However, if you have a global frame of reference in mind, and absolute orientation is important to you, the two shapes in figure 3.1a are very different; one is a square and one is a diamond. The orientation of the sides with respect to a global "up" allows one to discriminate between square and diamond, even though intrinsically the two figures are identical. In this case, position is still relative. One cannot transform "squareness" to "diamondness" simply by changing the position of the figure without rotating it.

Motions that are absolute in direction but relative in position—called displacements—are readily described by *vectors*. We can think of a vector as an arrow of definite length and direction but arbitrary position, pointing from beginning to end of the displacement. (Throughout the book we denote vectors by boldface symbols such as **v** and **w**.) In order to make a turtle produce squares and diamonds, imagine handing it a collection of vectors. A program to draw a figure tells the turtle when to make the displacement described by each vector. The following procedures correspond to figure 3.1b and c.

```
TO SQUARE
    DISPLACE.BY S₁
    DISPLACE.BY S₂
    DISPLACE.BY S₃
    DISPLACE.BY S₄

TO DIAMOND
    DISPLACE.BY D₁
    DISPLACE.BY D₂
    DISPLACE.BY D₃
    DISPLACE.BY D₄
```

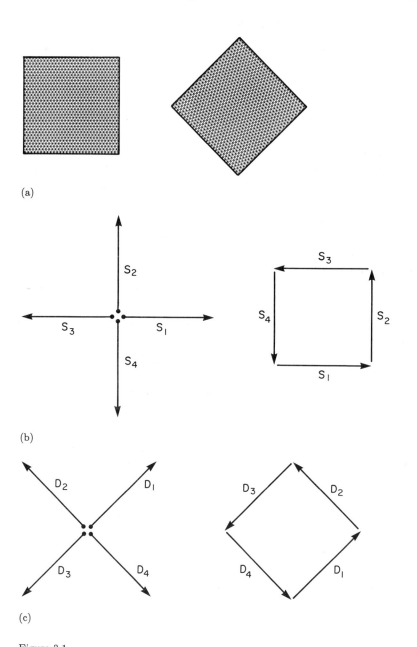

Figure 3.1
(a) Rotating a square produces a diamond. (b–c) Vector decompositions of square and diamond.

3.1.1 Vector Operations: Scalar Multiplication and Addition

There are a number of relations between vectors that can be useful
to a vector-following turtle. If the turtle knows how to walk along a
particular vector $\mathbf{v}$, then it should be able to walk along a vector of
the same length pointing in exactly the opposite direction. Naturally
enough, we denote this displacement by $-\mathbf{v}$. Similarly, a displacement
in the direction of $\mathbf{v}$, but 5 times as far, can be denoted by $5 \times \mathbf{v}$ (or simply
$5\mathbf{v}$). In general, $a\mathbf{v}$ (where a is a number) is a vector in the direction of $\mathbf{v}$,
but a times as long. (If a is negative, $a\mathbf{v}$ is opposite in direction.) This
operation is called *scalar multiplication* of numbers and vectors. It is
essentially just changing the scale used to measure displacement. Scalar
division can be defined by the formula $\mathbf{v}/a = (1/a) \times \mathbf{v}$.

Besides scalar multiplication (and the special case $-1 \times \mathbf{v} = -\mathbf{v}$)
there is one other fundamental method of producing new vectors from
old ones. Observe that performing two displacements in sequence defines
a net displacement, a net change in position. A displacement $\mathbf{v}$ followed
by a displacement $\mathbf{w}$ yields a net displacement called the *vector sum*,
denoted $\mathbf{v} + \mathbf{w}$. Having defined addition of vectors, we can define vector
subtraction as adding the negative:

$$\mathbf{v} - \mathbf{w} = \mathbf{v} + (-\mathbf{w}) \qquad \text{(by definition)}.$$

Vector addition satisfies the commutative property

$$\mathbf{v} + \mathbf{w} = \mathbf{w} + \mathbf{v}$$

for any vectors $\mathbf{v}$ and $\mathbf{w}$. This is illustrated in figure 3.2a, which shows
how following along $\mathbf{v}$ and then along $\mathbf{w}$, or alternatively $\mathbf{w}$ and then $\mathbf{v}$,
forms a parallelogram whose diagonal is the vector sum.

Figures 3.2b and c illustrate two more simple but important formulas
that relate scalar multiplication to addition of vectors:

$$(a + b)\mathbf{v} = a\mathbf{v} + b\mathbf{v},$$
$$a(\mathbf{v} + \mathbf{w}) = a\mathbf{v} + a\mathbf{w}.$$

The special vector $\mathbf{0}$ represents no displacement at all; its length is
zero. This *zero vector* is analogous to the number zero, and it has many
of the same properties:

$$\mathbf{v} - \mathbf{v} = \mathbf{0},$$
$$\mathbf{0} + \mathbf{v} = \mathbf{v},$$
$$0 \times \mathbf{v} = \mathbf{0}.$$

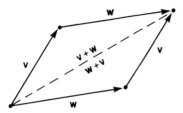

Commutativity: $\mathbf{v} + \mathbf{w} = \mathbf{w} + \mathbf{v}$

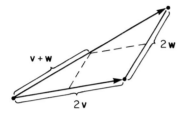

$a\mathbf{v} + a\mathbf{w} = a(\mathbf{v} + \mathbf{w})$

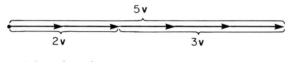

$a\mathbf{v} + b\mathbf{v} = (a + b)\mathbf{v}$

Figure 3.2
Properties of vector addition.

3.1.2 Vector Representations of Closed Paths

Now we'll take advantage of vectors to rephrase some of our analyses of
familiar turtle-geometric programs and look at some new phenomena.
We will be using the following fundamental correspondence between vectors and turtle programs: Each FORWARD step by the turtle is a displacement and can be described by a vector; successive displacements can
be described by vector addition. Notice that the RIGHT and LEFT commands are not directly represented by vectors; rather, they determine
the direction of the vectors generated by FORWARD commands.

Suppose the turtle makes its first move according to some initial vector
$\mathbf{v}_0$. If the second move is along $\mathbf{v}_1$, then the net displacement is just
$\mathbf{v}_0 + \mathbf{v}_1$. The turtle's net displacement after n steps, as shown in figure
3.3, will be

$$\mathbf{v}_0 + \mathbf{v}_1 + \cdots + \mathbf{v}_{n-1}.$$

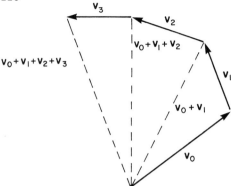

Figure 3.3
Turtle's displacement as a sum of vectors.

If the path is closed in these n steps the turtle must have returned to its starting point, and thus the net displacement from the initial position must be zero:

$$\mathbf{v}_0 + \mathbf{v}_1 + \cdots + \mathbf{v}_{n-1} = \mathbf{0}.$$

So if we ignore the question of whether or not the turtle's final heading is the same as its initial heading, then we can say the turtle's path is closed precisely when the vectors that represent the position changes add up to zero.

3.1.3 POLY Revisited: Rotations and Linearity

Let's look carefully at a simple special case: POLY, our archetypal looping program from chapter 1. We'll give a new interpretation of the POLY closing theorem of subsection 1.2.2. To keep things simple let the ANGLE of the POLY be $360/n$, where n is a positive integer. The POLY closing theorem says closure will be achieved in n steps. Reinterpreting the closure in terms of vectors, we see that proving the theorem boils down to verifying the equation

$$\mathbf{v}_0 + \mathbf{v}_1 + \cdots + \mathbf{v}_{n-1} = \mathbf{0}.$$

In order to do this we need some way of capturing in vector terms the simple relationship among the vs: They are all just $\mathbf{v}_0$ rotated by various multiples of the POLY angle. To express this relation we define, for any vector $\mathbf{v}$ and angle A, a new vector Rotate$(\mathbf{v}, A)$, also written $R_A(\mathbf{v})$, to be the vector obtained by rotating $\mathbf{v}$ through A. Using this rotation operation allows us to express the special property of the POLY segments:

$$\mathbf{v}_k = R_{kA}(\mathbf{v}_0) \qquad (A = 360/n).$$

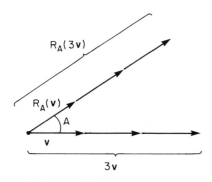

$$R_A(a\mathbf{v}) = aR_A(\mathbf{v})$$

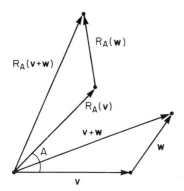

$$R_A(\mathbf{v} + \mathbf{w}) = R_A(\mathbf{v}) + R_A(\mathbf{w})$$

Figure 3.4
Linearity of the rotation operation.

Now we can restate the POLY closing theorem as follows:

POLY Closing Theorem (Vector Form) Given any vector $\mathbf{v}_0$ and positive integer n, let $A = 360/n$ and let $\mathbf{v}_k = R_{kA}(\mathbf{v}_0)$. Then

$$\mathbf{v}_0 + \mathbf{v}_1 + \cdots + \mathbf{v}_{n-1} = \mathbf{0}.$$

The proof of this theorem will be based on two fundamental properties of the rotation operation R_A for any angle A. As figure 3.4a illustrates, the rotation of any scalar multiple of a vector $\mathbf{v}$ can be obtained simply by scaling $R_A(\mathbf{v})$:

$$R_A(a\mathbf{v}) = aR_A(\mathbf{v}).$$

This is called the *scaling* property of rotation. Rotation has another property called *additivity*, which means that for any vectors **v** and **w**

$$R_A(\mathbf{v} + \mathbf{w}) = R_A(\mathbf{v}) + R_A(\mathbf{w}).$$

Figure 3.4b demonstrates that rotation satisfies additivity; just rotate the whole picture for vector addition and note that each of the parts **v** and **w** and the sum **v**+**w** get rotated while preserving their configuration as a sum. If an operation has both the scaling and additivity properties, then it is said to be *linear*. Linearity will soon take its place beside local vs. global and intrinsic vs. extrinsic as one of the recurring mathematical themes of this book.

Returning to the POLY theorem, we wish to demonstrate that the sum

$$\mathbf{V} = \mathbf{v}_0 + \cdots + \mathbf{v}_{n-1}$$

satisfies $\mathbf{V} = \mathbf{0}$. The insight that proves this is that the collection of **v**s that make up **V** is perfectly symmetrical. The sum of them could hardly point in any direction favoring one **v** over another, and so must point in no direction at all: $\mathbf{V} = \mathbf{0}$.

To turn this observation into a proof, let us rotate **V** through angle A and use linearity:

$$R_A(\mathbf{V}) = R_A(\mathbf{v}_0 + \mathbf{v}_1 + \cdots + \mathbf{v}_{n-1})$$
$$= R_A(\mathbf{v}_0) + R_A(\mathbf{v}_1) + \cdots + R_A(\mathbf{v}_{n-1}).$$

But $R_A(\mathbf{v}_0) = \mathbf{v}_1$ (by the definition of $\mathbf{v}_k$), and in general each $\mathbf{v}_k$ is transformed into $\mathbf{v}_{k+1}$ all the way until $\mathbf{v}_{n-1}$, which gets transformed into $\mathbf{v}_0$ (since $nA = 360$). Therefore,

$$R_A(\mathbf{V}) = \mathbf{v}_1 + \mathbf{v}_2 + \cdots + \mathbf{v}_{n-1} + \mathbf{v}_0 = \mathbf{V}.$$

Note that the last equality follows from commutativity of vector addition (the fact that order doesn't matter in a sum).

Having demonstrated that **V** doesn't change when rotated by A, we complete the proof by observing that the only vector that can remain unchanged by a rotation is the zero vector. (This statement is geometrically obvious, although later on we'll develop the machinery to prove this using algebra rather than geometry; see exercise 2 of section 3.2.) In summary,

$$R_A(\mathbf{V}) = \mathbf{V} \quad \text{implies that} \quad \mathbf{V} = \mathbf{0},$$

and this completes the proof of the theorem.

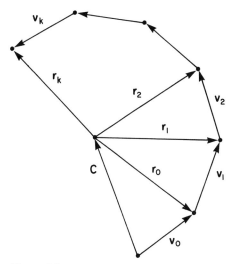

Figure 3.5
The POLY equation $\mathbf{v}_0 + \mathbf{v}_1 + \cdots + \mathbf{v}_k = \mathbf{c} + R_{kA}(\mathbf{r}_0)$.

We began this chapter by introducing vectors as a more global method
of describing turtle paths. We can capitalize on that perspective by
phrasing a global description of POLY in terms of vectors. The description
we have in mind specifies that the vertices of POLY lie on a fixed circle
where the angular measure of the arc between vertices is exactly the
angle input to the POLY (see chapter 1, section 1.2, exercise 15). This
fact means that, instead of following along POLY segments to reach a
particular vertex, we can obtain the same displacement by walking first
to the center of the circle and then along a radius. This gives

$$\mathbf{v}_0 + \mathbf{v}_1 + \cdots + \mathbf{v}_k = \mathbf{c} + \mathbf{r}_k$$

where $\mathbf{c}$ is a constant vector pointing to the center of the circle, and the
various $\mathbf{r}_k$ are all radii pointing to the POLY's vertices and hence equal
in length. Using the correlation between the amount of arc between
vertices on the circle and POLY angle, A, we can rewrite this as

$$\mathbf{v}_0 + \mathbf{v}_1 + \cdots + \mathbf{v}_k = \mathbf{c} + R_{kA}(\mathbf{r}_0).$$

Figure 3.5 shows this equation geometrically. In the next subsection
we'll see how to use this formula to good advantage.

If we let k become a continuous parameter, then $\mathbf{c} + R_{kA}(\mathbf{r}_0)$ represents
all the points along the circle in which POLY is inscribed. We now
have three complementary descriptions of a circle—turtle (FORWARD 1,
LEFT 1, etc.), Cartesian ($x^2 + y^2 = r^2$), and vector ($\mathbf{c} + R_{kA}(\mathbf{r}_0)$).

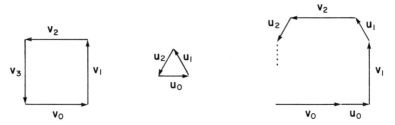

Figure 3.6
Interleaving segments of two POLYs.

3.1.4 MULTIPOLYs: Another Application of Vector Analysis

Let's turn now from the familiar POLY to apply vector techniques to
some new programs. Our aim will not be to supply complete analyses,
but rather to sketch some partial results and suggest further problems
for you to tackle on your own.

Our first example is an elaboration of POLY called DUOPOLY. It is
constructed by taking two ordinary POLYs and interleaving them as
shown in figure 3.6. This is the natural way of doing two POLYs at
the same time if one views POLY as a sequence of vectors rather than
as a sequence of turtle commands. (See NEWPOLY in subsection 1.1.4 for
comparison.) The DUOPOLY procedure takes four inputs, specifying the
sidelengths and the angles of the individual POLYs. The interleaving is
accomplished by alternately drawing sides of the two POLY figures POLY1
and POLY2, while making sure that the sides of the two POLYs have the
same headings they would have if the POLYs were drawn individually.
That is to say, if the first POLY's angle is ANGLE1 the headings of the
sides will be the successive multiples of ANGLE1, while for the second
POLY the headings will be the successive multiples of ANGLE2. Here is
the procedure:

```
TO DUOPOLY (SIDE1, ANGLE1, SIDE2, ANGLE2)
    C ← 0
    REPEAT FOREVER
        VECTOR (C * ANGLE1, SIDE1)
        VECTOR (C * ANGLE2, SIDE2)
        C ← C + 1
```

The procedure for drawing vectors takes two inputs specifying direction
and length of the vector to be drawn:

```
TO VECTOR (DIRECTION, LENGTH)
   SETHEADING DIRECTION
   FORWARD LENGTH
```

(To make the headings of our turtle vectors agree with standard mathematical conventions for directions, we specify that a heading of 0 is horizontal facing right, and that headings increase counterclockwise.)

One of the nice things about DUOPOLY is the great variety of figures that can be obtained by varying the four inputs. Figure 3.7 gives a small sample.

Closure

The first thing to notice about these figures is that they are all closed. By using vector methods, it is easy to see why this is true. Think of the DUOPOLY as a sum of vectors, and separate the vectors into two groups corresponding to the sides of POLY1 ($\mathbf{v}$) and POLY2 ($\mathbf{u}$). Then the net displacement is

$$\mathbf{v}_0 + \mathbf{u}_0 + \mathbf{v}_1 + \mathbf{u}_1 + \cdots + \mathbf{v}_k + \mathbf{u}_k$$
$$= (\mathbf{v}_0 + \mathbf{v}_1 + \cdots + \mathbf{v}_k) + (\mathbf{u}_0 + \mathbf{u}_1 + \cdots + \mathbf{u}_k).$$

The first group is just the net displacement of POLY1, and the second that of POLY2. Whenever each POLY closes, the corresponding part (vs or us) of the DUOPOLY net displacement will sum to zero. The trick is to show that there is some point where the two POLYs close simultaneously.

Suppose that POLY1 closes in n_1 steps—we saw in subsection 1.4.1 how to determine n_1 as the least common multiple of ANGLE1 and $360 \div$ ANGLE1. Whenever C (the "loop counter" in the DUOPOLY program) is a multiple of n_1, the vectors in the first group can be reassembled to form some number of complete copies of POLY1 and hence will sum to zero. Similarly, whenever C is a multiple of n_2 (the number of vertices in POLY2), the vectors in the second group will sum to zero. So if C is a common multiple of n_1 and n_2, both groups will sum to zero at the same time. In particular, taking C to be $n_1 \times n_2$, or (better yet) the least common multiple of n_1 and n_2, will produce a closed figure (see exercise 7 below). For example, figure 3.7a is a DUOPOLY with ANGLE1 = 90° ($n_1 = 4$) and an ANGLE2 of 320° ($n_2 = 9$). It closes in LCM(4, 9) = 36 steps. You can easily see nine complete squares, and the remaining segments can be reassembled to form four 9-gons.

In summary: DUOPOLY closes because vector addition is commutative. That allows us to reassociate an alternate sum of vectors from two POLYs into two pieces, each of which represents a POLY and hence sums to zero.

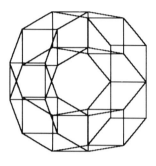

DUOPOLY (150, 90, 150, 320)

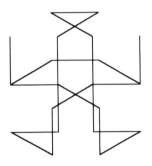

DUOPOLY (200, 90, 200, 300)

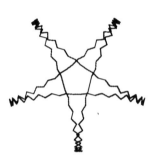

DUOPOLY (40, 10, 40, -15)

DUOPOLY (4, 2, 8, -2)

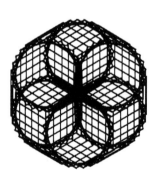

DUOPOLY (200, 62, 200, 300)

DUOPOLY (60, 19, 60, -20)

Figure 3.7
Some examples of DUOPOLY.

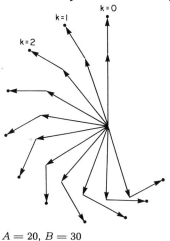

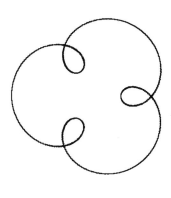

$A = 20,\ B = 30$ k continuous; $B = 4A$

Figure 3.8
Spirographs.

Symmetry

The global vector view of POLY, discussed at the end of subsection 3.1.3, furnishes additional insight by allowing us to write a global equation for the net displacement in DUOPOLY. (The equation is particularly simple if we consider only those displacements formed by an equal number of **v**s and **u**s, that is, the displacement at every other vertex of the DUOPOLY figure.) If we use A and B as the angles of the two POLYs, we have

$$\mathbf{v}_0 + \mathbf{v}_1 + \cdots + \mathbf{v}_k = \mathbf{c}_v + R_{kA}(\mathbf{r}_v),$$
$$\mathbf{u}_0 + \mathbf{u}_1 + \cdots + \mathbf{u}_k = \mathbf{c}_u + R_{kB}(\mathbf{r}_u)$$

where $\mathbf{c}_v$ and $\mathbf{c}_u$ are the centers of the two POLY circles, and $\mathbf{r}_v$ and $\mathbf{r}_u$ are the initial radii. Thus, the vertices of the DUOPOLY are given by

$$\mathbf{c}_v + R_{kA}(\mathbf{r}_v) + \mathbf{c}_u + R_{kB}(\mathbf{r}_u) = \mathbf{c} + R_{kA}(\mathbf{r}_v) + R_{kB}(\mathbf{r}_u).$$

The vector $\mathbf{c} = \mathbf{c}_v + \mathbf{c}_u$ represents the constant "center" of the DUOPOLY. Remember from 3.1.1 how making k a continuous parameter described the whole circle circumscribing POLY? We can do the same here. Geometrically,

$$\mathbf{c} + R_{kA}(\mathbf{r}_v) + R_{kB}(\mathbf{r}_u)$$

represents a "two-armed spirograph" figure formed by rotating one vector about the end of another rotating vector. As k increments by 1, $R_{kA}(\mathbf{r}_v)$ rotates by A and $R_{kB}(\mathbf{r}_u)$ rotates by B (figure 3.8a). Figure 3.8b shows a typical continuous spirograph figure (with no radii). We have shown that every DUOPOLY is inscribed in a two-armed spirograph.

Let's determine the symmetry of the spirograph. Imagine watching the figure being generated, starting from a time when the two arms are lined up. As soon as the two arms line up again, the figure will have completed one "loop-the-loop" and will be about to make another identical one, offset at some angle from the original. If B denotes the larger of the two angles, then the arms become realigned when the B arm has gone a full $360°$ plus some to catch back up to the slower A arm. The new loop-the-loop will be rotated by the amount the A arm turned between lineups; hence, that is the symmetry angle, S, of the spirograph. In equations this is expressed as follows:

$$kB = 360 + kA,$$

$$k = \frac{360}{B-A},$$

$$S = kA = \frac{360A}{B-A} = \frac{360}{B/A - 1}.$$

For example, a DUOPOLY with ANGLE1 equal to 45 and ANGLE2 equal to 9 has symmetry angle

$$S = \frac{360}{\frac{45}{9} - 1} = 90,$$

so we should expect fourfold symmetry, and this is what we observe in figure 3.9a. The symmetry angle depends only on the ratio of B to A. All DUOPOLYs with proportional angles are inscribed in similar spirographs.

Fortunately (since we're looking for good problems rather than easy answers), the full story of DUOPOLY's symmetry is more complicated than this one formula. Remember, the formula gives the symmetry of the associated spirograph figure; the symmetry of the actual DUOPOLY figure may be different. Figure 3.9b shows DUOPOLY with $A = 4$ and $B = 32$. Then $B/A = 8$, which implies $S = 360/7$. Indeed, the figure appears to have sevenfold symmetry. But this symmetry is not exact; the seven lobes are not identical. We call this curious phenomenon "approximate symmetry." We'll leave it to you to work out the conditions under which approximate symmetry can occur and find a way to compute the exact symmetry of a DUOPOLY figure rather than that of the spirograph (see exercise 5 below).

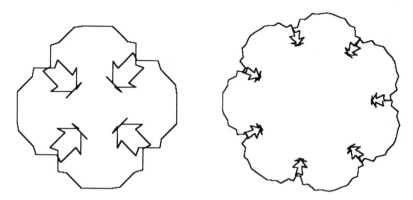

Figure 3.9
(a) DUOPOLY (100, 45, 40, 9) with fourfold spirograph symmetry.
(b) DUOPOLY (35, 32, 20, 4) with sevenfold spirograph symmetry.

Beyond DUOPOLY

The DUOPOLY procedure can be generalized to MULTIPOLY, which can interleave any number of POLYs. The input to MULTIPOLY is a list of [SIDE ANGLE] pairs. The number of pairs in the list is the number of POLYs to interleave. For example,

```
MULTIPOLY [ [100 90] [50 60] [20 30] ]
```

interleaves three POLYs.

The MULTIPOLY procedure first draws a side of the first POLY in the list, then a side of the second POLY, and so on until the list is exhausted. Then it starts again at the beginning of the list, and this process is repeated over and over:

```
TO MULTIPOLY INPUT.LIST
    C ← 0
    REPEAT FOREVER
        REPEAT FOR [SIDE ANGLE] IN INPUT.LIST
            VECTOR (C * ANGLE, SIDE)
        C ← C + 1
```

(See appendix A for explanations of the REPEAT FOR ... IN ... construct and the "structure-directed assignment" feature that is used to set both variables SIDE and ANGLE at once.)

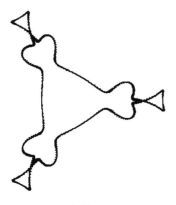

ANGLEs: 1, —8, 16, —2

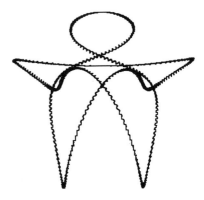

ANGLEs: 2, —3, 5, —7

ANGLEs: 20, —30, 40, —50

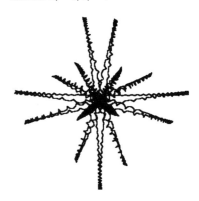

ANGLEs: 7, —8, 9, —10

Figure 3.10
Examples of equal-sided QUADRAPOLYs.

There are many different kinds of MULTIPOLYs. Figure 3.10 illustrates some QUADRAPOLYs (MULTIPOLYs with the number of POLYs equal to 4). Notice that figure 3.10a has exact symmetry, while c and d are only approximately symmetric. QUADRAPOLYs are a rich domain of phenomena in which to challenge your imagination at systematic investigation.

3.1.5 Unexpectedly Closed Figures

Unexpectedly closed figures, introduced in subsection 1.3.2, are figures drawn by looping programs in which the basic loop is itself closed—that is, figures whose POLY skeletons have zero sidelength. In terms of vectors this means that the vectors in the basic loop "unexpectedly" sum to zero.

Spirolaterals

When we introduced spirolaterals in subsection 1.3.2 we mentioned that the figures we called generalized spirolaterals could be unexpectedly closed. These figures are drawn, you recall, by the GSPIRO program:

```
TO GSPIRO (SIDE, ANGLE, MAX, LIST)
   REPEAT FOREVER
      SUBGSPIRO (SIDE, ANGLE, MAX, LIST)

TO SUBGSPIRO (SIDE, ANGLE, MAX, LIST)
   COUNT ← 1
   REPEAT
      FORWARD SIDE * COUNT
      IF MEMBER (COUNT, LIST)
         THEN RIGHT ANGLE
         ELSE LEFT ANGLE
      COUNT ← COUNT + 1
   UNTIL COUNT > MAX
```

The inputs to the program specify the sidelength of the initial side, the angle that the turtle turns at each vertex, the number of sides in the basic loop, and the steps at which the turtle turns RIGHT instead of LEFT.

As an example of an unexpectedly closed spirolateral, we'll take an ANGLE of $360/3 = 120$, a MAX of 11, and a LIST of [3 4 6 7]. To see why the corresponding GSPIRO (figure 3.11) is unexpectedly closed, notice first that any vector in the basic loop must be a multiple of either v_0, v_1, or v_2, that is, the initial vector v_0 rotated counterclockwise $0°$, $120°$, or $240°$, respectively. Now we compute what these multiples are. The turtle starts out pointing along v_0 and goes forward distance 1. (We suppose, for simplicity, that SIDE is 1.) Now the turtle turns left to point along v_1 and goes forward 2; that is, it, moves by the vector $2v_1$. The next move adds in $3v_2$. Now comes a right turn (since 3 is in the LIST), and so the next move adds in $4v_1$. Continuing in this way, we find that the sum of the vectors in the basic loop is

$$0_0 + 2v_1 + 3v_2 + 4v_1 + 5v_0 + 6v_1 + 7v_0 + 8v_2 + 9v_0 + 10v_1 + 11v_2$$
$$= 22(v_0 + v_1 + v_2).$$

But we know from the vector form of the POLY closing theorem (see subsection 3.1.3) that $v_0 + v_1 + v_2 = 0$. Therefore, the sum of the vectors in the basic loop is zero and the figure is unexpectedly closed.

Generalizing this analysis, we see that we'll get unexpectedly closed spirolaterals with an ANGLE of $A = 360/n$ whenever we can arrange

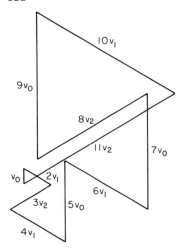

Figure 3.11
GSPIRO with ANGLE = 120, MAX = 11, LIST = [3 4 6 7] is unexpectedly closed.

things so that the sum of the vectors in the basic loop is a multiple of $\mathbf{v}_0 + \mathbf{v}_1 + \cdots + \mathbf{v}_{n-1}$. So, given $A = 360/n$ and MAX, we can attempt to find values of LIST that satisfy this property by the following "slot process": Start by setting up n "slots" (corresponding to the vectors $\mathbf{v}_k$). Now take the numbers from 1 through MAX (corresponding to the amount the turtle goes forward at each step) and distribute these among the n slots so that the sum of the numbers in each slot is the same (that is, so that in the end all the $\mathbf{v}_k$ will be weighted the same amount). There is one more restriction on assigning the numbers: If the number i goes into slot k, then $i + 1$ must go into either slot $k - 1$ or $k + 1$ (mod n); That is, the turtle can only rotate through the fixed ANGLE, left or right, between successive steps). We'll use the term "regular unexpectedly closed spirolateral" to refer to the kind of spirolateral produced by this slot process, the kind for which the basic loop vector sum is a multiple of $\mathbf{v}_0 + \mathbf{v}_1 + \cdots + \mathbf{v}_{n-1}$. But there are also irregular unexpectedly closed spirolaterals. One example is drawn by ANGLE = 90, MAX = 8, and LIST = [4]. The vector sum for this basic loop is

$$8\mathbf{v}_0 + 10\mathbf{v}_1 + 8\mathbf{v}_2 + 10\mathbf{v}_3,$$

which equals zero, since, for $A = 360/4$, $\mathbf{v}_0 = -\mathbf{v}_2$ and $\mathbf{v}_1 = -\mathbf{v}_3$.

As it turns out, if $A = 360/n$ where n is a prime number ($n \neq 2$), all unexpectedly closed spirolaterals are regular, whereas if $A = 360/n$ where n is an even integer no unexpectedly closed spirolaterals are regular (see exercises 17 and 19 below).

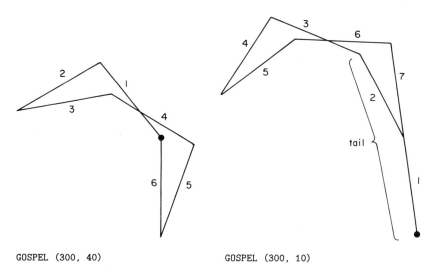

GOSPEL (300, 40)   GOSPEL (300, 10)

Figure 3.12
Looping and initial tail of GOSPEL figures.

GOSPEL

Our final example for vector analysis is a very simple program, but the analysis of whether or not the program draws a closed figure turns out to be surprisingly difficult. The program is GOSPEL, named after the two people who first studied it, Bill Gosper and Richard Schroeppel:

```
TO GOSPEL (SIDE, ANGLE)
    LEFT ANGLE
    FORWARD SIDE
    GOSPEL (SIDE, 2 * ANGLE)
```

For an example, suppose that ANGLE is 40 (see figure 3.12a). Then the sequence of turns in the resulting GOSPEL figure will be

$$40, 80, 160, 320, 640, 1280, 2560, 5120, \ldots$$

or, reducing modulo 360,

$$40, 80, 160, 320, 280, 200, 40, 80, \ldots$$

So GOSPEL with an ANGLE of 40 is equivalent to the fixed instruction loop

```
LEFT 40 FORWARD SIDE
LEFT 80 FORWARD SIDE
LEFT 160 FORWARD SIDE
LEFT 320 FORWARD SIDE
LEFT 280 FORWARD SIDE
LEFT 200 FORWARD SIDE
```

repeated over and over.

But GOSPEL is not always precisely equivalent to a fixed instruction loop. For instance, if we had taken the initial ANGLE to be 10 the sequence of turns (reduced modulo 360) would be

$$10, 20, 40, 80, 160, 320, 280, 200, 40, 80, \ldots,$$

or the same loop as before with an extra

```
LEFT 10 FORWARD SIDE
LEFT 20 FORWARD SIDE
```

added on at the beginning. This is illustrated in figure 3.12b.

In general, the sequence of angles turned is

$$\text{ANGLE}, 2 \times \text{ANGLE}, 4 \times \text{ANGLE}, 8 \times \text{ANGLE}, \ldots,$$

and this will start repeating over from the beginning if and only if there is some integer n for which

$$2^n \times \text{ANGLE} = \text{ANGLE} \ (\text{mod } 360).$$

If ANGLE $= 360 \times p/q$ where p and q are integers with no common factors, the above equation reduces (see exercise 24) to $2^n \times p = p$ (mod q). This equation can always be satisfied if q is an odd number, because if q is odd there is always some n for which $2^n = 1$ (mod q) (see exercise 25). The smallest positive integer n that satisfies $2^n = 1$ (mod q) is called the order of 2 modulo q. Thus,

if ANGLE $= 360 \times p/q$ where q is odd, then GOSPEL is equivalent to a fixed instruction loop. The number of steps in the basic loop is equal to the order of 2 modulo q.

One interesting fact about GOSPEL is that the heading change for this basic loop is always a multiple of $360°$ (see exercise 26). Therefore, whenever the figure is closed, it is automatically unexpectedly closed.

For a vector analysis of the basic loop, suppose that ANGLE $= 360 \times$ p/q, let n be the order of 2 modulo q, and let $\mathbf{v}_k$ denote the vector $\mathbf{v}_0$ rotated counterclockwise through (ANGLE $\times k$), where $\mathbf{v}_0$ points in the turtle's initial direction. Now compute the position of the turtle at the end of the basic loop in terms of the vectors $\mathbf{v}_k$. First the turtle turns through ANGLE and goes forward along the displacement $\mathbf{v}_1$. (We'll suppose that SIDE $= 1$). Then the turtle turns $2 \times$ ANGLE, which makes the heading ANGLE $+ 2 \times$ ANGLE $= 3 \times$ ANGLE, and goes forward. So the resulting position is $\mathbf{v}_1 + \mathbf{v}_3$. Now the turtle turns $4 \times$ ANGLE, which makes the heading $7 \times$ ANGLE, and goes forward to position $\mathbf{v}_1 + \mathbf{v}_3 + \mathbf{v}_7$. Continuing for the n steps of the basic loop, we see that the final position is

$$\mathbf{v}_1 + \mathbf{v}_3 + \mathbf{v}_7 + \cdots + \mathbf{v}_{2^n - 1},$$

and the loop closes if and only if this sum is zero. (Note that by the choice of n the last term in the sum above is equal to $\mathbf{v}_0$.)

In our example above, we had ANGLE $= 40$, $= 360/9$. The powers of 2 modulo 9 are $2, 4, 8, 7, 5, 1$, so the order of 2 modulo 9 is 6, the basic loop has 6 segments, and the vector sum is

$$\mathbf{v}_1 + \mathbf{v}_3 + \mathbf{v}_7 + \mathbf{v}_6 + \mathbf{v}_4 + \mathbf{v}_0.$$

We leave it to you (exercise 27) to verify that this sum is zero and that hence the figure is closed.

Exercises for Section 3.1

1. Give geometric interpretations of vectors (displacements) in three dimensions. Draw pictures to illustrate vector addition and scalar multiplication.

2. Give a geometric definition, in terms of displacements, of vector subtraction. Give one that does not involve "adding the negative." [A]

3. [D] Using vectors, prove that POLYSPI (subsection 1.1.4) cannot close. [HA]

4. State the vector form of the POLY closing theorem in the case where $A = 360 \times p/q$, and p/q is a fraction reduced to lowest terms. [A]

5. We saw in subsection 3.1.4 how to compute the symmetry of the spirograph associated with a given DUOPOLY. Now find the exact symmetry. In particular, show that DUOPOLY starts looping (in the sense

defined in section 1.3) when

C $\times$ (ANGLE1 $-$ ANGLE2) $= 0$ (mod 360)

where C is the loop counter, and that the symmetry angle will be C $\times$ ANGLE1 where C is the smallest positive integer that satisfies the above equation. [H]

6. Predict the symmetry of DUOPOLYs with ANGLE1 $= 17$, ANGLE2 $= 1$; with ANGLE1 $= 18$, ANGLE2 $= 2$; with ANGLE1 $= 28$, ANGLE2 $= 3$; with ANGLE1 $= 101$, ANGLE2 $= 1$; with ANGLE1 $= 102$, ANGLE2 $= 2$. Check your answers by drawing the figures. [A]

7. [P] In our analysis of DUOPOLY we saw that if POLY1 closes in n_1 steps and POLY2 closes in n_2 steps then the DUOPOLY will close when the loop counter C is a common multiple of n_1 and n_2. But can DUOPOLY close for other values of C? In particular, is there a value of C smaller than LCM(n_1, n_2) for which the DUOPOLY will generally be closed? What about special circumstances?

8. [P] Compare the patterns drawn by DUOPOLY (S1, A1, S2, A2) with those in which the second POLY is drawn by VECTOR (-A2, S2) rather than VECTOR (A2, S2). How about VECTOR (A2, -S2)? What about QUADRAPOLYs where the sign of the angle input to VECTOR alternates? What if the sign of the distance alternates (is positive for the first and third POLYs, negative for the second and fourth)? Can you make any generalizations? (Pay attention to symmetry!)

9. Generalizing our analysis of DUOPOLY, show that every nth vertex of an n-fold MULTIPOLY lies on an n-armed spirograph figure. Can you compute the symmetry of the spirograph? [A]

10. [D] Suppose we have a MULTIPOLY whose sequence of angles is $1, -n, n^2, -n^3, \ldots$. Prove that the MULTIPOLY has $(n + 1)$-fold approximate symmetry. Show that $1, n, n^2, n^3, \ldots$ produces $(n - 1)$-fold symmetry. In what sense does an ordinary clock mechanism have 11-fold symmetry? [A]

11. [D] Generalize the exact symmetry rule for DUOPOLYs (exercise 5 above) to a corresponding rule for MULTIPOLYs.

12. Find MULTIPOLYs with 3-, 4-, 5-, and 7-fold approximate symmetry.

13. [D] All of our symmetry considerations have been about rotational symmetry. There is another kind of symmetry, called bilateral symmetry. Bilaterally symmetric figures have a symmetry reflection through

an axis. (Figures 3.7a, b, and d are clearly bilaterally symmetric. Are 3.7c, e, and f?) When is DUOPOLY exactly bilaterally symmetric? Approximately bilaterally symmetric? What is the axis of symmetry? (It's not always the initial heading!) [HA]

14. [P] Write and explore a DUOPOLY (or MULTIPOLY) program that adds the vectors from one iteration of the REPEAT loop and then just moves according to that sum vector. This can be accomplished by inserting at the beginning of the loop a step called STARTVECTOR, which puts the pen up and remembers the turtle's current position, and a step at the end of the loop called ENDVECTOR, which notes the final position and then draws the line from initial position to final. Study properties of figures drawn by this program.

15. [P] Study the behavior of parametrized classes of MULTIPOLYs. For example, what happens to DUOPOLY ($k \times$ A1, S1, $k \times$ A2, S2) or DUOPOLY (A1, $k \times$ S, A2, $(1 - k) \times$ S) or DUOPOLY ($k \times$ A1, $k \times$ S1, $k \times$ A2, $k \times$ S2) as k varies? Pay particular attention to critical values of k such as positive or negative k near zero, $k = 1$, k large, etc. Invent your own parametrized classes with interesting behavior.

16. [P] A "multi-looping program" is one that interleaves (in the sense of MULTIPOLY) any number of looping programs. (Looping programs were discussed in section 1.3.) Try to formulate a general theorem that tells how to find the symmetry of any multi-looping program.

17. There is a partial converse to the vector form of the POLY closing theorem of subsection 3.1.4: Suppose that ANGLE $= 360/n$. As before, we define vectors $\mathbf{v}_k$ to be the initial vector $\mathbf{v}_0$ rotated through ($k \times$ ANGLE) and set

$$\mathbf{V} = \mathbf{v}_0 + \mathbf{v}_1 + \cdots + \mathbf{v}_{n-1}.$$

We know that $\mathbf{V} = \mathbf{0}$. The converse result (which we do not prove) says that if n is a prime number, then any collection of the $\mathbf{v}_k$ that sums to zero must do so by being a multiple of $\mathbf{V}$. (Give an example to show that this is false for nonprime n.) Using this converse to the theorem, prove that any unexpectedly closed spirolateral with ANGLE $= 360/n$ (n prime) must be regular. [A]

18. Show that if there is a regular unexpectedly closed spirolateral with ANGLE $= 360/n$, then n divides MAX $\times$ (MAX $+ 1)/2$. [HA]

19. [D] Show that if n is even there are no regular unexpectedly closed spirolaterals with ANGLE $= 360/n$. [HA]

20. For n an odd integer, show that we get a regular unexpectedly closed spirolateral by taking ANGLE $= 360/n$, MAX $= n^2$, and LIST $=$ [n $2n$ $3n$ ... n^2].

21. With ANGLE $= 360/n$, n odd, show that we get another regular unexpectedly closed spirolateral by taking MAX $= n^2 - 1$ and LIST $=$ [$n - 1$ $2n - 1$ $3n - 1$ ... $n^2 - 1$].

22. [P] Write a computer program to do a "brute force" search for unexpectedly closed spirolaterals. Given values for ANGLE and MAX, the program should test all possible values for LIST and record which ones give basic loops that are closed. Can you think of ways to increase the efficiency of this program?

23. [P] Write a program that uses the slot method to search for regular unexpectedly closed spirolaterals. Can you make this search any more efficient than the "brute force" search of the previous exercise?

24. Show that, for ANGLE $= 360 \times p/q$ where p and q have no common factors, $2^k \times$ ANGLE $=$ ANGLE (mod 360) if and only if $2^k p = p$ (mod q). [A]

25. Prove that if q is odd there is an integer k for which $2^k = 1$ (mod q). [H]

26. Prove that the heading change for the basic loop in the GOSPEL program with $A = 360 \times p/q$ (q odd) must be a multiple of 360. [H]

27. Verify that if $A = 360/9$ and $\mathbf{v}_k = R_{kA}(\mathbf{v}_0)$, then

$$\mathbf{v}_1 + \mathbf{v}_3 + \mathbf{v}_7 + \mathbf{v}_6 + \mathbf{v}_4 + \mathbf{v}_0 = \mathbf{0}. \quad [H]$$

28. Show that if p is a prime ($p \neq 2$) the order of 2 modulo p is at most $p - 1$. Use this to prove that if ANGLE $= 360/p$ the resulting GOSPEL figure is never closed. [HA]

29. [D] Let p be a prime, n an integer > 1, and ANGLE $= 360/p^n$. Show that the resulting GOSPEL figure is closed whenever the following condition is satisfied: For every positive integer r, $2^r + p$ is congruent modulo p^n to a power of 2.

30. [DDP] Schroeppel claims that a complete solution to the GOSPEL problem is that the figure will be closed for ANGLE $= 360 \times p/q$ where p/q is a fraction reduced to lowest terms if and only if, for every prime s dividing q, s^2 also divides q; and none of the primes dividing q have the

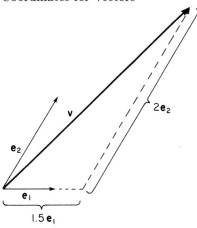

Figure 3.13
Any vector can be decomposed as $\mathbf{v} = a\mathbf{e}_1 + b\mathbf{e}_2$.

"exceptional property" that $2^{s-1} = 1 \pmod{s^2}$. Can you prove or disprove this claim? Write a computer program to find some "exceptional primes."

31. [DP] Consider variations on GOSPEL; for example, where ANGLE is multiplied by 3 each time or by an arbitrary fixed amount each time. How does this change the analysis of the program?

3.2 Coordinates for Vectors

So far we have dealt with the vectors as arrows having fixed direction and length. Sooner or later, however, we will want to manipulate vectors using the computer. This means we will have to represent vectors in terms of numbers and ordinary arithmetic operations.

Perhaps the most straightforward approach is to represent each vector by the pair of numbers giving direction and length. We have already used this method in the VECTOR command, which was part of the DUOPOLY and MULTIPOLY programs. But the calculation needed if we are to add vectors and express the result in the same format is difficult, and translating from vectors to numbers in this way is not much help.

Fortunately there is a better way. We saw in subsection 3.1.1 that vector addition and scalar multiplication allow us to construct new vectors from old ones. But you may not have noticed at that time that, if we start with any two vectors that are not scalar multiples of each other, every vector can be expressed as a sum of scalar multiples of these two. Figure 3.13 shows a general vector expressed in this way. So if we use a pair of reference vectors, say $\mathbf{e}_1$ and $\mathbf{e}_2$, we can decompose any vector $\mathbf{v}$ as a sum $\mathbf{v} = a\mathbf{e}_1 + b\mathbf{e}_2$ for some appropriate numbers a and b. The reference pair $\mathbf{e}_1, \mathbf{e}_2$ is called a *basis,* and the parts of the decomposition $a\mathbf{e}_1$ and $b\mathbf{e}_2$ are called the *components* of $\mathbf{v}$. The numbers a and b are called the *coordinates* of $\mathbf{v}$. (Sometimes a and b are themselves referred to as components.) We can create a correspondence between vectors and pairs of numbers as follows:

$\mathbf{v}$ corresponds to the pair (a, b) precisely when $\mathbf{v} = a\mathbf{e}_1 + b\mathbf{e}_2$.

It is important that this correspondence is one-to-one. That is, if $\mathbf{v}$ corresponds to (a, b) and $\mathbf{w}$ corresponds to (c, d) and if $\mathbf{v} = \mathbf{w}$, then we are justified in concluding that $a = c$ and $b = d$ (see exercise 5). This simple realization allows us to translate vector equations into numerical equations at will. It is also important to realize that the correspondence between vectors and number pairs is defined only relative to a basis. Each basis gives rise to a different system of coordinates. Notice, however, a few basis-invariant relations; $(0, 0)$ is always the zero vector $\mathbf{0}$; $(1, 0)$ is always $\mathbf{e}_1$; $(0, 1)$ is always $\mathbf{e}_2$.

3.2.1 Vector Operations in Coordinates

Now let's add vectors and see how the coordinates behave. Suppose $\mathbf{v}$ corresponds to (a, b)—that is, $\mathbf{v} = a\mathbf{e}_1 + b\mathbf{e}_2$—and $\mathbf{w}$ corresponds to (c, d). Then

$$\mathbf{v} + \mathbf{w} = a\mathbf{e}_1 + b\mathbf{e}_2 + c\mathbf{e}_1 + d\mathbf{e}_2 = (a + c)\mathbf{e}_1 + (b + d)\mathbf{e}_2.$$

Thus, $\mathbf{v} + \mathbf{w}$ corresponds to $(a+c, b+d)$. What could be simpler! Adding vectors is equivalent to adding corresponding coordinates. Furthermore, scalar multiplication by a number K is equivalent to multiplying both coordinates by K.

To teach our computer to manipulate vectors we need only represent vectors as pairs of numbers (coordinates relative to a basis) and define the procedures ADD, which takes as inputs two pairs of numbers, and MULTIPLY, which takes as inputs a number and a pair:

```
TO ADD ([A B], [C D])
   RETURN [ (A + C) (B + D) ]
```

```
TO MULTIPLY (K, [A B])
   RETURN [K*A K*B]
```

(For simplicity, we'll pretend that the computer is smart enough to know

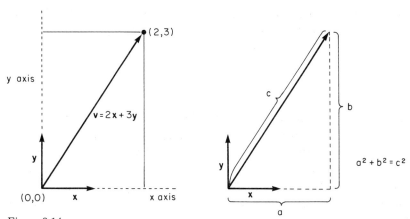

Figure 3.14
(a) Cartesian coordinates and the standard basis for vector coordinates. (b) The length of a vector $\mathbf{v} = (v_x, v_y)$ is given by $|\mathbf{v}|^2 = v_x^2 + v_y^2$.

that + is the symbol for "ADD," so that it will now know how to interpret expressions like "[1 2]+[2 3]" or "V + W" where V and W have been defined as pairs of numbers. Similarly, the definition of MULTIPLY should tell the computer how to interpret expressions like "4*[5 6]" and "4*V." And knowing both how to add and how to multiply should tell it how to subtract using the rule V−W = V+(−1)×W. Of course, most computer languages are not this clever, so in practice you will need to spell things out a bit more.)

Although we can use any basis for our vector coordinates, it is convenient to specify a pair of reference vectors whose lengths are 1 (*unit length*) and whose directions are perpendicular to each other. The standard choice is to use a horizontal vector $\mathbf{x}$ and a vertical vector $\mathbf{y}$, and to name the coordinates of a vector $\mathbf{v}$ by (v_x, v_y). In that way the vector coordinates are precisely the same as the Cartesian coordinates of the tip of the vector, provided the tail is put at the Cartesian point $(0, 0)$ (see figure 3.14a). Another advantage of the $\mathbf{x}, \mathbf{y}$ basis is that the length of a vector $\mathbf{v}$ is easily expressed in terms of the coordinates: If $\mathbf{v} = (v_x, v_y)$, then the length of $\mathbf{v}$, denoted $|\mathbf{v}|$, is equal to the square root of $v_x^2 + v_y^2$. The proof of this formula, illustrated in figure 3.14b, is a simple application of the Pythagorean theorem for right triangles.

A Note on Computer Languages and Vectors
Some computer languages aren't capable of handling vectors as single entities. Even with these languages, the methods of this chapter will still be useful; you just have to keep track of the separate vector components.

For example, instead of writing expressions like Z ← V + W (where Z, V, and W are pairs of numbers) or [ZX ZY] ← [VX VY] + [WX WY], you could use a pair of instructions:

```
ZX ← VX + WX
ZY ← VY + WY
```

But this is not as good as being able to deal with vectors as vectors. After all, one of the reasons for regarding vectors as conceptual entities in their own right is that they capture the geometric intuition of displacement, which is obscured if we constantly have to deal with components separately. So if our computer language is to be a good vehicle for thinking about problems (rather than just some way of getting a machine to do computations), then it helps to be able to deal with vectors directly. Some computer languages (such as APL) have vector operations built in so that it is not necessary to define them explicitly.

3.2.2 Rotation in Coordinates: The Linearity Principle

Now that we have seen that vector addition and scalar multiplication are very simple when expressed in terms of coordinates with respect to a basis, let's look at a more complex operation: rotation of vectors, which we introduced in subsection 3.1.3. Rotation is trivial if we use direction and length to represent a vector; the direction merely gets increased or decreased and the length is unchanged. So let's hope that computing rotations in basis coordinates is sufficiently simple that the advantage of easy vector addition will not be offset. That hope turns out to be more than justified, since when we tackle the problem of rotating in three-dimensional space (section 3.4) we will see that direction-length representation becomes hopelessly complex but computing with basis coordinates still works nicely.

In solving the rotation problem, we take an indirect but instructive approach. Rather than computing the coordinates of Rotate(**v**, A) directly in terms of the coordinates of **v**, we will instead look for an intrinsic intermediate representation that makes no reference to a particular choice of coordinates. Phrasing things in such terms will be simpler and more general; it will be the key to computing rotations in three dimensions, as we shall see in section 3.4.

One trick that often helps in solving vector problems is to construct a basis from vectors that have some intrinsic relation to the quantities involved in the problem and to decompose the vector we wish to compute in terms of this basis. In this case **v**, the vector to be rotated, is

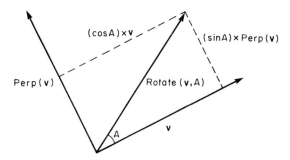

Figure 3.15
The rotation formula Rotate($\mathbf{v}$, A) = $(\cos A)\mathbf{v} + (\sin A)$Perp($\mathbf{v}$).

an obvious choice for one of the basis vectors. As a mate we can take Perp($\mathbf{v}$), which we define to be equal to $\mathbf{v}$ rotated 90° (in the direction of Rotate). Thus, we propose the decomposition

Rotate($\mathbf{v}$, A) = $a\mathbf{v} + b$Perp($\mathbf{v}$)

and try to solve for the quantities a and b. But these quantities are the proportions of the rotated vector which project, respectively, parallel and perpendicular to the original vector. As shown in figure 3.15, these are by definition precisely the cosine and the sine of the rotation angle A. Therefore, we have the rotation formula

Rotate($\mathbf{v}$, A) = $(\cos A)\mathbf{v} + (\sin A)$Perp($\mathbf{v}$).

As a computer procedure which takes as inputs a vector (a pair of numbers) and an angle, this is

```
TO ROTATE (V, A)
    RETURN COS(A) * V + SIN(A) * PERP(V)
```

This rotation computation requires only the operations of vector addition and scalar multiplication, which we already know how to perform using coordinates, and the new operation Perp. So the rotation problem will be completely solved if we discover how to compute the coordinates of Perp($\mathbf{v}$). We'll do this by using another important concept from section 3.1.3: linearity. Since Perp is a special case of rotation, it has the two properties which define linearity—scaling and additivity—and we can use those properties in computing with it:

Perp($\mathbf{v}$) = Perp($v_x\mathbf{x} + v_y\mathbf{y}$) = v_xPerp($\mathbf{x}$) + v_yPerp($\mathbf{y}$).

So we can express Perp($\mathbf{v}$) in terms of Perp applied to the basis vectors $\mathbf{x}$ and $\mathbf{y}$. And it is easy to see that Perp($\mathbf{x}$) and Perp($\mathbf{y}$) are just $\mathbf{y}$ and $-\mathbf{x}$, respectively. In net we have

$$\begin{aligned}
\text{Perp}(\mathbf{v}) &= v_x\text{Perp}(\mathbf{x}) + v_y\text{Perp}(\mathbf{y}) \\
&= v_x\mathbf{y} + v_y(-\mathbf{x}) \\
&= (-v_y)\mathbf{x} + v_x\mathbf{y},
\end{aligned}$$

which in coordinates means

$$\text{Perp}(v_x, v_y) = (-v_y, v_x).$$

As a computer procedure this is expressed as

```
TO PERP [VX VY]
    RETURN [-VY VX]
```

which completes the reduction of rotation to operations the computer can perform.

It's worth a moment to reflect on the particular use of linearity here, as it expresses the important general compatibility of linear operations with basis coordinatization. By taking advantage of scaling and additivity, we reduced the problem of computing Perp($\mathbf{v}$) to the much simpler problem of computing Perp for the basis vectors $\mathbf{x}$ and $\mathbf{y}$. This reduction to special cases is important enough to warrant a special name: the *linearity principle*.

Linearity Principle If L is a linear vector operation and we know how L acts on some basis $\mathbf{e}_1$ and $\mathbf{e}_2$, then we can compute $L(\mathbf{v})$ for any vector $\mathbf{v}$ by expressing $\mathbf{v}$ in terms of the basis. More precisely,

If $\mathbf{v} = a\mathbf{e}_1 + b\mathbf{e}_2$ then $L(\mathbf{v}) = aL(\mathbf{e}_1) + bL(\mathbf{e}_2)$.

Let's rephrase this principle. Expressing a vector in terms of a basis is a way of decomposing the vector into two pieces (an $\mathbf{e}_1$ and an $\mathbf{e}_2$ piece), and linear operations are "compatible" with this kind of decomposition. Compatible really means that in applying a linear operation, one can work with the pieces separately. Another way to say this is that linear situations are those in which it really is true that "the whole is equal to the sum of the parts." Linearity is a technical form of the kind of assumption that allows complex problems to be broken into pieces that can be worked on independently.

Exercises for Section 3.2

1. Using the coordinate equations we derived, verify that Perp and Rotate are linear. Suppose we define the operation L by $L(\mathbf{v}) = |\mathbf{v}|$ (the length of $\mathbf{v}$). Show that L satisfies scaling but not additivity.

2. Using the rotation formula in coordinates, give an algebraic proof of the "obvious" final step to the proof of the vector POLY closing theorem of subsection 3.1.3. That is, show that if $R_A(\mathbf{V}) = \mathbf{V}$ for some A which is not a multiple of 360, then $\mathbf{V} = \mathbf{0}$. [A]

3. Use the vector form of the POLY closing theorem to deduce that if $A = 360/n$ where n is a positive integer, then

$$\sin A + \sin 2A + \cdots + \sin(n-1)A = 0,$$
$$\cos A + \cos 2A + \cdots + \cos(n-1)A = -1.$$

Use the computer to check these equations numerically for various values of n. [A]

4. Show how to translate between the (v_x, v_y) and the heading-length representations of vectors. [A]

5. When can two vectors be used as a basis? In particular, given $\mathbf{v}_1 = (v_{1x}, v_{1y})$ and $\mathbf{v}_2 = (v_{2x}, v_{2y})$ (with coordinates given with respect to the standard $\mathbf{x}, \mathbf{y}$ basis), what are the algebraic conditions on the four numbers v_{1x}, v_{1y}, v_{2x}, v_{2y} which correspond to the geometric condition "$\mathbf{v}_1$ and $\mathbf{v}_2$ do not point along the same line." Show that if v_{1x}, v_{1y}, v_{2x}, and v_{2y} satisfy this condition, then $\mathbf{v}_1$ and $\mathbf{v}_2$ actually are a basis. That is, show that for every vector $\mathbf{v}$ there is exactly one pair of numbers (a, b) with $\mathbf{v} = a\mathbf{v}_1 + b\mathbf{v}_2$. [HA]

6. As a particular example of the previous exercise, show how to express the standard basis vectors $\mathbf{x}$ and $\mathbf{y}$ in the form

$$\mathbf{x} = a\mathbf{v}_1 + b\mathbf{v}_2,$$
$$\mathbf{y} = c\mathbf{v}_1 + d\mathbf{v}_2.$$

That is, solve for a, b, c, and d in terms of v_{1x}, v_{1y}, v_{2x}, and v_{2y}. [A]

7. When do $\mathbf{v}_1$ and $\mathbf{v}_2$ form a basis such that, if one uses the coordinates given by the basis, one always has the relation $\mathrm{Perp}(a, b) = (-b, a)$? Answer in terms of algebraic conditions on v_{1x}, v_{1y}, v_{2x}, v_{2y}, and also in terms of geometric conditions on $\mathbf{v}_1$ and $\mathbf{v}_2$. [HA]

8. Show that DUOPOLY (A, B, C, -B) draws an ellipse when A, B, and C are small. [HA]

3.3 Implementing Turtle Vector Graphics on a Computer

In the first part of this chapter we got acquainted with vectors primarily as a language for analysis. Now that we have an important set of vector operations implemented on the computer, we are in a position to build computer representations of complex geometric phenomena. We can even construct and explore worlds beyond planar turtle geometry.

We'll begin by using vectors to implement the most important features of an ordinary planar turtle. This will form a basis for constructing a turtle that moves in three dimensions.

3.3.1 Turtle State

We said in chapter 1 that the state of a turtle is specified by giving the turtle's position and heading. Once we decide how to represent those in terms of vectors we will need to represent the state-change operators, FORWARD, BACK, LEFT, and RIGHT, in terms of basic vector operations.

Although we have used vectors so far only to represent displacements, there is an obvious way to represent positions with them. Simply select some fixed reference point (call it the origin) and represent an arbitrary position by the vector that points from the origin to the point of interest. This is like telling someone where something is by saying how to get there from some agreed reference point. Since what we're interested in is getting lines to appear on a computer display, it's only natural to choose the origin to be the $(0,0)$ point on the display. We'll call the position vector **P**. Furthermore, we can choose the size and orientation of the basis vectors **x** and **y** so that the coordinates (v_x, v_y) of any vector **v** are precisely the Cartesian x and y coordinates of the corresponding point on the display screen.

Besides representing positions, we must also have some way to get lines to appear on the screen. To accomplish this, we'll assume that our computer graphics system is equipped with a display command

DRAWLINE([START$_x$ START$_y$], [END$_x$ END$_y$])

which takes as input two Cartesian coordinate pairs and draws a line between the specified points. Most graphics systems include this command, or something similar.

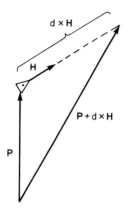

Figure 3.16
Position and heading vectors for a planar turtle.

Now how about heading? You've probably been thinking of turtle heading as an angle, but there is a very direct way to specify heading as a vector: Simply take any vector that points in the direction the turtle is pointing. To standardize matters we'll use the vector of length 1, and we'll call this $\mathbf{H}$.

So there we have it: Turtle state is specified by $\mathbf{P}$, which can be an arbitrary vector, and $\mathbf{H}$, which can be an arbitrary vector of length 1. Next we must specify how the state-change operators change $\mathbf{P}$ and $\mathbf{H}$.

3.3.2 State-Change Operators

As shown in figure 3.16, going forward some distance d displaces the turtle's position along a vector of length d which points in the heading direction. That is, the displacement vector is $d \times \mathbf{H}$. The new position is $\mathbf{P} + d\mathbf{H}$. Of course, FORWARD doesn't change $\mathbf{H}$ at all. Besides changing the turtle's state, FORWARD must also draw a line on the display screen, if the pen is down. We haven't mentioned details about how to keep track of the pen. We'll leave it to you to outline a more complete turtle implementation that takes care of this and other matters. See the exercises at the end of this section.

LEFT and RIGHT are even easier than FORWARD, as they just rotate the heading vector and do nothing else; $\mathbf{H}$ ← ROTATE($\mathbf{H}$, ANGLE).

Summary: A Vector-Based Turtle Implementation

Here in capsule form are the state and state-change operators for a turtle, expressed in terms of vectors. See the exercises below for details needed in actually implementing a turtle.

Turtle State

The turtle's state is represented by two vectors, **P** and **H**. By convention, **H** is always a vector of length 1.

State-Change Operators

```
TO FORWARD DISTANCE
   NEW.P ← P + (DISTANCE * H)
   IF PEN.IS.DOWN THEN DRAWLINE (P, NEW.P)
   P ← NEW.P

TO BACK DISTANCE
   FORWARD (- DISTANCE)

TO LEFT ANGLE
   H ← ROTATE(H, ANGLE)

TO RIGHT ANGLE
   LEFT (- ANGLE)
```

Subprocedures Used in Computing Rotations

```
TO ROTATE (VECTOR, ANGLE)
   RETURN COS(ANGLE) * VECTOR + SIN(ANGLE) * PERP(VECTOR)

TO PERP [VX VY]
   RETURN [ -VY VX]
```

Basic Vector Operations

```
TO ADD ([A B], [C D])
   RETURN [(A + C) (B + D)]

TO MULTIPLY (N, [A B])
   RETURN [N*A N*B]
```

Exercises for Section 3.3

The exercises below are concerned with fleshing out the details of the vector turtle implementation. Doing them will help prepare for pro-

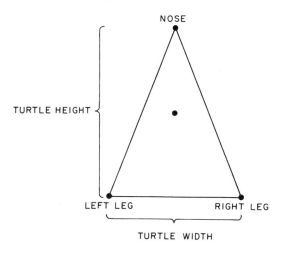

Figure 3.17
Specification of triangular turtle indicator.

graming nonplanar turtles, which is to come.

1. [P] Show how to keep track of the turtle's pen using the PEN.IS.DOWN variable, which is checked by the FORWARD procedure. Give procedures for PENUP and PENDOWN.

2. [P] We ignored the problem of actually drawing the little triangular turtle indicator. This involves erasing and redrawing the indicator each time we change the turtle's state. To keep things simple, suppose there is an ERASELINE command that takes inputs as DRAWLINE does and erases the specified line. Suppose the turtle is specified as an isosceles triangle of a given TURTLE.WIDTH and TURTLE.HEIGHT (see figure 3.17). Show how to compute the three vertices of the turtle triangle (which we can call, say, NOSE, LEFT.LEG, and RIGHT.LEG) in terms of TURTLE.WIDTH, TURTLE.HEIGHT, **P**, and **H**. Use this to implement procedures DRAWTURTLE and ERASETURTLE which are used by FORWARD and LEFT to redraw the turtle indicator. [H]

3. [P] Add to your implementation the procedures for XCOR and YCOR, which output the (x, y) coordinates of the turtle, and HEADING, which gives the angle of **H** with respect to some fixed direction.

3.4 Maneuvering a Three-Dimensional Turtle

We (and the turtle) now proceed into new, three-dimensional territory. If you like, you can now begin to think of the turtle as a spaceship that moves freely in space, leaving an indication of its trail. Maneuvering the turtle in three dimensions is the most substantial project we've discussed so far. It contains two main parts: deciding how to move the turtle and deciding how to display the three-dimensional path on a two-dimensional screen. We'll treat the first of these problems here and the second in section 3.5. Vectors play a central role in both parts of the project.

First of all, we will need three-dimensional vectors to represent three-dimensional space. Conceptually this is no problem at all; a vector is still an arrow with a certain length and with a certain direction representing a displacement. In terms of coordinates we simply need to add a third vector to the $\mathbf{x}, \mathbf{y}$ basis. Call it $\mathbf{z}$, and for convenience make it of length 1 (unit length) and perpendicular to both $\mathbf{x}$ and $\mathbf{y}$. The correspondence between vectors and coordinates is now

$\mathbf{v}$ corresponds to (v_x, v_y, v_z) provided $\mathbf{v} = v_x\mathbf{x} + v_y\mathbf{y} + v_z\mathbf{z}$.

Vector addition and scalar multiplication still follow the same patterns: addition and multiplication of each component, respectively.

As in two dimensions, position can still be specified by a vector which we will call $\mathbf{P}$, running from the origin $(0, 0, 0)$ to the turtle's position. Heading can still be a vector with length 1 which we'll call $\mathbf{H}$, and FORWARD is still

$\mathbf{P} \leftarrow \mathbf{P} + \text{DISTANCE} \times \mathbf{H}.$

Now we are done with FORWARD.

3.4.1 Rotating the Turtle

Although the FORWARD command in three dimensions is a straightforward modification of the two-dimensional version, generalizing the rotation commands is not so simple. In fact, the problem is deeper than the technical issue of computing rotations in three dimensions: We must decide which three-dimensional rotation we wish to represent, which is to say, though "left" has an unambiguous meaning in the plane there are many different possibilities in three-dimensional space.

The real problem is that $\mathbf{H}$ by itself is insufficient to specify the orientation of the turtle, as it only tells which way the turtle's nose is pointing.

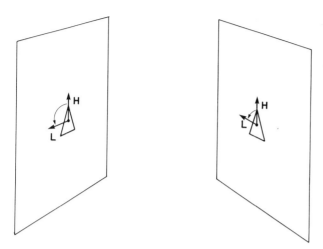

Figure 3.18
Turtles in three dimensions need an extra vector, **L**, to specify the plane in which to rotate.

Two turtles with the same **H** can rotate "LEFT" in different directions (see figure 3.18). To solve the ambiguity we can add to the turtle's state a new unit-length vector **L** which is perpendicular to **H**. We can interpret **L** as pointing to the turtle's left. Now LEFT can be geometrically specified as a rotation of both **H** and **L** in the plane containing them (see figure 3.18).

Here we are rotating three-dimensional vectors through an arbitrary angle in some arbitrary plane. Surely that seems like a terribly difficult computation. But no, it is simple! The reason is this: When we discussed two-dimensional rotations, we wrote down the answer in intrinsic terms. Recall the rotation formula of subsection 3.2.2:

Rotate($\mathbf{v}, A$) = $(\cos A)\mathbf{v} + (\sin A)$Perp($\mathbf{v}$).

Now, Perp(**H**) is **L**. Therefore we have

Rotate($\mathbf{H}, A$) = $(\cos A)\mathbf{H} + (\sin A)\mathbf{L}$.

And Perp(**L**) is $-\mathbf{H}$, so

Rotate($\mathbf{L}, A$) = $(\cos A)\mathbf{L} - (\sin A)\mathbf{H}$.

Does that seem too simple? By writing down the rotation of a two-dimensional vector in intrinsic form, we automatically have a completely general formula for rotating any vector through any angle about any axis (perpendicular to the vector) in any dimensional space, provided only that the perpendicular vector is known. Such reasoning is extremely important and is worth thinking through. So let's run through the argument again, slowly.

Consider the plane that contains both **H** and **L**. We must rotate **H** and **L** inside that plane by some angle A. But forget about the rest of the three-dimensional world outside the plane—it is entirely irrelevant to the rotation operation. In a plane, however, we have solved the problem of rotating a pair of perpendicular vectors. All that remains to be done is the translation back to three dimensions. And that is easy, provided we have been prudent enough to express the answer in a form that makes no commitment to using a coordinate system that is restricted to the plane. The rotation formula makes no commitment to any coordinate system at all. Merely regarding

$$\text{Rotate}(\mathbf{v}, A) = (\cos A)\mathbf{v} + (\sin A)\text{Perp}(\mathbf{v})$$

as a vector equation in three dimensions solves the problem of translating from the planar case to three dimensions.

If the fundamental vector operations on your computer accept (or can be modified to accept) vectors with three components, then the rotation equation readily translates into the program

```
TO ROTATE (VECTOR, PERPVECTOR, ANGLE)
    RETURN (COS ANGLE) * VECTOR + (SIN ANGLE) * PERPVECTOR
```

Notice that the perpendicular to the vector must be supplied as an input, since the rotation is not well defined without it. In fact, the only differences between this program and the planar rotation program of section 3.3 is that Perp(**V**) is accessed as a variable rather than computed, and the additions and scalar multiplications are performed on vectors with three components rather than two.

In terms of coordinates, the rotation equation translates into three component equations, which give the components of the rotated vector (**rv**) in terms of the components of **v** and its perpendicular (**pv**):

$$\mathbf{rv}_x = \mathbf{v}_x \cos A + \mathbf{pv}_x \sin A,$$
$$\mathbf{rv}_y = \mathbf{v}_y \cos A + \mathbf{pv}_y \sin A,$$
$$\mathbf{rv}_z = \mathbf{v}_z \cos A + \mathbf{pv}_z \sin A.$$

3.4.2 Rotation Out of the Plane

Are we done with state-change operators? If we stop here the turtle will certainly walk around in three-dimensional space, but only in one plane:

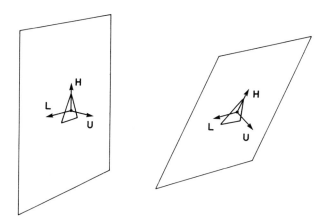

Figure 3.19
The pitch operation rotates **H** about the axis determined by **L**. Adding **U** to the turtle's state makes the rotation easy to compute.

that specified by the initial pair **H** and **L**. To gain full motion in three dimensions we also need to be able to pitch the turtle out of that plane by rotating about the **L** axis, and to roll it by rotating around the **H** axis.

The pitch operation is illustrated in figure 3.19. **L** remains invariant, but we must rotate **H** out of the plane of **L** and **H**. To compute this we need have in hand a vector that is perpendicular to **H** and perpendicular to **L** (the axis of rotation). If you are clever you should be able to construct this vector out of **H** and **L**, but let's be even more clever: Let us always carry along, as part of the turtle's state, a third unit-length vector, **U** (for "up"), perpendicular to both **H** and **L**. This will be a slight extra burden, since we will need to rotate **U** as well as **H** when the turtle pitches. However, such rotation will be easy because −**H** is Perp(**U**) for that rotation.

So now we have a neat and symmetrical set of rotation operators to change the turtle's orientation, represented as three mutually perpendicular vectors **H**, **L**, and **U**. In fact, we can use the parallel term YAW instead of LEFT so that in controlling our "spaceship turtle" we can employ the standard three-dimensional navigational terms roll, pitch, and yaw. In making any of these rotations, two of these vectors change and the third remains fixed. For rotating one vector **v** of the changing pair, the other changing vector (or its negative) serves as Perp(**v**).

3.4.3 The State-Change Operators, in Summary

The position of the three-dimensional turtle is represented as a three-component vector **P**. The orientation (the three-dimensional equivalent of the heading part of the state) is represented by a trio of mutually perpendicular unit-length vectors, **H**, **L**, and **U**. These can be initialized to be the basis vectors **x**, **y**, and **z**, which in coordinates are $(1, 0, 0)$, $(0, 1, 0)$, and $(0, 0, 1)$. The state-change operators are

```
TO FORWARD DIST
    P ← P + DIST * H

TO YAW ANGLE
    TEMP ← ROTATE (H, L, ANGLE)
    L ← ROTATE (L, -H, ANGLE)
    H ← TEMP

TO PITCH ANGLE
    TEMP ← ROTATE (H, U, ANGLE)
    U ← ROTATE (U, -H, ANGLE)
    H ← TEMP

TO ROLL ANGLE
    TEMP ← ROTATE (L, U, ANGLE)
    U ← ROTATE (U, -L, ANGLE)
    L ← TEMP

TO ROTATE (VECTOR, PERPVECTOR, ANGLE)
    RETURN (COS ANGLE) * VECTOR + (SIN ANGLE) * PERPVECTOR
```

Note the use of the variable TEMP to avoid deleting the old values of **H** and **L** before we are done using them. If you use the rotation equation in coordinate form you will have to be even more careful not to delete old variables by assigning new values before you're done using the old ones.

3.5 Displaying a Three-Dimensional Turtle

Our problem, simply put, is to make some marks on the computer display screen that will fool us into believing that the screen is a window looking out onto the three-dimensional world of the turtle. Imagine we are looking at something in space—say, a green line segment drawn by our turtle. The mechanism of seeing is that the green light reflected off the line segment travels in straight rays to our eye. Suppose there is a window between us and the turtle. If we draw green marks on the window along the line of sight between the eye and the line segment, we can erase the real line segment and still see the same image; the rays of green light reaching our eye will be unchanged. That's the geometrical process we need: projecting along the line of sight onto a plane which is going to be our computer display "window."

3.5.1 Parallel Projection

Actually, in order to project a line segment we need only worry about how to project the endpoints of the segment, since the projection of the line segment is just the segment on the window connecting the projections of the endpoints. (This can be proved by projecting a line segment point by point using the formulas we are about to derive for point projection.)

Rather than starting out with the general projection problem, it will be to our advantage to begin with simpler and more specialized cases and to proceed in stages toward more general and realistic but also more complex projections. In particular, let's first imagine that the eye is far enough from both the screen and the object being looked at that the lines of sight from the eye to all points on the object are essentially parallel. This is known as *parallel projection*. Moreover, if we assume that the eye is looking along the **z** axis of our coordinate system, then we can imagine the window to be the **x, y** plane. With these assumptions, projection amounts simply to sliding a point parallel to the **z** axis until the z coordinate is zero, but with x and y remaining the same (see figure 3.20). This is equivalent to "losing" the **z** component of the vector-basis decomposition of the position. In coordinates we have

$$(\text{display}_x, \text{display}_y) = \text{Project}(v_x, v_y, v_z) = (v_x, v_y).$$

For many purposes this trivial projection is quite sufficient. But suppose we want to move the eye around to look at the turtle's drawing from other perspectives. Consider first a window, still centered at the origin of our coordinate system, but pitched, rolled, and yawed with respect to the standard **x, y, z** basis as shown in figure 3.21a. This is equivalent to having three new (but still mutually perpendicular and unit-length) basis elements, which we call **ex**, **ey**, and **ez** (e for "eye"). In fact, we could produce these vectors by pitching, rolling, and yawing **x**, **y**, and **z** in exactly the same way we operated on the turtle's **H**, **L**, and **U**.

In order to solve this new projection problem we need to find the x and y coordinates of the point we want to project, but now with respect to

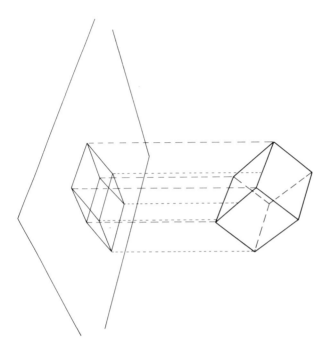

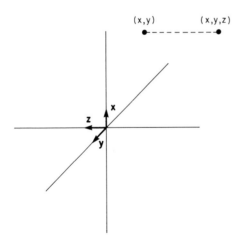

Figure 3.20
Simple parallel projection amounts to "losing" the **z** component at each point.

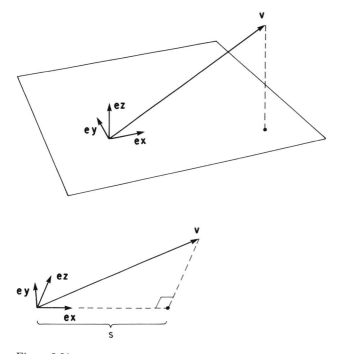

Figure 3.21
(a) Projection onto an arbitrary plane involves finding components with respect to a new basis. (b) The **ex** component of **v** is found by projecting **v** onto the line determined by **ex**.

the new basis **ex**, **ey**, **ez**. As you might expect, this problem of finding the coordinates of a point in an arbitrary basis is of great general importance and is worth a little time and energy.

Suppose we have **ex**, **ey**, **ez** and a vector **v**, and we want to compute the components of **v** with respect to **ex**, **ey**, **ez**. Focus on **ex**. First draw the line continuing **ex**. Next draw a perpendicular through the line that intersects the point of interest (the tip of **v**). The component we want is precisely the length of the segment **s** from the origin to the base of the perpendicular (figure 3.21b). This is because the construction effects a decomposition **v** = **s** + **p**, where **s** is a scalar multiple of **ex** and **p** is in a plane perpendicular to **ex** and can thus be subsequently decomposed into a sum of multiples of **ey** and **ez**. In other words:

The **ex** component of a vector **v**, that is, the value a in the decomposition

$$\mathbf{v} = a\mathbf{ex} + b\mathbf{ey} + c\mathbf{ez},$$

is precisely the perpendicular projection of **v** onto the line of **ex**.

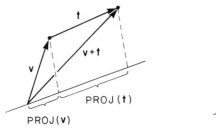
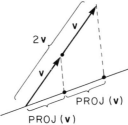

$$\mathrm{Proj}(\mathbf{v} + \mathbf{t}) = \mathrm{Proj}(\mathbf{v}) + \mathrm{Proj}(\mathbf{t}) \qquad \mathrm{Proj}(a\mathbf{v}) = a\mathrm{Proj}(\mathbf{v})$$

Figure 3.22
Proj is linear.

The **ey** and **ez** components are found similarly. So now we are led to the problem of studying, in vector terms, the geometric operation of projecting a vector onto a line.

3.5.2 Dot Product: Another Application of Linearity

Given two vectors **v** and **w**, we wish to compute the length of the perpendicular projection of **v** onto the line determined by **w**. We denote this length by $\mathrm{Proj}(\mathbf{v}, \mathbf{w})$. It is natural to think of $\mathrm{Proj}(\mathbf{v}, \mathbf{w})$ as an operation on **v**, but one that, of course, depends on **w**. We can suppress **w** in our notation and just write $\mathrm{Proj}(\mathbf{v})$ to emphasize this way of thinking about $\mathrm{Proj}(\mathbf{v}, \mathbf{w})$.

If subsection 3.2.2 is still fresh in your mind, you may be able to guess the observation that solves the projection problem: Proj is linear! Figure 3.22 demonstrates that Proj satisfies both scaling and additivity:

$$\mathrm{Proj}(a\mathbf{v}) = a \times \mathrm{Proj}(\mathbf{v}),$$
$$\mathrm{Proj}(\mathbf{v} + \mathbf{t}) = \mathrm{Proj}(\mathbf{v}) + \mathrm{Proj}(\mathbf{t}).$$

From experience with the rotation operator you should expect that this fact in itself is sufficient to allow us to compute projections in terms of coordinates. But rather than grinding out the answer, let's try a more insightful approach. We begin by indulging in some wishful thinking (a much-underrated method of doing mathematics). Remember that $\mathrm{Proj}(\mathbf{v}, \mathbf{w})$ is an operation with two arguments, **v** and **w**. Wouldn't it be nice if the order of the arguments didn't matter, that is, if $\mathrm{Proj}(\mathbf{v}, \mathbf{w})$ were always equal to $\mathrm{Proj}(\mathbf{w}, \mathbf{v})$? We now make two observations:

1. This relation could not be true in general, because $\text{Proj}(\mathbf{v}, \mathbf{w})$ doesn't depend on the length of $\mathbf{w}$ yet scales as $\mathbf{v}$ is enlarged.

2. If $\mathbf{v}$ and $\mathbf{w}$ happen to have the same length, then $\text{Proj}(\mathbf{w}, \mathbf{v})$ is equal to $\text{Proj}(\mathbf{v}, \mathbf{w})$, since the diagrams for projecting $\mathbf{v}$ onto $\mathbf{w}$ and for projecting $\mathbf{w}$ onto $\mathbf{v}$ will be symmetric.

Let's go farther by causing the accident in 2. Force $\mathbf{v}$ and $\mathbf{w}$ to have the same length by multiplying each by the length of the other to produce $|\mathbf{w}|\mathbf{v}$ and $|\mathbf{v}|\mathbf{w}$. That is, forget for the moment about Proj and concentrate on a a new operation called Sproj, for "scaled projection," defined by

$$\text{Sproj}(\mathbf{v}, \mathbf{w}) = \text{Proj}(|\mathbf{w}|\mathbf{v}, |\mathbf{v}|\mathbf{w}).$$

Now it's an easy matter to check algebraically that Proj doesn't lose its linearity as a function of $\mathbf{v}$ in its metamorphosis into Sproj. Because of the symmetry in arguments, Sproj must be linear in both arguments:

$$\text{Sproj}(\mathbf{v}, a\mathbf{w} + b\mathbf{t}) = a \times \text{Sproj}(\mathbf{v}, \mathbf{w}) + b \times \text{Sproj}(\mathbf{v}, \mathbf{t}),$$
$$\text{Sproj}(a\mathbf{v} + b\mathbf{t}, \mathbf{w}) = a \times \text{Sproj}(\mathbf{v}, \mathbf{w}) + b \times \text{Sproj}(\mathbf{t}, \mathbf{w}).$$

This looks so much like multiplication of numbers that Sproj is called a product—a *dot product*—and denoted

$$\text{Sproj}(\mathbf{v}, \mathbf{w}) = \mathbf{v} \cdot \mathbf{w}.$$

Compare the properties of dot product,

$\mathbf{v} \cdot \mathbf{w} = \mathbf{w} \cdot \mathbf{v}$	(symmetry),
$\mathbf{v} \cdot (a\mathbf{w} + b\mathbf{t}) = a\mathbf{v} \cdot \mathbf{w} + b\mathbf{v} \cdot \mathbf{t}$	(linearity in second variable),
$(a\mathbf{v} + b\mathbf{t}) \cdot \mathbf{w} = a\mathbf{v} \cdot \mathbf{w} + b\mathbf{t} \cdot \mathbf{w}$	(linearity in first variable),

to the properties of ordinary multiplication of numbers,

$$xy = yx,$$
$$x(ay + bz) = axy + bxz,$$
$$(ax + bz)y = axy + bzy.$$

Notice that because dot product is just mutually scaled projection, it is *exactly* projection for unit-length vectors. For example, taking the standard $\mathbf{x}$, $\mathbf{y}$, and $\mathbf{z}$ basis vectors, we have

$$\mathbf{x} \cdot \mathbf{x} = 1, \quad \mathbf{x} \cdot \mathbf{y} = 0, \quad \mathbf{x} \cdot \mathbf{z} = 0,$$
$$\mathbf{y} \cdot \mathbf{y} = 1, \quad \mathbf{y} \cdot \mathbf{z} = 0, \quad \mathbf{z} \cdot \mathbf{z} = 1.$$

Finally, we are left with the job of computing the dot product $\mathbf{v} \cdot \mathbf{w}$ in terms of coordinates. But since dot product is linear, the linearity principle ought to reduce that computation to special cases. Those special cases are just the dot products of all pairs of basis vectors, which we wrote down immediately above. If you carry out the details (exercise 1 below) you'll find that dot product has the remarkably simple form

$$\mathbf{v} \cdot \mathbf{w} = v_x w_x + v_y w_y + v_z w_z.$$

Our shift in attention from Proj to dot product has led us to an operation that can be simply described in terms of coordinates. In making the transformation we lost very little, since for unit-length vectors dot product is absolutely identical to projection. Even if only one of the vectors (say, $\mathbf{w}$) has unit length, we can still interpret $\mathbf{v} \cdot \mathbf{w}$ as a projection, the projection of $\mathbf{v}$ onto $\mathbf{w}$, because in scaling $\mathbf{v}$ by $|\mathbf{w}|$ no change is made. For arbitrary $\mathbf{v}$ and $\mathbf{w}$, the projection can be computed as

$$\mathrm{Proj}(\mathbf{v}, \mathbf{w}) = \frac{\mathrm{Sproj}(\mathbf{v}, \mathbf{w})}{|\mathbf{w}|} = \frac{\mathbf{v} \cdot \mathbf{w}}{|\mathbf{w}|}.$$

3.5.3 Parallel Projection in Coordinates; Generalizations

In subsection 3.5.1 we saw that the projection problem reduces to computing the components of a vector $\mathbf{v}$ with respect to an arbitrary basis $\mathbf{ex}, \mathbf{ey}, \mathbf{ez}$. Dot product enables us to do the computation. For example, suppose we want the projection of $\mathbf{v}$ onto $\mathbf{ex}$. Since $\mathbf{ex}$ is of length 1, that projection is exactly $\mathbf{ex} \cdot \mathbf{v}$. In other words, the coordinates of $\mathbf{v}$ are just the dot products of $\mathbf{v}$ with the corresponding basis vectors.

Notice how important it is that dot product is defined intrinsically in terms of vectors. That means it is independent of the coordinate system used to compute it. Thus, in computing $\mathbf{ex} \cdot \mathbf{v}$, we can use the standard $\mathbf{x}, \mathbf{y}, \mathbf{z}$ basis. In a computer program, that's the only basis that would be actually used for computation. In summary:

To find the projection of a point with respect to an eye whose orientation is described by the triple $\mathbf{ex}, \mathbf{ey}, \mathbf{ez}$, what we use for coordinates on the display screen are the first and second coordinates of the point in the $\mathbf{ex}, \mathbf{ey}, \mathbf{ez}$ basis; that is,

$$(\mathrm{display}_x, \mathrm{display}_y) = \mathrm{Projection \ of \ } \mathbf{v} \mathrm{\ onto \ } \mathbf{ex}, \mathbf{ey} \mathrm{\ plane}$$
$$= (\mathbf{ex} \cdot \mathbf{v}, \mathbf{ey} \cdot \mathbf{v}).$$

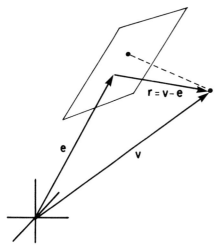

Figure 3.23
Projecting with respect to plane centered at some arbitrary position, **e**.

A simple modification of this formula allows even more general projections. Suppose the center of the window is located at some point other
than the origin—say, **e** (figure 3.23). Then we want to have **ex**, **ey**, **ez** sit
at their own origin, the tip of **e**. With respect to that origin the position
vector is

$$\mathbf{r} = \mathbf{v} - \mathbf{e} \qquad (\mathbf{r} \text{ for relative position}),$$

so the projection is still computed in the same way, only using **r** instead
of **v**:

$$(\text{display}_x, \text{display}_y) = \text{Project}(\mathbf{v}) = (\mathbf{ex} \cdot \mathbf{r}, \mathbf{ey} \cdot \mathbf{r}) \text{ where } \mathbf{r} = \mathbf{v} - \mathbf{e}.$$

Notice in passing that we have solved the general problem of finding
coordinates of vectors with respect to a new basis and a new origin: Set
$\mathbf{r} = \mathbf{v} - \mathbf{e}$ (where **e** points to the new origin from the old one), and then
just pick off the coordinates of **r** in the new basis using dot product:

$$(x, y, z) \text{ coordinates in new coordinate system } = (\mathbf{ex} \cdot \mathbf{r}, \mathbf{ey} \cdot \mathbf{r}, \mathbf{ez} \cdot \mathbf{r}).$$

3.5.4 Perspective Projection

The parallel projection we've just computed lacks some important features of real vision. It doesn't make distant objects smaller, nor does
it have "vanishing point" behavior. (This follows from our simplifying
assumption in 3.5.1 that the eye was located very far from both the
window and the object.) We'll now see how to be more realistic.

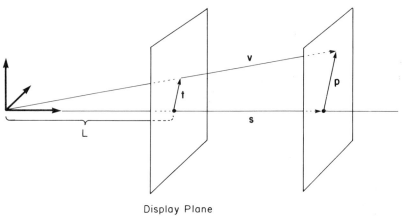

Display Plane

Figure 3.24
Perspective projection of **v** onto the display plane.

Start with the eye located at the origin facing directly along the **z** axis. Now imagine our display window located some distance L down the **z** axis and perpendicular to it (figure 3.24). In order to find the projection of the endpoint of **v** onto the window, we need to compute (in x and y coordinates) the vector marked **t** in the diagram. To do this, introduce the vector **p** in the plane perpendicular to **z** going through the point to be projected. This is just the familiar decomposition of a vector into a **z** component and a component perpendicular to **z**, which is to say,

$$\mathbf{v} = v_x\mathbf{x} + v_y\mathbf{y} + v_z\mathbf{z} = \mathbf{s} + \mathbf{p}$$

where

$$\mathbf{s} = v_z\mathbf{z} \quad \text{and} \quad \mathbf{p} = v_x\mathbf{x} + v_y\mathbf{y}.$$

But note that our desired vector **t** is parallel to **p**; in fact it is just **p** scaled by the ratio of size of similar triangles L/v_z:

$$\mathbf{t} = \frac{L}{v_z} \times \mathbf{p}.$$

(The similar triangles have common vertex at **0** and sides opposite that vertex of **t** and **p** respectively.) So, in terms of coordinates,

$$\text{Projection of } \mathbf{v} = (t_x, t_y) = \frac{L}{v_z} \times (v_x, v_y).$$

That's all there is. Perspective projection in this special case is just picking off the **x** and **y** components of position (like parallel projection) and then scaling by the ratio of L to the **z** component.

In the completely general case, let an eye be located at **e** with orientation given by basis **ex, ey, ez** (looking along **ez** with **ey** being "up" and **ex** "to the right"). Then, with the above answer transformed to the new origin (at **e**) and to the new basis, the display coordinates are just

$$(\text{display}_x, \text{display}_y) = \text{Projection of } \mathbf{v} = \frac{L}{\mathbf{ez} \cdot \mathbf{r}} \times (\mathbf{ex} \cdot \mathbf{r}, \mathbf{ey} \cdot \mathbf{r})$$

where $\mathbf{r} = \mathbf{v} - \mathbf{e}$.

3.5.5 Outline of a Three-Dimensional Turtle Project

This subsection outlines a number of possible implementations of a three-dimensional turtle. Pick the level of complexity at which you feel comfortable and work out the details there. You can always upgrade your implementation.

I. Implement the internal vector representation for a three-dimensional turtle, including FORWARD, ROLL, PITCH, and YAW.

II. Implement a PROJECT procedure that takes a three-component vector input and outputs a two-component vector for the display. Now you can furnish the turtle with a FORWARD operation that draws lines on the display:

```
TO FORWARD DIST
   P ← P + DIST * H
   IF PEN.IS.DOWN
       NEW.2D.P ← PROJECT P
       DRAWLINE (2D.P, NEW.2D.P)
       2D.P ← NEW.2D.P
```

This format saves computation by projecting only when PEN.IS.DOWN. (But this means that the PENDOWN command will have to project to update 2D.P to account for moves made while the pen was up. Of course, the simplest implementation could leave out the PENUP possibility altogether.) The major decision to be made here is whether to use parallel projection or true perspective.

III. Implement a movable eye.

A. For either parallel projection or a true perspective projection, a rotating eye can be an advantage. This amounts to being able to roll, pitch, or yaw the basis **ex, ey, ez**.

B. For either type of projection, one can move the origin around to change point of view. The eye can be considered to be just another turtle, with position given by some vector **e** and orientation by a trio **ex**, **ey**, **ez**. So the eye can be "flown around" with FORWARD, ROLL, PITCH, and YAW commands. For moving the eye, it may be convenient to supplement FORWARD ($\mathbf{e} \leftarrow \mathbf{e} + \mathrm{DIST} \times \mathbf{ez}$) with two new position-changing commands: JUMPUP ($\mathbf{e} \leftarrow \mathbf{e} + \mathrm{DIST} \times \mathbf{ey}$) and JUMPRIGHT ($\mathbf{e} \leftarrow \mathbf{e} + \mathrm{DIST} \times \mathbf{ex}$).

IV. Implement optional features.

A. Changing L amounts to "zooming" the lens of the eye. Implement a zooming feature.

B. Some displays may not be able to deal with coordinates bigger than some limit. The "right thing to do," of course, is for DRAWLINE to display only the portion of the line segment that is within the bounds of the display. If you want a "dumb" DRAWLINE to clip off what you don't see in this way, rather than just giving out-of-bounds errors, then you will have to implement a procedure to clip the segment before displaying it. We urge you to try this using vector methods. If you have a hard time, look ahead to subsection 6.1.3.

C. You may have noticed that the projection formulas we derived will also project things from behind the eye. If you object to this, we leave it to you to implement a fix.

D. Whenever the eye is moved, you will have to clear the screen and rerun from scratch the turtle commands and programs which drew things. If you plan on moving the eye a lot (for example, implementing a three-dimensional spaceship docking program where what you see on the screen is a changing view of a fixed object), then this may become a serious problem. One way to help matters is to build up a display list of connected sequences of three-dimensional points which gets added to each time a FORWARD (with the pen down) is issued. The whole list must then be redisplayed each time the eye is told to rotate or move. You will have a special problem if you are displaying a turtle itself, because that part of the list must change after every turtle command rather than only on moving the eye. One simple way to handle this is to have the first sublist in the display list be the picture of the turtle, to be treated specially. It must be erased and redrawn after each move.

E. Our outline of the project shows that, as far as internal representation is concerned, an eye is exactly the same thing as a turtle. So why not implement a three-dimensional system that is just a multiple turtle setup (having no special eye at all), in which you can issue commands to any of a number of turtles? Then you can change perspective merely by telling the projection operation which turtle's point of view you want to take. A fancy version of this system can display each turtle in a different way (for example, one as an airplane, one as a pyramid, etc.) and will allow you to talk to several turtles at once and thus choreograph turtle dances!

Exercises for Section 3.5

1. Taking advantage of the linearity in both arguments, verify the formula for dot product in terms of coordinates.

2. Compute the perpendicular projection (not mutually scaled) of one vector onto another in terms of coordinates. [HA]

3. Prove the following special cases of dot product: $\mathbf{v} \cdot \mathbf{w} = 0$ for any pair of perpendicular vectors; $\mathbf{v} \cdot \mathbf{v} = |\mathbf{v}|^2$. [H]

4. Show that $\mathbf{v} \cdot \mathbf{w} = |\mathbf{v}||\mathbf{w}| \cos A$ where A is the angle between $\mathbf{v}$ and $\mathbf{w}$. Notice that this formula shows how to evaluate dot product in coordinate independent terms. [HA]

5. Represent a triangle's sides as vectors $\mathbf{v}$, $\mathbf{w}$, and $\mathbf{t}$, and, using the above formula, derive the law of cosines:

$$|\mathbf{t}|^2 = |\mathbf{v}|^2 + |\mathbf{w}|^2 - 2|\mathbf{v}||\mathbf{w}| \cos A$$

where A is the angle opposite $\mathbf{t}$. [HA]

Try the following exercises after you have implemented a three-dimensional turtle system.

6. [P] Study analogs to POLY on your three-dimensional system. Should the analog be

```
TO POLY
    REPEAT FOREVER
        FORWARD
        ROLL
        YAW
        PITCH
```

or

```
TO POLY
    REPEAT FOREVER
        FORWARD
        ROLL
        JUMPUP
        YAW
        JUMPRIGHT
        PITCH
```

or what? Do you expect these to draw simple figures like cubes or tetrahedra? When do these close? Is there a general behavior analogous to POLY laying down equal chords of a circle? [H]

7. [D] POLYs in three dimensions often wander off to infinity. What goes wrong with the proof that POLYs are closed, which we gave in subsection 1.2.2? [HA]

8. [PD] Implement three-dimensional analogs to DUOPOLY or MULTIPOLY. To start, restrict each POLY to a simple closed planar figure (FORWARD, YAW, FORWARD, YAW, etc.) but put different POLYs in different planes. There are lots of options for how to do this. You may want to generate the set of vectors for each POLY first and then just circle your way through each set. Or keep two orientation bases around, YAWing each in turn and alternating **H** vectors for the increment to position in FORWARD. Compare figures using the same YAW angle but many different initial orientations. Look particularly at figures where the planes of the POLYs are perpendicular. Look at figures where each POLY is a circle, but where one takes 2 or $2\frac{1}{2}$ or 3 times as many steps as the other. Some of the most interesting planar DUOPOLYs happen when the symmetries of the two POLYs are relatively prime. Does this still hold true? Take one simple special case, such as squares in mutually perpendicular planes (DUO- or TRI-POLYs), and do an exhaustive study of possible figures depending on initial orientation within each plane.

9. [PD] An interesting problem arises if we want the eye to shift its gaze toward some specified point **p**. The **ez** vector should now point towards **p**. But where should **ex** and **ey** be pointing? One way to settle this is to make the "minimal" rotation of the **ex, ey, ez** basis which moves **ez** from its old direction to the new; that is, rotate **ez** in the plane of **ez** and **p** toward **p**. This is a rotation about an axis perpendicular to the **ez, p** plane, and we can imagine **ex** and **ey** just carried along. (Think of

the trio **ex, ey, ez** as a rigid body. Skewer it through their origin with a line perpendicular to the plane **ez, p** and rotate.) Can you invent a way to carry out this rotation with ROLL, PITCH, and YAW, or by any other means? Use this to implement a LOOKAT command that turns the eye toward a specified point. [H]

10. For each view of the standard **x, y, z** basis shown in figure 3.25a, say where the eye is located to produce that view. If this is hard for you, practice with your three-dimensional simulator. Imagine looking down at a square-tiled floor. Which angles appear greater than 90°; which less? For example, the edges of tiles far away may appear as in figure 3.25b.

11. [P] Implement an airplane that can fly around, from which what you see on the display screen is the landing strip (with mountains in the distance) from the view of the pilot.

12. [P] Implement a spaceship and a docking situation similar to that of the airplane in exercise 11. Spaceship controls are different, however: A rocket burst increments (vector) velocity by adding on a vector in the direction the ship is pointing, a roll burst starts continuous rotation around the ship's **H**, etc.

13. [PDD] Make a four-dimensional turtle system! There are lots of options for projecting. Although parallel projection to two dimensions is easiest, you may want to think of the perspective projection process in this way: Imagine a four-dimensional turtle sitting at $\mathbf{0} = (0, 0, 0, 0)$ looking down the **t** axis (**x, y, z, t** basis) through a "three-dimensional window" at $t = L$. The turtle sketches on (in) the "window" the object it sees, and hands this three-dimensional image to you to walk around and look at in ordinary three-dimensional space. Suppose the object the turtle is looking at is a four-dimensional cube. [Subproblem 1: Describe a four-dimensional cube by considering the sequence square (two-dimensional cube), three-dimensional cube, four-dimensional cube. Describe it in such a way that your turtle can draw it.] What do you see when you walk around or rotate the three-dimensional image? What do you see as the four-dimensional cube is rotated but your position with respect to the three-dimensional image remains fixed? What can you say about the three-dimensional "thing" that is the projection of the four-dimensional cube? [Subproblem 2: Describe four-dimensional rotations in the same way we did three-dimensional. Do things rotate around lines, as in three dimensions, or around planes? Correspondingly,

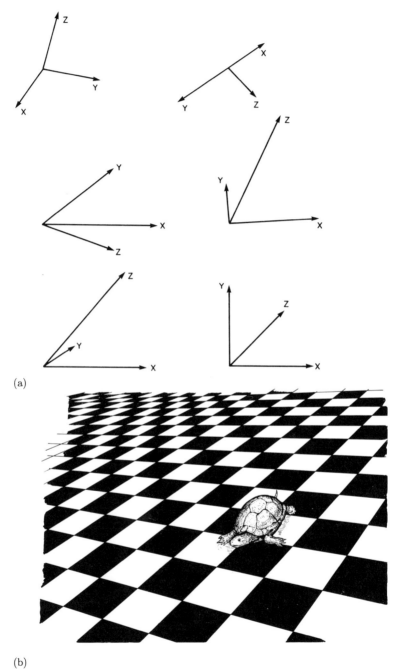

(a)

(b)

Figure 3.25
(a) A basis from various points of view. (b) Square tiles viewed obliquely.

will there be four fundamental rotations (one for each or the mutually perpendicular axes) or six (one for each mutually perpendicular plane)?] Use your simulation to help you, but try above all to get an intuitive feel for what you will see if you rotate the cube or change your point of view. You may wish to forget about implementing a turtle to draw the cube and, instead, just project vectors representing edges of the cube. [H]

14. [P] If you have a color display, implement a three-dimensional display "for two eyes," where what the right eye sees is in green and what the left eye sees is in red. With glasses having red right and green left lenses you should get a good three-dimensional effect. Such glasses are available with books that have three-dimensional pictures in them. (A simpler color system would "use only one eye," but would encode depth as, say near being red, gradually mixing in blue until far distance is pure blue.) If you can make hard-copy printouts of your screen, but not in color, you can get the same effect by tracing separate left and right eye printouts in red and green onto a single sheet of paper. There are also special glasses for reading three-dimensional topographical maps for which you can use two black-and-white printouts directly.

15. [P] Design some three-dimensional space-filling curves—for example on the model of FILL of chapter 2, except winding through 27 cubes to make a larger cube instead of 9 squares to make a larger square. Can you make a three-dimensional analog of HILBERT? These may be quite impressive in a two-eye version of a three-dimensional display such as suggested above.

16. [P] Grow some three-dimensional spirals, horns, and trees analogous to the work done in chapter 2 in two dimensions. (Spirals that wind in three dimensions are called *loxodromic spirals*.)

4

Topology of Turtle Paths

Any path is only a path ...
Carlos Castaneda

Turtle geometry has so far been the study of the process of drawing paths and patterns. In this chapter we study another kind of geometric process: how a turtle path can gradually *change*. For the most part we will be studying closed paths, and we'll of course be representing those paths as turtle programs. But in addition we'll be paying close attention to a more familiar representation of paths: pictures. Our starting point will be the closed-path theorem, which says that the total turning of any closed path is an integer multiple of 360°. By focusing on how the total turning of a path changes as we vary the path, we will be introducing the branch of mathematics concerned with the *topology* of curves in the plane. As an application of ideas from topology, we'll describe an algorithm that enables the turtle to escape from any maze.

4.1 Deformations of Closed Paths

Look at the three paths in figure 4.1a–c. By the closed-path theorem of subsection 1.2.1, the total turning of each path must be an integer multiple of 360°. It happens that each of these paths has total turning 720°. How can we be sure of that? For the first path, which has only 90° angles, it's easy to add the turns by inspection. But the other two paths have rounded parts consisting of many small segments and turns. Adding up the total turning vertex by vertex would be an extremely laborious task. Nonetheless, most people are extremely confident that path b, and even path c, has the same total turning as path a. Good mathematics supports their intuition. You may wish to take a moment now to test your own intuition in figuring out the mathematics behind this phenomenon.

Start with any closed curve. Now make a very small change in it to produce a second closed path (figure 4.1, d and e). How does this change affect total turning? Since the path and the turning at each vertex are changed only a little, the total turning over the path can change only a little. But we are assured by the closed-path theorem that if the total

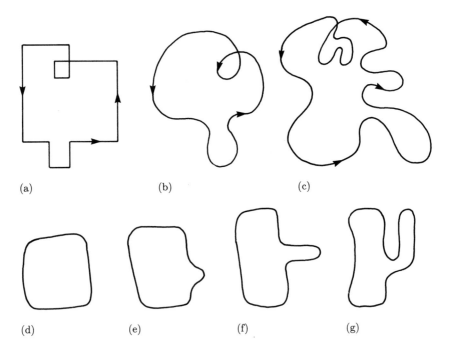

Figure 4.1
(a–c) Three paths with total turning 720°. (d–g) A deformation as a sequence of small changes.

turning changes at all it must change by at least 360°. Therefore our tiny change in the path cannot change the total turning.

Now, if one small change cannot affect total turning, a second one can't either, and we see that even a long sequence of small changes cannot affect total turning. A sequence of small changes is called a *deformation* (figure 4.1, e–g), and we conclude that making a deformation in a closed path cannot change the total turning. In figure 4.1, we can easily imagine a sequence of small changes which defines a deformation from a to b to c. This ensures that all three paths have the same total turning.

The general form of reasoning here is very important. If we have any quantity associated with a geometric figure that satisfies the conditions that small changes in the figure cannot change it very much and that permissible values of the quantity are spaced far apart (in this case, 360°), then the quantity can never change under any deformation. Something that doesn't change under deformations is called a *topological invariant*.

We will have much to say about other topological invariants in future chapters. For now, remember the following principle:

Deformation Principle Anything that satisfies the two conditions above must be a topological invariant.

Using these terms, we can augment the closed-path theorem of 1.2.1:

Closed-Path Theorem Total turning is a topological invariant for closed paths. For any closed path, the total turning is an integer multiple of $360°$.

(In later chapters we will find it convenient to measure angles in radians as well as in degrees. When we use radian measure, we'll say that total turning is an integer multiple of 2π.)

4.1.1 Turtle Paths: Pictures and Programs

If the reasoning of the preceding paragraphs seemed precise, you may be surprised to discover that a crucial point, the definition of deformation as "a sequence of gradual changes in a path," was left extremely ambiguous. To demonstrate this, we present three examples of "a sequence of gradual changes" and ask you to decide whether or not each should be considered a legitimate deformation. The first example, pictured in figure 4.2a, shows how to remove a loop from a closed curve by forming a kink. This certainly looks like a small change at each step, but it changes the total turning of the curve from $720°$ to $360°$. Surely something is wrong here! Figure 4.2b gives an even more blatant example of two curves that look "the same" and yet have different total turning. Here we have two circles which are identical except for orientation (the direction in which the turtle draws them). Are these circles the same, or not? Finally, figure 4.2c illustrates a phenomenon we'll call an overlap. Again, there is only a gradual change at each step—in fact, total turning does not change throughout the entire process—and yet the overlap creates crossing points where there weren't any before. Are we to allow this as a topological deformation?

The point of these examples is that in deciding what constitutes a "small change" to a curve, we must consider more than just the picture of the curve (the set of points belonging to the curve). One way to think of the additional information that must be taken into account is to regard the closed curve as the path traversed by a turtle. (We can always

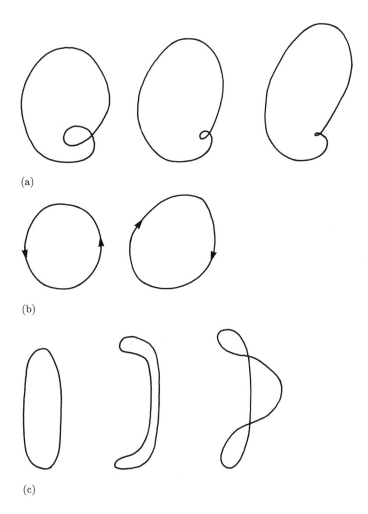

Figure 4.2
(a) Removing a loop by forming a kink. (b) The "same" path with two different values for total turning. (c) Creating an overlap.

regard a truly curved line as approximated by a turtle path consisting of many short segments as with arc and circle programs of subsection 1.1.2.) Then a "small change" should be required to be "small" not so much with respect to changes in the picture of the curve as with respect to changes in the *process followed by the turtle* in traversing the curve.

Let's apply this reasoning to the second of our two mysterious examples, the two circles that are "the same" except for orientation. Of course, it's only the pictures, the set of points, that are the same. Seen as process, the turtle is constantly turning left while drawing one circle and right while drawing the other. So the two processes are different, and it's not at all mysterious that they can have different total turning.

We can make a similar observation about the kink. Note that the turtle does a complete 360° loop-the-loop in the kink, except at the last step. It's clear that there is going to have to be a violent change in the turtle program, such as throwing away a whole bunch of steps (which contain the loop-the-loop turning) in moving to the final figure. So the tendency to regard kink removal as a deformation is just a trick of your intuition coming from the fact that you usually think of paths as pictures rather than as turtle programs.

In our third example, the overlap, we are in the opposite situation— the appearance of the two crossing points seems like a big change in the picture, but in terms of process the paths are not very different. The overlap is a legitimate deformation. Indeed, those crossing points are totally invisible from a local, turtle point of view. If we assume that the turtle doesn't leave any marks, then there's no way for the turtle to tell if it is crossing its own path. A crossing point is a global, not a local phenomenon. There is no way to see a crossing point on the basis of the local information that describes what the turtle is doing at a particular instant.

4.1.2 Correlating Pictures and Programs

We've seen how the idea of deformation is clarified when we regard paths as turtle programs. But any picture of a path, such as figure 4.1a, can be implemented as a program in many ways. For example, one of the LEFT 90 turns could be replaced with a RIGHT 270. This would change the total turning of the path, subtracting 270° at the vertex rather than adding adding 90°. If we want to assign a single number for total turning to a path (picture) then we had better resolve this ambiguity.

The easiest thing to do is to agree on a convention that only angles less than 180° should be allowed in translating a picture to a program.

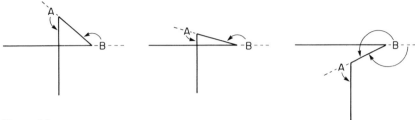

Figure 4.3
Unkinking viewed as a turtle program.

This will establish a unique contribution to total turning between 180°
(LEFT 180) and −180° (RIGHT 180) for each vertex of a path. The
convention can be restated by saying one should use the minimum turn
necessary to align the turtle for the next segment.

Let's take a closer look at how removing a kink changes total turning.
Figure 4.3 shows an unkinking viewed as a changing turtle program.
Notice that turn *A* gradually decreases in a very regular manner. It is
not responsible for the change in total turning. On the other hand, *B*
gradually increases to LEFT 180, at which point two of the segments
cross over—unkinking. Notice that it is exactly at that point that our
convention of using angles less than 180° insists we start using RIGHT.
So the sequence of changing turns throughout the unkinking process is

LEFT 179, LEFT 180 (= RIGHT 180), RIGHT 179, ...

Hence total turning is reduced in a jump by 360°. You can see how
our convention catches the unkinking; it is a good convention. This
particular configuration, the crossing over of two segments that caused
a shift from LEFT 180 to RIGHT 180 above, is called a *scissors*. You can
create many interesting figures by incorporating scissors as modules in
POLYlike programs. Some of these are presented in the exercises for this
section. Though a scissors is not a deformation, it does change total
turning in a predictable way. Thus, it is a good thing to look for as you
try to understand changing paths.

In summary: We've made progress in understanding deformations of
closed paths by representing them in terms of FORWARD, LEFT, and RIGHT
turtle commands. We can regard a deformation as a sequence of small
changes to the turtle program (see exercise 14).

4.1.3 Topological Classification of Closed Paths

We've been discussing curves that can be deformed into one another—
curves that are "the same" as far as topology is concerned. Such curves

are said to have the same *topological type*. We've also seen that total
turning is a topological invariant for closed paths. Any two closed paths
of the same topological type must have the same total turning. It is
natural to ask whether the converse is true: If two paths have the
same total turning, does that mean that they can be deformed into one
another? This is indeed the case, as was first proved in 1936 by H.
Whitney and W. C. Graustein.

Whitney-Graustein Theorem Two closed paths in the plane can be deformed
into one another if and only if they have the same total turning.

We won't give a proof of the Whitney-Graustein theorem, but you
should note that it is another example of a classification theorem, like the
classification of looping programs given in subsection 1.3.3. We saw there
that all the information about the symmetry or boundedness of a looping
program is contained in one number: the heading change in the basic
loop. We can express this by saying that heading change completely
determines the "symmetry type" of a looping program. Similarly, the
Whitney-Graustein theorem tells us that the topological type of a closed
path is completely determined by the total turning. As an interesting
exercise, you might think about the relation between topological type
and crossing points. The overlap phenomenon shows that deformations
do not preserve the number of crossing points, and hence one cannot
simply count crossing points to determine topological type. But there is
a relationship, which is developed in exercises 15–18.

Exercises for Section 4.1

1. [P] A scissors is a good dynamic building block to incorporate in a
turtle program.

```
TO SCISSOR (DISTANCE, PHASE)
   RIGHT PHASE
   FORWARD DISTANCE
   LEFT 2 * PHASE
   FORWARD DISTANCE
   RIGHT PHASE
```

Angular state transparency and symmetrical "scissor action" are ensured
by the arrangement of FORWARDs and turns. Start with an ordinary POLY
and replace the FORWARD with a scissors:

```
TO SCISSOR.POLY (D, A, PHASE)
   TOTAL.TURNING ← 0
   REPEAT
      SCISSOR (D, PHASE)
      LEFT A
      TOTAL.TURNING ← TOTAL.TURNING + A
   UNTIL REMAINDER (TOTAL.TURNING, 360) = 0
```

Watch how SCISSOR.POLY deforms as the phase of the scissor changes
(figure 4.4):

```
TO DEFORM.SCISSOR.POLY (D, A, PHASECHANGE)
   PHASE ← 0
   REPEAT FOREVER
      CLEARSCREEN
      SCISSOR.POLY (D, A, PHASE)
      PHASE ← PHASE + PHASECHANGE
```

Study programs like this with respect to symmetry, topological type,
and change in topological type.

2. [P] In the above program the phases of all the SCISSOR parts of the
SCISSOR.POLY are the same; they all close and open at the same time.
This need not be the case. For example:

```
TO SCISSOR.POLY (D, A, LOCAL.PHASECHANGE)
   LOCAL.PHASE ← 0
   REPEAT FOREVER
      SCISSOR (D, LOCAL.PHASE)
      LEFT A
      LOCAL.PHASE ← LOCAL.PHASE + LOCAL.PHASECHANGE
```

Show that this program always closes. Invent a stop rule for it. Study
these figures, particularly when LOCAL.PHASECHANGE and A are simply
related. [H]

3. [P] The local phase-changing SCISSOR.POLY of exercise 2 (with stop
rule) can be used just as in exercise 1 to produce a sequence of gradually
changing figures by incrementing the initial phase at which each figure
starts (use LOCAL.PHASE ← PHASE instead of LOCAL.PHASE ← 0 in the
SCISSOR.POLY; then DEFORM.SCISSOR.POLY runs through a sequence of
SCISSOR.POLYs as PHASE is incremented). Study these figures.

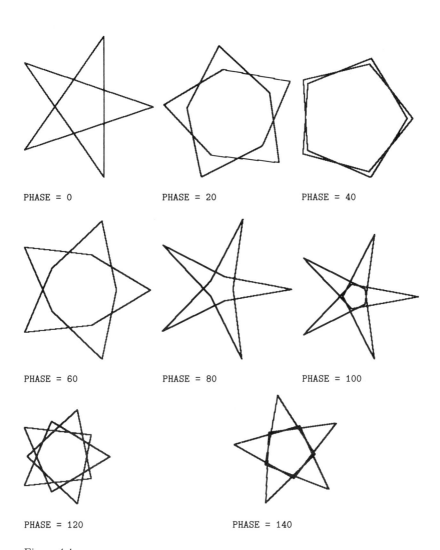

PHASE = 0   PHASE = 20   PHASE = 40

PHASE = 60   PHASE = 80   PHASE = 100

PHASE = 120   PHASE = 140

Figure 4.4
A deforming SCISSOR.POLY, $A = 144$.

4. [P] Suppose one alternates inward and outward SCISSORs as follows:

```
TO SCISSOR.POLY (D, A, LOCAL.PHASECHANGE)
   LOCAL.PHASE ← 0
   REPEAT FOREVER
      SCISSOR (D, LOCAL.PHASE)
      LEFT A
      LOCAL.PHASE ← - (LOCAL.PHASE + LOCAL.PHASECHANGE)
```

Study this program and the analogous DEFORM version (as in exercise 3).

5. [P] In addition to the scissor process, one can use segment disappearance as a dynamic building block:

```
TO SHRINKSEG (D, AMOUNT)
   FORWARD D * COS(AMOUNT)
```

The segment disappears at AMOUNT = 90. This is relatively uninteresting in POLY unless one changes the PHASE of the SHRINKSEGs:

```
TO SHRINKPOLY (D, A, LOCAL.PHASECHANGE)
   LOCAL.PHASE ← 0
   REPEAT FOREVER
      SHRINKSEG (D, LOCAL.PHASE)
      LEFT A
      LOCAL.PHASE ← LOCAL.PHASE + LOCAL.PHASECHANGE
```

Figure 4.5 shows how a SHRINKPOLY varies as LOCAL.PHASECHANGE varies. Study these figures with respect to closing, stop rules, etc. Embed SHRINKPOLYs (with stop rule) into a continuously changing family as we did with phase-changing SCISSOR.POLYs, and study how the the topological types vary.

Exercises 6–13 discuss a project for making the computer automatically generate deformations of closed paths. The idea is to start with two different figures (turtle programs) and to try to find a gradual "interpolation" from one to the other.

6. [P] Suppose we have two turtle paths, each given as a sequence of pairs

```
FORWARD SOMEDISTANCE
LEFT SOMEANGLE
```

and suppose, for simplicity, that there are the same number of FORWARD, LEFT pairs in each path. Write a program that "interpolates" one path

LOCAL.PHASECHANGE = 0

LOCAL.PHASECHANGE = 20

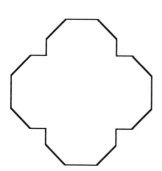

LOCAL.PHASECHANGE = 30

LOCAL.PHASECHANGE = 40

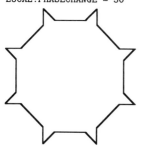

LOCAL.PHASECHANGE = 60

LOCAL.PHASECHANGE = 120
(3 × size)

Figure 4.5
SHRINKPOLY, A = 45.

to the other by slowly varying each of the distances and angles from its value in the first path to its value in the second. For example, use

```
DISTANCE ← N*DISTANCE₂ + (1 - N)*DISTANCE₁
```

as N goes from 0 to 1.

7. [P] If the initial turtle paths have a different number of pairs, you will want to modify them to have the same number. One way to do this is to add FORWARD 0, LEFT 0 pairs to the shorter one, but this is unsymmetrical if done just at the end of the program. A better way is to "expand" both programs to a length which is the least common multiple of the lengths of the original programs. Then we can do the expansion uniformly through the program. For example, if an expansion by 3 is necessary, then FORWARD D should be replaced by FORWARD D/2, LEFT 0, FORWARD D/2, and LEFT A should be replaced by LEFT A/2, FORWARD 0, LEFT A/2. Experiment with "expansion" techniques until you have one that satisfies you and works in all instances.

8. [P] Show, by example, that this kind of interpolation has a problem: Even if the two original paths are closed, the intermediate paths need not be closed. However, if your expansion technique is uniform (symmetrical) enough, and if the two original paths are closed POLYs with the same total turning, then the intermediate paths will be closed.

9. [P] Find a way to fix up the intermediate paths so that they will be closed. (For instance, you could compute, for each intermediate path, the vector by which it misses closing, and distribute this in small pieces among the vertices of the path.) Add this modification to the interpolation program. Show how this modification can introduce kinks.

10. [P] Try the modified program (exercise 9) on lots of examples. Notice that if the two original paths do not have the same total turning, the interpolation must produce kinks. But suppose the paths do have the same total turning. Can you be sure (or modify the program to make sure) that the interpolation won't produce any kinks and therefore will give a valid deformation?

11. [P] Rather than starting the interpolation process at the first of the original paths and stopping at the other one, why not let the variations continue beyond the second path (corresponding to taking N > 1 in the formula in exercise 6), thus extrapolating to get some new figures? Or run the interpolation backwards, finding figures "before" the first path (this corresponds to taking N < 0). See figure 4.6 for examples.

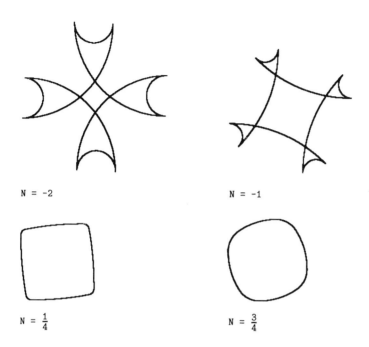

N = -2   N = -1

N = $\frac{1}{4}$ N = $\frac{3}{4}$

Figure 4.6
Interpolations and extrapolations based on a square and a circle.

12. [P] So far these interpolations have been based on interpolating inputs to turtle commands. If we think of a path as a sequence of vectors, other interpolation schemes come to mind. If $VECTOR_1$ is to be changed into $VECTOR_2$, then one might interpolate using $INT(VECTOR_1, VECTOR_2)$ where INT is the same "linear interpolation" function we used with number inputs above (exercise 6), but using vector addition and scalar multiplication:

```
TO INT (START, END)
   RETURN N*END + (1 - N)*START
```

Experiment with such schemes. Is intermediate state closure ensured, or can you patch it up? Does the scheme kink?

13. [P] Think of and experiment with other methods of interpolation. For instance, alternate commands from the two programs and continue looping in each program (if necessary) until you are simultaneously done

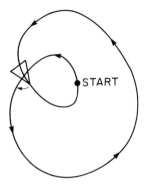
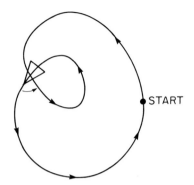

Figure 4.7
A crossing point can be regarded as a position that the turtle passes through twice.
By comparing the turtle's heading the first time it passes through the point with its
heading the second time (seeing whether it is facing more to the right or more to the
left) one can assign to the crossing point a sense of "right-handed" or "left-handed."
The "handedness" of a crossing point depends, not only on the curve, but also on
where the turtle starts traversing the curve.

with both programs. Now slowly "turn on" the distances and/or angles
of one while you "turn off" the other. Investigate closure and kinking in
the intermediate figures.

14. [D] Suppose we have a closed turtle path, specified as a sequence of
FORWARD and LEFT instructions. Give definitions of "small change" and
"deformation" in terms of allowable changes to the inputs for FORWARD
and LEFT. [H]

Exercises 15–17 ask you to deduce a formula, originated by Whitney,
that relates the crossing points of a curve to the total turning.

15. A closed curve has exactly one crossing point. What are the possible
values for its total turning? How about two crossing points? Or three?
[A]

16. At each crossing point of a closed curve there are two arcs. Suppose
we know which of the two arcs the turtle traveled along first. Show that
this allows us to define two kinds of crossing points—"right-handed"
and "left-handed." Show that whether a crossing point is right- or left-
handed depends on where the turtle starts drawing the path. (Consider
an inside loop, as in figure 4.7.) Invent some simple way to make "right-
handed" and "left-handed" unambiguous. [A]

17. [D] Show that if we know the number of left-handed crossings and
the number of right-handed crossings of a curve, then there are only two
possible values for the total turning. Moreover, the total turning will be

completely determined if we add one piece of information. What is this piece of information? Give a formula for total turning. [HA]

4.2 Local and Global Information

We turn now to the other theorem of subsection 1.2.1, the simple-closed-path theorem, which describes the total turning around a simple closed path (a path with no crossing points). Recall that we stated the theorem, but did not provide a proof.

Simple-Closed-Path Theorem The total turning in any simple closed path is equal to $\pm360°$ (or $\pm2\pi$ if we measure angles in radians).

This theorem is deeper than the closed-path theorem, and its proof is considerably more complicated. The reason that we say the theorem is deep is because it forms a link between local and global information. In the case at hand, remember that crossing points of a curve are nonlocal phenomena—there is no way for the turtle to sense a crossing point as it is walking. Sensing a crossing point requires stepping back and looking at the entire curve at once. But total turning is locally computable, and the theorem relates total turning to the existence of crossing points.

The following is an example of the link between local and global contained in the theorem: Suppose that the turtle walks around a closed path accumulating total turning, and that when it completes the path it finds that the total turning is not equal to $\pm360°$. Then the turtle can assert that somewhere the path must have at least one crossing point. The turtle doesn't know where the crossing point is, and was unable to observe it while traversing the path. Nevertheless, by applying the theorem one can deduce that a crossing point must exist.

Seen in this light the simple-closed-path theorem is an instance of a powerful principle:

The Local-Global Principle One can often determine global properties by accumulating local information.

We've already seen other examples of this principle in action. The POLY closing theorem (subsection 1.2.2) predicts closing, which is a global property of a path, from a sum of turnings, which are local information. In chapter 2 we saw animals navigating toward some global goal, like the warmest or wettest place, using a feedback mechanism based only

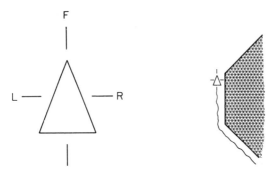

Figure 4.8
(a) Turtle with touch sensors. (b) Using touch sensors to follow along a wall.

on local measurements of the surroundings. Later on, we'll see how the local-global principle applies to the study of surfaces.

As we said above, the proof of the simple-closed-path theorem is more involved than those of the other theorems we have dealt with so far. In fact, we'll delay discussing the proof until section 4.3, where we'll describe how this theorem relates to some other results in the topology of curves. For now, we'll turn to an application of the theorem in a particularly nice example of the local-global principle: teaching the turtle to escape from a maze.

4.2.1 Escaping From a Maze

Suppose that the turtle is equipped with touch sensors—one in front, one in back, and one on each side (figure 4.8a)—which allow it to detect whether it is bumping against an obstacle. (You may want to simulate this on the display screen. See exercise 1 below.) In writing programs for this "touch turtle" we can imagine that the set of basic turtle commands includes FRONT.TOUCH, LEFT.TOUCH, and RIGHT.TOUCH, operations which register TRUE or FALSE according to whether the corresponding touch sensor is activated. Using these commands it is not difficult to write a procedure, FOLLOW, that causes the turtle to follow along a wall, say, keeping the wall to the right (see figure 4.8b). Writing the FOLLOW procedure is left as an exercise (see exercise 2).

Now, can the turtle use this new ability to circumvent any obstacle in its path by FOLLOWing the obstacle around to the other side? An arbitrary obstacle might be very complicated. In fact, the ability to get around any obstacle would entail the ability to escape from any maze. What we are asking for is a universal maze-solving algorithm.

Here is a first attempt at such an algorithm. The idea is to keep the turtle heading in a preferred direction, say "north," whenever you can, and whenever the turtle hits an obstacle, to have it walk around the obstacle until it can walk freely again.

Maze Algorithm 1:

1. Select an arbitrary initial direction, call it "north," and face that way.

2. Walk straight "northward" until you hit an obstacle.

3. Turn left until the obstacle is to your right.

4. Follow the obstacle around, keeping it on your right, until you are once again facing "northward."

5. Go back to step 2.

Notice that the turtle can determine when it has completed step 4 by keeping track of total turning. As soon as the total turning in following the wall (including the initial turn in step 3) is an integer multiple of 360°, the turtle knows that it is once again facing "north." Figure 4.9a illustrates the algorithm in action.

But this procedure does not work in general. Figure 4.9b shows how the turtle can become trapped. The turtle can be fooled into thinking that it has gotten around an obstacle while in fact it ends up traveling in a loop forever.

It is remarkable that a simple modification to maze algorithm 1 will avoid not only the trap in figure 4.9b, but also any other trap—it will produce a universal maze-solving algorithm. The modification is in step 4: The turtle should follow the obstacle, not until the total turning is a multiple of 360°, but until the total turning is exactly equal to zero. This procedure is the Pledge algorithm, named for John Pledge of Exeter, England, who at age 12 developed this method for navigating the turtle through mazes.

Pledge Algorithm

1. Select an arbitrary initial direction, call it "north," and face that way.

2. Walk straight "northward" until you hit an obstacle.

3. Turn left until that obstacle is on your right.

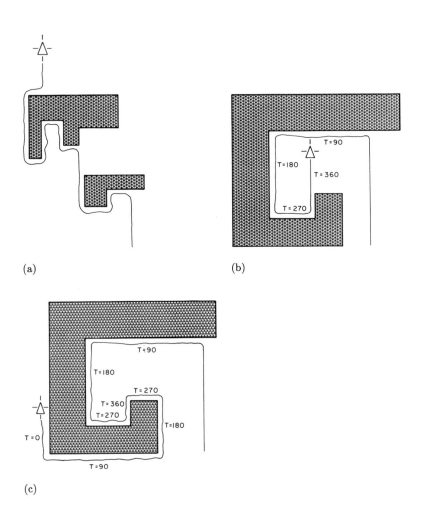

Figure 4.9
(a) Maze algorithm 1 in action. (b) A trap for maze algorithm 1. The turtle will loop forever, trying to head "north." (c) The Pledge algorithm allows the turtle to get out of the trap, by keeping track of total turning.

4. Follow the obstacle around, keeping it on your right, until the total turning (including the initial turn in step 3) is equal to zero.

5. Go back to step 2.

Figure 4.9c shows how the Pledge algorithm gets the turtle out of the trap. The reason why the algorithm works is intimately related to the simple-closed-path theorem. The idea is to suppose that the turtle gets trapped in a loop, going round and round the same path. Then we can show that the path has two mutually incompatible properties: It can be deformed into a simple closed curve, and yet the total turning around the path is zero. These two things together would contradict the simple-closed-path theorem. Thus we conclude that the algorithm cannot fall into a loop, and so the turtle cannot get trapped. Of course, many details must be filled in to turn this sketch into a proof. We will give a full proof in section 4.4.

Try the Pledge algorithm on a few mazes and observe how it gets the turtle out of traps. Remember that the driving force behind this algorithm is another application of the local-global principle: By observing local information (total turning) the turtle can be assured of fulfilling some global criterion (not getting trapped in a loop).

Exercises for Section 4.2

1. [P] Implement a "touch turtle" on the computer display. Your turtle should have the ability to sense when it is about to cross a previously drawn line. Your task can be made easier if you restrict the lines to be vertical and horizontal. Alternatively, take a look at subsection 6.2.3, which explains how to compute the intersection of two lines. A way to implement the touch turtle without computing any intersections is to divide the display screen into a large number of small squares and construct "obstacles" out of square bricks. Then the turtle is not allowed to move into a square already occupied by an obstacle.

2. [P] Use your touch turtle to implement the FOLLOW procedure discussed in the text. Do you see how to use a feedback mechanism to ensure that the program will work even if the turtle's sensors are slightly inaccurate?

3. [P] Implement the Pledge algorithm and try it out on some mazes. Also try some other maze algorithms (such as algorithm 1) and construct mazes that serve as "traps" for the algorithms.

4.3 Deformations of Curves and Planes

The purpose of this section is to provide proofs of the simple-closed-path theorem and some related theorems about the topology of simple closed curves. Recall that we want to show that, if we have a simple closed path (a path with no crossing points), then the total turning around the path is equal to $\pm 360°$. There are many paths for which this result is obvious; perhaps the simplest is a square. This suggests a strategy for proving the theorem: Try to show that any simple closed path can be deformed to a square. Since we know that total turning is invariant under deformations, we will therefore have shown that any simple closed path has the same total turning as a square: $\pm 360°$, depending on which direction the turtle goes around the square. This reduces the problem of proving the simple-closed-path theorem to showing that any simple closed curve can be deformed to a square. In fact, we're going to prove something a bit better: Given any simple closed path, not only can the path itself be deformed to a square, but we can imagine the deformation being done in a very special way; the entire plane can be deformed, pulled and stretched, so that the path becomes a square.

The difference between the two notions of deformation—deformation of a path versus deformation of the plane—requires some explanation. Until now we've been talking about deformations of paths. We focused on a turtle walking around a closed path, and imagined how the path would change as we made small modifications to the turtle's program. But we can also consider deformations of the plane. Imagine that the plane is an arbitrarily stretchable rubber sheet. Then any kind of stretching or shrinking (but not cutting or tearing) can be viewed as a deformation.

These two kinds of deformation are closely related. In particular, if we draw a closed path on the "rubber sheet" plane, then any deformation of the plane will give rise to a deformation of the path. (See figure 4.10a and imagine for the moment that the rubber sheet is stretched over a flat surface so that it remains flat.) Of course, straight turtle segments may become curvy under such a deformation, and that may require us to use an "approximate program" (as POLY with small inputs approximates a circle). But if you can tolerate such approximate curves, then a deformation of a plane always bends a turtle path drawn on it gently enough so the new path is a turtle-program deformation of the original. On the other hand, many of the changes that are legitimate for deformations of curves, such as the innocuous overlap phenomenon we met in 4.1.1, cannot happen with plane deformation. In general, crossing

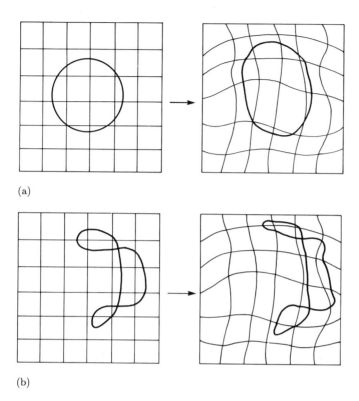

Figure 4.10
(a) A rubber-sheet deformation of the plane yields a deformation of any curve drawn on the plane. (b) A rubber-sheet deformation preserves crossing points.

points can be neither created nor destroyed during plane deformation (see figure 4.10b).

In summary: Plane deformations are "gentler" than path deformations; every plane deformation is a path deformation, but path deformations that introduce crossovers are too violent to be plane deformations. Incidentally, if you were suspicious about admitting the crossover phenomena as valid deformations of curves, it's probably because you had the rubber-sheet rather than the turtle-program model of deformation in mind. (The technical mathematical term for a turtle-path deformation is *regular homotopy,* while a rubber-sheet deformation is called an *ambient isotopy.*)

The main theorem of this section asserts that any simple closed path can be deformed to a square, and, moreover, that this can be done with a "gentle" deformation, that is, a plane deformation.

Deformation Theorem for Simple Closed Curves For any simple closed curve in the plane, there is a "rubber sheet" deformation of the plane that reduces the curve to a square.

We'll give the proof of this theorem in subsection 4.3.1. As we've already said, the simple-closed-path theorem follows as an immediate consequence.

There is another result about the topology of simple closed paths that also follows from the deformation theorem. This is the Jordan curve theorem:

Jordan Curve Theorem Any simple closed curve in the plane divides the plane into exactly two regions (an "inside" and an "outside").

This result may seem intuitively obvious, but simple closed curves can be rather convoluted (see figure 4.11a), so we should be prepared to justify our intuition. Also, notice that the theorem is definitely false if we consider curves on surfaces other than the plane. For example, the curve drawn on the torus in figure 4.11b is a simple closed curve, and yet it does not divide the torus into two regions. We'll have more to say about turtle paths on tori and other nonplanar surfaces in later chapters.

Do you see how the Jordan curve theorem follows from the deformation theorem? The point is that properties such as "dividing the plane into two pieces" and "having an inside and an outside" are invariant under rubber-sheet deformations of the plane. Since the curve after deformation (that is, the square) has these properties, then so must the original curve before the deformation.

The deformation theorem implies a bit more than the Jordan curve theorem: Not only does the curve have an inside and an outside, but the inside itself can be deformed, in the rubber-sheet sense, to the interior of a square. A region that can be deformed to the interior of a square is called a *topological disk* (as far as rubber-sheet deformations are concerned, a disk is as good as a square). Note that deforming a rubber-sheet region does not require that we keep the region a part of the flat plane—figure 4.11c illustrates some topological disks of both the planar and the nonplanar variety. In later chapters we will see that topological disks play a key role in the study of the turtle geometry of nonplanar surfaces.

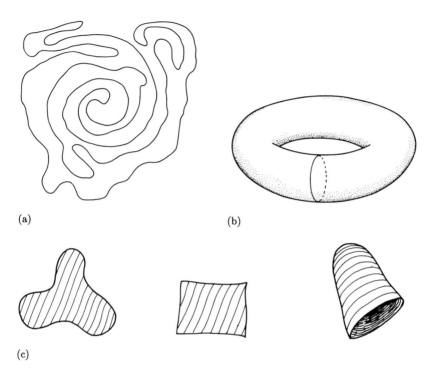

Figure 4.11
(a) A simple closed curve in the plane can be very convoluted, but it always has an inside and an outside. (b) A simple closed curve on a torus that does not divide the torus into two pieces. (c) Topological disks. The third disk is non-planar.

4.3.1 Proof of the Deformation Theorem

The aim of this section is to prove the deformation theorem by showing how to construct, for any simple closed path in the plane, a rubber-sheet deformation that reduces the path to a square. This proof is more involved than the proofs we've discussed so far (it should be, since both the simple-closed-path theorem and the Jordan curve theorem follow as immediate consequences), and you may want to skip this section your first time through the chapter.

The first step in the proof is to imagine that the plane is divided into a fine grid, and that the curve is made up of grid lines, as shown in figure 4.12. If the grid is fine enough, then we can always deform any normal turtle path into a "grid path." In fact, you've probably been working with grid paths all along, since most computer displays draw

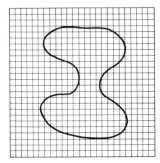 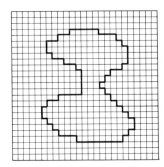

Figure 4.12
Approximating a curve by a path on a grid.

pictures that are actually made up of dots on a very fine grid. (Many of the difficult technical parts of topology are concerned with providing precise mathematical definitions for such terms as "closed curve" that are consistent with the intuition that any closed curve can be deformed onto a suitably small grid. By considering curves to be turtle paths, we can avoid most of these technicalities. Exercises 5–7 of this section give more details on deforming turtle paths to lie on a grid.)

Since any turtle path can be deformed to a grid path, we need only prove the deformation theorem for grid paths, in which all angles are 90°. The basic idea of the proof is to "collapse" a simple closed curve down to a single square of the grid. We do this by defining a process that successively eliminates every "southwest corner" of the curve. In other words, we take every vertex of the curve that is oriented as in figure 4.13a and push it, as shown, towards the "northeast." Notice that this "push" can be accomplished by a rubber-sheet deformation of a small piece of the plane surrounding the vertex (figure 4.13b).

We will prove the deformation theorem by showing two things: that this pushing process can always be done with a simple closed curve, and that enough successive pushes will eventually reduce the curve to a square. Consider the first assertion. When might we not be able to remove a southwest corner by pushing it to the northeast? The answer is: If the curve already passes through the new, northeast vertex we would create by the push, then we cannot perform the pushing process, because the resulting curve would intersect itself and hence not be a simple closed curve.

Let's examine all the ways in which the vertex northeast to a southwest corner can already be occupied by the curve. Since each of the two

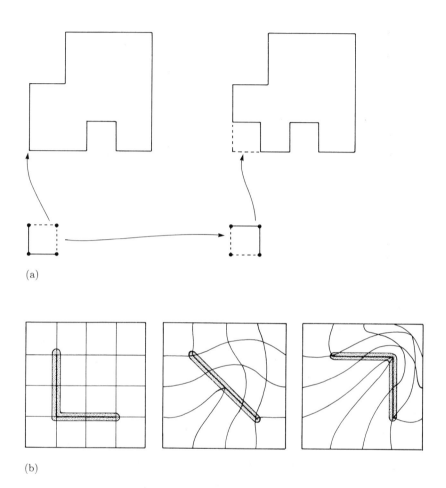

Figure 4.13
(a) Deforming a curve by removing a "southwest" corner. (b) Pushing a southwest vertex northeast, viewed as a rubber-sheet deformation of the plane.

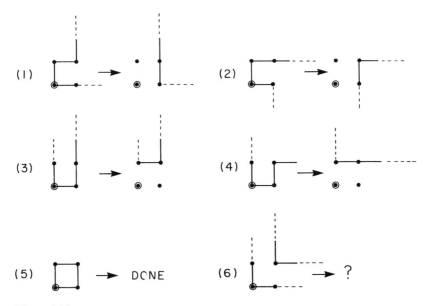

Figure 4.14
The six ways that the northeast vertex can already be occupied. In all but the last
case, this causes no problem.

segments of the curve meeting at the northeast vertex can come from
one of four directions, and the directions for the two segments must
be different, there are six different possible local configurations in all.
These are illustrated in figure 4.14, which also shows how in four of the
six cases we can easily eliminate the southwest vertex by a deformation.
Notice that in each case the required deformation can be accomplished
as a rubber-sheet deformation of the plane. The fifth case shown in
the figure can only arise if the curve is already a single square, which is
where we wish the deformation process to stop.

It is only in the sixth case, where our northeast vertex is itself occupied
by a southwest corner of another part of the curve, that we run into
trouble. We must move the curve away from the northeast vertex before
we can perform the collapse. The clearest way to do this is to first apply
the collapsing process to the northeast vertex (regarded as a southwest
corner of its own part of the curve), and then return and continue with
the original southwest corner (figure 4.15 shows an example). There is
still a problem, for it is certainly possible for this northeast square to
be blocked, in turn, by another corner to its northeast, and so on. But
this sequence of blocking northeast corners cannot go on indefinitely,
because the curve has only a finite number of vertices to begin with and

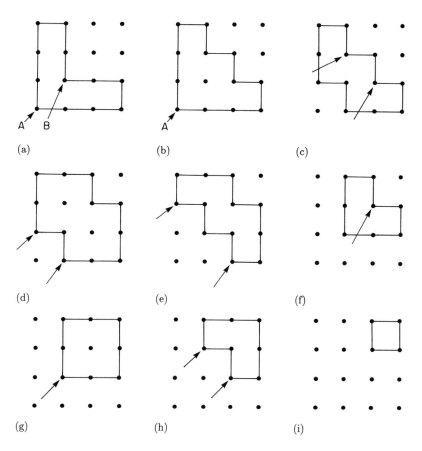

Figure 4.15
Example of the collapsing process in action. Notice that in going from (a) to (b) we collapse vertex B before vertex A, since B is blocking A. Also note that collapses in (e) and (h) illustrate cases (2) and (3), respectively, of figure 4.14.

so cannot stretch infinitely far to the northeast. Thus, we can always do the collapse if we are sure to begin collapsing each sequence of blocking corners by starting at the most northeast end of the sequence.

To review our collapsing process: We get rid of southwest corners, one by one. This is straightforward when the southwest corner is not blocked to the northeast. If it is blocked, the blocking configuration is one of those shown in figure 4.14, so we apply the deformations shown there. In one of the cases (case 6) this may entail applying the collapsing process recursively to the northeast corner. We can describe this process using the format of our turtle computer language as follows:

```
TO REDUCE a simple closed curve
    REPEAT
        FIND a southwest vertex
        COLLAPSE the vertex you found
    UNTIL curve is reduced to a square

TO COLLAPSE a vertex
    IF vertex is not blocked
        THEN apply the process shown in figure 4.13
        ELSE BLOCKED.COLLAPSE the vertex

TO BLOCKED.COLLAPSE a vertex
    IF in cases 1–4 of figure 4.14
        THEN apply deformation shown in figure 4.14
    IF in case 5 of figure 4.14
        THEN curve is reduced to a square
    IF in case 6 of figure 4.14
        THEN
            COLLAPSE the vertex to the northeast, and then
            COLLAPSE the original vertex
```

This completes the definition of the collapsing process.

Now we must show that this process actually terminates with the curve reduced to a single square. Do you see the problem here? In collapsing a southwest corner we create some new southwest corners, and these must in turn be collapsed, which might create more southwest corners, and so on. So how can we be sure that this process doesn't go on forever? The answer is that the process keeps squeezing the curve into smaller and smaller pieces of the plane. Each collapsing of a vertex pushes a piece of the curve to the north and/or east. On the other hand, if we draw a line directly above the original curve and another line directly to the east of the curve, we can see that the collapsing process never moves the curve past these lines (figure 4.16). So the region occupied by the curve gets smaller and smaller, and the process must therefore eventually terminate. This can happen only when the curve is reduced to a single square.

We have now completed the proof of the deformation theorem.

Exercises for Section 4.3

1. Suppose the turtle walks around the boundary of a simple closed curve. By the Jordan curve theorem, the curve divides the plane into

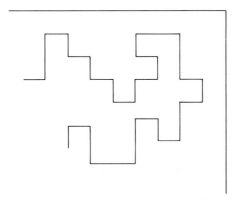

Figure 4.16
The collapsing process will never push the curve beyond its northern and eastern borders.

two regions, one lying to the turtle's left and one to the right. How can the turtle tell which region is the inside and which is the outside of the curve? [HA]

2. To test your understanding of the proof given above, can you pinpoint exactly where the argument breaks down if we assume that the original curve has crossing points? [A]

3. [D] To test your understanding of the proof given above, can you pinpoint exactly where the argument breaks down if we assume that the curve is drawn on some nonplanar surface, such as a torus? After all, figure 4.11b demonstrates that the theorem must be false for such curves. A cheap answer is to protest that we haven't said how to define a "grid" for such curves. Assume we can do that. What is the real problem with the proof? [HA]

4. [D] In a rubber-sheet deformation, any two distinct points must remain distinct throughout the deformation, and any arc joining the two points must be transformed to an arc joining the transformed points. Show that this implies that a rubber-sheet deformation cannot change the topological type of a curve drawn on the plane.

The following exercises deal with the problem of showing that any turtle path can be deformed to lie on a grid. The key to the demonstration is estimating how fine a grid is necessary. What we want is a "safety zone" around every part of the path such that no deformation within the zone can run into any other part of the curve. Then if we choose a grid size much smaller than the width of the safety zone, we can use

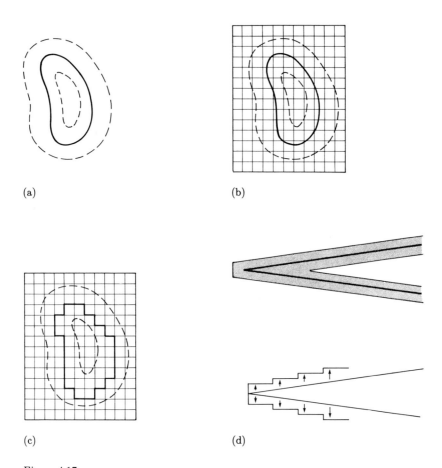

Figure 4.17
Deforming within "safety zone" eliminates possibility of overlaps and crossing points.
(a) Path with safety zone. (b) Grid chosen smaller than zone. (c) Deforming within
zone. (d) Deforming a curve to a grid near an acute vertex.

any sort of deforming algorithm to deform within the zone without risk of producing crossing points (see figure 4.17a–c). Consider now in detail a simple closed turtle path with a finite number of segments:

5. [D] Show that, except in the case of points on adjoining segments, points on one segment cannot be arbitrarily close to points on other segments. That is to say, given any turtle path, show that there is some number $D > 0$ such that for any two points p and q on nonadjacent segments of the path, the distance from p to q is at least D. Thus, the safety zone can be taken to have width D and there can be no overlap. Such a D may not exist if the path has an infinite number of segments. [HA]

6. [DD] Points on adjacent segments can be arbitrarily close, so the safety zones for the two segments must overlap. Show in such an instance that, perhaps by making the grid a bit finer, one can still deform in safety by pushing the segments away from each other within the zone (see figure 4.17d). Combine this idea with the result of exercise 5 and describe in detail a complete method for deforming a simple closed turtle path to lie on a grid. [A]

4.4 Correctness of the Pledge Algorithm

In subsection 4.2.1 we described the Pledge algorithm for guiding a turtle through a maze. Here we will prove that the Pledge algorithm is a universal maze-solving algorithm (that is, one that will allow the turtle to escape from any maze). Here is an overview of the proof:

• The only way the algorithm can fail is if the turtle falls into an infinite loop, traversing the same path over and over in a way reminiscent of the turtle trap that defeated the first version of maze algorithm 1 in subsection 4.2.1. The validity of this assumption is discussed below in 4.4.3.

• The only way the turtle can end up traveling in a loop is if it winds up following around and around the same simple closed path of wall. We prove this in 4.4.2 by applying the simple-closed-path theorem.

• The only way the turtle can be fooled into following the same simple closed path of wall over and over again is if the mazemaker has cheated and placed the turtle in a maze with no way out, such as that shown in figure 4.18a. We prove this in 4.4.1.

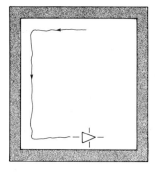 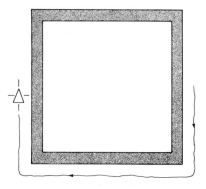

Figure 4.18
The maze may be unfair, with the turtle trapped inside a simple closed path of wall
with no way out. Since it keeps the wall to the right, a turtle traversing the outside
of the wall will make a net 360° right turn and a trip around the inside of the wall
will make a net 360° left turn.

Putting these three facts together shows that the only way the Pledge
algorithm can fail is if the maze is unfair. The rest of this section is
concerned with spelling out the details of these three steps. As with the
proof of the deformation theorem, you may want to skip this on a first
reading.

4.4.1 Unfair Mazes

We want to show that the turtle will keep following the same simple
closed path of wall only if the maze is unfair. Let's consider how the
turtle could recognize an unfair maze. An unfair maze will contain a
simple closed path of wall that seals the turtle in. But the presence of
a simple closed path of wall does not necessarily mean that a maze is
unfair—the turtle may be stupidly walking around the outside of the
wall. Our first task will be to show that the algorithm is not that
stupid—that if the turtle keeps retracing a simple closed path of wall
then it really is trapped on the inside. To show this, recall that the turtle
does its wall-following keeping the wall to the right. Then, as figure
4.18b shows, a trip around the outside of a wall will be a net 360° right
turn for the turtle whereas a trip around the inside of a wall will be a net
360° left turn. Now imagine that the turtle has a counter that registers
the accumulated total turning while following a wall. Left turns cause
the count to increase and right turns cause it to decrease. So a right-
turn (outside) loop will subtract 360° from the count, and for a turtle
trapped following an outside loop forever, the count would keep getting
smaller and smaller. On the other hand, the counter registering zero is

precisely the signal for the turtle to stop following the wall and start heading northward again (step 4 of the algorithm), so the turtle will not run forever in an outside loop. So if the turtle does run forever around a simple closed path of wall, it must indeed be sealed inside an unfair maze.

4.4.2 The Body of the Proof

Here we will establish the second point in the proof outline given at the beginning of this section: If the turtle runs in a loop, that loop must be a simple closed path of wall. The structure of the Pledge algorithm reveals that the turtle's wanderings can be divided into two kinds: "free running" (traveling north without contacting a wall), and following a wall. We will first prove that if the turtle does fall into a loop then it traces a path that can be deformed to a simple closed path. We will then prove that any closed path containing both "free running" and "wall following" sections must have zero total turning and hence (by the simple-closed-path theorem) be unamenable to such deformations. Together these assertions show that if the turtle does loop, then the repeated part of the path must consist only of "wall following" parts (a loop clearly cannot consist of all northward-pointing "free running" parts) and hence the turtle is tracing a simple closed path of wall.

Suppose that the turtle retraces the same closed path over and over. By considering all the ways this closed path can touch itself, we will show that the path can be deformed to a simple closed curve. One way the path might touch itself would be for the turtle to "free run" more than once along the same northward line segment at different times in the same loop, as shown in figure 4.19a. We leave it to you (exercise 1) to prove that this can never happen.

The only other way the path can overlap itself is in the situation shown in figure 4.19b: The turtle, while running northward, bumps against a wall it has already followed, or else starts following a wall it has previously bumped against (it doesn't matter which happened first, the bumping or the following, since we're assuming that the turtle is in a loop and will be doing one and then the other over and over).

Let's take a closer look at this situation. Let A be the part of the path corresponding to the time the turtle followed along the obstacle, and let B be the part of the path that has just bumped against the obstacle while running northward. We would like to deform the turtle's path to eliminate the overlap. Whether or not we can do this depends on where A and B leave the obstacle.

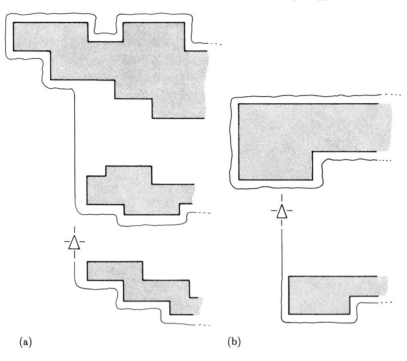

(a)   (b)

Figure 4.19
(a) Example of how the turtle's looping path might cover the same northward segment twice. (In fact, this cannot happen.) (b) Sample intersection in the path: The turtle, while running north, bumps against a wall it has previously followed.

If B leaves the wall before A (as in figure 4.20a) there is no problem; we simply deform the path as shown. If A leaves the obstacle first, as in figure 4.20b, there is no obvious way to deform the path to eliminate the overlap. We claim that this troublesome situation will never arise. To see this, think about the counter that the turtle is using to accumulate total turning. Examine the counter at corresponding points of A and B, at a point shortly after B reaches the obstacle and the turtle has turned left to face along it (see figure 4.20c). On B the counter registers some angle θ between $0°$ and $180°$, depending on how much the turtle had to turn in order to begin following the wall. How about the counter on A? Since at that point the turtle's heading is the same as at the corresponding point on B, the count must equal θ plus some integer multiple of $360°$. Furthermore, the integer cannot be negative, since that would make for a negative accumulated total turning, which is not possible with the Pledge algorithm. So the A count must be greater than or equal to the B count, and both are greater than zero. Now, in continuing to follow along the object, both the A and the B count will

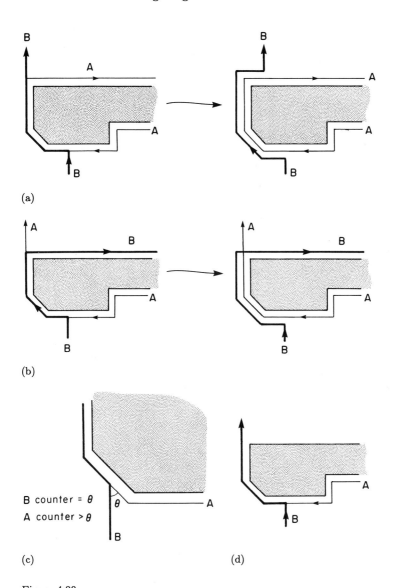

(a)

(b)

B counter = θ

A counter > θ

(c)   (d)

Figure 4.20
(a) If B leaves the obstacle before A, then a simple deformation removes the intersection. (b) If B leaves after A, then there is still an intersection after deforming. (c)
Compare the total turning count for A and B at a point just after the overlap. (d)
A and B might conceivably also leave the obstacle together.

be reduced (or increased) by the same amount. So the A counter cannot reach zero before the B counter does. Thus, A must continue to run along the obstacle longer than B does.

We should also consider the possibility that A and B leave the wall at the same place (figure 4.20d)—that is, start with equal turning indicators. But this is a particular case of the turtle beginning to follow the same northward line twice, and we've already said that such a thing cannot happen.

In summary: We've shown that of the three situations shown in figure 4.20 (a, b, and d), only the first is possible, and in this case we can deform the path to eliminate the overlap. Thus we have shown that if the turtle does get into a loop, the path can be deformed to a simple closed curve.

Suppose now that the turtle retraces the same closed path over and over, and that this path contains both "free running" and "wall following" sections. Such a path must have zero total turning. Certainly the "free" sections have zero total turning, since the turtle is simply running northward there. But, as step 4 of the algorithm shows, any completed "following" section must have zero total turning as well. Hence, the entire path has zero total turning, and, by the simple-closed-path theorem, cannot be deformed to a simple closed curve.

We have proved our two assertions; that is, we have shown that if the turtle runs in a loop it must be running around a simple closed path of wall.

4.4.3 Looping and Finite-State Processes

To tie up all the loose ends, we must discuss the first point in the proof outline given at the beginning of section 4.4—that the only way the algorithm can fail is by going into a loop, driving the turtle in the same path over and over. The reasoning we will use here is an instance of a very general principle, the concept of a *finite-state process*. The point is this: If we are watching the turtle wander through a maze following the Pledge algorithm, then we can predict what the turtle will do next, provided that we know three things: the turtle's position, the turtle's heading, and the accumulated total turning registered in the turtle's counter. These three pieces of information—position, heading, count—give a complete description of the state of the process as far as the Pledge algorithm is concerned; at any instant the turtle's entire future path in the maze is determined solely by this threefold state. So if we want to show that the algorithm falls into a loop we need only show that there is some state that the turtle reaches more than once. Consider: The turtle proceeds from some state and eventually comes back to the same state. So, proceeding once more from this state, the turtle must do the same thing that it did the first time, which brings it back to the same state again, and so on, and so on. (Compare this reasoning with the argument used in the proof of the POLY closing theorem in subsection 1.2.3.)

Let's assume that the Pledge algorithm fails for some maze—the turtle wanders around forever without ever getting out. How can we show that there is a loop, or, equivalently, how can we show that there must necessarily be some state that the turtle reaches more than once? The key idea is this: Suppose we could show that there are only a finite number of different states that the turtle can be in. Then, since we are assuming that the turtle wanders around forever, there must be some state that is entered more than once.

So we are reduced to showing that there are only a finite number of states—position, heading, count—that the turtle can be in while following the Pledge algorithm. Unfortunately, there are situations where this is not true. For example, if the maze has infinitely many walls, then the number of possible turtle positions, and hence the number of states, will surely be infinite. In fact, our entire proof breaks down for infinite mazes.

Let's retreat, then, from such infinities, and restrict our attention to finite mazes—say, a maze that has a finite number of straight walls and is entirely contained within some bounded region of the plane. Even in these cases, it appears that there can be an infinite number of different states. There are an infinite number of possible positions (points) in the region, the heading can be any angle, and the count can be any non-negative number. So we need to be more subtle, and consider not all possible different states but rather all possible "effectively different" states (states whose difference actually affects what the algorithm will do next).

Even though there are infinitely many different positions the turtle can be at, we can lump together in a single state sequences of positions (all with the same heading and total turning) that always occur together, such as all points along the same section of wall or along the same segment of some "northward" line between obstacles. With this proviso, the number of effectively different positions is finite so long as the maze has a finite number of segments. We can make a similar remark for heading: The number of different headings cannot be more than the number of different segments in the maze, plus one (to allow for a northward heading).

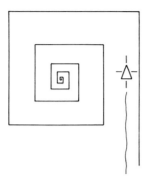

Figure 4.21
Will the turtle get lost in an infinite spiral?

If we restrict all angles to be integers, then there are only a finite number of possibilities for the count part of the state, as well. This is because the count cannot become arbitrarily large. To see this, observe that, each time the turtle finishes following a wall, the counter registers zero total turning. So consider the largest total turning that the turtle can accumulate while performing the "following" phase of the algorithm, without retracing the path. (This maximum turning must be less than the total number of wall segments in the maze times the maximum possible turn, 180°.) If the turtle's count becomes larger than this number, it must have followed a wall all the way around and begun retracing its path. But, as noted in 4.4.1, the turtle can be fooled into following all the way around a closed path of wall only if the maze was unfair to begin with. Thus, for any fair maze, the possible values of the total turning counter are bounded.

In summary: We have shown that for any finite and fair maze there are only a finite number of effectively different states. Hence, if the turtle wanders around forever it must get into a loop. This is the final assumption we needed to check, so we have completed the proof that the Pledge algorithm is a universal maze-solving algorithm.

Exercises for Section 4.4

1. Fill in the part of the proof we left out in subsection 4.4.2: that through one round of the looping path the turtle cannot run along the same northward segment twice. [HA]

2. [D] Suppose the turtle is dropped into an infinite spiral maze (figure 4.21). If the turtle is idealized as a point, the Pledge algorithm will take

an infinite number of steps—winding in and in and in, then out and out and out—if it is to succeed at all. Even if we allow an infinite number of steps, what happens in such a situation? Can spirals have infinite length, infinite total turning? Do these doom the Pledge algorithm? [H]

3. [D] Suppose a maze is really made up of curved lines rather than a finite number of line segments. Show that in a wide range of situations the number of effectively different states is still finite. Be as explicit as you can in defining and enumerating the effective states and in specifying the conditions under which you can be sure the number of effectively different states is finite. Do circles meet those criteria? Do spirals?

5

Turtle Escapes the Plane

"But how do I get there?" asked Boots. "That's
easy," the old man replied. "Just put one foot
before the other and follow your nose."

fairy tale

We have seen how turtle geometry, with its emphasis on procedural
descriptions and local methods, can be a useful alternative to Euclidean
axioms and Cartesian coordinates in exploring plane geometry. Now
it's time to leave Euclid behind and consider what life is like for a turtle
crawling on a curved surface. The branch of mathematics that deals with
the geometry of curved surfaces is known as *differential geometry,* and
this chapter presents a turtle's-eye view of some of the basic concepts in
this subject.

We'll begin our survey of turtle geometry on curved surfaces with a
discovery: For a turtle on a sphere, the closed-path theorem—that the
total turning around any closed curve must be an integer multiple of
360°—is false. You may well ask how we can hope to gain any benefit
from turtle geometry without the closed-path theorem. After all, the
theorem is one of the cornerstones of the work we've done so far. It
formed the basis for the symmetry analysis of looping programs, not to
mention the entire topological classification of closed curves which we
discussed in chapter 4. But instead of throwing up our hands in despair,
we'll take a close look at some turtle paths in order to get to the nub of
how it can be that this basic theorem doesn't hold. And a very rewarding
nub it is. In fact, we shall see that the breakdown of the closed-path
theorem is, in a sense, the very essence of what it means for a surface
to be curved. Pursuing this idea, we'll give a definition of curvature
that satisfies the turtle criteria of being local and intrinsic. We'll also
introduce the total curvature of a surface, a topological invariant that
plays a role analogous to that of the total turning for curves in the plane.

5.1 Turtle Geometry on a Sphere

Imagine that a turtle is crawling on a sphere—the earth's surface, for
example. Suppose the turtle walks around the closed path shown in
figure 5.1. Starting at the equator and facing north, the turtle goes

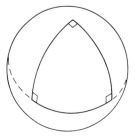

Figure 5.1
A $3 \times 90°$ triangle on a sphere.

straight north until it reaches the north pole. There it turns $90°$ and goes straight south until it gets to the equator. Again it turns $90°$ and runs along the equator to get back to its initial position, where a final $90°$ turn restores the initial heading. That's certainly a closed path, but the total turning is $3 \times 90°$, or $270°$ in all. This contradicts the closed-path theorem (subsection 1.2.1), which says that the total turning should be an integer multiple of $360°$. Even worse, it's easy to see that on a sphere there can be closed paths with any amount of turning whatsoever: Start the turtle at the equator walking north as before. This time, when the turtle reaches the north pole, have it turn some arbitrary angle θ, then march south to the equator, then back along the equator to the initial position, and turn as before to restore the initial heading. The total turning for this trip is $180° + \theta$, so by varying θ we can produce arbitrary total turning. Try this on a globe.

This should bother you a fair amount. After all, the proof we gave of the closed-path theorem in subsection 1.2.1 was very straightforward and made no explicit mention of the fact that the turtle was walking on a plane. So how can it break down so badly as soon as we put the turtle on a sphere? Of course, you might think we are being overly naïve in expecting our planar turtle theorems to carry over to the sphere. The turtle is walking on a curved surface, the sphere, and surely this must have something to do with turning. Is it fair even to regard these turtle paths as made up of straight lines?

5.1.1 Turtle Lines

Let's begin with that last question: What is a straight line for a turtle on a sphere? When the turtle walked along the equator, we said that it was walking straight. Can we give some justification for regarding the equator as a sphere's version of a straight line?

First of all, the lines we're talking about are not straight in Euclid's sense: They don't lie in a plane. To save confusion let's refer to this kind of straight line as a *turtle line*. Because we've shifted our attention from the abstraction of "straightness" to crawling turtles, it's natural to try to define a turtle line as the path followed by a turtle that walks along the surface without turning. Of course, this is progress only if we can say what we mean by "without turning." In other words, how can the turtle know how to walk straight?

Suggestion 1 Turtle cannot possibly walk straight on a curved surface, and we shouldn't waste time trying to make sense of such a notion.

Suggestion 2 Indeed the turtle can't really walk straight if it's restricted to the sphere's surface. In order to really walk straight the turtle has to walk in a plane. But the next best thing may be good enough: The turtle can walk along the *intersection* of the sphere with a plane. We should therefore define a turtle line on a sphere to be the intersection of the sphere with a plane. According to this definition, the equator is a turtle line. So is any great circle, and any line of latitude. (Do you agree that these should all count as turtle lines?)

Suggestion 3 One thing we expect about a straight line segment is that it should be the shortest distance between its two endpoints. So we should admit as turtle lines only those paths that give the shortest distance between their endpoints. By this definition it is not hard to see (although it's hard to prove) that any turtle line must be part of a great circle. Latitudes other than the equator don't satisfy the criterion.

Suggestions 2 and 3 are reasonable, but they have a serious shortcoming: They are not local. That is, they are not phrased in such a way that the turtle can tell if it's walking straight *as it is walking*. Consider suggestion 2. The turtle would have to stand back, move off the sphere altogether, and look at the intersection of the path with a plane before it could be sure that it was walking straight. Suggestion 3, based on shortest distance, is at least intrinsic; it allows the turtle to remain on the sphere. But the definition still isn't local. In order to be sure of walking in a turtle line between two points, the poor turtle would have to measure every possible path between the two points and then pick the shortest.

There's something wrong here. "Walking straight without turning" seems like a simple idea. The turtle should be able to tell that it is

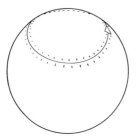

Figure 5.2
Is the line of latitude an equal-strided turtle walk?

walking straight as it is walking, without getting off the sphere to look for planes or finding all possible paths between two points. Can't we find such a local definition? After all, couldn't you walk without turning on a sphere (the earth)?

Here's an idea: Imagine the turtle's legs churning away. We'll say that the turtle is going straight if its left legs take the same number of steps, of the same length, as its right legs. If the turtle starts taking shorter steps on one side (or even backward steps), it will turn. This leads to the following definition:

A (turtle) line is an equal-strided turtle walk.

Now, is any latitude a turtle line? If the turtle straddles a (northern hemisphere) latitude and starts walking, its "south" legs travel a bit below the latitude and its "north" legs a bit above (figure 5.2). Marching all the way around the sphere, has the turtle taken the same-size steps with north as with south legs? Of course not. The farther north the latitude, the smaller the round-trip path. Take a look at a globe again. The equator is the longest latitude, and as you get closer and closer to the north pole the latitudes get smaller and smaller and eventually reach zero length at the north pole. So the turtle must take different-size steps with its left and right legs, and therefore a nonequator latitude is not a turtle line. Equators and longitudes, on the other hand, are turtle lines. (Stare at a globe if you're not convinced.)

There are some interesting points to notice about this way of looking at "straight" turtle lines. First of all, the definition can be used on any surface, not only planes or spheres. Any bent-up surface will do. Just set the turtle down and have it take even strides, left and right, and it will walk in a turtle line. Second, this idea of "even strides," and therefore the determination of what is "straight," reduces to measuring

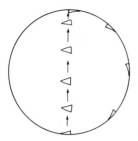

Figure 5.3
Turning without "turtle turning."

small distances. It is as if the turtle carries a little ruler, constantly checking that its left and right sides are moving equally. We'll return to these points later.

5.1.2 Turtle Turning and Trip Turning

Now let's go back to the sphere and the closed path in figure 5.1. The sides are straight in a turtle sense, but the path still requires three 90° turns. Should we just abandon the closed-path theorem? Not yet! Let's at least see exactly what went wrong in the turtle proof given in subsection 1.2.1 that the total turning around any closed path should be a multiple of 360°. Remember the key idea in the proof: When the turtle completes the path, it is once again facing in the initial heading, so the total turning (the net change in heading) must be a multiple of 360°.

In terms of net state change on this spherical triangle, we cannot dispute that the turtle has at the end returned to its initial heading. So in this sense the change in heading must be 360° (or some multiple). The problem is evidently that, in contrast with a plane, net heading change is not equal to turtle turning.

Can we focus on what causes turning not to equal heading change? Get your globe out again and try this: Start the turtle at the north pole and notice which way it is pointing. Walk the turtle straight ahead until it gets to the south pole. Now, without letting the turtle turn at all, walk it sideways (a good straight turtle walk, but sideways) all the way back up to the north pole. Presto! The turtle has been turned 180° without "turning" at all. That's the problem with spheres; the turtle can *get turned* even if it's not turning. If you examine figure 5.3 you will easily see the sphere turning the turtle without the turtle knowing.

So there are two kinds of turning: actual "turtle turning" and "trip turning." The turtle thinks it is turning only when it is "turtle turning," but it can be turned by going on a trip even without "turtle turning."

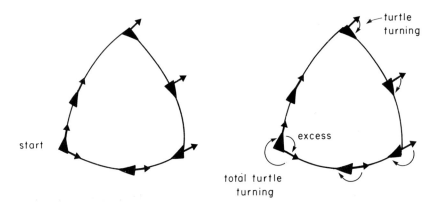

Figure 5.4
(a) Turtle carrying a pointer around the 3 × 90° triangle. (b) Comparison of pointer direction with turtle direction.

Now that we realize that spheres can turn the turtle without the turtle knowing it, we can hypothesize about that extra 90° in the 90°-90°-90° path: While the turtle was walking and turning 270°, it must have been turned an additional 90° by the sphere.

Can we compute trip turning other than as the amount by which the closed-path theorem fails? We want a method for seeing trip turning—something like ..gure 5.3, but more general and more intrinsic. If there were some general way to think of something traveling around a closed path without turtle turning at all, then the extra (trip) turning would become visible directly. One way to do this is as follows: Suppose turtle carries a pointer. While the turtle is walking straight, it always keeps the pointer from turning by keeping it at a constant bearing from turtle's own heading. And whenever the turtle does some (turtle) turning, it again makes sure not to turn the pointer. In other words, the turtle is carrying the pointer around the path without (turtle) turning the pointer. Therefore, any heading change in the pointer must be due to trip turning.

Let's try that idea out on the 90°-90°-90° path. Turtle starts on the equator with the pointer facing north as shown in figure 5.4a. It walks to the north pole, turns right 90°, and returns to the equator. But now the pointer is facing west. The turtle returns to the initial position with the pointer facing west. There is the 90° trip turning that fooled us into thinking that the turtle must have turtle-turned 360°, whereas in actuality it only turtle-turned 270° and was trip-turned the other 90° The bug in the closed-path theorem has been isolated. It is this change in pointer heading—trip turning, pure and simple. In a plane, trip turning doesn't exist.

5.1.3 Angle Excess

We've made some real mathematical progress because we have run across a new concept. The concept is what mathematicians call *angle excess,* or simply *excess.* Excess is, by definition, the trip turning that the pointer gets turned when being carried around a closed path. Right away there are some nice things to notice about angle excess: You can ask what it is for a closed path around any polygon, not just a triangle, and you can ask about angle excess on any surface, not just a sphere (because we know how to make the turtle walk in a "straight line" on any surface).

Excess is a rather general concept. It is an angle associated to any closed path on any surface. In fact, we can restate the closed-path theorem so that it holds for simple closed paths on arbitrary surfaces:

If the turtle walks around a simple closed path on a surface, then

(total turtle turning along the path) + (excess along the path)
$$= 2\pi \text{ radians} = 360°.$$

Figure 5.4b illustrates this equation on our $3 \times 90°$ triangle and shows that the turtle can directly measure total (turtle) turning at any time by seeing how far it has turned away from the pointer direction.

This formula and the pointer measuring process are a beginning, but they don't really tell us much unless we know more properties of excess. Here are some questions we might ask about this quantity:

• Can we ever compute angle excess without directly measuring it? We've hinted at a partial answer: An excess angle on a plane is always zero. That's precisely another way of stating the original closed-path theorem for paths in a plane. This leads to the question of whether the plane is the only surface with zero excess for all closed paths.

• Is angle excess always greater than zero for any surface, or might there be surfaces for which the turtle must turn more than 360° in going around a simple closed path?

• In general, what does knowing excess tell you about a surface?

• What does angle excess really mean?

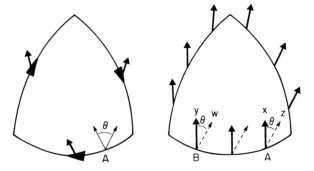

Figure 5.5
(a) Measuring excess around a triangle starting from point A. (b) Measuring excess around a triangle starting from two different locations. The angle from x to z is the same as the angle from y to w.

But let's not get too far ahead of ourselves. We should make sure the excess concept is nailed down. That means asking some simple questions about it. For instance, we've been talking about the "excess around a path." But is this notion really well defined? That is, does carrying a pointer around a path really specify exactly one number to be associated with the path? In particular:

Question 1 Does the measured excess depend on the initial direction of the pointer?

Question 2 Does it depend on where the turtle starts on the boundary?

Answer 1 No. Suppose the turtle carried two different pointers around the same path. While the turtle is walking, both pointers must maintain the same heading with respect to the turtle line, since otherwise they would be (turtle) turning. And neither pointer does anything at all while the turtle turns. So the angle between the two arrows is always constant, and the turtle might as well carry a disk with two arrows marked on it. Therefore, we see that the difference between the initial and final headings for either pointer is just the net rotation of the disk. Both pointers measure the same excess.

Answer 2 No. Look at a diagram (figure 5.5a) of a turtle measuring the excess around a path by starting at A and carrying a pointer all the way around. The excess is marked θ. Suppose instead that the turtle measures the angle excess starting at some other point B. In order to compare the two measurements, we'll imagine that the turtle does both measurements at once, as shown in figure 5.5b. The turtle starts at A, and the direction of the pointer is labeled x. Then the turtle moves to B, and the pointer direction is labeled y. Next we go all the way around to A again, where the pointer direction is labeled z. The difference between x and z is, by definition, the excess θ as measured from A. Finally, let the turtle continue to B once more, where the pointer direction is labeled w. The excess as measured from B will be the difference between y and w. But now regard x and z as two different pointers being carried simultaneously from A to B. The angle between them remains constant. (Remember the disk with two pointers on it from answer 1?) Since the angle between pointers is θ at A, it must also be θ at B.

The result of answers 1 and 2 is that it doesn't matter where the turtle starts along a given closed path, or at what heading. The excess will be the same.

5.1.4. Excess is Additive

Let's get back to more investigation and less formalization by concentrating on the sphere for a while. We started on the sphere with a path of fairly large excess, 90°. Can you imagine a closed path with a bigger excess? How about the equator? The turtle starts anywhere and travels all the way around. The total turning is zero, so by our formula the excess is 360°. How about a path with smaller excess? That's no problem. Just take a path that is very small in comparison with the size of the sphere. If the turtle remains in a very small region, the sphere looks almost flat, almost like a plane, so the excess must be close to zero.

It appears as if paths around small regions have small excesses and paths around large ones have large excesses. If you haven't already noticed, the path around the equator has 4 times the excess of the $3 \times 90°$ path, and the hemisphere bounded by the equator can be constructed by pasting together exactly four of the $3 \times 90°$ triangles. Could it be that excesses add? Take a look at any triangle made up of two 90° angles at the equator and n degrees (interior angle) at the pole. It has excess of n degrees and can be made up of n triangles of 1° excess (see figure 5.6). This is beginning to look like a theorem.

Theorem If a triangle is subdivided into two subtriangles, then the excess of the triangle is the sum of the excesses of the pieces.

Notice that the theorem doesn't mention anything about spheres in particular. Neither will the proof; it is true for triangles on any surface.

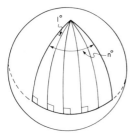

Figure 5.6
The excess of the large triangle is the sum of the excesses of the small triangles.

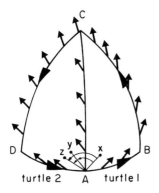

Figure 5.7
Excess BCD (x to z) = Excess ABC (x to y) + Excess ACD (y to z).

Proof Look at a record of a turtle using a pointer to measure the excess in triangle ABC (figure 5.7). The pointer starts out with heading x and ends up with heading y. Now measure the excess of triangle ACD. To make things simple imagine a second turtle that starts from A with the same heading, y, at which the first turtle ended measuring ABC. Then the second turtle's pointer should agree with the first turtle's all along the line AC. In particular, the pointers of the two turtles will agree at point C. The second turtle then continues to D and ends up at A with pointer heading z. Now we'll measure the excess in the large triangle BCD as follows: Start at A with pointer heading x and follow the first turtle's path as far as C. At C, pick up the second turtle's path (this can be done without changing the pointer heading) and follow it around clear back to A. The pointer winds up with heading z. So the excess of the large triangle is the angle from x to z, which is just the sum of the excesses (x to y and y to z) of the two smaller triangles.

This is a pretty good theorem. It is the core of a really great one:

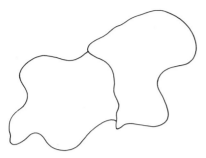

Figure 5.8
Two regions joined along a common arc.

Excess Additivity Theorem The excess of any polygon is the sum of the excesses of the pieces in any polygonal subdivision.

Can you see how to prove this? One way is to notice that the reasoning in the proof above still works even if we combine whole polygons at a time. It doesn't really depend on the pieces being triangles. All we need is a situation like the one shown in figure 5.8, in which the two pieces are pasted together along a single arc. In fact, we don't even need polygons and vertices. The proof depends only on topology, how pieces are hooked together. We'll have more to say about this in section 5.2.

5.1.5 Excess and Area

Compare the excess additivity theorem to the following obvious and familiar theorem:

Theorem The area of any polygon is the sum of the areas of the pieces in any polygonal subdivision.

Excess acts like area in this respect. Could it be that excess is proportional to area, that is, $E = kA$, where E is the excess around a polygon, A is the area of the polygon, and k is some constant? This would account for the additivity of excess. But it is obvious that k couldn't be a universal constant like π. After all, k must be zero for a plane but it can't be zero for a sphere. Not only that, but it can't even be the same constant for all spheres. Consider our $3 \times 90°$ path on a sphere the size of the earth and on one the size of a ping-pong ball. They have the same excess, but certainly not the same area. So how about the hypothesis that k depends on the surface, and every surface may have a different

k? Let's try that out. Obviously any plane has $k = 0$. The following theorem shows that the hypothesis is also true for spheres:

Theorem For any polygon on a sphere of radius r, $E = kA$ where $k = 1/r^2$ (if E is measured in radians).

Proof First we'll show that the ratio E/A is the same for all polygons on the sphere. (Then, denoting this constant ratio by k, it will be simple to find out what k is.) The idea is to measure both excess and area by subdividing a large polygon into a lot of tiny identical pieces and adding them all up. For example, you can subdivide any polygon into tiny standard-sized squares. (Of course there can be a little bit of surface left over, but not much. You can always use smaller squares to get a better approximation. And calculus buffs know how to talk about the limit of small squares.) Then the area of the polygon is the sum of the areas of the individual small squares. Similarly, the additivity theorem ensures that the excess of the polygon is the sum of the excesses of the individual squares.

Now, since the sphere is the same all over, the individual squares can be taken to be absolutely identically shaped pieces of the sphere. Thus, not only will they all have the same area, they will also all have the same excess. Let a be the area of any one of these small square pieces, and let e be the excess. Then the area of any large polygon that consists of N small squares is $A = Na$ and the excess is $E = Ne$. So $E/A = e/a$ is a constant that is independent of the size or shape of the large polygon.

Finally, since the ratio E/A, which we will denote by k, is the same for all polygons on the sphere, we can compute k by considering any particular polygon for which we know both the excess and the area. Take, for instance, the equator bounding half the sphere. For that path we have

$$A = \frac{1}{2} \text{ sphere area} = 2\pi r^2$$

and

$$E = 2\pi \text{ radians,}$$

so

$$k = \frac{E}{A} = \frac{2\pi}{2\pi r^2} = \frac{1}{r^2}.$$

This completes the proof.

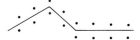

Figure 5.9
Is this a turtle line?

We can combine this theorem with the definition of excess as the correction factor in the total-turtle-trip theorem to get a formula (originally due to Gauss) which relates the area of a spherical polygon to the total turning around its boundary:

For a turtle walking around a polygon on the surface of a sphere,

$$\text{total turning (in radians)} = 2\pi - \frac{A}{r^2}$$

where A is the area of the polygon and r is the radius of the sphere.

Exercises for Section 5.1

1. [D] We proved a formula relating the excess around a closed path to the area of the interior. But any closed path on the sphere bounds *two* regions, which in general do not have the same area. Which region do we take as the inside? Can you clarify the definitions of excess and "inside" so that the area formula in 5.1.5 will work for both of the regions bounded by a closed path? [HA]

2. Give a formula for the sum of the interior angles of a triangle on a sphere in terms of the area of the triangle. [A]

3. Convince yourself again that an equator must be a turtle line. Is the path of a boat with rudder aimed straight a turtle line? How about a jet plane flying "straight"?

4. Look at the record of turtle tracks in figure 5.9. The left legs take the same number of steps as the right legs, and all steps are the same length, so why isn't the track a turtle line? (It obviously isn't one.) Can you apply the principle of "a line must be everywhere the same"? Can you answer the question without the principle? Another problem along the same lines is as follows: If a line must be "everywhere the same," then what happens to a turtle line on a flattened sphere as it goes from the round part to the flat part? Can you reformulate the "a line is everywhere the same" principle so that it really applies to turtle lines? [H]

5. Would a little turtle (say, one you might use for measuring turtle lines on a ping-pong ball) draw the same turtle lines on a big sphere as a big turtle? What do you have to say about turning a turtle loose to draw triangles in your back yard? Would the turtle's size matter? Think about a tiny, tiny turtle crawling over each pebble in your back yard. Does that make you nervous about what a turtle line really is? After all, you know pretty much what a triangle of turtle lines, say, 20 feet on a side should look like, but wouldn't a tiny turtle get all confused by the pebbles and blades of grass? Who tells you what size turtle to use? [H]

6. [D] In 5.1.4 we used the formula Total Turning + Excess = 360° together with the fact that the equator is a turtle line to deduce that the excess around the equator is 360°. But can you use the pointer method to see directly that Excess = 360° rather than 0° or 720°? [HA]

7. Imagine that a turtle is a two-wheeled creature with a motor on each wheel. Can you convince yourself that the total turning of this turtle is simply the distance rolled by one wheel minus the distance rolled by the other wheel divided by the distance between wheels? Does this mean that a car going over a bump with its left wheels but not its right will be turned by an amount which is equal to the extra distance traveled going up and over bump, divided by the distance between wheels? [A]

8. Exercise 7 gives some remarkable information about staggered starts on race tracks. Show that the difference in pathlengths of adjacent lanes in going around any non-self-intersecting track on a plane is $2\pi \times$ (width of lane). Show that a figure-eight track does not need a staggered start. Are these statements true if the track is banked? [HA]

5.2 Curvature

We've cleared up the mystery of non-360° turtle trips on the sphere, and discovered a relation between angles and areas for spherical polygons. The wonderful thing is that much of our insight carries over to geometry on arbitrary surfaces as well. This is because our methods of investigation are local and intrinsic. The whole theory, remember, depended on having a notion of the difference between "straight" and "turning," and we were careful to define "straight line" in a way that doesn't rely on coordinate systems, intersecting spheres with planes, or anything else, except for a turtle walking along, locally marking off equal distances with its left and right legs. Thus, anywhere a turtle can walk we have turtle lines, excess, and the additivity theorem. Let's see how the other observations we made about spheres might carry over to arbitrary surfaces (figure 5.10).

5.2.1 Curvature Density

Does the relation between excess and area $E = kA$ hold true on an arbitrary surface? Pretty clearly not. Suppose we have a sphere that is squashed flat on one side. The excess is zero for polygons on the flat part, but regions on the rounded part will have nonzero excess. Where does the proof we gave for spheres in 5.1.5 break down? Exactly here: We divided our polygon into small square patches and then noted that, for a sphere, all the squares are identical; each square has the same $k = e/a$. That's not true for the flattened sphere. Little square patches taken from the flat side will be flat, with $k = 0$, while squares taken from the curved side will not be flat. So $k = e/a$ is different on the two parts.

In general, for an arbitrary surface, we can think of k as a measurement that can be made at any point on the surface. The value of k at a point is the excess per unit area of a small patch of surface containing the point. We call k the *curvature density* of the surface at a point. It is "density" because it is "stuff per unit area" (in this case, excess per unit area). And it is called "curvature density" rather than "excess density" because, although it is measured using excess, we can interpret it as telling how "curved" the surface is at the point. Think of it this way: Suppose we want to approximate a small patch of an arbitrary surface by a small patch of some surface we know very well. Within a small area almost any surface will appear flat like a plane, but we can make an even better approximation by using a small piece of a sphere. We'll choose the approximating sphere to have the same excess per unit area as the patch of surface. So if k doesn't change radically in the small patch, all the geometry there—angles, total turning, and so on—will be very close to the geometry on a sphere whose excess per unit area is k, that is to say, a sphere whose radius is determined by $k = 1/r^2$. The smaller the radius of the approximating sphere (that is, the greater the curvature density), the more "curved" we say the surface is. A football, for example, is not too curved in the middle; k is small there. But at the pointed ends the football is curved as much as a sphere of small radius. From the middle to the pointed ends, k gradually increases. The surface of a very smooth lake will be well approximated by a patch of a sphere as big as the earth; the density of curvature is so low that you might think it was flat.

Figure 5.10
Turtle investigating an arbitrarily curved surface. (Drawing by Joseph Coté.)

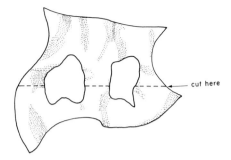

Figure 5.11
A figure that is not a topological disk can nevertheless be divided into topological disks.

5.2.2 Total Curvature

Curvature density is a local quantity that we can measure in the vicinity of a point on an arbitrary surface. In this subsection we show how to define a global version of curvature density called *total curvature*. Start with a region of an arbitrary surface and divide it into polygonal pieces. For each polygon, compute the excess. Now sum the excesses for all the pieces. The result is called the total curvature, K, of the region. Of course, in order for this definition to make sense, we have to know that if we chop up a region into polygons in two different ways, then the sum of the excess of the pieces is the same in both cases. This is true, and we leave the proof to you (exercise 4).

If the region we started with was itself a polygon, then the additivity theorem implies that K is precisely equal to the excess around the boundary of the polygon. So we can think of K as a sort of "excess over the region," except that it works for *any* region on a surface, not just for polygons. For example, the boundary of the surface shown in figure 5.11 is not a single simple closed path, so there is no obvious excess to relate to the total curvature K. Nevertheless, we can divide the surface into two polygonal pieces and sum the excesses to get total curvature. (There is more to say on this; see exercise 15.)

Even better, we can compute K for a region that has no boundary at all: the sphere. Divide a sphere into two pieces, the northern and southern hemispheres. Each of these is bounded by the equator, which, as we know, has excess 2π. So the two hemispheres each have excess 2π, giving 4π for the total curvature of the sphere. This is somewhat striking: The curvature density k of a sphere depends on the radius, but the total curvature K is the same for all spheres.

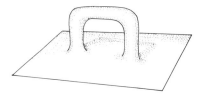

Figure 5.12
Square with handle.

Can we say exactly which regions have K equal to excess around the boundary? The answer is found in the proof of the additivity theorem: whichever regions we can build up by pasting together polygonal pieces, always joining pieces two at a time along a single arc. Notice that this ensures that when we're done, the boundary of the region will be a simple closed curve. For example, we can't build the surface in figure 5.11 this way, because we can't add a piece to close one of the rings without connecting to the rest of the surface along two separate arcs. (Incidentally, the fact that a region is bounded by a simple closed curve does not guarantee that it can be built up from pieces according to the required scheme. The "square with handle" shown in figure 5.12 is one example.)

If you remember our discussion of the deformation theorem of subsection 4.3.1 you may suspect that these regions that can be built up from small polygonal pieces, each piece joined on along a single arc, are precisely the things we called topological disks (that is, regions that can be deformed to a disk). And indeed this is the case. So the relation between total curvature and excess can be restated as follows:

Theorem For any topological disk on an arbitrary surface, the angle excess around the boundary is equal to the total curvature of the interior.

In summary: Thinking about angle excess has led us to two versions of curvature, curvature density and total curvature. We can clarify the relation between these two notions by making an analogy between curvature and paint. Think of the surface as covered with paint. The curvature density is analogous to how much paint you have per little chunk of surface area. Spheres have uniform coats of paint—that is, the curvature density is the same at all places. If you want to know the total amount of paint P on some surface with constant paint per unit area p, the answer is simple: $P = pA$, where A is the total area. In the same way the total curvature K of a surface of constant curvature density k

is just $K = kA$. But just as in the case of a room that has one coat of paint on the wall, a double coat on the woodwork, and no paint at all on the windows, the curvature density of a surface may vary from place to place. If the paint density varies from place to place, how do you find out how much total paint there is? The answer is to divide your surface into tiny pieces so that the paint density is pretty much constant on each piece. You find out how much paint is on each little piece by multiplying paint density times area, and then adding to find the total paint.

There are two different ways to compute the total curvature of a region. The first is the paint method: Divide the region into tiny pieces, so that k is approximately constant on each piece, and add up k times area for all the pieces. The second method you cannot do with paint: Divide the region into topological disks of any size at all, and total up the excess around the boundaries. With this method you need not look to see if the curvature is uniform or examine every bit of the surface to see how dense the curvature is there.

It is remarkable that these two processes end up computing the same thing, that total curvature—something spread out over a whole region— can be measured by a method that looks only at the boundaries of the pieces in a subdivision. In fact, you may recognize this as another instance of the "local-global" principle of section 4.2. That is to say, we can determine a global quantity (total curvature) by accumulating information (excess) that is measured locally at the boundaries of the pieces in a subdivision. In section 5.3 we'll see how to put this property of curvature to good use.

5.2.3 Cylinders

We've been talking a lot about arbitrary surfaces, but so far our only concrete example has been the sphere. Let's look at another surface, the cylinder (a tin can without top or bottom). What is k for a cylinder?

The answer is that $k = 0$ at every point, just as for a plane (and therefore $K = 0$ as well). The reason is profound: A cylinder is just a plane rolled up, and rolling something up doesn't change any pathlengths on the surface. (If you are not convinced, glue a rubber band to a piece of paper. Now try to stretch the rubber band without ripping the paper. Rolling the paper up won't do it, except for a tiny bit of stretching that happens because the rubber band is not in the surface but a little above.)

If pathlengths don't change, then a straight (turtle) line in the plane

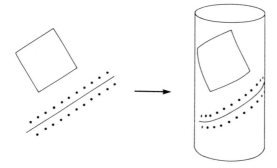

Figure 5.13
Turtle line and square are still turtle line and square when rolled into a cylinder.

remains a turtle line when the plane is rolled up into a cylinder. How can we be so convinced that turtle lines are preserved? Because the determination of what is a turtle line depends only on measuring small distances: The turtle knows it is walking in a straight line when its left legs and its right legs are moving the same distance in each step. Look at the straight line in figure 5.13 and the turtle tracks around it. Now imagine the paper rolled up. The turtle will still walk in the same tracks, because no distances have changed. Angles don't change when you roll something up either, so in any polygon of turtle lines on a cylinder we will measure the same vertex angles as in the "unrolled" polygon on the plane. Therefore the polygon will have zero excess.

There is an important lesson here. When we began with planes and spheres, it was pretty clear that $k = 0$ meant what people usually mean by "flat" and $k \neq 0$ meant "curved." But here is a surface, the cylinder, that most people would say is curved. You have to decide now whether you want to go on saying a cylinder is curved, as you always did, or change your definition of "flat" to mean $k = 0$ and then say that a cylinder is flat. The latter possibility may sound very strange, but it is a good thing to do if you are interested in a geometry that reflects properties that are *intrinsic* to the surface, rather than how things look to an observer outside of the surface. From an intrinsic point of view, a cylinder is much more like a plane than it is like a sphere. In fact, a turtle that wasn't allowed to go all the way around the cylinder and discover its different topology would never be able to tell the difference between that cylinder and a plane at all! So if you were talking to your friends who haven't read this book you'd be better off saying that a cylinder is curved, but a turtle living on the surface of a cylinder would be happier to hear you say that its world is flat.

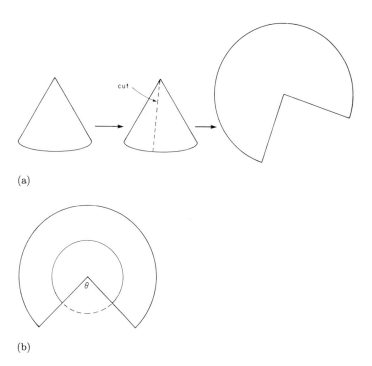

(a)

(b)

Figure 5.14
(a) Flattening a cone. (b) Turtle circle on cone is missing turning done in the gap
from 2π; excess $= \theta$.

5.2.4 Cones

Almost any little piece of a cone can be easily laid flat on a plane.
This means that the cone is just about everywhere a zero-curvature-
density object; $k = 0$ almost everywhere. But there is an exception:
The tip won't flatten out without ripping. All the curvature in a cone
is concentrated at the tip.

We can compute how much curvature is in the tip by seeing how much
excess is contained in some path around the tip. A little trick makes it
easy to keep track of turtle turning on the cone: Slit the cone up the side
and lay it out flat to get a figure like a pie with a slice missing (figure
5.14a). Turtle turning can now be easily seen as change of heading in
the usual planar way, except in crossing the cut. So look at a simple
turtle circle centered around the tip (figure 5.14b). The total turning
along that path is short of 2π by the turning that would have been done
in the pie gap to make a complete planar circle. But excess is, by our
excess formula, exactly what is missing in total turning from 2π. So

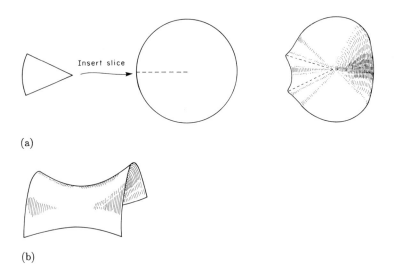

(a)

(b)

Figure 5.15
(a) Concentrated negative curvature: a pie with an extra slice. (b) Saddle surface—
spread-out negative curvature.

the turning in the gap is excess, and since that turning is precisely the
central angle of the pie gap, θ, we conclude that θ is the excess of the
path.

What is nice about cones, then, is that you can see the angle excess
directly: It is the angle you need to cut from a flat piece of surface to
make it into a cone.

Notice that this result, "excess of path around tip equals pie angle,"
does not depend at all on how big the path around the tip is. So you can
see by pushing the path closer and closer to the tip and always getting
the same excess that the curvature must be concentrated in the tip, and
that the curvature is zero everywhere else.

What is K for a region on the cone? It is zero unless the region
contains the tip, in which case $K = \theta$. How about k? We said that
$k = 0$ at every point except the tip. At the tip, k is infinite. Don't
let that infinity upset you. After all, k is a density: stuff per unit area.
And on a cone, all the curvature is concentrated at a single point. With
a finite amount of curvature in a region of zero area (a point), density
must be infinite.

Suppose we make a cone using too much paper rather than too little—
not a pie with a slice taken out, but a pie with an extra slice, as shown in
figure 5.15a. You can't push such a thing flat—not because you have too

little circumference and will rip the cone trying to flatten it, but because you have too much circumference (for a given radius) and can't cram it all into a plane. This cone has *negative curvature*. A path around the tip contains more than 360°; hence excess is negative. The saddle surface shown in figure 5.15b is an example of a surface with negative curvature density at each point (see exercise 9).

5.2.5 Curvature for Curves and Surfaces

By way of a brief review, let's explore the analogy between the curvature of surfaces and the total turning of curves in the plane, which we studied in chapters 1 and 4.

First of all, the definitions we gave for both surface curvature and curve turning were local and intrinsic. They could be expressed in terms of a turtle crawling along a curve or a surface without recourse to coordinate systems.

What is the analog of total curvature K for a curve? It is simply the total turning of a turtle walking along the curve. What corresponds to curvature density k? By analogy with excess per unit area on a surface, we should define curvature density of a curve to be turning per unit length. So for any segment of a curve, we can define k_{curve} to be the total turning along the segment divided by the length of the segment. This is the same thing we called simply "curvature" in previous chapters.

Just as a sphere has constant k, a circle has constant k_{curve}: In traversing a circular arc subtended by a central angle of θ (in radians) the turtle turns the same angle, θ, and goes a distance $d = r\theta$. Hence, by the above definition, $k_{\text{curve}} = \theta/r\theta = 1/r$, which is analogous to $k = 1/r^2$ for a sphere. (The analogy goes farther; see exercise 18.)

Comparing curvature in one and two dimensions can be misleading, however, when we think about negative curvature. For a curve, the difference between positive and negative curvature depends on the direction in which the turtle turns. Turning right rather than left changes the sign of the curvature. So you might expect that a similar kind of reflecting will change positive to negative curvature in two dimensions. For example, it is easy to imagine that a turtle crawling on the inside of a sphere would see negative curvature. But this is false. If we look carefully, we can see that polygons on spheres always have positive excess, whether measured from the inside or the outside. To find negative curvature, we need to look at something like the saddle surface shown in figure 5.15b. Actually, this whole notion of inside versus outside a surface is misleading. It is better to think of the turtle as a two-dimensional

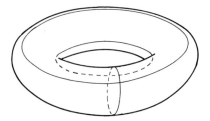

Figure 5.16
Which of these paths on a torus are turtle lines?

creature who lives *in* a curved world, rather than *on* it, just as plane
geometry is about figures lying in the plane, rather than on top of or underneath it. Here is another way to say the same thing: We should think
of an idealized two-dimensional surface like the sphere as just that—a
two-dimensional surface—not as a shell with separate inside and outside
surfaces.

Exercises for Section 5.2

1. Suppose turtle walks all the way round a cylinder on a path perpendicular to its length. That is a closed path with zero turtle turning,
hence 360° excess. But didn't we say that a cylinder has zero curvature?
Doesn't zero curvature mean that there can't be any excess? Explain.
[HA]

2. Which surfaces have no excess anywhere? Can you formulate a
general description of such a surface? [A]

3. Figure 5.16 shows some paths drawn on a torus. Which of these are
turtle lines? [A]

4. [D] Show that total curvature K is well defined. That is, show that
if you chop up a region into topological disks in two different ways, and
sum up the excess around the boundaries, you'll get the same answer in
both cases. [HA]

5. The cone is an example of a surface where curvature is concentrated
at a point. Can you find an example of a surface where curvature is
concentrated along a curve? [A]

6. Prove that a "radial circle" drawn around the tip of a cone (by taking
points of equal distance from the tip) really is a circle from the turtle's
point of view—that it can be drawn by going FORWARD a little and turning
a little, over and over. Is a radial circle centered about some point

other than the tip of the cone still a turtle circle? What do turtle circles look like on a sphere? How about radial circles on spheres? [A]

7. Show that a football has total curvature 4π. [HA]

8. What is the total curvature of a cube? What is k? Is there concentrated curvature? If so, where and how much? [A]

9. Envision a point on some surface, and the shape of the surface near the point. Show that if the surface looks like a hill or a depression the curvature density k is positive at the point, whereas if the surface looks like a saddle k is negative. Do this geometrically, by drawing some turtle lines and estimating excess. Even better, make a model of the surface and draw some turtle paths on it.

10. Suppose that you make a scale model of a surface, say scaled by a factor of s. Show that K remains unchanged. How does k change? [A]

11. Using the fact that changing the scale of a surface does not change total curvature, conclude once again that all the curvature in a cone is in its tip. [HA]

12. Suppose that a turtle is a bit out of adjustment and takes slightly longer (by 2%) strides with its left legs than with its right. (Assume that the distance between turtle's right and left legs is the same as its right-side stride.) What is the radius of the circle such a turtle would walk on a plane if it did not "turtle turn?" (Use turtle stride as your unit of distance.) Suppose this turtle walks 25 steps on some surface and finds it has returned to the initial position and heading. What is the total curvature interior to this path, if the interior is a topological disk? How about a 400-step trip? [A]

13. [P] Suppose that a turtle is sitting at the tip of a cone. It goes a distance r away and draws a circle around the tip. According to the turtle's measurement, r is the radius of the circle. But of course it finds that the circumference of the circle is not $2\pi r$, but something less. (It is missing exactly the "defect pie" from being $2\pi r$.) The turtle will discover the same sort of thing on a sphere: The circumference of a circle is not $2\pi r$, but a little less. Suppose we define "global π" on a surface to be equal to the circumference of a circle divided by twice the radius. What is global π for a cone? For a sphere? Does it depend on how big a circle you draw? Does it depend on where you draw the circle? If you cannot give the precise value, can you give upper and lower bounds for

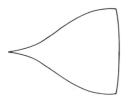

Figure 5.17
Segment of an umbrella.

global π? Define "intrinsic π" to be the circumference divided by twice the radius of curvature and answer the same questions for it. [H]

14. [P] Suppose somebody told you that not only is the earth not flat, our *universe* is not flat either. What could that mean? Answer in terms of angles, circumferences and radii of circles, and perhaps surface areas and radii of spheres. Notice before starting that we never had to leave the surface of a sphere to discover that it was curved, as long as we had drawn turtle lines. (Einstein decided that the universe was not flat. He thought it was curved in a very special way to account for the existence of gravity. In fact, he hypothesized that the paths objects follow under the influence of gravity are just "turtle paths" in our curved universe. We'll have much more to say about this in chapter 9.)

15. Can you find the total curvature of a surface with holes in it (figure 5.11) in terms of the excesses of the boundaries of the surface? [HA]

16. An umbrella is made by sewing together six pieces, as shown roughly in figure 5.17. Where does the umbrella have negative curvature? How can you tell? [HA]

17. We have ignored the problem of non-simply-closed curves. Show that additivity still works for the situation shown in figure 5.18 in the following way:

Total turning around the closed path

$\quad = (2\pi -$ total curvature contained within the outer loop)

$\quad\quad + (2\pi -$ total curvature contained within the inner loop).

18. Extending the analogy between curvature for circles and spheres, the central angle θ of a circular arc has a counterpart called solid angle, Ω. Just as θ measures how much of a plane lies between two rays (or how much plane can be seen from the center through a gap in a circle), Ω measures how much "sky" can be seen through a window in a

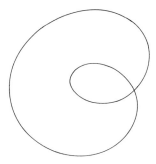

Figure 5.18
What is the relation between excess and total curvature for this curve?

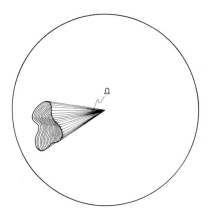

Figure 5.19
Solid angle for a region on a sphere measures the opening subtended by it.

sphere (figure 5.19). By analogy with the formula $\theta = k_{\text{curve}}d = d/r$, Ω is defined to be $\Omega = kA = A/r^2$, where A is the area of the window. Notice that θ can be measured as the turning done by turtle along the arc. In an analogous way, can you relate Ω to things that the turtle can measure on the sphere's surface? [A]

5.3 Total Curvature and Topology

We ended the previous section with an analogy between the total curvature of a surface and the total turning of a curve. But there is one property of total turning that we haven't seen reflected in our study of surfaces: topological invariance. Remember that the total turning of a closed curve is a topological invariant (section 4.1). However you deform

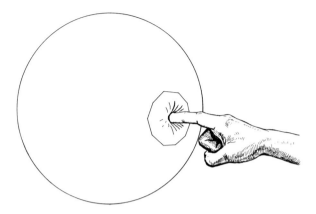

Figure 5.20
Pushing a dent in a sphere and surrounding the dent by a turtle path.

the curve, the total turning remains the same. Now we'll see that this same fact is true for the total curvature of a closed surface.

5.3.1 Dents and Bends

Suppose you put a small dent in a sphere. What happens to the total curvature? Perhaps it depends on the dent—if it is a flattening maybe that reduces the curvature; if it is a pointy kind of outward dent maybe that increases the curvature. But the answer is that *total curvature is unchanged.*

Proof Surround the dent with a closed path, which isolates within a topological disk the region affected by the dent, but make sure that the path is far enough away from the dent so that the immediate vicinity of the path is unaffected by the dent (see figure 5.20). The curvature outside the disk obviously has not changed at all. What is happening inside? Think of a turtle measuring the total curvature within the disk by computing the excess along the path. Before and after denting, the turtle treks the same territory. The excess must be the same before and after denting, and so the total curvature does not change at all.

This fact illustrates what a strong statement we are making when we assert that we can measure something spread out over a region (the total curvature of a topological disk) by measurements made only at the boundary of the region (in this case, the excess along the boundary). The consequence is that any deformation of the region that doesn't affect the boundary must leave the total curvature invariant.

Figure 5.21
Topological sphere = Cylinder + Two caps.

So total curvature is invariant under small deformations. But this means it must be invariant under *any* topological deformation. The point is that any topological deformation can be made by doing a bunch of small deformations one at a time, each small deformation affecting only a part of the surface that can be isolated within a disk.

You can dent, bend, smash, buckle, push, or pull a sphere one small piece at a time into any shape you choose and the total curvature remains the same. It doesn't change no matter what you do to the sphere as long as you don't rip it or in some other way change its topology. A football has total curvature 4π. A Mickey Mouse balloon, ears and all, has total curvature 4π. That sphere we flattened on one side still has total curvature 4π. (Suppose we smash the southern hemisphere flat. That part has total curvature zero, and the northern hemisphere has only 2π. Where did the other curvature go? It's there; find it.)

Suppose you take a sphere and pull it to make a cylinder capped on each side with a hemisphere (see figure 5.21). The resulting topological sphere still has total curvature 4π. But each cap has 2π, so that doesn't leave you anything for the cylinder. This is another way to show that cylinders have zero total curvature (and, since a cylinder is the same all over, that the curvature density is zero as well).

What happens to total curvature when we deform a cylinder? To be sure, any deformation whose effects we can isolate within a topological disk will always preserve total curvature. But, for example, suppose we take the cylinder and spread it out at the end to create flanges (figure 5.22a). Can we assert that this flanged cylinder has total curvature zero? No, we can't, even though the flanged cylinder is topologically the same as a regular cylinder. Look carefully what happens when we deform the cylinder in a little patch near the edge (figure 5.22b). We can't surround that deformation by a closed turtle path, simply because the turtle would have to run off the edge of the cylinder to get around the deformed part. There is no turtle-path barrier, so you can push curvature off the edge. On the other hand, any deformation that does not affect the boundary of the cylinder (as in figure 5.22c) cannot affect the total curvature.

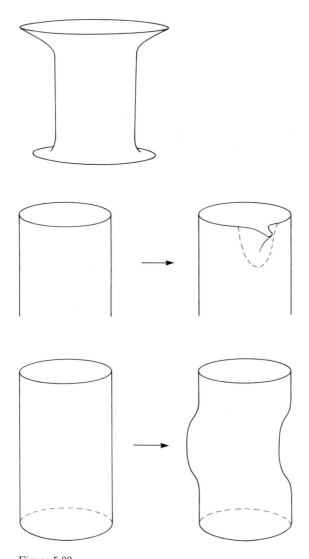

Figure 5.22
(a) Flanged cylinder. (b) Deforming the cylinder near the boundary may change total
curvature. (c) A deformation of the cylinder that preserves total curvature.

There is an important class of surfaces for which this problem of deformations near the boundary cannot arise. These are the *closed surfaces*—those surfaces that, like the sphere, have no boundary to begin with. (We disallow planes or infinitely long cylinders as closed surfaces, by stipulating that a closed surface must not stretch off "to infinity.")

The following theorem summarizes the preceding observations:

Theorem Total curvature K is a topological invariant for closed surfaces. For surfaces with boundary, the total curvature is unchanged by deformations that do not affect the vicinity of the boundary of the surface.

Once again, the situation for the total turning of a curve is analogous. For closed curves, total turning is a topological invariant. But it is certainly not a topological invariant for nonclosed curves, since any nonclosed curve can be deformed to a straight line segment. On the other hand, if we make a deformation of a curve that keeps the curve fixed in a vicinity of the endpoints, total turning will be unchanged.

5.3.2 Concentrated Curvature

Are you puzzled by the sphere with one hemisphere squashed flat? The flattened side has no curvature and the other hemisphere has total curvature 2π, yet the entire surface is topologically a sphere and has total curvature 4π. Where is that missing 2π of curvature? It must be concentrated in the edge between the two hemispheres.

Here is another example of the same phenomenon. Take a cylinder and close it at the top and bottom with two flat disks. The resulting "tin can" is topologically a sphere, but the disks and the cylinder each have zero curvature. There must be 4π worth of total curvature concentrated in the edges that form the rims of the can. This concentrated curvature arises because the pieces joined together are not matched: To a turtle walking on the cylinder that forms the side of the can the rim is a straight turtle line, but to a turtle on the top of the can the rim is a circle, not a straight line. This "difference of opinion" shows up as excess in a strip near the rim. Figure 5.23 shows a rectangular path surrounding a part of the rim given by an arc of angle θ. The "rectangle" consists of four right angles, two straight sides crossing the rim, and two paths measuring the turning in the arc from opposite sides of the rim. Now the four right angles, the two straight sides, and the arc on the side of the can contribute 2π total turning. So the arc on the lid accounts for the whole excess, and it has a turtle turning of θ. In other words,

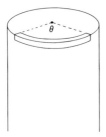

Figure 5.23
A rectangle enclosing part of the rim of a tin can.

there is θ worth of curvature concentrated in this piece of the rim. Since
all parts of the rim look the same, there must be 2π worth of curvature
in the entire rim, or 4π in both rims. The tin can does indeed have the
same total curvature as the sphere. The curvature density k for the tin
can is zero on the side, top, and bottom, and infinite along the rims.

In general, we can construct surfaces by pasting together pieces, but
before we can assert that the total curvature of the surface is the sum of
the curvature of the pieces we must check to make sure that there isn't
any curvature concentrated along the edges or in the corners between
the pieces. How do we check such a thing? If the pieces fit together
smoothly with no sharp edges and with no sharp points (such as the peak
of a cone), then there won't be any concentrated curvature. If there is a
sharp edge, then we can measure the total curvature concentrated there
as the difference of opinion between two turtles, each one computing
the turning along the edge as viewed from its piece of the surface (see
exercise 5). The curvature at a sharp point can be measured by a turtle
trip around it.

5.3.3 Cutting and Pasting

What is the total curvature of a torus (the surface of a donut)? The first
thing to notice is that any torus has the same total curvature as any
other. A fat torus with a small hole and a skinny torus like the inner
tube of a bicycle tire are topologically the same and therefore have the
same total curvature. We can make a torus by pasting together surfaces
whose curvature we do know: cylinders. Take a cylinder (for which $k =
0$) and bend it as shown in figure 5.24a. If we're careful not to do any
stretching at the boundary of the cylinder, then this bent cylinder still
has total curvature zero. Now paste two bent cylinders together (figure
5.24b) to get a torus. Each half of the torus has total curvature zero.
Therefore, the whole torus does also.

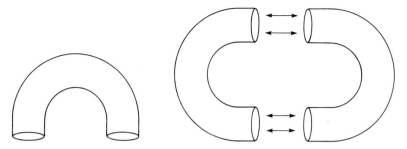

Figure 5.24
Joining two bent cylinders to make a torus.

Theorem Any torus has zero total curvature.

We are not asserting that a torus is flat, like a cylinder or a plane. That would be saying that the curvature density is zero everywhere. What the theorem does say is that any torus has just as much negative curvature as positive curvature.

So now we know the total curvature for two kinds of closed surfaces, spheres and tori. A sphere is not topologically the same as a torus, yet there is a relation between them. The torus can be described as a "sphere with a handle attached." The process of "handle attaching," though not a deformation, is a good, general way of making new surfaces from old. We say "good" because it is easy to keep track of how total curvature changes in the process. Here is how this is done for a sphere and a torus:

Start with a sphere and flatten out two regions on it. From each region cut out a flat disk. Now paste a "handle" in the holes left by the disks (figure 5.25a). The handle is topologically a cylinder, but the edges of the cylinder have been flanged out to match smoothly with the flat regions around the disks. The result is a torus. In other words, we have the equation

(sphere) $-$ (2 disks) $+$ (handle) $=$ torus.

Now compute the total curvature on each side of the equation. The sphere has $K = 4\pi$. The disks were flat and so have $K = 0$. The torus, as we just saw, also has $K = 0$. So in order for the equation to be balanced, the handle must have total curvature -4π.

We can also attach a handle to any surface by the same flattening, cutting, and gluing operation. Since we know the curvature in the handle now, we see that this always decreases the total curvature by 4π. What is the total curvature of a two-holed torus (figure 5.25b)? It is the same

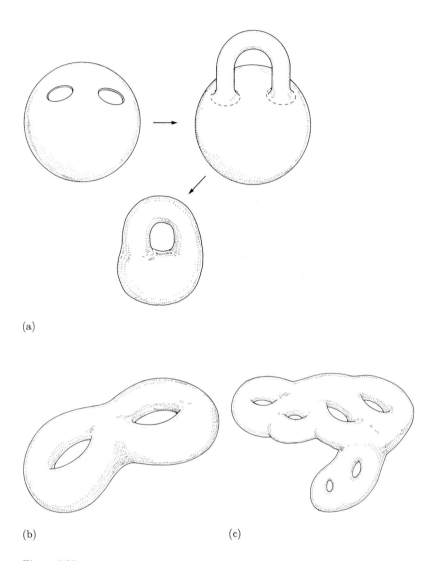

(a)

(b)   (c)

Figure 5.25
(a) Adding a handle to a sphere to make a torus. (b) Two-holed torus. (c) Surface
equivalent to topological sphere with six handles.

as that of a torus with a handle attached or a sphere with two handles attached:

K(two-holed torus) $= 4\pi - 4\pi - 4\pi = -4\pi$.

More generally, if we have a surface that is topologically the same as a sphere with n handles attached, then the total curvature is given by

K(sphere with n handles) $= 4\pi(1 - n)$.

The importance of knowing about spheres with handles is this: Any closed surface in three-dimensional space is topologically equivalent to a sphere with a bunch of handles attached. For example, the surface in figure 5.25c is equivalent to a sphere with six handles. So we see from the equation above that the total curvature of any closed surface in three-dimensional space is an integer multiple of 4π.

We won't give the proof that any surface in three dimensions is equivalent to a sphere with handles, but we will whet your mathematical appetite by informing you that there are closed surfaces that do not have total curvature a multiple of 4π and, as a consequence, are "too twisted" to fit into three-dimensional space. We'll meet some of them in chapter 8. As it turns out, any closed surface, including these "twisted ones," must have total curvature a multiple of 2π. We'll get to that in chapter 8 as well.

One final comment in our study of curvature on surfaces: We saw that for closed plane curves the total turning is always an integer multiple of 2π. Now we find a similar thing for closed surfaces in three-dimensional space. All that arbitrary denting and bending and all those excess angles must somehow combine to give exactly and precisely an integer multiple of 4π. That seems almost miraculous. You would have thought it possible to change the total curvature of a surface a little bit by making a small change to the surface. But no; in changing the total curvature of a closed surface you must change it by a multiple of 4π or not at all.

Exercises for Section 5.3

1. Show how to divide a cone into two pieces, neither of which has any curvature. [A]

2. Consider a surface with a "knotted handle" (figure 5.26). How does adding a knotted handle change the total curvature of a surface? [HA]

3. Take a plane and push a dent into it. Since this dent is just a topological deformation, the total curvature is still zero. That means there must

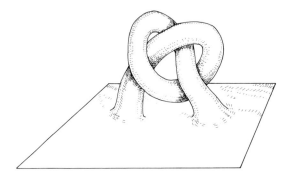

Figure 5.26
Knotted handle on a flat square.

be places of both positive and negative curvature density. Where is k positive? Negative? Zero? When is k a maximum? A minimum? [A]

4. In subsection 5.3.3 we computed k for a torus by making the torus out of two cylinders. But couldn't we have done the same thing by making a torus out of one cylinder? [A]

5. [D] Justify the following recipe for measuring curvature concentrated along an arc: Take two turtles, one on each side of the arc, and have each turtle measure the total turning along the arc from its side. Show that the difference between the two measurements is equal to the curvature concentrated in a small strip around the arc. (How do you decide which turtle's measurement to subtract from which?) [HA]

6. [D] The discussion in subsection 5.3.2 shows that, strictly, the excess additivity theorem of 5.1.4 is false because it doesn't allow for the possibility of concentrated curvature. But, remarkably, the proof of the theorem is not at fault. The proof is true, but the theorem is false! Find the part of the proof that needs to become a condition stated in the theorem, and formulate that condition carefully. [HA]

7. The surface shown in figure 5.27 is formed by placing a smaller cube on top of a larger one. What is the total curvature? How much is at each vertex? [A]

8. [D] Must any torus have at least one point where the curvature density is zero? [A]

9. In section 3.3 we showed by cutting and pasting that

(sphere) — (2 disks) + (handle) = torus.

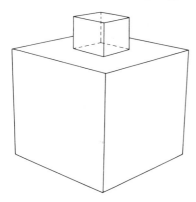

Figure 5.27
Double cube.

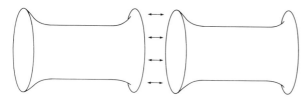

Figure 5.28
Pasting two flanged handles together.

Find another cutting-and-pasting construction that demonstrates that

(2 spheres) — (2 disks) + (handle) = sphere,

and use this equation to compute the total curvature of a handle. [A]

10. Two flanged handles are pasted together as shown in figure 5.28. What is the total curvature? How much is concentrated along the circle where the handles are joined? [HA]

11. Look at some familiar objects and consider their topology and curvature. For example, your hand. Your wrist has an equatorlike turtle path of excess 2π. That must be the total curvature of the topological disk contained (your hand). Can you imagine deforming the surface of your hand to a disk? Each of your fingertips looks much like a hemisphere (has 2π total curvature). Where is the $-4 \times 2\pi = -8\pi$ curvature to balance out the $5 \times 2\pi$ on the fingertips and give the net 2π curvature measured from the wrist? Isn't this a nice way to show that if you have n fingers, you must have $n - 1$ spaces between them?

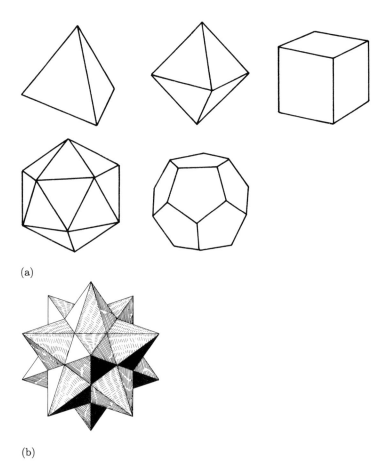

(a)

(b)

Figure 5.29
(a) The five Platonic solids: tetrahedron, octahedron, cube, icosahedron, and dodecahedron. (b) The starlike dodecahedron, a rectangular solid with faces which are
five-pointed stars (with a point protruding through the central pentagon).

12. [DD] Show that any closed surface in three-dimensional space must
have a place where the curvature density is positive. [HA]

13. [D] Suppose you have a closed surface in three-dimensional space
that has non-negative curvature density at every point. Using the result
of exercise 12, show that the surface is topologically equivalent to a
sphere. [HA]

14. [D] A Platonic solid is any object that is flat almost everywhere
and otherwise is as "regular" as can be. That means its surface is made

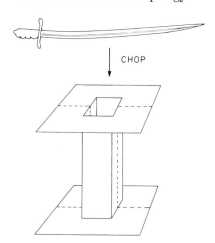

Figure 5.30
Chopping a handle into two bent-up rectangles.

up of a number of faces which are all identical regular polygons pasted together. Each vertex of the solid is also identical to any other (has the same number of faces adjoining). Use the result of exercises 12 and 13 to deduce that any Platonic solid must be topologically equivalent to a sphere. Now, using the fact that you know the total curvature, show that there can be no more than five Platonic solids. (There are in fact exactly five: tetrahedron, octahedron, cube, icosahedron, and dodecahedron. See figure 5.29a.) [H]

15. [D] After doing exercise 14, look at the object shown in figure 5.29b, the "starlike dodecahedron" discovered by Johannes Kepler. It can be viewed as a regular solid with twelve faces, each of which is a five-pointed star. The faces meet at twelve vertices, five faces meeting at a vertex. Shouldn't this count as a Platonic solid? Now go over your proof that there can be no more than five Platonic solids. What assumptions did you make that will disallow the starlike dodecahedron? [HA]

16. Compute the total curvature of the basic flange (handle) by dividing it into two bent-up rectangles and measuring the excess in each rectangle (figure 5.30). You can compute the turning for the parts of the square on the flange edges by remembering that that part is supposed to be "planelike."

17. What is the total curvature of the "square with handle" shown in figure 5.12? [A]

6

Exploring the Cube

Of course, in one sense mathematics is a branch of
knowledge—but still it is also an *activity*.
Ludwig Wittgenstein

We learned a great deal in chapter 5 about the geometry of surfaces in
general, but that is not at all to say that we know a great deal about the
geometry of any particular surface. This chapter and the following one
are meant to open up two worlds whose geometries are as interesting and
mathematically rich as plane geometry. The fact that these geometries
are much less well known than plane geometry makes them ideal areas
for your exploration.

Take on the role of explorer. Be daring but patient, look for interesting phenomena, and try to make useful definitions and ask interesting questions. (One deep question is worth more than many shallow
answers.) Formulate guesses and maybe some theorems. Can you prove
your theorems? Can you find useful new ways to look at these worlds?
Take your time; a good exploration is probably weeks long, even if you
concentrate on some small aspect of these geometries. Take a friend or a
group of friends along. Sharing ideas and explaining your special way of
understanding something or your method for accomplishing something
are as valuable as uncovering any particular "mathematical truth."

The next two chapters have a common format. We start with an
introduction to the geometric world. The first main section of the
chapter will give you some help in building a computer simulation,
which is perhaps the best tool for basic "brute force" experimentation.
The next section contains observations, questions, and suggestions for
problems to solve. Finally, we include a few answers and proofs. (Use
the last two sections sparingly. We have provided them only to help
out should your imagination get tired, or to show you other perspectives
once you think your own exploration is finished.)

Figure 6.1 shows the surface of a cube. As you can see, it is a
symmetrical surface. Topologically it is a sphere, but it is flat almost
everywhere. All the curvature is concentrated in the eight vertices. In
particular, no curvature is concentrated along any edge. To a turtle
walking on the cube, crossing an edge causes no difficulty whatsoever.
In fact, a two-dimensional turtle living in the cube's surface will not be

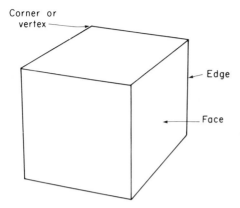

Figure 6.1
A cube.

able to tell an edge from the middle of any face. To convince yourself
of this, remember that the turtle can only feel distances *within* its
two-dimensional world, and observe that a piece of surface does not
need to change shape in crossing an edge. Figure 6.2a shows how an
unstretchable "rug" can slide over an edge without being deformed
(changing distances). The edge is therefore no different intrinsically
from the flat part of a cube. Compare this with trying to push an
unstretchable rug around on a football, or over a vertex of the cube. Or
think of an edge as being a quarter of a very small cylinder, which has
no curvature (figure 6.2b). (Look back to the sections in chapter 5 on
cones and cylinders if you still think an edge should have curvature.)

So crossing an edge is no problem for a turtle. Convince yourself in
any way you can that a straight turtle path will continue on the other
side of an edge in such a way as to preserve the angle of intersection with
the edge, as shown in figure 6.2c. It is a good exercise to see how many
ways you can justify this equal-angle edge-crossing rule as the "right"
way for a turtle to cross an edge.

What happens to a turtle path that runs into a cube vertex? Unlike
edges, vertices have concentrated curvature, which makes it a bit difficult
to imagine equal-strided turtle walks through them. For example, parallel turtle paths through points close to the vertex can go off in very
different directions. This suggests that there really may be no good
choice for how a turtle path should continue after hitting a vertex.
Perhaps the path should continue in a random direction, or even disappear into oblivion. We will leave this for your consideration. Note that,
from the point of view of a cube-walking turtle, this issue is a minor

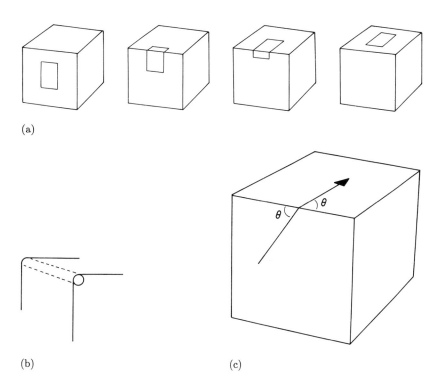

Figure 6.2
(a) A sliding unstretchable "rug." (b) An edge as a quarter of a small cylinder. (c)
The equal-angle edge-crossing rule.

one. Running into a particular point like a vertex is such an unlikely
thing that you may well choose to ignore the possibility entirely.

What kinds of tools should you have to explore a cube? Naturally your
imagination is most important, but having a real cube is a big help. A
model cube big enough to draw on yet small enough to hold in your hand
would be ideal. Pencil and paper are good tools, too, especially if you
do to a cube what we did to the cone in subsection 5.2.4: cut it up and
lay it flat, as in figure 6.3. But probably the most useful tool would be
a computer simulation of a cube with a turtle wandering around on its
surface. The following section gives some abbreviated but useful advice
for writing such a program. Read it even if someone else has written
a cube program for you to use. There are some important messages in
teaching a computer to walk a turtle on a cube. In particular, we will
take the time to discuss some of the design principles we used in earlier
projects but didn't mention explicitly.

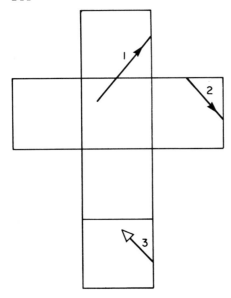

Figure 6.3
A cut-up, flattened cube, showing part of a turtle line.

6.1 A Computer Cube

Developing a computer cube is a large project, and it is best to start
out by dividing the task into parts. We'll follow the same strategy
that we used in chapter 3 when we implemented a three-dimensional
turtle. First, we'll forget about drawing things on a display screen and
concentrate on describing the state of a turtle walking on the cube. The
next step is to specify how this state is changed by the state-change
operators FORWARD and LEFT. The main problem here will be to figure
out how to determine when and where the turtle crosses an edge. Finally,
we'll worry about how to go from this internal representation to pictures
on a display screen.

6.1.1 Internal Representation

In writing a program to simulate a cube-bound turtle perhaps the most
important question is: How should the computer program represent the
cube? Though the kind of representation we're after is one that is good
for the computer and not necessarily good for you (in thinking about
cube problems), the representation we propose will turn out to be very
good for conceptualizing the cube's geometry.

You might think that the simplest and most natural way to make a computer cube is to start with a three-dimensional turtle and in some way constrain it to the surface of the cube. But this method is clearly not intrinsic; all of three-dimensional space is not relevant to the geometry on a cube. And on reflection there are some difficulties. How do we embody the constraints that restrict the turtle to the cube's surface? In particular, the rotation of the turtle in crossing an edge at an oblique angle is not a simple roll, pitch, or yaw. These are not grave difficulties, but they encourage us to look for alternative representations.

Let's go back to secure ground. One thing our computer certainly knows about is planar turtle geometry; it already knows everything about walking and turning in a plane. But except for the vertices, a turtle on a cube *is* always in one plane or another. So why not pretend the turtle always stays in the same plane, even inside the same square? Then we will just have to keep track separately of what face the turtle actually is on. Think of it this way: We are looking through a window at the cube (figure 6.4a). The frame of the window coincides with the front face of the cube. A turtle walks on the front face. When it hits the edge of the cube we just rotate the cube till the new face appears in the window.

Crossing an edge amounts to just moving the turtle (parallel to an edge) to the opposite edge of the window and remembering that we've rotated the cube. (The process of sliding the turtle across the window upon edge crossing is called *wrapping*. Standard computer display systems often do this kind of "wraparound" automatically.) There is no need to worry about changing planes at all; that is automatically taken care of merely by realizing we're on a new face. We also have a bonus: In figuring out when the turtle changes faces, we have to check for crossing only four edges (the window edges) rather than all 12 different edges of the cube.

So a large part of the state of a turtle on a cube will be summarized by two-dimensional position and heading "window coordinates" that describe the turtle relative to the current face. If the turtle never crossed any edges, then these window coordinates would be all we'd ever need to worry about.

How should we keep track in the computer of what face the turtle is on? More important, notice that we need to know more than just which face we're on, because a face can fit into the window in four different ways. Consider the path shown in figure 6.4b: The turtle can go up

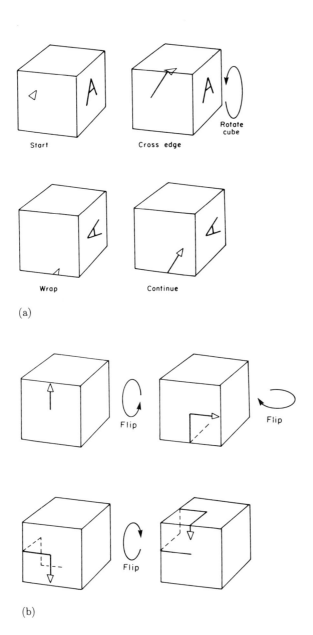

Figure 6.4
(a) Walking on a cube—the window picture. (b) A trip that leaves the turtle at the top of the window, but at the side of the first face.

across an edge, then right 90°, forward across another edge, and finally right 90° again and across a third edge, to come back to the top of the window, but the side of the first face. So what we really need is to keep track of the whole "rotational state of the cube" behind the window, not just which face is in the window frame.

Here is a good scheme for keeping track of the cube's rotational state: Create a variable, or slot, for each place a face can occupy, FRONT, BACK, TOP, BOTTOM, RIGHTSIDE, and LEFTSIDE. Now slip into each of those slots the names of the initial faces that occupy them:

```
FRONT ← "INITIAL.FRONT"
BACK ← "INITIAL.BACK"
         .
         .
         .
```

Whenever the turtle crosses a window edge, we merely shuffle the contents of the slots in the way dictated by the particular edge crossed. For example, in crossing the top edge, the face that was in the top slot gets flipped down into the front position, the back face becomes the new top, the bottom becomes the back, and the front face ends up on the bottom. We can accomplish this by the following sequence of instructions:

```
TEMP ← FRONT
FRONT ← TOP
TOP ← BACK
BACK ← BOTTOM
BOTTOM ← TEMP
```

(The extra TEMP slot is needed to fix the standard "shuffle bug" that always appears when we reorder variables. Compare with the YAW, PITCH, and ROLL procedures in 3.4.3.) Notice that the face in the window is always in the FRONT slot.

This may be the first time you have encountered this kind of symbolic encoding of mathematical information, and it may take a while for you to get comfortable with it. Right now you should make sure you believe that all the information is there; given the current state of the FRONT, TOP, and the other variables and the heading and position of the turtle in the window, one does indeed know the position and heading on the cube.

Another way to keep track of the rotational state of the cube is to shuffle not faces, but vertices. If we label the cube's eight vertices as

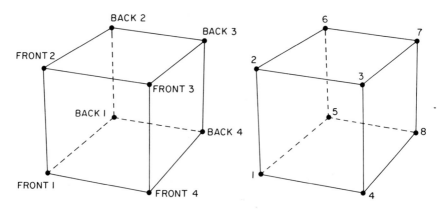

Figure 6.5
(a) Labeling vertices. (b) Numbering vertices.

shown in figure 6.5a, then flipping the cube when the turtle crosses the
top edge of the window corresponds to

```
TEMP ← FRONT1
FRONT1 ← FRONT2
FRONT2 ← BACK2
BACK2 ← BACK1
BACK1 ← TEMP
TEMP ← FRONT4
FRONT4 ← FRONT3
FRONT3 ← BACK3
BACK3 ← BACK4
BACK4 ← TEMP
```

When we consider the problem of drawing the cube on the display
screen, we will see that shuffling vertices turns out to be more convenient
than shuffling faces. Shuffling edges is another possible method, but we'll
stick with vertices in implementing the cube program. (Chapter 8 will
discuss another program, which uses the face-shuffling method.)

6.1.2 Permutations

Shuffling things around in slots is a standard mathematical operation
called a *permutation*. The above considerations show that the symmetry
rotations of the cube can be represented as permutations in several ways
(faces, edges, vertices). By numbering slots, we can represent a permuta-

tion simply as a list of numbers. For example, [2 6 7 3 1 5 8 4] is interpreted as

the contents of slot 2 get moved to slot 1,
the contents of slot 6 get moved to slot 2,
the contents of slot 7 get moved to slot 3,
the contents of slot 3 get moved to slot 4,
the contents of slot 1 get moved to slot 5,
the contents of slot 5 get moved to slot 6,
the contents of slot 8 get moved to slot 7,
the contents of slot 4 get moved to slot 8.

So if we number the vertices of the cube as shown in figure 6.5b, then crossing the top of the window permutes the vertices exactly as in this example. Similarly, crossing over the right edge of the window invokes the permutation [4 3 7 8 1 2 6 5]. As an exercise, write down the permutations corresponding to the left and bottom edges of the window.

To keep track of how the vertices get shuffled, assign a permutation to each of the four edges of the window corresponding to the flip made when the turtle crosses that edge. Then develop a procedure called SHUFFLE.VERTICES that takes as input the number of the edge crossed and shuffles the contents of the eight slots according to the appropriate permutation.

In net, the "coordinate system" we have chosen to represent turtle state on a cube has two parts: the window coordinates (position, heading), and a permutation (the shuffled vertices represent a net permutation of the initial configuration) that describes the rotational state of the cube behind the window. State-change operators change both parts of this state, and, in particular, one of four special permutations operates on the rotational state when an edge is crossed. Note that with this method we have avoided any reference to three-dimensional space.

6.1.3 Crossing Edges Using Dot Product

A problem that must be solved regardless of representation is this: How do we know when the turtle has crossed an edge of the cube? We have to check whether the line segment that is the turtle's intended path intersects any edge of the window. So let's consider the following general problem: Given two line segments in the plane (an "edge" and an "intended turtle path"), how can we tell whether they intersect and compute the point of intersection?

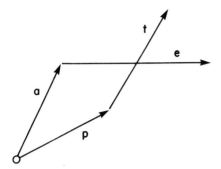

Figure 6.6
Two segments intersect.

As you might guess from our experience in chapter 3, vectors are a useful tool for solving this problem. Let **a** and **b** be vectors running from the origin to the endpoints of a given line segment. Then $\mathbf{e} = \mathbf{b} - \mathbf{a}$ is the vector running from **a** to **b**, and the line segment itself is the set of points represented by $\mathbf{a} + \lambda\mathbf{e}$ where λ (a number between 0 and 1) specifies the fraction of the way from **a** along **e** the particular point is. In our application, **a** and **b** will be the endpoints of an edge of the window, and **e** the edge vector itself. Similarly, if the turtle's path is the vector **t** running from **p** to **q** (that is, if $\mathbf{t} = \mathbf{p} - \mathbf{q}$) then the points on the path are given by $\mathbf{p} + \mu\mathbf{t}$ where μ is between 0 and 1 (figure 6.6).

Now, if the two segments intersect, this can be expressed by

$$\mathbf{a} + \lambda\mathbf{e} = \mathbf{p} + \mu\mathbf{t}. \tag{1}$$

What remains is merely to solve this equation for λ and μ and check that they are both between 0 and 1. (See exercise 4 of this section.) This looks like one equation with two unknowns, but think for a moment: The vector equation implies a numerical equation for each component. One could write out these two equations, but there is an even better way to obtain the solution, which goes along with the vector philosophy of using intrinsic descriptions and operations.

Algebraically speaking, we want to eliminate one of the unknowns, say λ, from equation 1. We can do that by looking at the component of the equation in the direction perpendicular to **e**. Since **e** itself has no such component, it and λ will both disappear from the equation. You can think of this operation as setting up coordinates parallel and perpendicular to **e** and looking at the perpendicular component. Projecting both sides of the vector equation onto a line perpendicular to **e** amounts to the same thing.

Dot product (subsection 3.5.2) and the Perp operation (subsection 3.2.2) are precisely the algebraic tools we need to carry out this projection easily. We take the dot product of Perp(**e**) with both sides of our intersection equation:

$$\text{Perp}(\mathbf{e}) \cdot (\mathbf{a} + \lambda\mathbf{e}) = \text{Perp}(\mathbf{e}) \cdot (\mathbf{p} + \mu\mathbf{t}).$$

Using linearity and the fact that $\text{Perp}(\mathbf{e}) \cdot \mathbf{e} = 0$ we can solve for μ:

$$\text{Perp}(\mathbf{e}) \cdot \mathbf{a} + \lambda\text{Perp}(\mathbf{e}) \cdot \mathbf{e} = \text{Perp}(\mathbf{e}) \cdot \mathbf{p} + \mu\text{Perp}(\mathbf{e}) \cdot \mathbf{t}$$

$$\text{Perp}(\mathbf{e}) \cdot \mathbf{a} = \text{Perp}(\mathbf{e}) \cdot \mathbf{p} + \mu\text{Perp}(\mathbf{e}) \cdot \mathbf{t}$$

$$\mu = \frac{\text{Perp}(\mathbf{e}) \cdot (\mathbf{a} - \mathbf{p})}{\text{Perp}(\mathbf{e}) \cdot \mathbf{t}}. \tag{2}$$

Because of the symmetry in the intersection problem we can solve for λ by interchanging **a** with **p** and **e** with **t**:

$$\lambda = \frac{\text{Perp}(\mathbf{t}) \cdot (\mathbf{p} - \mathbf{a})}{\text{Perp}(\mathbf{t}) \cdot \mathbf{e}}. \tag{3}$$

Equations 2 and 3 give a quick and simple way to solve for λ and μ. If both are between 0 and 1, an intersection has occurred at the point $\mathbf{p} + \mu\mathbf{t}$ (or $\mathbf{a} + \lambda\mathbf{e}$, which is the same).

We can implement these formulas in a computer procedure called CHECK.EDGE, which takes as inputs the two endpoints of a window edge and the two endpoints of the turtle's path (each of these points should be expressed as a vector):

```
TO CHECK.EDGE (EDGE.START, EDGE.END, TURTLE.START, TURTLE.END)
    P ← TURTLE.START
    A ← EDGE.START
    E ← EDGE.END - A
    T ← TURTLE.END - P
    MU ← DOT(PERP(E), A - P) / DOT(PERP(E), T)
    LAMBDA ← DOT(PERP(T), P - A) / DOT(PERP(T), E)
    IF BOTH (BETWEEN(MU, 0, 1), BETWEEN (LAMBDA, 0, 1))
        THEN
            INTERSECTION ← P + MU * T
            FRACTION ← MU
            RESULT ← "INTERSECTION FOUND"
        ELSE RESULT ← "NO INTERSECTION"
```

The procedure checks whether the turtle's path intersects the edge, and sets a variable called RESULT to indicate whether or not an intersection occurred. If there is an intersection the procedure sets variables that give the point of intersection and the number μ, which specifies the fraction of the turtle path that was traversed before the intersection occurred (see exercise 1). This procedure uses the PERP subprocedure, as given in subsection 3.2.2, and also a procedure that takes two vectors as inputs and outputs the dot product:

```
TO DOT ([VX VY], [WX WY])
   RETURN (VX * WX) + (VY * WY)
```

In addition, a simple BETWEEN subprocedure is used to tell whether a number lies within a specified range.

The complete solution to the edge-crossing problem can now be given by a procedure called CHECK.INTERSECTIONS, which takes as inputs the turtle's current position and the endpoint of the path:

```
TO CHECK.INTERSECTIONS (POSITION, END.POINT)
   REPEAT FOR I = 1 TO 4
      CHECK.EDGE (EDGE.START(I), EDGE.END(I), POSITION,
                  END.POINT )
      IF RESULT = "INTERSECTION FOUND"
         THEN
               EDGE.HIT ← I
               RETURN
```

This procedure uses CHECK.EDGE to see whether the path crosses any of the edges. After the procedure is run the variables RESULT, INTERSECTION, and FRACTION can be examined by other procedures to determine whether an intersection occurred, and, if so, where. Also, the variable EDGE.HIT specifies which edge was intersected. (In order for this CHECK.INTERSEC-TIONS procedure to work, you need to supply subprocedures EDGE.START and EDGE.END that output the endpoints of the appropriate window edges.)

Note that the RETURN statement in the last line prevents the CHECK.IN-TERSECTIONS procedure from going on to try the next edge if an intersection is found before the last time through the loop.

6.1.4 Implementing the State-Change Operators

Now that we know how to tell if the turtle crosses an edge of the window, let's get on to the problem of moving around generally on the cube. This entails specifying the state-change operators FORWARD and LEFT (and their "opposites" BACK and RIGHT) with respect to the internal representation (the window position and heading and the permutation).

We must say how each state-change operator modifies these quantities. Turning the turtle with LEFT and RIGHT is a simple operation—just let the heading change as usual.

To implement FORWARD, start by letting **p** be the position of the turtle in the window. If the turtle is to go a distance D, first try the full distance, ending at **q**. Now we need to know whether **q** is inside or outside the window. This can be done with the CHECK.INTERSECTIONS procedure above. If there is no intersection with any of the edges, then we're done; the turtle's end position is **q**. If there is an intersection, then INTERSECTION $= \mathbf{p} + \mu\mathbf{t}$ tells where to go on the current face, and FRACTION $= \mu$ determines how far the turtle needs to go on the new face: $D_{\text{new}} = (1 - \mu)D$.

More explicitly, here's what to do when there is an intersection:

Step 1 Move the turtle from the current window position **p** to the intersection point $\mathbf{p} + \mu\mathbf{t}$. (If we're drawing the turtle's path on the display, we should also draw a line between the corresponding points on the display screen. We'll discuss how to do this in subsection 6.1.5.)

Step 2 Wrap the turtle across the window to the opposite edge. Algebraically, this entails adding or subtracting the length of the window edge from the turtle's x or y coordinate. (This part of the path doesn't get drawn, of course.)

Step 3 "Rotate" the cube by shuffling vertices according to the permutation associated with EDGE.HIT, the window edge that the turtle crossed.

Step 4 Now go back and repeat the entire FORWARD process with the turtle starting out from the window position computed in step 2, and going forward a distance $(1 - \mu)D$.

6.1.5 Displaying the Cube; Capitalizing on Linearity

We have left for last the problem of displaying the lines drawn by the turtle on our cube. The problem may seem difficult because of our decision to represent a position on the cube by x and y "window" coordinates together with the rotational state of the cube, which is remembered as a permutation of vertices. Wouldn't it have been easier to use three-dimensional vectors all along, so that the display could proceed using the projection procedures of chapter 3? Surprisingly, despite our peculiar internal representation, display will not be hard—and as a bonus we'll get another look at the power of linearity.

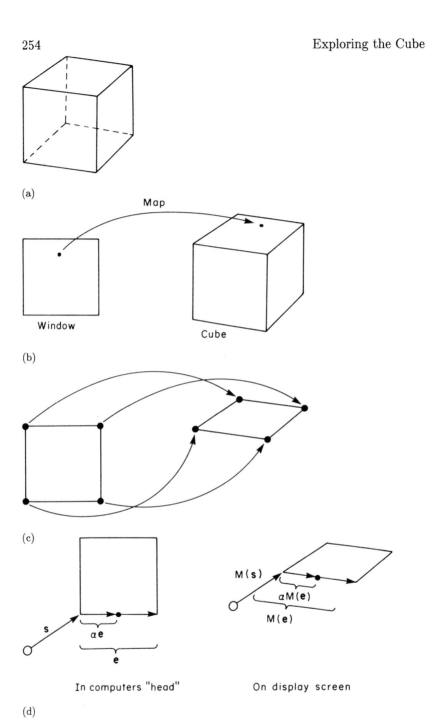

(a)

(b)

(c)

(d)

Figure 6.7
(a) Cube on a display screen. (b) The map from window to display. (c) Vertices are
mapped to vertices. (d) Mapping along an edge is easy.

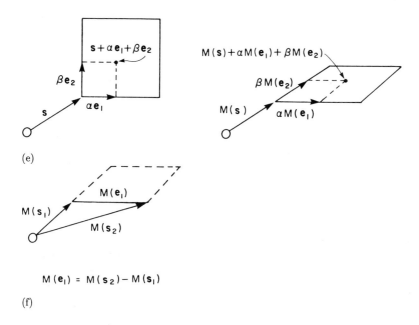

(e)

$$M(e_1) = M(s_2) - M(s_1)$$

(f)

Figure 6.7 (cont.)
(e) Linearity! (f) Edges are the differences between vertices.

Imagine you have the cube drawn on the display in the usual perspective way, with parallel edges drawn parallel on the screen as shown in figure 6.7a. Now assume that the cube-simulation program knows where the turtle is in the window frame and which permutation describes the cube. The problem is to map (translate) the position on the window to the appropriate point on the display cube, as shown in figure 6.7b.

Notice that this mapping is from a plane (the window) to a plane (display screen). There is no hint of three dimensions as with the projection in chapter 3. What else do we know about that mapping? Certainly vertices get mapped into vertices (figure 6.7c). And if you're α percent of the way from one vertex to another in the window, it is reasonable (and true) that you should be α percent of the way on the display cube as well. In vectors, if you are at $\mathbf{s} + \alpha\mathbf{e}$, where $\mathbf{s}$ points to the start of the window edge and $\mathbf{e}$ is the window edge vector, and if $M(\mathbf{s})$ and $M(\mathbf{e})$ stand for the "mapped" vectors on the display screen (figure 6.7d), then $\mathbf{s} + \alpha\mathbf{e}$ is mapped into $M(\mathbf{s}) + \alpha M(\mathbf{e})$, or

$$M(\mathbf{s} + \alpha\mathbf{e}) = M(\mathbf{s}) + \alpha M(\mathbf{e}).$$

Even better, if the turtle is in the interior of the window at some point $s + \alpha e_1 + \beta e_2$ (figure 6.7e) then the corresponding point on the display screen is

$$M(s + \alpha e_1 + \beta e_2) = M(s) + \alpha M(e_1) + \beta M(e_2). \tag{4}$$

In other words, the mapping M from window coordinates to display screen is a linear mapping. Consequently, the components αe_1 and βe_2 can be mapped independently and then added. To apply this formula we must know the mapped positions of the vertices, $M(s)$, and the mapped edges $M(e_1)$ and $M(e_2)$. (In fact, knowing just the vertices is enough, because the edges can be determined as the vector differences of the vertices, as shown in figure 6.7f.) Can our internal representation tell us those vertices? Yes. Suppose that what gets shuffled around in the vertex slots are the (x, y) coordinates *on the display screen* of the appropriate vertex, that is, each $M(s)$ in x and y coordinates. Then the mapped vertex positions that we need will be found precisely in the slots FRONT1, FRONT2, FRONT3, and FRONT4 (or in slots 1 through 4 if we use slot numbers rather than slot names). This is why we chose to shuffle vertices in constructing the representation of the cube in 6.1.1.

You might as well simplify things by setting up the window coordinates so that $(0, 0)$ corresponds to the bottom left corner of the window. That way α and β are just the window x and y coordinates divided by the length of the window edge. We have thus reduced the problem of locating display points to terms that appear in the representation: window coordinates (x, y) and the vectors contained in the vertex slots FRONT1 through FRONT4, each of which represents a vertex position on the display. As a vector equation we have

$$\text{DISPLAY} = \text{FRONT1} + \alpha(\text{FRONT4} - \text{FRONT1}) \\ + \beta(\text{FRONT2} - \text{FRONT1}). \tag{5}$$

We can implement this formula in a procedure that takes as input a vector whose components are the (x, y) window coordinates of a point, and outputs (in vector form) the coordinates of the corresponding point on the display screen:

```
TO DISPLAY.COORDS [X Y]
   EDGE1 ← FRONT4 - FRONT1
   EDGE2 ← FRONT2 - FRONT1
   ALPHA ← X / LENGTH (EDGE1)
   BETA ← Y / LENGTH (EDGE2)
   RETURN FRONT1 + (ALPHA * EDGE1) + (BETA * EDGE2)
```

6.1.6 Summary Outline of the Cube Program

Step 1 Draw your display representation of a cube, making sure to keep parallel cube edges parallel on the display. Store the display x and y coordinates of each vertex in the appropriate variable slot FRONT1,..., FRONT4, BACK1,..., BACK4.

Step 2 Use equations 2 and 3 and the procedure given in subsection 6.1.4 to walk a turtle around on the cube, making all computations with respect to the internal representation.

Step 3 Use formula 5 to find the position of the turtle on the display screen.

We can combine steps 2 and 3 into a single FORWARD procedure. (We assume below that heading is kept as a vector.)

```
TO FORWARD DIST
   ENDPOINT ← POSITION + DIST*HEADING
   CHECK.INTERSECTIONS (POSITION, ENDPOINT)
   IF RESULT = "NO INTERSECTION"
      THEN FORWARD.WITHIN.FACE (ENDPOINT)
      ELSE FORWARD.ACROSS.EDGE
```

The FORWARD procedure uses CHECK.INTERSECTIONS (6.1.3) to determine whether the turtle's path intersects any edge of the window. If not, it simply moves the turtle to the point on the screen that corresponds to the endpoint of the path and resets the turtle's current position to this new location:

```
TO FORWARD.WITHIN.FACE (NEW.POSITION)
   MOVE.TO (DISPLAY.COORDS (NEW.POSITION))
   POSITION ← NEW.POSITION
```

(This procedure uses a simple MOVE.TO subprocedure, which places the turtle at the appropriate point on the screen and draws a line from the current position if the pen is down.)

When the path does cross an edge we proceed as described in 6.1.4, first moving to the intersection point, then wrapping across the screen, shuffling the vertices, and going FORWARD the remaining distance:

```
TO FORWARD.ACROSS.EDGE
   FORWARD.WITHIN.FACE (INTERSECTION)
   POSITION ← WRAP (POSITION)
   SHUFFLE.VERTICES (EDGE.HIT)
   FORWARD (DIST * (1 - FRACTION))
```

All the rest—drawing the cube and turtle in perspective, maintaining a HEADING vector, providing and keeping track of a pen for drawing lines, and making dotted lines for lines drawn on the back of the cube—we leave to you.

Once you have a working cube, you may want to try some variations. For example, vary the display part of your cube so that it looks like figure 6.3. This should be very easy; all you need do is to permute the 14 vertices shown on that figure rather than the 8 in the perspective drawing. Do you find this display useful?

6.1.7 Comments on the Cube Program

The above discussion of the program was not just to help you write an efficient simulation. It brings out some essential points, both about mathematics and about programing.

Representations

Note how rich is the issue of selecting the computer's internal representation of the cube. In particular, the representation chosen above takes advantage of thinking of a cube as one face (with wrapping) together with a group of permutations. The permutations are easily handled, and the turtle motion on one face is also very simple. This has advantages over the obvious three-dimensional representation: We avoid three-dimensional rotations altogether. Heading changes only when a turtle turn command is given. In the "window representation" the method for display is carried out almost trivially because of linearity and the fact that vertices are chosen as permutation elements. Finally, the problem of checking whether a turtle segment crosses an edge entails examining only four fixed edges of the window rather than four of the twelve different edges of the cube. There is also a conceptual advantage in thinking of a cube in this way, one face and rotations. This may not be apparent yet, but in later sections of this chapter we will use this representation to demonstrate some remarkable facts about cube geometry. Beyond our particular concerns here, the general scheme of forgetting about the nonidentity of similar parts (for example, using one "window" instead of six faces of the cube) and keeping track separately

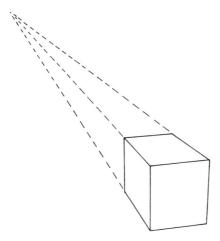

Figure 6.8
Cube in perspective, with vanishing point.

how the parts are shuffled is a potent mathematical technique. The "window picture," as we will call this representation, divides the state of the turtle into two parts: the window state and the rotational state. The remarkable observations to come arise out of the fact that these two parts of the state often change independently.

Linearity
Our method of displaying lines on the cube gives a good image of the meaning of linearity and of its power of simplification. The linear mapping from computer window to display screen allows us to map every point if we know only where the corners of the window are mapped. Even changing the map so that it is nonlinear by using a vanishing point to draw the cube in perspective (figure 6.8) is not a difficult perturbation of the linear case.

Intrinsic or Invariant Methods
Vectors provide an improvement over bare-bones analytic geometry by eliminating the need for coordinate systems, or at least leaving the choice of a coordinate system until near the end of the solution, when coordinates can be chosen in a more appropriate way than might be evident at the onset. Furthermore, vectors carry along meaningful entities, such as $\mathbf{e}$ =edge vector and λ =proportion of distance along edge, rather than just coordinate numbers, which depend as much on how you select coordinates as on the meaning of the quantities involved. Also, vectors

have operations, such as dot product, that support algebraic manipulations while retaining geometric meaning. Linking geometric with algebraic operations gives alternate and often helpful views. Finally, and this is not to be scorned, vector equations handle several component equations at once, and mean less writing and fewer chances for mistakes. (As an exercise, go back and do the edge-intersection problem using analytic geometry, without vectors.) In summary: Think geometrically, and compute with vectors.

Modular Planning

Notice that the three main problems we selected for study—internal representation, edge crossing, and display—were tackled independently. This kind of modular planning is an excellent heuristic method for undertaking any programing project. It is generally necessary in large, complex projects. Only after you have fleshed out the separate parts is it time to make decisions about interactions between the parts, such as choosing the internal coordinates to be Cartesian rather than polar to help with display considerations, or choosing to permute vertices rather than faces, or using vertex coordinates rather than vertex names. These interactions can often force you to modify your original plan, but interfacing the subplans is generally fairly easy, and in this case positively rewarding (for example, much of the display work can be done with the internal cube representation).

Modular Programing

The computer implementation of the program should reflect the modular plan. For example, designing the FORWARD command to operate in the internal representation, as in 6.2.4, means that the command can be used independently of the particular way of displaying the cube. Moreover, our presentation suggests some building blocks that can be used on the way toward the final cube program, such as a general method for handling permutations (exercises 1 and 2) and routines for dot products and vector arithmetic. Not only do these building blocks make implementation of the cube program easier by encouraging a modular approach, but they can also be useful in creating similar programs (see exercise 5). Finally, the fact that separate but meaningful programs such as CHECK.INTERSECTIONS are written independently means that these parts can be checked out by themselves before you run the main program, which improves the probability that the whole program will work and simplifies debugging if there is a problem.

Exercises for Section 6.1

The main exercise for this section is, naturally, to implement the turtle geometry cube as described above. The following questions suggest some extensions and variants of this project.

1. There is a bug in the CHECK.EDGE procedure of 6.1.3: We might attempt to divide by zero in computing λ and μ. What does this mean geometrically, and how should the procedure be modified to avoid the bug? [A]

2. [P] We have seen how crossing an edge leads to a shuffling of the variables FRONT1, FRONT2, etc. This shuffling can be realized as a sequence of assignment statements, as illustrated in 6.1.1. Writing down such a sequence is not much of a problem when there are only a few different permutations to keep track of. (There are only four to worry about in the cube program). But this method becomes cumbersome when one wants to shuffle things according to an arbitrary permutation. A better strategy would be to keep the things to be shuffled in a list and then reorder the list according to a given permutation. Write a SHUFFLE procedure that takes two inputs—a list of items and a permutation (represented as a list of numbers, as explained in 6.1.2)—and outputs the list of items reordered according to the permutation. (Beware of the "shuffle bug.")

3. [P] In keeping with exercise 2 you may wish to redesign the cube program so that, instead of variables FRONT1, FRONT2, etc., there is a single list, VERTICES, that contains the vertex coordinates. The procedure SHUFFLE.VERTICES can then reorder this list using the SHUFFLE procedure of exercise 2. Show how to rewrite the other pieces of the cube program to use the VERTICES list rather than the FRONT1, FRONT2, etc., variables.

4. [P] Suppose you take a normal POLY figure and collect the sides as vectors. If you draw the sides in sequence you'll obtain the POLY figure, of course. But suppose you first shuffle the sides according to some permutation. We'll call this a "permuted POLY." Write a procedure to draw permuted POLYs and study these figures. Do you see why they are closed?

5. We saw how solving for λ and μ using equations 2 and 3 of subsection 6.1.3 provided a way to determine whether two line segments intersect: The intersection occurs if and only if λ and μ are both between 0 and 1. What is the geometric interpretation of other values of λ and μ? For

example, what would it mean if you solved the equations and found that $\lambda = -1$ and $\mu = 4$? [A]

6. [P] Many of the techniques we developed for building a cube program carry over to a program to enable the turtle to crawl around on a regular tetrahedron. Describe the modifications to the cube program that will change it into a tetrahedron program. For example, what are the permutations corresponding to the three edges of the window?

6.2 Observations and Questions About Cubes

DO NOT READ THIS SECTION until you have played around a bit with geometry on the cube.

6.2.1 Monogons

There are no one-sided closed polygons in a plane. On the cube, however, monogons are a diverse and interesting class of figures. The simplest monogons may well be called "equators." As shown in figure 6.9a, there are at least two equators through most points on a cube. Find a third monogon through an arbitrary point on the cube. ("Arbitrary" excludes vertices, edges, and maybe the centers of faces, all of which are clearly not arbitrary.) Find all monogons through a given point. Notice that each of the equators in figure 6.9a lies in a plane. Is this true for all monogons? Classify monogons. What are good classification schemes? Prove that any example you have really is a monogon, rather than a path that just comes close to closing. The general monogon problem can be phrased like this: If the turtle starts out somewhere with some heading and walks straight, under what conditions will that eventually make a monogon? How does this depend on heading and starting point? Classify exceptions—for example, starting from nonrandom places on the cube.

In your search for monogons you will quickly discover a different kind of monogon: one that comes back to its original position but not its original heading, as shown in figure 6.9b. Such a monogon may be called an *irregular* monogon. What do you notice about the way irregular monogons close? Prove your conjecture. Note that a monogon cannot close with the turtle facing opposite to its initial heading (see figure 6.9c). Prove this.

An irregular monogon, if extended, may turn into a regular monogon with crossings (figure 6.9d). Such monogons are like star polygons, in

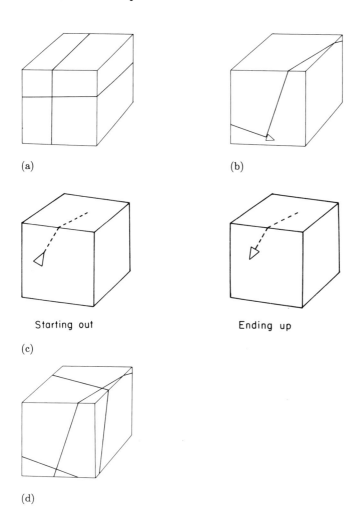

(a)

(b)

Starting out   Ending up

(c)

(d)

Figure 6.9
(a) Two equators through an arbitrary point. (b) An irregular monogon. (c) An impossible "reverse trip" monogon. (d) A starry monogon—figure (a) extended.

that they have crossings. We will call them "starry monogons." They should not be neglected in the search for regular monogons. Is there a longest regular monogon? Is there a longest nonstarry regular monogon?

In looking for regular monogons you may decide that any turtle walk, if extended far enough, will close, or at least come very close to closing. However, you should be able to find a line that you know will never close to form a regular monogon. Show also that any such nonclosing path must intersect itself. These two problems are not very difficult, but consider on the other hand the following conjecture: Every straight turtle line will, if extended far enough, come as close as you wish to its starting point, and may in fact close. In other words, if a turtle leaves a small spot at its starting point and walks straight away, it will always eventually run into the spot, no matter how small the spot is.

You may wish to catalog the lengths of regular monogons and look for surprising regularities.

6.2.2 POLY

The POLY program does interesting things on the cube. Play with it. For example, investigate "squares," that is, POLYs with 90° angles. Note that some squares become starry, which can't happen in a plane. How many sides do such squares have? Look for pretty or unusually symmetric or asymmetric squares. Can a square have two or three sides? How about five sides?

All POLYs that close in a plane also seem to close on the cube, only they may have a different number of sides. This is an excellent medium-hard theorem to try to prove. (Give it at least a week.) You may want to study general fixed instruction programs on the cube.

6.2.3 Other Gons

How about bigons? Are they interesting creatures? Or should one let bigons be bygones?

Can you find a right equilateral triangle, or a right equiangular non-equilateral triangle? What are the restrictions on the sum of interior angles of a triangle? You will find, in particular, triangles with 270° of interior angle. Can this 270° be distributed in any possible way among the three angles? In a plane the 180° of interior angle can be distributed arbitrarily, but this may not be true on a cube for non-180° triangles. Does the size of the triangle affect what shapes are allowed? On a plane, size doesn't matter—hence we have the usual theory of similar triangles ignoring size. (Perhaps in your studies you will want to omit starry triangles.)

Circles (that is, POLYs where both distance and angle are small) are good objects to study on a cube. Do circles have centers? How about the radius of a circle? Recall (section 1.1, exercise 2) that one can define a radius without reference to a circle's center as the radius of curvature, equal to the distance traveled divided by the angle turned. What values can the ratio of circumference to radius of curvature have on a cube?

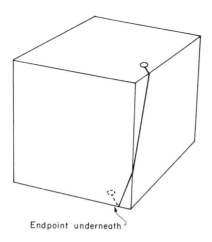

Endpoint underneath

Figure 6.10
A shortest distance.

6.2.4 Lines and Distance

How many turtle lines are there connecting any two points on the cube?
Are there exceptions to the general rule? Is one of those straight lines
guaranteed to be the path of shortest distance between the two points?
If you think you know an algorithm to find the path of shortest distance
between any two points, consider the example shown in figure 6.10.
Explore the analog of the Pythagorean theorem on the cube. Perhaps
you will want to start with equiangular right triangles.

6.2.5 More Projects

Can you formulate a maze problem on the cube, as in the discussion of
the Pledge algorithm in chapter 4? Will the Pledge algorithm itself work
on the cube? If not, is there a modification of the algorithm that will
work? If not, is there a modification of the maze problem that does have
a Pledge-type solution? Consider also the cube analogs of the theorems
on the topology of plane curves discussed in chapter 4.

   Try out the cubical versions of the random-walk procedures of section
2.1:

```
TO RANDOM.MOVE (D1, D2, A1, A2)
    REPEAT FOREVER
        LEFT RAND (A1, A2)
        FORWARD RAND (D1, D2)
```

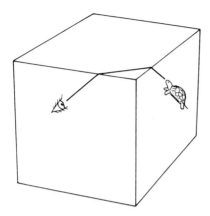

Figure 6.11
Line of sight on a cube.

After a long time (say, long enough so that the average distance traveled
is many times around an equator), is the turtle equally likely to be
anywhere on the cube, or it be more likely to find itself near a vertex (for
example) than near the center of a face? Can you devise an experiment
to find out? Can your prove your conjecture?

Is the program

```
TO LEAP
   SETHEADING RAND(0, 359)
   FORWARD 10000
```

a good approximation to a random walk? That is, do the points found
by LEAPing over and over from the same starting point seem to be
distributed over the cube like the endpoints of random walks? Note
that on a plane such a program would have all of its endpoints on a
circle. In fact, one might still think of the set of points reachable by
going FORWARD some fixed distance as a "circle." But to distinguish it
from a POLY circle (it is different on a cube), call it a *radial circle*. Is
there an interesting theory of radial circles as the radius varies from 0
to infinity? (Radial circles break up into many pieces as the radius gets
larger. The circumference of such a circle will have to be defined as the
sum of the lengths of the pieces.)

6.2.6 Things to Think About

One very foggy morning, the turtle looks out into the distance on the cube. The turtle can see only a distance of about one edge length, so the only vertices it sees are the four corners of the current face. (Never having decided what to do if it should run into a vertex, the turtle sees them as ominous black holes.) As the fog begins to lift and the turtle can see farther, it sees four more vertices, the remaining ones of the cube. (Remember, the turtle's universe is the surface of the cube, and even light rays travel on it. See figure 6.11.) The fog thins some more and turtle sees another set of four vertices dimly in the distance. Which vertices are these? Thinner and thinner fog brings more and more vertices! The turtle begins to wonder if, when the fog finally clears, there will be a vertex in every direction. Show that on a clear day when turtle can see forever, it will see an infinite number of vertices, and indeed will detect vertices in almost every direction; however, there will still remain directions in which there are no vertices. Also, between any two "vertex seeing" directions there will be a direction with no vertices (and vice versa).

DANGER—The next section contains "premade" (already discovered) mathematics. It may be harmful to your imagination and should be used only as a last resort. TURN THE PAGE AT YOUR OWN PERIL.

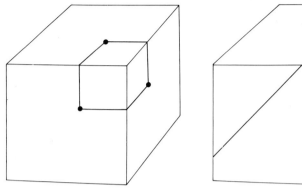

Equilateral right triangle and three-sided
square.

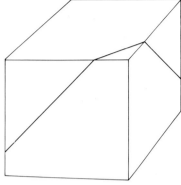

A 45° equator.

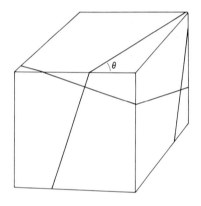

A short regular monogon, $\theta = \arctan 3$.

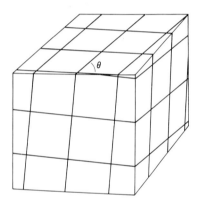

A longer regular monogon, $\theta = \arctan 11$.

Figure 6.12
Some interesting figures on the cube.

6.3 Results

Figure 6.12 gives some pictorial results. We invite you to study it.

6.3.1 The Monogon Problem

Theorem A turtle line can intersect itself only at right angles. Segments
of the same line that appear on a given face can have (window) heading
only θ, $\theta + 90°$, $\theta + 180°$, or $\theta + 270°$.

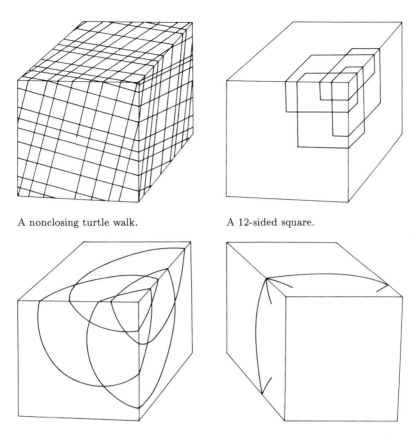

A nonclosing turtle walk.   A 12-sided square.

A POLY circle; FORWARD a bit, RIGHT a bit,... A radial circle, points equidistant from a
Circumference= $6\pi r$.   center. Circumference= $2\pi r$.

Figure 6.12 (cont.)

We give three different proofs of the first statement. The second statement follows easily from the first.

Excess method The cube's curvature is concentrated at its vertices; 4π
total curvature (remember, the cube is topologically a sphere) distributed
among eight identical vertices makes $\pi/2 = 90°$ at each vertex. Hence:
Observe the part of a turtle path between times when turtle is at the
point of the first self-intersection. There is no turtle turning, so any
change in heading must be trip turning (excess, that is, curvature contained within this closed circuit). But curvature comes in lumps of $90°$,
so the difference in heading must be a multiple of $90°$.

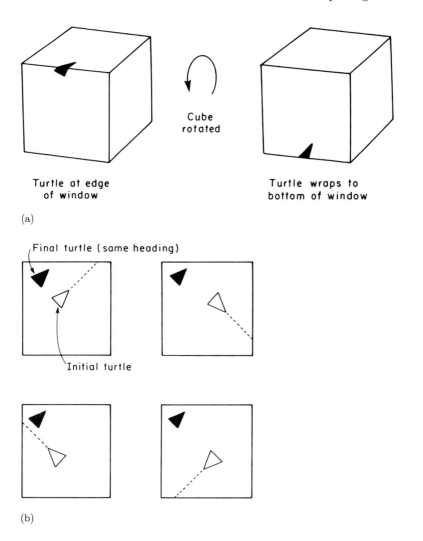

Figure 6.13
(a) Crossing an edge in the window picture. (b) A face can appear in the window in
four different ways.

Window method Recall the window method of imagining a turtle walk
on a cube, which was the basis for the computer's internal representation
of the cube in section 6.1. One always sees the turtle walking in a single
window with the rest of the cube behind. When the turtle reaches the
edge of the frame, the cube rotates behind the frame to keep the turtle
in the window (see figure 6.13a). In going forward without turning, the

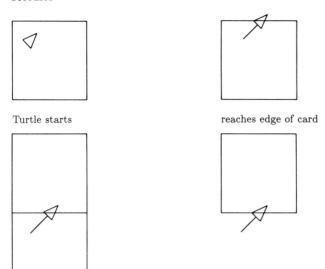

Turtle starts   reaches edge of card

next card laid down   First card picked up, showing ink mark
                                       underneath

Figure 6.14
The card picture.

turtle never changes its heading as seen in the window. So if the turtle ever returns to the starting face it will have the same window heading. But the actual face, which can fit into the window in four different ways, may have rotated underneath the turtle by some multiple of 90° from the initial state (see figure 6.13b). Thus, the relative heading from start to finish must be some multiple of 90°.

Card method This variant of the window view of cube walking adds its own insight to many cube problems. Imagine the faces of a cube as cards cut apart, but with edges labeled to show how they fit together. Lay down the starting face and start the turtle walking. Draw the turtle line with ink that penetrates to the table underneath the card. When turtle gets to the edge of the card, carefully lay down the new connecting card in the appropriate way. Now pick up the first card and continue. (See figure 6.14.) Clearly, the line on the table top will always keep the same heading. If the first card is ever laid down again it will be in one of four orientations, differing from the original by a multiple of 90°, and the continuation of the turtle line onto it will be at that multiple of 90° from the original heading of the turtle.

Notice that the translation from card picture to window picture merely involves having the window follow the current card, like a mobile TV camera.

It is impossible to define a heading on a cube in the usual 0°-to-360° way—at least, it is impossible if you want heading to change only when a RIGHT or a LEFT command is given. The impossibility is demonstrated by the existence of turtle lines that, because they do not have any turning, shouldn't change heading, but do cross themselves. But the above theorem says there *is* a sort of heading if you are willing to put up with 90° ambiguity: If your compass needle has four indistinguishable arms at 90° to each other, and four norths, then walking straight around on a cube will never change your heading. Examine the compass in figure 5.10. That may be an unconventional compass, but it's better than nothing.

6.3.2 Headings for Monogons

Theorem Any regular monogon must have a heading with a rational tangent.

Proof Look at the "card" picture of walking along a regular monogon from the starting point to the return to the starting point (figure 6.15a). If the path is to close regularly (that is, wind up with the same heading it started with), then the final card must be the same as the initial card and also must have the same orientation. From the figure, though, one sees that $\tan \theta = p/q$, which is a rational number. As a corollary, if $\tan \theta$ is irrational then the above picture cannot be achieved, and the turtle's path will never close.

A converse theorem If the tangent of the heading is rational, then the turtle line will close to form a regular monogon.

Partial proof If $\tan \theta = p/q$, the above card picture shows what happens in the first $\sqrt{p^2 + q^2}$ cardlengths of walking. But there is no guarantee that the card at the end of such a trek is the first card. To make progress we must change our view from the card method to the window method. Translating from the card method, we can see that in the window the turtle will appear at the initial position (and heading) after a trek of $\sqrt{p^2 + q^2}$ cardlengths. But each wrap has flipped the cube around, and

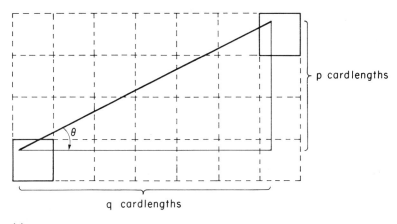

p cardlengths

θ

q cardlengths

(a)

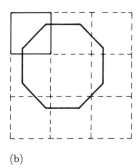

(b)

Figure 6.15
(a) A straight line in the card picture. (b) A POLY in the card picture.

the face now showing may not be the same as the first, or it might be the first but not in the correct orientation. To summarize: The turtle traveling along a heading that has a rational tangent will close its path as far as the window part of the position state is concerned, but may undergo a net cube rotation, causing the permutation part of the state to be different.

Now consider the net flip made by the cube behind the window. If the turtle continues walking for another $\sqrt{p^2 + q^2}$ distance, the cube will undergo the same flip again. And then again. And again. Is it possible that the cube can be flipped again and again in the same way and never return to its initial position? If the cube ever did return to the

initial position, that would make the turtle's path close. The possibility
that each of a whole infinite sequence of flips could fail to restore the
initial position of the cube is even more unlikely in view of the fact that
there are only 24 possible cube positions to choose from. A proof that
a sequence of identical rotations must eventually return the cube to its
initial rotation state is given in the next subsection.

6.3.3 POLYs and Other Looping Programs

Theorem Any turtle program that closes in the plane will close on a cube
(if repeated enough).

Proof Run any turtle program on a cube. Notice that the path drawn
on the table in the card view is just the path the program would draw
when run on a plane (figure 6.15b). So we see that a planar closing
program will draw a path in which the window part of the turtle's state
will come back to its initial state after a single run of the program.
Unfortunately, we have the same problem as with the monogons above:
The final card may not be the same one in the same orientation as the
first card. In other words, the cube may have rotated away from its
initial state behind the window.

The saving fact is that repeating the program over and over performs the
same rotation on the cube again and again. If the initial cube orientation
is eventually restored, then at this point the program will have closed
on the cube. So to finish the proof of the theorem, and of the theorem
in 6.3.2 we must prove the following lemma:

Lemma If a given symmetry rotation (the "net flip") is performed over
and over, the initial rotational state will eventually be restored.

You should recognize this as an example of a finite-state process, such as
encountered in subsection 4.4.3. But now we need a bit more information
than that the process winds up in a loop. We need to know that the
loop includes the initial state.

Proof The key idea is that the same rotation is applied over and over,
so if the cube ever finds itself in some given state twice, the sequence of
subsequent rotational states must be the same. Not only that, but the
preceding sequence must also be the same, because applying the inverse

rotation to a given state always does the same thing: It results in the same (previous) state. More precisely, imagine the sequence of states all laid out in a row:

$$S_1, S_2, S_3, S_4, \dots .$$

Each state is obtained from the preceding one by applying the same fixed "flip." Eventually some state must repeat, because there are only 24 to choose from. Hence, $S_n = S_{n+m}$ for some n and m:

$$S_1, \dots, S_{n-1}, S_n, S_{n+1}, \dots, S_{n+m-1}, S_{n+m}, S_{n+m+1}, \dots .$$

But now applying the inverse flip to $S_n = S_{n+m}$ shows that S_{n-1} must be the same as S_{n+m-1}:

$$S_1, \dots, S_{n-1}, S_n, S_{n+1}, \dots, S_{n+m-1}, S_{n+m}, S_{n+m+1}, \dots .$$

For the same reason, $S_{n-2} = S_{n+m-2}$. Sliding this equality of states to the left, one step at a time, we arrive quickly (in fewer than 24 steps) at $S_1 = S_{1+m}$.

You can easily show that $m < 24$. In fact, with a good deal of work you can show that $m < 4$ for any flip, and so we have the following:

A Truly Remarkable Theorem Any looping program that closes in the plane will close on the cube, but it may take as much as 4 times as long.

Find programs that close in 1, 2, 3, and 4 times their planar closing runs. Isn't it remarkable that the number 4 is associated with cubes in this way, rather than, say, 6 (the number of faces)?

In summary: Any program that closes in the plane will, when run once, return the turtle to the same window state, but may rotate the cube. However, repeating the program at most 3 more times will return the cube to its initial rotational state, and will thus return the turtle to the initial position. By the same reasoning, any turtle line with heading satisfying $\tan\theta = p/q$ (where p/q is a fraction in lowest terms) will form a regular monogon whose length is between $\sqrt{p^2 + q^2}$ and $4\sqrt{p^2 + q^2}$ times the sidelength of the cube. Notice that monogons with headings of θ_1 (where $\tan\theta_1 = 2$) and θ_2 (where $\tan\theta_2 = 2.000000001 = \frac{2000000001}{1000000000}$), which are very nearly the same angle, close in vastly different lengths.

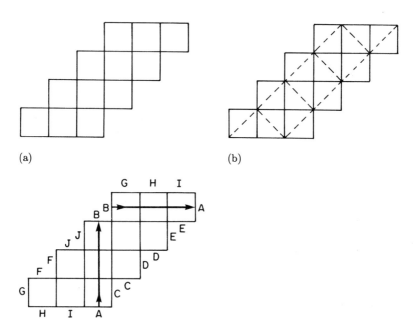

(a)   (b)

(c) Sides labeled the same get glued together.

Figure 6.16
Another dissection of the cube.

6.3.4 Another Representation

Notice that a cube can be cut up into cards in another way than that
shown in figure 6.3; it can be cut up as shown in figure 6.16a. Figure
6.16b shows how to fold this collection of cards into a cube by showing
some "usual" edges in dotted lines. In this representation it is clear that
edges are "flat." Figure 6.16c shows a 45° equator in this representation
of a cube. Does this make it easier to see that all 45° equators are the
same length? Did you discover that fact? (If you didn't, be sure to
measure the lengths of other monogons with the same cube heading.)

6.3.5 Another Representation Revisited

Suppose you happen to be an excellent billiards player—truly excellent,
so that you can cause the ball to bounce off the cushions many times and
return exactly to the same place. Of course you know that billiard balls
with no spin bounce according to an equal-angle law (see figure 6.17).
But now you want to know about cubes. Show how you can think of a
cube as a square billiards table together with some appropriate group of

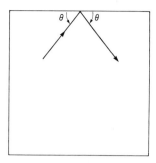

Figure 6.17
A perfect bounce on a square billiards table.

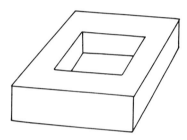

Figure 6.18
A rectangular torus.

permutation operations (name them). A turtle line will just be a bouncing billiard shot (the equivalent of a wrapping window) plus a change in the hidden part of state (the permutation) for each bounce. Explain this, and construct a regular monogon in this representation.

6.3.6 More Distance

Beyond the conjecture that all regular monogons with the same heading have the same length, distance on a cube can be the basis for a number of investigations. In general there are an infinite number of turtle lines between any two random points. (Are there exceptions to this when points are nonrandom, such as vertices or centers of faces?) It is true on a cube that one of those lines must be the path of shortest distance; but there are other surfaces, such as a rectangular torus (shown in figure 6.18), for which the shortest path between a pair of points need *not* be a single turtle line. (It is, however, a number of turtle segments glued together.) Can you give an example?

Finally, although the circumference of a POLY circle is not always $2\pi\rho$ (ρ =radius of curvature), the circumference of a radial circle (the points reached by a turtle walking a constant distance r in all directions from a given point) *is* always $2\pi r$.

6.4 Conclusion

We hope you have learned a lot about cubes, about representations, about geometry, about mathematical exploration. Don't judge your own results and insights by the results of the previous section. Those were end products of rough guesses and much searching for appropriate ways of looking at the cube. The hardest part of doing mathematics, and the real meat as well, is often hidden far beneath such a slick surface.

7

A Second Look at the Sphere

> Do not despair. Remember there is no triangle,
> however obtuse, but the circumference of some circle
> passes through its wretched vertices.
>
> Samuel Beckett, *Murphy*

We have already found out a great deal about geometry on the surface of a sphere, in chapter 5. But our concern there was to uncover facts about the sphere that would guide our exploration of arbitrary surfaces. Now is your chance to investigate carefully the peculiarities that make the sphere different from every other surface. Constructing a computer simulation of a sphere will be even easier than making one of a cube. The reason is that a sphere is "the same all over." In mathematical terminology, one says that the sphere is *homogeneous* (each point is just like every other point) and *isotropic* (at each point, every direction is just like every other direction).

Approaching the sphere fresh from turtle investigations of planes and cubes, we see that the salient feature of this new geometry is its curvature. Of course, the cube had curvature, too, but it was concentrated into eight identical vertices and hence easy to keep track of. The sphere, however, is everywhere curved, and, as we saw in chapter 5, the excess of a closed path is proportional to the enclosed area. So the total turning of a closed path depends on its size. Turning cannot be separated from going forward; the symmetry of a figure such as POLY(SIDE,ANGLE) depends on SIDE as well as ANGLE.

The theme of this chapter is that we can turn this complication to our advantage. We will find that not only are going forward and turning interrelated, but when viewed from the proper perspective they are absolutely identical. This natural symmetry between the basic turtle state-change operators FORWARD and LEFT will guide us in building the computer sphere as well as in exploring its geometry.

7.1 A Computer Simulation

Our design for a computer simulation of a turtle-geometric sphere adheres to the same two principles that proved so fruitful in our work with the cube. First, we'll separate the problem into modules, and, in particular, define the internal representation independent of concerns about drawing on the display screen. Second, we'll choose representations that, as much as possible, are intrinsic to the problem at hand.

7.1.1 Internal Representation

There does not seem to be any simple alternative to representing the sphere as part of three-dimensional space. (You are welcome to look for alternatives.) This means that our representation will not be entirely intrinsic. But we can at least use vectors to describe the situation, rather than jumping directly to Cartesian coordinates. We'll indicate the turtle's position by a vector $\mathbf{P}$ pointing from the center of the sphere to the current turtle position. In addition, we'll represent the heading as a vector $\mathbf{H}$ that points in the direction the turtle is currently facing (see figure 7.1a). Note that $\mathbf{H}$ is tangent to the sphere and therefore perpendicular to $\mathbf{P}$.

What is the FORWARD ("sphere forward") state-change operator in this representation? The key observation is that it is merely a *rotation* of $\mathbf{P}$ and $\mathbf{H}$ through some angle in the plane determined by those two vectors (see figure 7.1b and 7.1c). We can easily compute this rotation using the rotation formula of subsection 3.2.2:

$$\text{Rotate}(\mathbf{v}, A) = (\cos A) \times \mathbf{v} + (\sin A) \times \text{Perp}(\mathbf{v})$$

The vector $\mathbf{H}$ can serve as $\text{Perp}(\mathbf{P})$ if we select $\mathbf{H}$ to be the same length as $\mathbf{P}$. And then $-\mathbf{P}$ is $\text{Perp}(\mathbf{H})$. Therefore, we have in the plane determined by $\mathbf{P}$ and $\mathbf{H}$

$$\text{Rotate}(\mathbf{P}, A) = (\cos A)\mathbf{P} + (\sin A)\mathbf{H},$$
$$\text{Rotate}(\mathbf{H}, A) = (\cos A)\mathbf{H} - (\sin A)\mathbf{P}.$$

That's all; we are done with FORWARD.

What about RIGHT and LEFT? They just rotate $\mathbf{H}$ in the plane tangent to the sphere at $\mathbf{P}$ and leave $\mathbf{P}$ alone. Again, this is simple to compute if we can get our hands on $\text{Perp}(\mathbf{H})$. We do this in the same straightforward way in which we dealt with the three-dimensional turtle in section 3.4. Along with $\mathbf{P}$ and $\mathbf{H}$, include in the turtle's state a third vector $\mathbf{L}$ (for left), which is perpendicular to both $\mathbf{P}$ and $\mathbf{H}$. Then, in the plane determined by $\mathbf{H}$ and $\mathbf{L}$, $\mathbf{L}$ can serve as $\text{Perp}(\mathbf{H})$ and $-\mathbf{H}$ as $\text{Perp}(\mathbf{H})$. So in this plane we have

$$\text{Rotate}(\mathbf{H}, A) = (\cos A)\mathbf{H} + (\sin A)\mathbf{L},$$
$$\text{Rotate}(\mathbf{L}, A) = (\cos A)\mathbf{L} - (\sin A)\mathbf{H}.$$

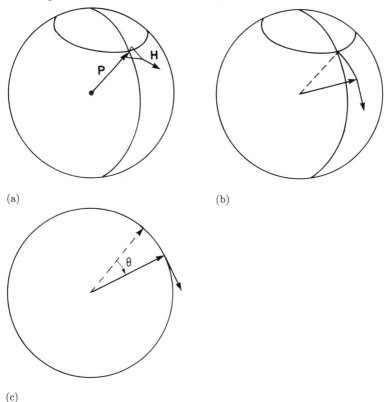

(a)   (b)

(c)

Figure 7.1
(a) Two perpendicular vectors **P** and **H** give position and heading for a turtle on a
sphere. (b) FORWARD in perspective. (c) FORWARD in the plane of the path. In (b) and
(c), going FORWARD corresponds to rotating **P** and **H** in the plane determined by these
two vectors.

Thus, the sphere simulation turns out to be the "turning" part of a
three-dimensional turtle (with different names attached to the rotation
commands).

In summary: The turtle's state is represented by three vectors **P**, **H**,
and **L**, which are initially set up to be mutually perpendicular and of
the same length. FORWARD is the operation

$$\mathbf{P} \leftarrow (\cos A)\mathbf{P} + (\sin A)\mathbf{H},$$
$$\mathbf{H} \leftarrow (\cos A)\mathbf{H} - (\sin A)\mathbf{P};$$

LEFT is the operation

$$\mathbf{H} \leftarrow (\cos A)\mathbf{H} + (\sin A)\mathbf{L},$$
$$\mathbf{L} \leftarrow (\cos A)\mathbf{L} - (\sin A)\mathbf{H}.$$

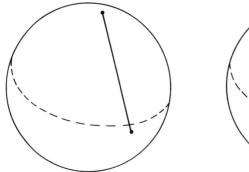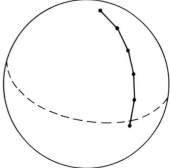

Figure 7.2
(a) The wrong way to draw a turtle path. (b) Breaking up the path into short
segments gives the right picture.

For computer implementation, see the rotation programs in subsection
3.4.3.

7.1.2 Display

With a three-dimensional position vector in hand, all we need do is
project onto a display plane. There seems little point in being fancy, so
we suggest simple parallel projection as described in subsection 3.5.1:

$$(\text{display}_x, \text{display}_y) = \text{Project}(\mathbf{P}) = (P_x, P_y).$$

We leave it up to you whether you want to display lines on the back side
of the sphere as dotted or in a separate projection, or whether you want
to invent some other display technique.

In drawing the turtle's path, there is one additional complication
that we didn't have to face in the cube simulation or with the three-
dimensional turtle. Straight turtle lines on a face of the cube and
in three-dimensional space will also *look* straight when drawn on the
display screen. But that's not true for the sphere. Suppose the turtle
goes FORWARD a large amount. Then rotation will compute the correct
new position, but you should not therefore indicate the turtle's path by
drawing a straight line on the display screen to join the old and new
positions as in figure 7.2a. Lines on the sphere should look curved when
projected onto the display screen. The easiest way to accomplish this is
to break up large FORWARDs into a sequence of small ones, as shown in
figure 7.2b. Each of the small steps can then be represented as a short
straight segment. (Increments of 5° or 10° will probably be short enough
to give a good picture.) If the pen is up, of course, you might as well
save computation time by having the turtle jump directly to the new
position.

7.1.3 Distances and Angles

Does it seem strange that our sphere simulation expresses FORWARD as
a rotation through an angle, the same as RIGHT or LEFT? You may
choose to make FORWARD take a distance as input rather than an angle,
but measuring distance in terms of angle has advantages. First, it is
an invariant measure of distance (invariant on moving to a sphere of
different size). Provided distance is measured as an angle, programs such
as POLY with fixed inputs will have the same behavior on a sphere of any
size. More important, it emphasizes that on a sphere FORWARD and LEFT
are the same kind of operation. They each rotate two of the turtle's state
vectors and leave the third fixed, so if you insist on measuring FORWARD
in units of, say, inches, give thought to measuring LEFT in inches also.

7.2 Exploring

One of the best heuristics in learning and problem solving applies in
exploring as well: Ask yourself "What do I know about similar things?"
How is a sphere like a plane or a cube? How is it different, and how do
those differences come about? In particular, a sphere is very much like
a plane when you're constrained within a small area or a narrow slice.
That observation has a lot of experimental and theoretical implications.
For example, every formula that applies on the sphere must approximate
the corresponding plane formula in an appropriately small domain. You
may wish to look carefully for such things.

One word of advice: In setting out to explore the sphere's geometry,
don't let your mathematical sight be clouded by too strong a fixation
on obtaining exact formulas. Of course, there are many exact formulas
to be discovered, but there are also many intriguing approximations and
qualitative results, which you won't want to miss. Be on the lookout.

7.2.1 POLY

An obvious area for turtle exploration on the sphere is the behavior of
the POLY program

```
TO SPHERE.POLY (α, β)
   REPEAT FOREVER
       FORWARD α
       LEFT β
```

Closure, symmetry, and all the other standard POLY results deserve your
attention. In some ways spherical POLYs and other fixed instruction

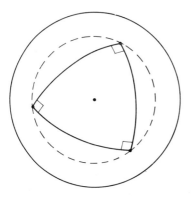

Figure 7.3
POLY(90,90) has threefold symmetry; $\theta = 120°$.

programs may be simpler than on a plane—for example, exceptional looping programs that march off to infinity on the plane cannot do so on a sphere. (What do they do?) In other ways, spherical POLYs may be much harder to understand.

A good way to get a handle on the general problem is to carefully examine one specific case—regular four-sided polygons, for example. Take experimental data on the set of α's and β's that produce such figures. Can you guess or derive a functional relationship between α and β? If not, can you find any qualitative features of such a relationship? Are there restricted domains where the relationship is simple? For a given value of α, is it possible that there are two different values of β that will both give four-sided figures? Or is the correspondence between α and β one-to-one? Are there "forbidden domains" (angles or distances that cannot have "squares" associated with them)? Now make a similar study for three-sided POLYs, or five-sided ones. What are the general phenomena for n-sided POLYs?

7.2.2 Symmetry Types

If you try a few POLYs you will observe that, just as the vertices of a POLY in the plane lie on a circle, so the vertices of a POLY on the sphere appear to lie on latitudelike paths, that is, on spherical circles. Can you prove this? Assuming it is true, note the special significance of the center of this circle. It is a point of the sphere that remains fixed as we rotate the sphere to produce a symmetry of the POLY. Figure 7.3, for example, shows how we can see a symmetry of POLY(90,90) by rotating the sphere about the center of the POLY circle. The amount of rotation needed for a symmetry (call it θ) relates directly to the order of the symmetry. Here POLY(90,90) has threefold symmetry, and $\theta = 120°$. This symmetry angle θ is a prime candidate for your investigation. Can you give a formula for θ in terms of the inputs α and β to the POLY program?

7.2.3 Circles

Notice that, on a sphere, constant-curvature circles (which are generated by POLY(α, β) with α and β both small) are the same as radial circles (points of fixed distance from a center), and that this is true in the plane but not true on the cube (see subsection 6.3.7). (Can you prove this?) But circles on the sphere differ from circles on the plane in that, on the plane, the radius of the circle, r, is related to the radius of curvature, $\rho = \alpha/\beta$, by $r = \rho$. What is the relationship between r and ρ on the sphere? Furthermore, the circumference of a circle is neither $2\pi r$ nor $2\pi\rho$; nor is the area πr^2 or $\pi\rho^2$. What are the correct formulas? (Hint: In investigating these relationships it is much easier initially to use r than ρ.)

What is the total turning of a spherical circle in terms of r or ρ? More qualitatively, is there a circle of greatest total turning? (On a cube the "truly remarkable theorem" of subsection 6.3.3 implies that a circle can have at most $4 \times 2\pi = 8\pi$ radians of turning.)

7.2.4 Distances

Distances in a plane satisfy a basic relationship called the *triangle inequality,* which states that the sum of the lengths of any two sides of a triangle must be greater than the length of the third side. What is the spherical triangle inequality? Can you prove it? What exactly are the restrictions on its validity? (Hint for proof: Assume that the triangle inequality holds for triangles of small area, such as long, thin slivers; then go back to prove that assumption later.)

7.2.5 Two New Views of Sphere

The "window view" of a cube—regarding the cube as a square together with a group of rotations that flip the cube whenever the turtle crosses an edge—played a key role in our study of the cube in chapter 6. Before you continue reading, answer this: What views of a turtle walking on a sphere correspond to the window and card views of the cube?

Just as a circle can be thought of as a POLY with an infinite number of sides, a sphere can be thought of as similar to a polyhedron but with

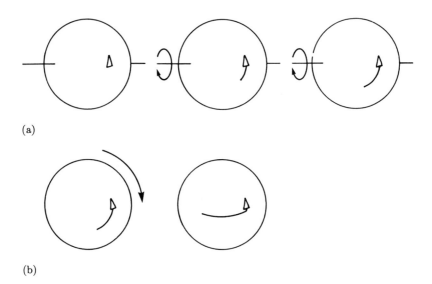

(a)

(b)

Figure 7.4
The window picture for a sphere turtle: (a) going forward; (b) turning (axis through
turtle coming out of page).

an infinite number of faces. Each face is infinitely small, and the turtle
is always crossing edges. The story is hard to make sense of in detail
but suggests the following view of walking and turning on a sphere: The
turtle stands still (within an infinitely small window) and the sphere
rotates behind the turtle as it walks (figure 7.4a). In a similar fashion,
the turtle again stands still while turning, and sphere rotates in the
opposite direction behind (figure 7.4b). (Notice that this is not exactly
analogous to the cube situation, where cube does not turn for LEFTs or
RIGHTs.) It is as if you set turtle on its back to hold up the world with
its feet. Walking and turning then rotate the world like a ball on the
feet of a "circus turtle," as shown in figure 7.5a.

Observe that FORWARD and LEFT are both represented by the same kind
of operation—a rotation of the sphere. Performing FORWARD is the same
as rotating the sphere about some axis, which we'll call the FORWARD
axis. The LEFT operation is a rotation about a different axis, the LEFT
axis, which is perpendicular to the FORWARD axis. Note that these axes
have a permanently fixed orientation in this view of the sphere.

The corresponding "circus" activity that gives a "card view" of walking on a sphere involves putting the turtle *inside* the sphere, which is
free to roll on a plane. As the turtle walks, the sphere rolls to keep the

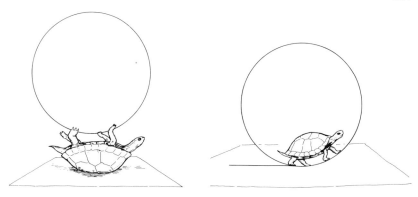

Figure 7.5
(a) A "circus turtle" with the world at its feet. (b) Rolling a ball from the inside: the "card view" of a sphere turtle.

turtle at the bottom. When the turtle turns, the sphere prepares to roll in a new direction. (See figure 7.5b.)

7.3 Results

This section answers some of the questions raised in the previous one. We urge you NOT TO READ FARTHER until you've explored some of these issues on your own.

The window view will be the basis of most of our analyses, so get it firmly in mind. The sphere stands skewered by two fixed, mutually perpendicular axes: one labeled FORWARD and one labeled LEFT. Each command causes a rotation of the sphere about the appropriate axis.

7.3.1 The FORWARD-LEFT Symmetry

Let's continue exploring the symmetry between α and β. FORWARD and LEFT are seen to be the same operation—a rotation of the sphere—except that the axes of rotation are different. Does this mean that POLY(α,β) and POLY(β,α) should do the same thing? An argument that they should goes something like this: Make an invariant description of POLY(α,β). It causes alternate rotations through angles α and β about mutually perpendicular axes. But that is exactly the description of POLY(β,α) as well. From an invariant point of view, there should be no difference between them.

On the other hand, the figure drawn by POLY(90,0) certainly does not look like that drawn by POLY(0,90). The question is, why not? The key to answering this is realizing that in our picture, it happens that the turtle is on the LEFT axis and the pen drags along the sphere whenever a

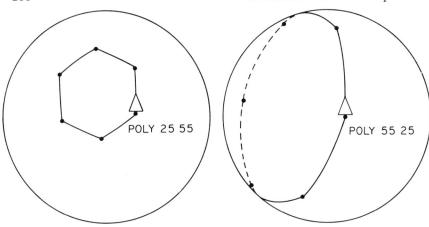

Figure 7.6
Dual figures.

FORWARD command rotates the sphere. Placing the turtle and pen down
on the LEFT axis distinguishes one axis from the other and hence breaks
the FORWARD–LEFT symmetry. If you put the pen down on the FORWARD
axis instead, you'll see lines drawn by the LEFT operation but not by
FORWARD. This second figure, drawn by a pen on the FORWARD axis, is
called the figure *dual to* the usually drawn one. If we include pen site in
the invariant descriptions of POLY figures, we see that POLY(α, β) and
POLY(β, α) are distinguished exactly by the fact that with POLY(α, β)
the pen is on the axis for which the rotation is β, while with POLY(β, α)
the pen is on the α axis. Changing the pen site to the other axis turns
POLY(α, β) into POLY(β, α); therefore, by definition, those POLYs are
dual to one another.

   How can we see what POLY(α, β) and POLY(β, α) have in common?
Let's concentrate on the state change. Suppose POLY(α, β) closes (position and heading) after n steps. At this point, the sphere has returned to
its initial state because the point where the turtle started is back under
the turtle, and the sphere is oriented so that the turtle will retrace its
initial step with another FORWARD. But with the sphere back to the initial
state, a pen on the FORWARD axis must have its starting point under it
as well—so it must draw a closed figure, too. This is expressed in the
following principle:

POLY duality principle On a sphere, POLY(α, β) closes in exactly the
same number of steps as POLY(β, α).

Figure 7.6 illustrates the dual figures POLY$(55, 25)$ and POLY$(25, 55)$.

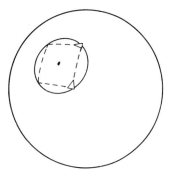

Figure 7.7
State change of FORWARD α, LEFT β (in a POLY "square") can be achieved by a single rotation about the center of the circumscribed circle.

No law says that we have to place the pen on either the LEFT or the FORWARD axis. Any point on the sphere will do, and the picture drawn by POLY(α,β) will vary with the selection of the pen site. For a general pen location, *both* FORWARD and LEFT commands will draw lines, but the resulting figure will still have the same symmetry as the usual POLY(α,β). Investigate these figures. How can you modify your computer sphere program so you can see these drawings on the display?

7.3.2 Net Rotation of a POLY Step

The fundamental insight in arriving at the duality principle was to use the window picture to describe the process of drawing a POLY figure—to focus on the rotational state of the sphere rather than fixing the sphere and keeping track of the moving turtle. We'll apply this now to elaborate upon the observation in subsection 7.2.2 that the vertices of any POLY lie on a circle.

Imagine rotating the sphere to produce the figure POLY(α,β). First make a FORWARD rotation, then a LEFT rotation. Each pair of rotations takes the pen to a new vertex. But we mentioned earlier that these vertices lie on a circle, just as if we were simply making a single rotation of the sphere about a fixed axis to get from one vertex to the next. This suggests that the combined operation FORWARD α followed by LEFT β is equivalent to a single rotation about some new axis, and the circle on which these POLY vertices lie is a circle of latitude for this axis (figure 7.7).

Net rotation theorem If we rotate the sphere by α about the FORWARD axis and then rotate it through β about the LEFT axis, the net effect will be the same as a single rotation (about some axis that depends on α and β).

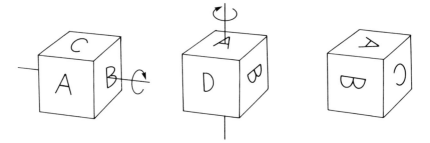

Figure 7.8
Rotating a cube 90° about two perpendicular axes in sequence is equivalent to rotating 120° about a diagonal.

Think about this remarkable theorem. Try making two sequential rotations of any object. Can you see the net axis and the amount of net rotation? This is a very hard problem in general. In fact, the proof of this theorem is hard enough so that we will show only that such an net rotation exists; we won't compute its axis. So as not to clutter more important issues, we will assume this theorem for now and draw some conclusions. We'll return to the proof in 7.3.6.

In case you failed miserably at visualizing a net rotation, we hope figure 7.8 will restore some faith in the theorem. It shows how a cube rotated 90° in sequence about two perpendicular axes through face centers winds up rotated 120° about an axis piercing two vertices.

It should be clear that the symmetry angle of POLY (α, β), which we called θ, must be the angle of net rotation of a POLY step. Does the FORWARD–LEFT symmetry say something about the relationship of α, β, and θ? To see this we add a bit more detail to our understanding of the way such symmetries work.

Think of the LEFT and FORWARD axes as coordinate axes. Now suppose someone happened to reverse the axis labels on a sphere diagram. Then FORWARD α, LEFT β,... would be read as LEFT α, FORWARD β,.... In other words, POLY (α, β) and POLY (β, α) are not only intrinsically the same (as far as sphere state is concerned), but we can think of them as descriptions of *exactly* the same process from two different coordinate systems. Since the angle θ that summarizes FORWARD α, LEFT β does not depend on any coordinate system, it must be invariant under the exchange. We thus obtain a stronger version of the duality principle of 7.3.1, which applied only to closed POLYs:

POLY (α, β) and POLY (β, α) always have the same symmetry angle.

7.3.3 The Spherical Pythagorean Theorem

There is a wonderful formula relating α, β, and θ:

$$\alpha^2 + \beta^2 \approx \theta^2.$$

The equation is not exact, but it is a good approximation for small angles. Small, however, does not mean tiny. In fact, the formula is off only by a degree or so for angles α and β as large as 45°. Again we postpone proof. The question is, did you discover this relation while exploring with your computer sphere? This is a remarkably simple and powerful formula. It is the equivalent of the Pythagorean theorem, only for rotations about perpendicular axes rather than sides of a plane right triangle. Go back and look at your experimental technique. What didn't you do that you should have done to discover the formula? What should you have done better? For example, what kind of graphing would have uncovered the relationship? What things might have prompted you to guess the relationship? A detailed study of why your exploration did not reveal some simple and powerful relationship may be more helpful to you than an accidental discovery of it. At the very least, look at the implications of such a formula and check them on your computer sphere simulation.

Although it is not exact, this formula makes some very concrete suggestions concerning POLYs. For one, it suggests the inequalities $\alpha < \theta$, $\beta < \theta$—the "hypotenuse" is always larger than the other "sides." These must hold whenever the error in the Pythagorean formula is less than any of the terms in it. When valid, these inequalities establish forbidden zones for n-gons. There are no four-sided figures with α or β greater than 90°, no three-sided figures with α or β greater than 120°, and so on. In such cases θ would be restricted to values too large to give the appropriate symmetry. Look for such forbidden zones.

We stress again that the approximation $\alpha^2 + \beta^2 \approx \theta^2$ is quite close even for fairly large angles. It predicts that the set of pairs α, β giving a particular symmetry (determined by θ) lies nearly on a circle which has radius θ centered at the origin in the α, β plane (see figure 7.9). The approximation is almost perfect for θ less than 45° (that is, for polygons with eight or more sides), and it is not bad even for squares. Because of the FORWARD-LEFT symmetry, the graph of pairs α, β giving a particular symmetry is always *precisely* symmetric in α and β (that is, about the 45°, $\alpha = \beta$ line). Furthermore, one finds that the forbidden zones $\alpha < \theta$ and $\beta < \theta$ are maintained even when α and β are large.

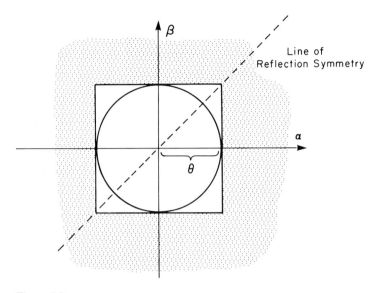

Figure 7.9
Graphing the pairs α and β that give a particular symmetry θ. The shaded area is the forbidden zone.

7.3.4 Exact Formula for θ

The exact formula for θ is tricky to find. Here is the result:

Theorem The symmetry angle θ for the combined operation FORWARD α, LEFT β satisfies the formula

$$\cos \frac{\theta}{2} = \cos \frac{\alpha}{2} \cos \frac{\beta}{2}.$$

How can we prove such a thing? It's not easy. First of all, we need some way to *see* θ in terms of the FORWARD and LEFT rotations. Let's use T to denote the combined operation FORWARD α, LEFT β. The transformation T is, by the theorem in 7.3.2, a rotation through angle θ about some axis. If we choose a point P on that axis, then P must return to its initial position after the two parts of the POLY step. So look at some vector $\mathbf{v}$ tangent to the sphere at P (figure 7.10a). The transformation T should have the net effect of rotating $\mathbf{v}$ by θ. Examine carefully how $\mathbf{v}$ and P move under T: First, the FORWARD α rotation moves P along along some circular arc A (an arc of a circle of latitude about the FORWARD axis) to end up at the point Q. Then the LEFT β rotation moves Q back to P, this time along an arc B on a circle of latitude for the LEFT axis.

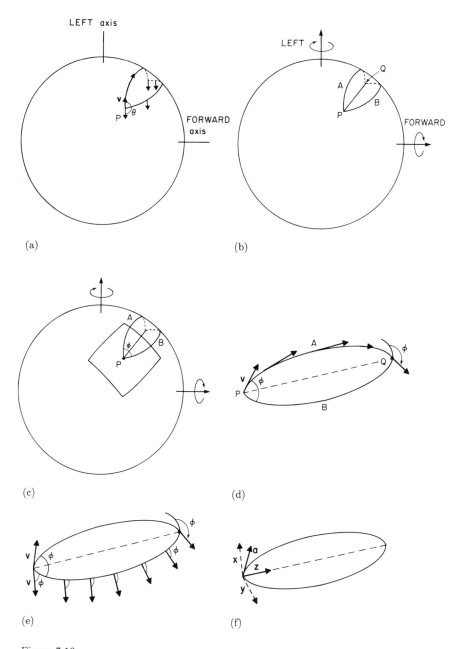

Figure 7.10
(a) Computing the symmetry angle θ by following the path of a vector $\mathbf{v}$ based at
the fixed point P. (b) The vector moves along two circular arcs A and B. (c) The
angle ϕ is the angle between A and B at P. (d) When $\mathbf{v}$ reaches Q, it makes there
an angle of ϕ with the arc B. (e) Moving back along B to P gives a total change of
2ϕ from its original heading. (f) The vector $\mathbf{a}$ can be decomposed into components
along the chord ($\mathbf{z}$) and perpendicular to the chord ($\mathbf{x}$).

Before following **v** on its trek, let's focus on the arcs A and B. They lie in perpendicular planes and intersect at the two points P and Q (figure 7.10b). Look at the intersection at P. Let ϕ be the angle between A and B at P (that is, the angle that a turtle crawling on the sphere along A would need to turn at P in order to face along B—see figure 7.10c). By symmetry the arcs intersect at the same angle ϕ at Q.

In determining what happens to **v**, the crucial observation is that the rigid rotations of the sphere we are about to perform maintain a constant angle between **v** and the latitudes of rotation. (Glue a vector to a globe latitude, rotate about the globe's axis, and watch what happens.) Keeping this observation in mind, start **v** pointing along A. It stays pointed along A as we rotate the sphere by α. Figure 7.10d shows that when **v** reaches Q it points at the angle ϕ with respect to the B circle. Rotating back by β returns **v** to P, maintaining the angle ϕ from B. Figure 7.10e shows that **v** has made a net rotation from start to finish of $\theta = 2\phi$.

Now that we've related θ to something that can be computed more directly in terms of α and β, we can complete the proof of the theorem. Our tool will be the relation between angles and dot products:

$$\mathbf{s} \cdot \mathbf{t} = |\mathbf{s}||\mathbf{t}| \cos \gamma$$

where γ is the angle of intersection between **s** and **t** (see section 3.5, exercise 4).

We'll apply this formula to unit vectors **a** and **b** pointing along arcs A and B, respectively, at P. The angle between **a** and **b** is, as we know, $\phi = \theta/2$, and so we have

$$\mathbf{a} \cdot \mathbf{b} = \cos \frac{\theta}{2}. \tag{1}$$

Now let's set up a coordinate system in which to compute $\mathbf{a} \cdot \mathbf{b}$. Let **z** be a unit-length vector at P pointing along the chord joining P to Q (figure 7.10f). Let **x** be a unit vector in the plane of A and perpendicular to **z**. Similarly, let **y** be a vector perpendicular to **z** lying in the plane of B. The angle between **a** and **z** is just the angle between the chord and the circular arc A, which is equal in turn to half the arc angle α. So we can produce the vector **a** by rotating **z** toward **x** through an angle $\alpha/2$. Therefore, we have

$$\mathbf{a} = \mathbf{z} \cos \frac{\alpha}{2} + \mathbf{x} \sin \frac{\alpha}{2}.$$

Similarly, we have

$$\mathbf{b} = \mathbf{z}\cos\frac{\beta}{2} + \mathbf{y}\sin\frac{\beta}{2}.$$

Taking the dot product of these two expressions, we find that since $\mathbf{z}$, $\mathbf{x}$, and $\mathbf{y}$ are mutually perpendicular, all the terms are zero except the term containing $\mathbf{z} \cdot \mathbf{z} = 1$. Thus,

$$\mathbf{a} \cdot \mathbf{b} = \cos\frac{\alpha}{2}\cos\frac{\beta}{2}.$$

Combining this with equation 1 gives

$$\cos\frac{\theta}{2} = \mathbf{a} \cdot \mathbf{b} = \cos\frac{\alpha}{2}\cos\frac{\beta}{2},$$

which proves the theorem.

As an application of this theorem, let's see how our formula for θ relates to the spherical Pythagorean theorem of 7.3.3. Have you seen the approximation formula for the cosine of an angle x (in radians),

$$\cos x = 1 - \frac{x^2}{2!} + \frac{x^4}{4!} - \frac{x^6}{6!} + \cdots ?$$

If x is small, then the first two terms of the series give a good approximation:

$$\cos x \approx 1 - \frac{x^2}{2!}.$$

Using this approximation in our theorem for θ gives

$$1 - \frac{1}{2}\left(\frac{\theta}{2}\right)^2 \approx \left[1 - \frac{1}{2}\left(\frac{\alpha}{2}\right)^2\right]\left[1 - \frac{1}{2}\left(\frac{\beta}{2}\right)^2\right],$$

which simplifies (if you leave out the very small term $\alpha^2\beta^2$) to the Pythagorean theorem $\theta^2 \approx \alpha^2 + \beta^2$.

7.3.5 Results for Circles

This subsection derives a fundamental result that relates the total turning around a circle to the radius.

We want to know the amount of turning a turtle will do in walking around on a spherical circle. We can consider the circle to be a latitude at an angle Θ down from the north pole. (The name of this angle is the

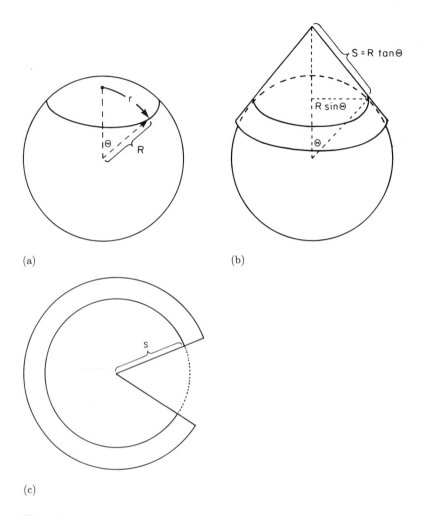

Figure 7.11
(a) An arc of radius r is part of a great circle subtending angle Θ from center; $\Theta = r/R$. (b) Draw a cone tangent to sphere along the latitude circle. (c) With the cone cut apart, the path is seen to be part of a planar circle.

colatitude.) From figure 7.11a one can see that $\Theta = r/R$, where R is the radius of the sphere and r is distance (measured on the sphere) from the turtle's path to the north pole.

The trick in determining the total turning done by a turtle in walking round a latitude is to invent a way to lay that total turning out on a plane so we can immediately see it as a change in heading. Imagine a cone placed over the sphere, tangent to it at the latitude of interest

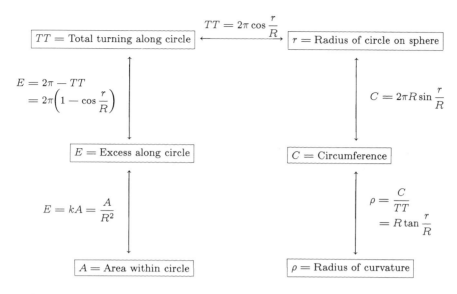

Figure 7.12
Relations among the various parameters of spherical circles.

(figure 7.11b). Now, a turtle walking on the conical latitude experiences locally (near its path) the same world as a turtle on a sphere; it would have the same total turning. We can cut up and lay out the cone to see that the turtle's path can be regarded as an arc of a regular planar circle (figure 7.11c). The heading change for the turtle's path can therefore be computed as 2π times the fraction of the planar circle the turtle traverses in covering the path:

$$TT = \frac{\text{length of path on sphere}}{\text{total circumference of planar circle}} \times 2\pi.$$

The length of the turtle's path is $2\pi R \sin \Theta$ (figure 7.11b). The circumference of the corresponding planar circle is $2\pi s$, where s is the distance to path from the peak of the cone. Returning to the uncut version of the cone, one sees that s is equal to $R \tan \Theta$. Hence,

$$TT = \frac{2\pi R \sin \Theta}{2\pi R \tan \Theta} \times 2\pi = 2\pi \cos \Theta = 2\pi \cos \frac{r}{R}.$$

This relation completes the chart shown in figure 7.12 of relationships among circle parameters on the sphere, and allows any one to be computed from any other.

7.3.6 Proof of Net Rotation Theorem

We'll tie up loose ends by giving the proof that a POLY step is equivalent to a single rotation about some axis. There are two parts to the proof. The first is to show that there is some fixed point of the pair of rotations. That is, if we let T denote the combined operation FORWARD α followed by LEFT β, and imagine how the points of the sphere are moved about by T, then there must be some point P that comes back to its initial position, $T(P) = P$. The second part of the proof is to show that, once we know a fixed point exists, then T must necessarily be a rotation of the sphere about the axis passing through P.

Proof that T has a fixed point Examine how T moves the sphere. Each of the rotations FORWARD α and LEFT β moves points around on the latitudes of their respective axes. If a point p gets moved to q by FORWARD α, then p and q must lie on the same latitude of the FORWARD axis. Similarly, since the subsequent LEFT β moves q to $T(p)$, q and $T(p)$ must lie on the same latitude of the LEFT axis (figure 7.13a). Now apply this reasoning, assuming that we start with a fixed point P of the transformation. The first rotation has P and its FORWARD-rotated image Q on the same FORWARD latitude, and the second rotation has Q and $T(P)$ on the same LEFT latitude. But $T(P) = P$, so P and Q are simultaneously on a latitude of both axes (figure 7.13b). Therefore, we can narrow our search for P and Q by considering only those points that share both a FORWARD latitude and a LEFT latitude. The set of such pairs p and q are symmetrically located above and below the great-circle longitude that passes through the FORWARD and LEFT poles (figure 7.13c). For reference, call this common longitude of the FORWARD and LEFT poles the Greenwich longitude. Those ps and qs must lie on the $\alpha/2$ (FORWARD) longitude above and below the Greenwich longitude in order for a rotation of α about the FORWARD axis to take ps and move them to qs located symmetrically (with respect to Greenwich). So all candidates for P and Q lie on the pair of FORWARD latitudes $\alpha/2$ above and below the Greenwich longitude. We need only ask now whether one of those qs is returned to its initial p by a LEFT β. Look at how much LEFT rotation would be needed to make one of those qs return to its p. At the LEFT pole, one needs 180° (figure 7.13d). Near the FORWARD pole one needs only a tiny fraction—approaching 0—of a whole revolution (figure 7.13e). Somewhere in between, there must be a place where the actual β will suffice (but not overdo) to bring q back to p; those are the P and Q we want.

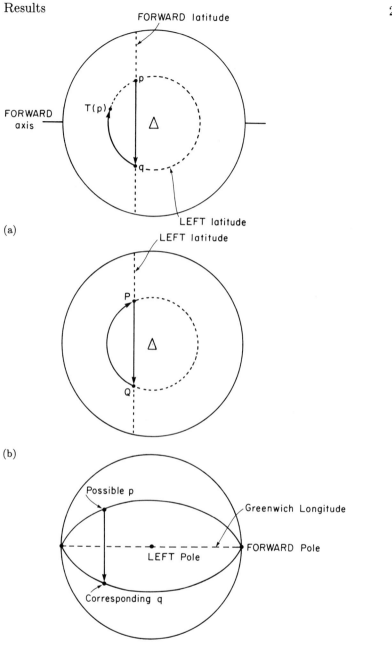

Figure 7.13
(a) The FORWARD operation moves each point p to some point q along a latitude of its axis. LEFT moves q to $T(p)$ along a latitude of its axis. (b) If P is a fixed point, then the LEFT rotation moves Q back to P along a LEFT latitude line. (c) The pairs p and q that share both a LEFT and a FORWARD latitude are symmetrically located above and below the great circle passing through the FORWARD and LEFT poles.

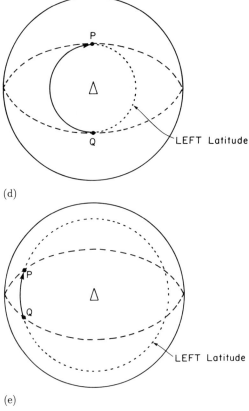

(d)

(e)

Figure 7.13 (cont.)
(d) The amount of rotation needed to make Q return exactly to P is almost 180° for P near the LEFT pole and (e) small near the FORWARD pole.

Proof that, if there is a fixed point, T is a rotation Now that we have a fixed point, we will show that T must be a rotation about the axis passing through P. The key idea here is that T is *distance-preserving—* that is, for any points p and q, the distance from p to q is equal to the distance from $T(p)$ to $T(q)$. (Distance, of course, is measured by a turtle crawling on the sphere.) Rotations and combinations of rotations, like T, must preserve distance. The following lemma completes the proof:

Lemma Any distance-preserving transformation of the sphere, if it has a fixed point, must be a rotation of the sphere about the axis containing the fixed point.

Think about stirring around all the points on the surface of a sphere so that distance between each pair is preserved and making sure one point does not move. How can we be sure that the stirring is actually a rigid rotation around an axis? To begin with, consider a latitude circle about the line containing the fixed point P and its opposite point on the sphere (the line we hope is the axis of net rotation). This circle consists of all points at some fixed distance from P. After we apply T they all must be the same distance from $T(P)$, since T is distance-preserving. But $T(P) = P$; hence T applied to any point on the latitude circle must also lie on the same latitude circle. As a special case, the point antipodal to P, which happens to be the only point in its particular latitude, must also be fixed under T.

So we see that each latitude must be stirred around within itself. But since distance within the latitude must be preserved, each latitude must be rigidly rotated. The final possibility to reject is that all latitudes are rotated, but not all by the same amount. The trouble with this is that longitudes would then "wriggle." But notice that T must transform turtle lines to turtle lines. (Remember, turtle lines are defined using only the ability to measure distance.) So each line of longitude, as a turtle line running from P to its antipodal point, must be transformed into another line of longitude. So all latitude circles must rotate the same amount. The whole skeleton of latitudes and longitudes must be moved intact, which shows that T must be a rotation. This completes the proof of both theorem and lemma.

Exercises for Chapter 7

In case you run out of things to think about, or in case you cheated and read section 7.3 before conducting your own investigation, here are some additional questions about turtle geometry on spheres.

1. [P] Experiment with different projections from sphere to plane in your turtle sphere simulation. For example, try stereographic projection (figure 7.14). (Note that the north pole on the sphere ends up "at infinity" on the plane.) Stereographic projection has the property that angles are preserved—for example, two lines intersecting at right angles on the sphere will intersect at right angles in the projection. This implies that straight turtle lines on the sphere are mapped to straight lines or circles on the plane. (Think about that.) Also, circles are mapped to circles. Other projections to try are the cartographers' standard Mercator and polar projections.

2. There is a slight gap in our proof of the POLY duality principle in subsection 7.3.1. We said that when the sphere returns to initial state

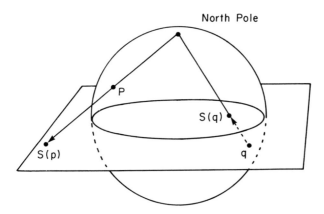

Figure 7.14
Stereographic projection maps points p and q on the sphere along a line through the north pole to the equatorial plane. Points in the northern hemisphere get mapped outside the equator, points on the southern hemisphere inside.

and POLY (α, β) is closed, then POLY (β, α) is also closed. Strictly, this only shows that POLY (β, α) cannot have more vertices than POLY (α, β), not that the two figures have the same number of vertices. Can you repair the proof? [A]

3. [DP] Which POLY inputs α and β will give closed figures?

4. [D] Do the operations FORWARD α, LEFT β and FORWARD β, LEFT α have the same associated θ? (Subsection 7.3.2 showed that FORWARD α, LEFT β and LEFT α, FORWARD β have the same θ.) Do they have the same axis of net rotation? If not, how do these compare? [A]

5. [P] Small figures should have small areas and hence small excesses, so $TT = 2\pi$ should be a passable approximation for the total turning around a small polygon. This approximation can be improved by using

$$TT = 2\pi - \text{excess} = 2\pi - \frac{\text{area}}{R^2}$$

and using the planar formula for area. (The latter is justified for small figures, which must be approximately planar.) Try this out for, say, squares. What area should you use to handle star POLYs? [A]

6. The planar approximation of exercise 5 can be helpful for figures with very large sides as well. A figure with large sides and small angles has the same symmetry as a figure with α and β reversed by the FORWARD–LEFT symmetry. But that's a small figure and hence nearly planar. Startle your friends by predicting offhand that a huge POLY with a side (α) of

120 and an angle (β) of 5 will be very nearly a triangle. Can you improve the approximations for these large figures in the same way we improved the formula that gave the total turning for small figures (exercise 5)?

7. Verify each relationship shown in figure 7.12. Derive direct relations between, for example, r and ρ; TT and circumference. [A]

8. In subsection 7.3.4 we deduced the spherical Pythagorean theorem from the exact formula by approximating the cosine by the first two terms of the cosine series. It can be shown that the error in this cosine approximation is bounded by the third term in the series, $x^4/4!$. Use this to deduce a bound on the accuracy of the Pythagorean theorem as an approximation to θ. Say also whether the approximation is too high or too low.

9. The cosine approximation used above is valid only for angles expressed in radians, but the Pythagorean theorem is also good for angles in degrees. Give a proof of this fact, and also investigate the error in the approximation. [A]

10. [D] Now that you know from 7.3.4 how to compute θ in terms of α and β, show that r, the radius of the POLY circle, can be computed as $\sin r = \sin\frac{\alpha}{2} / \sin\frac{\theta}{2}$. [H]

11. Generalize the theorem of 7.3.2 to show that any sequence of rotations of the sphere, about any axes, is equivalent to a single rotation. [H]

12. [D] Suppose we perform two consecutive rotations of the sphere about two axes that are not necessarily perpendicular. First rotate by α around one axis, then through β about the other axis. Show that the formula in 7.3.4 generalizes to give the following formula for the symmetry angle θ:

$$\cos\frac{\theta}{2} = \cos\frac{\alpha}{2}\cos\frac{\beta}{2} - \sin\frac{\alpha}{2}\sin\frac{\beta}{2}\cos\gamma$$

where γ is the angle between the two axes. [H]

13. Just as the result in 7.3.4 leads to the "Pythagorean theorem" as an approximation for θ, show that the result of exercise 12 leads to

$$\theta^2 \approx \alpha^2 + \beta^2 + 2\alpha\beta\cos\gamma,$$

which we could call the "spherical law of cosines." [H]

14. [PD] Can you extend the analysis of POLY to general fixed instruction programs? For example, what is the symmetry angle θ for an INSPI?

15. We noticed the FORWARD–LEFT symmetry in the vector triad method of representing turtle state on a sphere before we discovered the "window picture." But we did all our symmetry analysis in the latter and not in the former. Why?

16. The domain for validity of the spherical Pythagorean theorem, small α and β, is just the domain for circles. Use it to derive formulas for n (the number of steps to make the POLY circle close), for the total turning involved, and for the circumference of the circle. Show that these are consistent with what you can derive from figure 7.12. [A]

17. Each line on a sphere, being a great circle, has a special point associated with it—the "north pole" when you consider that great circle to be "the equator." Thus, any triangle has three new points associated with it—the "north poles" for each side of the triangle. Show that these three points determine another triangle (called a polar triangle), which is dual to the original triangle in the sense of subsection 7.3.1. [HA]

8

Piecewise Flat Surfaces

> "Now, this *third* handkerchief," Mein Herr proceeded,
> "has also four edges, which you can trace continuously
> round and round: all you need do is to join its
> four edges to the four edges of the opening. The
> Purse is then complete, and its outer surface—"
> "I see!" Lady Muriel eagerly interrupted. "Its
> *outer* surface will be continuous with its inner sur-
> face!..."
>
> Lewis Carrol, *Sylvie and Bruno, Concluded*

In exploring the topology and geometry of surfaces, we have investigated in detail two surfaces of particular interest: the sphere and the cube. We found a lot of interesting geometry on the sphere arising from the sphere's property of being everywhere the same. The cube's geometry was amenable to study because, except at the vertices, it is flat and planelike. That flatness simplifies the computer program for a cube-walking turtle; so long as the turtle remains within one face of the cube, we might as well think of it as walking in the plane.

As we continue our study, it makes sense to look for other "simple" surfaces. Unfortunately, everywhere-the-same surfaces like the sphere are very scarce. But surfaces that share the cube's simplifying properties are easy to come by. In this chapter we will study surfaces formed by taking a collection of planar pieces and gluing them together along the edges. These are called *piecewise flat surfaces,* since any surface formed in this way will surely be flat everywhere except possibly along the edges where the pieces are glued together. In fact, if all the planar pieces have straight edges, then, like a cube, the glued surface can have curvature only at the vertices (see exercise 16). Figure 8.1 shows some examples of piecewise flat surfaces.

As with cubes and spheres, the crucial step in designing a computer program to explore piecewise flat turtle geometry is deciding on a representation for these surfaces. A good representation will not only help us design the computer program, but should also lead to insights into the mathematical properties of piecewise flat surfaces. Perhaps the most straightforward representation is simply to describe each face separately and keep track of which edges are glued together. This kind of repre-

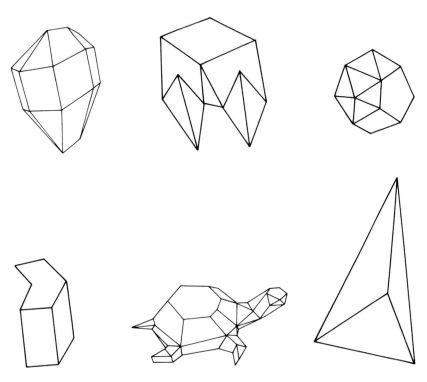

Figure 8.1
Piecewise flat surfaces.

sentation is called an *atlas*. Figure 8.2 shows a pyramid constructed from four triangles and a square, together with the corresponding atlas. You can think of this mathematical atlas as similar to a road atlas—a collection of separate maps together with information telling which map to use next when you run off the edge of the map you're using. And this is precisely how we shall use the atlas to implement a turtle for piecewise flat surfaces. As long as the turtle remains within a particular face, then we handle things just as for the familiar planar turtle. Whenever the turtle crosses the edge of a face, we consult the atlas to determine which face the turtle has moved to. In this chapter we'll consider only surfaces that are *closed* (that is, have no boundary). What this means in terms of the atlas is that each edge of every face must be matched with some other edge. No edge can be left "open," or else the turtle could run across the edge and find itself off the surface.

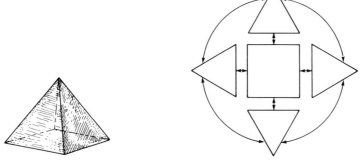

Figure 8.2
A pyramid and the corresponding atlas.

8.1 A Program for Piecewise Flat Surfaces

Now we'll turn to the problem of designing a program that allows the turtle to walk on a piecewise flat surface. Your experience with cubes and spheres should tell you that there are two main parts to such a program: maintaining an internal representation and translating the internal representation into a picture on the display screen. One way to greatly simplify the second problem is to have the program display only one face of the surface at a time—the face the turtle is currently on.

More generally, we will maintain the following design philosophy for the programs in this chapter: Proceed *locally*, that is, keep the representation as close as possible to what the turtle itself sees and senses. Accordingly, we will arrange the display so that when the turtle crosses an edge, the new face the turtle has walked onto will appear as the turtle sees it (not, therefore, in a standardized orientation as on a page of a road atlas). In particular, this means that the same face may appear on the display screen in different orientations. For example, the turtle trek around the vertex of a cube illustrated in figure 8.3a will be displayed by the program as in figure 8.3b. Although this complicates slightly the translation between internal representation and display, it does have the advantage that the turtle's heading as shown on the screen is not changed by crossing an edge. As a project, you might think about designing programs more in the style of the cube program of chapter 6, which attempt to display the entire surface on the screen in perspective. As we will see below, this cannot be done for every surface, because there are atlases whose corresponding surface simply does not "fit" into three dimensions. We'll discuss this point further in subsection 8.1.4.

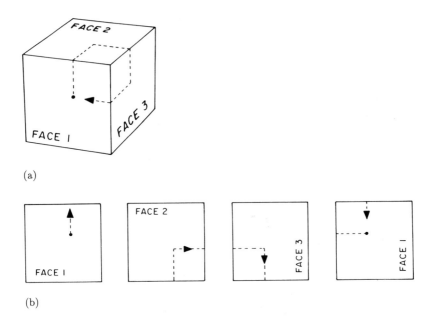

(a)

(b)

Figure 8.3
(a) Turtle trek around vertex of a cube. (b) The same trek as displayed by the program, one face at a time.

8.1.1 Internal Representation

In order to simplify our sketch of a piecewise flat turtle geometry program, we'll consider only those surfaces that, like the cube, are *piecewise square*, that is, are formed by gluing together equal-sized squares. (Topologically, this is no loss of generality. Surfaces of any topological type can be produced in piecewise square form.) If all faces are the same, then the part of the atlas that describes each individual face is redundant, so we need to record only how the edges are matched (glued together). We can therefore take as the atlas for a closed piecewise square surface the collection of matched edge pairs. Each edge can itself be labeled by a pair of numbers specifying which face and which edge of that face we are talking about. We'll number the faces sequentially starting from 1, and number the four edges of each face counterclockwise from 0 to 3. For example, the cube shown in figure 8.4 has as its atlas

```
[[1 0]  [6 2]]    [[1 1]  [4 3]]    [[1 2]  [2 0]]    [[1 3]  [3 1]]
[[2 1]  [4 2]]    [[2 2]  [5 0]]    [[2 3]  [3 2]]    [[3 0]  [6 3]]
[[3 3]  [5 3]]    [[4 0]  [6 1]]    [[4 1]  [5 1]]    [[5 2]  [6 0]]
```

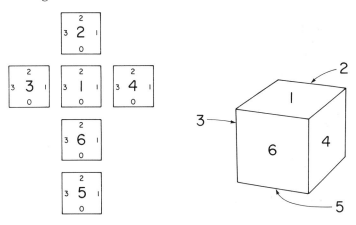

Figure 8.4
A cube and its corresponding atlas.

This is interpreted as "edge 0 of face 1 is matched with edge 2 of face 6" and so on.

We will design the program so that all information needed about the surface will be contained in the atlas. Programs for different surfaces will be identical, except for the fact that they consult different atlases. (This is another advantage of displaying only one face at a time on the screen.) So the first building block in our program should be a method for consulting the atlas, a procedure called LOOKUP which takes as its input a pair [FACE EDGE] and returns the matching face and edge. The details of how LOOKUP works will depend on how the atlas is represented in the computer (see exercise 2). The important thing to remember is that a modular style of programing ensures that the rest of the turtle program is independent of these details. We need only assume that we have some kind of LOOKUP procedure that works; we can deal with considerations of precisely how it works as a separate problem.

Since each individual face of the surface is flat, the turtle state is much the same as for the ordinary planar turtle. We have to keep track of the position and heading, for example, by POSITION and HEADING vectors, as explained in chapter 3. Notice that the RIGHT and LEFT commands work exactly as for the planar turtle—all they do is rotate the HEADING vector. Besides position and heading, we need to keep track of CURRENT.FACE, the number that specifies which face of the surface the turtle is on.

8.1.2 Maintaining the Display

The problem of maintaining the computer display in this program breaks up into two parts. First, we must draw the turtle's path as it moves

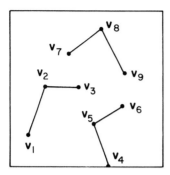

Figure 8.5
Sample path stored as $[[v_1 \; v_2 \; v_3] \; [v_4 \; v_5 \; v_6] \; [v_7 \; v_8 \; v_9]]$.

on the screen. This is relatively straightforward. Each face appears as a square on the screen, and as long as the turtle remains within this square we can handle things just as for the planar turtle. In particular, the coordinates of the turtle's POSITION vector can be taken to be the usual display coordinates.

The second and trickier problem is to keep track of the lines drawn by the turtle on a particular face and redraw them when the turtle returns to that face. We can do this by recording for each face a list of turtle paths, where each path is itself specified as a list of vectors representing positions. For example, in the list $[[v_1 \; v_2 \; v_3] \; [v_4 \; v_5]]$, the first sublist, $[v_1 \; v_2 \; v_3]$, is a list of three points to be connected by lines in a sequence. The next sublist is another such plot. Of course, there may be more sublists (see figure 8.5). A PENDOWN command (or coming onto a new face with the pen down) should start one of these sublists. When the pen is down, a FORWARD command should add a point to the last sublist. Note that each v_i is a vector which, using the techniques of chapter 3, may itself be represented as a list of two coordinates.

There is a complication in saving and redrawing these paths: The face need not appear on the screen with its zero edge at the bottom. In fact, a particular face may appear on the screen in any one of four different orientations. So the "same" stored turtle paths as specified by the v_i may have to be drawn on the screen in different ways (figure 8.6). We'll solve this problem by using a different coordinate system for storing the points v_i. Instead of display coordinates, which specify the x, y coordinates of points as drawn on the screen, we'll use "face coordinates," which are an x, y coordinate system having the 0 and 1 edges of the face as axes. The advantage of these coordinates is that lines will be stored in a form independent of the orientation of the face on the screen when

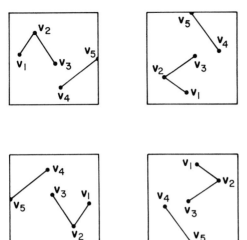

Figure 8.6
The same path may appear on the screen in different orientations.

the lines are drawn. The appearance of the face on the display screen in different orientations will be reflected in the program by different transformations between face and display coordinates. So, whenever we wish to record the turtle's position in one of the lists, we first translate the turtle's POSITION vector (which is kept in display coordinates) into face coordinates. When we redraw the stored paths, we must translate the v_i into display coordinates.

To accomplish these coordinate translations, we must keep track of how the face appears on the display screen. Think of the square drawn on the display screen as a "face" in its own right, with its own edges numbered. (We'll refer to the edges of the display square as "slots" to distinguish them from the edges of the atlas faces.) We can specify how a face appears on the display by noting which display slot corresponds to edge 0 of the face. Our program will keep track of this ZERO.EDGE.SLOT. If we know ZERO.EDGE.SLOT then we can compute the transformations between face and display coordinates as follows: Let A be the angle (ZERO.EDGE.SLOT) $\times 90°$. Then transforming face coordinates to display coordinates is simply a matter of rotating counterclockwise through angle A about the center of the screen (figure 8.7). Provided we choose $(0,0)$ to be the center of the square, we have

display coordinates = Rotate(face coordinates, A),

and the opposite transformation is therefore given by

face coordinates = Rotate(display coordinates, $-A$).

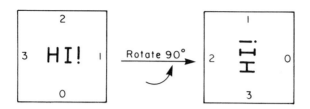

Figure 8.7
To transform from face coordinates to display coordinates, rotate counterclockwise through ZERO.EDGE.SLOT × 90°. (a) Picture on face. (b) As it appears on display with ZERO.EDGE.SLOT = 1.

If you prefer formulas expressed in terms of x and y coordinates, you are welcome to derive them by applying the rotation formula of 3.1.3. The answers, expressed as computer procedures, are the following:

```
TO DISPLAY.COORDS.OF [X Y]
    RETURN [(X*COS(A) - Y*SIN(A)) (Y*COS(A) + X*SIN(A))]

TO FACE.COORDS.OF [X Y]
    RETURN [(X*COS(A) + Y*SIN(A)) (Y*COS(A) - X*SIN(A))]
```

With this outline, we'll leave to you (exercise 3) the task of writing the following subprocedures to be used by the piecewise square turtle program:

• RECORD.POSITION, which takes the turtle's current POSITION, translates it into face coordinates, and adds it to the last sublist in the list of paths associated with the current face,

• START.NEW.PATH, which starts a new sublist in the list of paths associated with the current face, and

• DRAW.PATHS, which clears the screen and draws all the paths saved for the current face (after translating the saved points into display coordinates).

8.1.3 Implementing the FORWARD Command

The main problem in implementing the FORWARD command is to determine if the turtle's path intersects one of the edges of the display square, and, if so, to shift to the new face. This is much the same kind of computation that we had to do for the cube in chapter 7, and we can use the same method to do most of the work. We need a CHECK.INTERSECTIONS procedure that takes the turtle's current position and the endpoint of the proposed FORWARD walk as inputs and does one of two things:

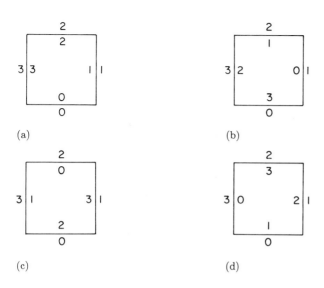

Figure 8.8
The correspondence between display slots and face edges is given by EDGE = SLOT −
ZERO.EDGE.SLOT (mod 4). ZERO.EDGE.SLOT = 0 in (a), 1 in (b), 2 in (c), and 3 in (d).

If the line joining the two points does not intersect any of the edges of
the display square (the "slots"), then CHECK.INTERSECTIONS should set
the variable RESULT equal to the message "NO INTERSECTIONS."

If the line does intersect one of the slots, then CHECK.INTERSECTIONS
will set RESULT to "INTERSECTION FOUND." In addition, the variables
SLOT.HIT, INTERSECTION, and FRACTION will be set to the number of
the slot hit, the intersection point of the turtle's path with the slot, and
the fraction of the turtle's path that was traveled before the intersection
occurred.

We'll leave CHECK.INTERSECTIONS as an exercise for you. It is virtually
identical to the analogous program developed for the cube in 6.1.3.
    When the turtle's path intersects a slot, the first thing to do is to
compute which edge of the current face this corresponds to, via the
formula

EDGE.HIT = SLOT.HIT − ZERO.EDGE.SLOT (mod 4).

For example, if the turtle goes off the top of the screen (slot 2), and
ZERO.EDGE.SLOT is 3, then that corresponds to crossing edge 2 − 3 =
−1 = 3 (mod 4) (see figure 8.8). Once we know which edge is crossed,

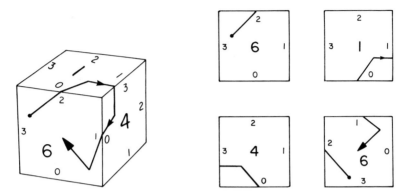

Figure 8.9
Turtle trek on a cube. Notice that crossing an edge always appears as a wrap on the screen.

the new face and edge hit can be found in the atlas with the LOOKUP procedure of 8.1.1. Because of the way face transitions are displayed, turtle heading (as seen on the display) doesn't change in going to the new face, and the turtle's new position is just a wrap on the display square, as shown in figure 8.9. However, the new ZERO.EDGE.SLOT must be computed. This can be done as follows: Suppose the new display slot to which the turtle has wrapped is called NSLOT (NSLOT = SLOT.HIT + 2 (mod 4)). Then

new ZERO.EDGE.SLOT

$\quad$ = NSLOT — ⟨new edge number as found in the atlas⟩ (mod 4).

So the complete computation of the parameters for the new face is

```
TO COMPUTE.FACE.PARAMETERS
    EDGE.HIT ← REMAINDER (SLOT.HIT - ZERO.EDGE.SLOT, 4)
    [NEW.FACE NEW.EDGE] ← LOOKUP [CURRENT.FACE EDGE.HIT]
    NSLOT ← REMAINDER (SLOT.HIT + 2, 4)
    ZERO.EDGE.SLOT ← REMAINDER (NSLOT - NEW.EDGE, 4)
```

Next we use the DRAW.PATHS procedure (subsection 8.1.2) to redraw the paths that were recorded for this face. The final step, as with the cube program, is to go FORWARD the distance remaining, computed from FRACTION.

Here is the complete program for moving FORWARD on a piecewise square surface:

```
TO FORWARD (DIST)
   ENDPOINT ← POSITION + DIST*HEADING
   CHECK.INTERSECTIONS (POSITION, ENDPOINT)
   IF RESULT = "NO INTERSECTION"
      THEN FORWARD.WITHIN.FACE (ENDPOINT)
      ELSE FORWARD.ACROSS.EDGE
```

You can see how similar this is to the cube implementation given in subsection 6.1.6. FORWARD calls two main subprocedures. The first, used when the turtle does not leave the current face, merely moves the turtle to the new position and records the position in the list of vertices:

```
TO FORWARD.WITHIN.FACE (NEW.POSITION)
   MOVE.TO NEW.POSITION
   POSITION ← NEW.POSITION
   RECORD.POSITION
```

The MOVE.TO procedure above, as in section 6.1, simply moves the turtle to the new screen coordinates and draws a line if the pen is down. We will use below a JUMP.TO procedure, which is almost like MOVE.TO except that it never draws a line.

When the turtle does cross an edge, we first move the turtle forward to the edge, then determine the new face and face parameters, erase the screen, and redraw any previous paths that should appear on the new face. The turtle's initial entry position on the new face is found by wrapping across the display square from the intersection point. So we move the turtle there, start a new sublist in the list of paths, and go forward the distance remaining:

```
TO FORWARD.ACROSS.EDGE
   FORWARD.WITHIN.FACE (INTERSECTION)
   COMPUTE.FACE.PARAMETERS
   CURRENT.FACE ← NEW.FACE
   DRAW.PATHS
   POSITION ← WRAP (POSITION)
   JUMP.TO POSITION
   START.NEW.PATH
   FORWARD (DIST * (1 - FRACTION))
```

We'll leave to you the details of allowing for PENUP and PENDOWN. You will also need to determine appropriate initial values for the necessary parameters.

8.1.4 Starting to Explore: Surfaces with Only One Face

We invite you to fill in the details in the preceding sections and begin your own computer investigation of piecewise square surfaces. You may want to embellish the basic program—for example, by displaying the current face number on the screen. Alternatively, you might not display this information, and then challenge a friend to figure out the geometry of an unknown surface by steering a turtle around on it. To get you started on your exploration, we'll acquaint you with two surfaces that can be made with one square face.

Pointy Sphere
Figure 8.10a shows the edge-gluing corresponding to the atlas

[[1 0] [1 1]]   [[1 2] [1 3]].

Since the edges of the square are glued in pairs, the resulting surface has only two distinct edges. Two of the four vertices of the square are merged by the gluing, so the surface has three distinct vertices, as shown in figure 8.10b. The figure shows turtle paths around the three vertices. By counting total turning you can see that two of the vertices have excess $3\pi/2$ and the remaining one has excess π. Therefore, the surface has total curvature 4π. Topologically, the surface is equivalent to a sphere, as illustrated in figure 8.10c.

Flat Torus
If we glue opposite edges of the square, that is, if we glue according to the atlas

[[1 0] [1 2]]   [[1 1] [1 3]],

we get a surface with two edges and one vertex which is topologically equivalent to a torus (figure 8.11a). Can you see that the surface has only one vertex? Counting vertices is not always easy, since what appear as separate vertices on the individual faces may actually become one via gluing.

One interesting fact about this torus is that the total turning for a turtle moving around at its single vertex is 2π, and hence the excess is zero, so the surface is flat near the vertex (figure 8.11b). Since it is also flat away from the vertex, we see that this torus not only has zero total curvature (as does any torus), it has zero curvature density everywhere. Every closed path has a multiple of 2π for total turning.

But how can there be a torus that is flat everywhere, when all the tori we've ever run across (for example, in chapter 5) have regions of both

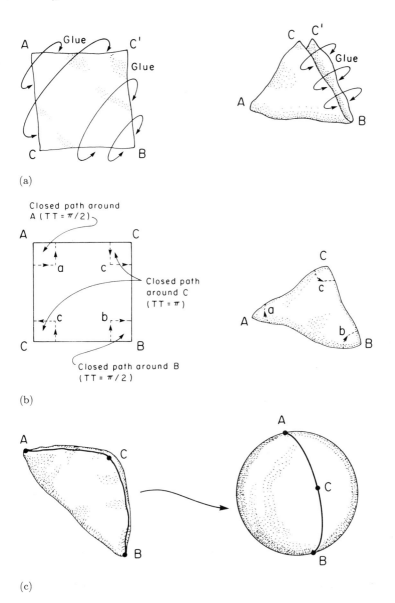

Figure 8.10
(a) Gluing the sides of a single square in accordance with the atlas [[1 0] [1 1]]
[[1 2] [1 3]]. (b) Closed paths and total turning around the three vertices of the
surface. (c) The surface is topologically equivalent to a sphere.

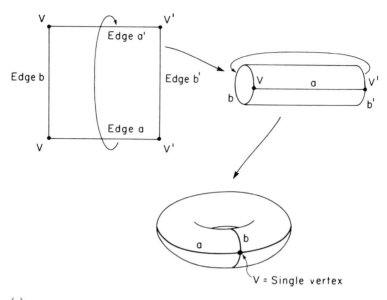

(a)

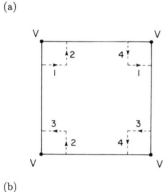

(b)

Figure 8.11
(a) Gluing opposite edges of a square gives a torus with two edges and a single vertex.
(b) A closed path around the single vertex has total turning 2π and hence excess 0.

positive and negative curvature? The answer is that, although this flat torus is topologically equivalent to an ordinary "inner tube" torus (both can be constructed from the same square, making the same gluings), nevertheless the two tori are different geometrically.

   Examine figure 8.12, which shows in detail the construction of an ordinary torus by starting with a square sheet of rubber and physically making the gluings indicated in the atlas. First glue edges 0 and 2 together to make a tube. Next, bend the tube around to glue 1 and 3

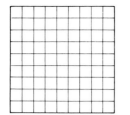
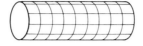

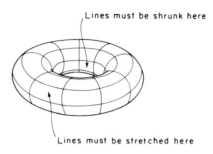

Figure 8.12
Bending a square into a torus requires us to distort distances. (No stretching is required to get from the square to the cylinder.)

together. In doing this second step you must stretch the tube and make the curvature density positive on the outside and negative on the inside. Of course, the total curvature must be zero because the resulting surface is topologically a torus. But geometrically, it is not the same torus as the flat one described by the above atlas and simulated by using that atlas in the program of the previous sections. Distances and the distribution of curvature density have changed.

We have seen topologically identical, yet geometrically different surfaces before. The new twist in this is example is that it is impossible to fit a flat torus into three-dimensional space without distorting distances. (This follows from exercise 12 of section 5.3). Nevertheless, the square together with the atlas which matches edges defines a perfectly consistent world for a turtle to live in. You can predict the result of every walk or turn a turtle might take with no difficulty. Intrinsically (from the turtle's point of view), the surface makes perfectly good sense; your extrinsic three-dimensional perspective makes it hard to imagine what the flat torus looks like. (A flat torus will fit in four-dimensional space, and there one can deform back and forth between flat and "inner tube" tori.)

Note the phenomenon exhibited here: Trying to make a model of the surface by actually bending and gluing (in your head or with a paper

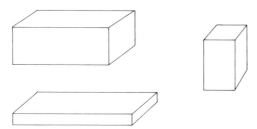

Figure 8.13
Rectangular parallelopipeds.

or rubber sheet) may require distorting the surface depicted in an atlas. And yet the atlas itself defines a perfectly good surface. Because of this, mathematicians are satisfied to declare that the two edges marked in an atlas are "the same." That is called *identifying* (as in "making the same"). The process of visualizing the actual bending and gluing is not necessary; it becomes merely an optional (and only sometimes possible) procedure to help you visualize such surfaces.

Exercises for Section 8.1

1. [P] Describe in detail an atlas representation and the associated LOOKUP procedure. How efficient is the procedure? That is, how many atlas entries must you inspect (on the average) before you find the information you're looking for? Can you think of a way to speed things up?

2. [P] One common way to speed up information retrieval is to store the answer to each possible question and then label the answer by the question. Sometimes this is too expensive in prior computation and storage. In the case of an atlas, neither of these is true—prior computation is minimal, and there are only twice as many questions as pairs of sides in an atlas. Implement a LOOKUP procedure that uses this method and therefore requires no search time at all. [H]

3. [P] Implement the procedures RECORD.POSITION, START.NEW.PATH, and DRAW.PATHS described in this section.

4. [P] Modify the FORWARD implementation described in 8.1.3 to include PENUP and PENDOWN commands.

5. [PD] Use your piecewise square surface programs to investigate the geometry of rectangular parallelopipeds (figure 8.13). What are the analogs of the phenomena we found in the geometry of the cube? In

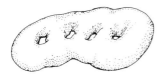 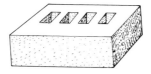

Figure 8.14
An n-holed torus and a topologically equivalent piecewise-square version.

particular, which headings give closed monogons? (Compare subsection 6.3.2.)

6. [PD] We saw in 6.3.3 that any looping program that closes in the plane will also close on the cube but may take as much as four times as long. How does this generalize to rectangular parallelopipeds?

7. Describe a family of atlases that give n-holed tori, as shown in figure 8.14.

8. [D] What is the minimum number of square faces needed to make an n-holed torus? Can you prove that? [HA]

9. [D] Show that, if we allow faces that are arbitrary topological disks (rather than just squares), an n-holed torus can be made with *one* face and $2n$ pairs of matching edges. [A]

10. [P] Look at the vertices of large POLYs drawn on the flat torus. Explain the qualitative features (such as symmetry) of the distribution of dots. Explain the placement of the "center" of the distribution. (Calculate it in advance.)

11. Is it true that there is a turtle line of shortest distance between any two (nonvertex) points of a piecewise flat surface? [A]

12. [P] Subsection 5.3.3 described the handle-attaching process, which changes the topological type of closed surfaces. For a piecewise square surface this involves removing two faces that have no edge in common and replacing them with a handle. Write a computer program that takes as input an atlas for a piecewise square surface and returns a new atlas describing the surface "with a handle attached."

13. [P] Use your program to construct a surface consisting of some specified number (say, four) of square faces. Challenge a friend to determine its topological type as quickly as possible. Let your friend prepare by writing whatever turtle procedures he or she would like to use as an aid in the exploration. Can you do better?

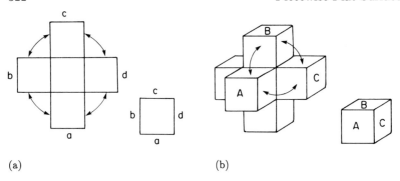

Figure 8.15
Atlases for (a) a cube and (b) a tessaract.

14. [P] Generalize the program of this section to allow as faces other regular polygons besides squares. Investigate, in particular, piecewise triangular versions of spheres and n-holed tori. Further generalize the program to handle arbitrary piecewise flat surfaces.

15. Show that an edge of a piecewise flat surface formed by gluing together two planar pieces along a straight edge can have no concentrated curvature except at the vertices. [HA]

16. [DD] Imagine what it would be like to construct a closed surface by identifying two faces along edges with *different* lengths. (It seems hard to visualize this identification as a gluing process; just think of this as an abstract identification.) Suppose, for example, we identify the edge of a square of side 100 with the edge of a square of side 50. A turtle crawling along the surface finds that, one side of the edge, each turtle step is $\frac{1}{100}$ of the way across a face, while on the other side each step is $\frac{1}{50}$ of the way across a face. Is it still true that the surface is flat except at the vertices, or is there concentrated curvature along the "funny" edge? What does a turtle line look like near this edge? If the line crosses the edge making an angle of A as measured on the 100-unit face, then what angle should it make as measured on the 50-unit face? [HA]

17. [PD] You can generalize a piecewise flat surface simulation to a piecewise flat *space* simulation in which to fly a three-dimensional turtle. Figure 8.15 shows an atlas for a *tessaract* (the three-dimensional equivalent of the surface of a cube) constructed in strict analogy to the way in which a cube's atlas is made from squares: Glue six solid cubes onto the faces of a central cube, close up the gaps, and identify the six faces of an eighth cube with the six open faces left from the previous steps. Explore the geometry of the space interior to those cubes.

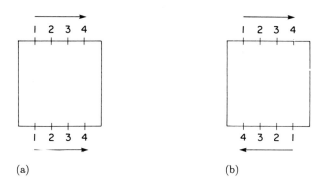

Figure 8.16
(a) Orientation preserving identification. (b) Orientation reversing identification.

8.2 Orientations

The program outlined in the preceding section will enable you to construct a wide variety of piecewise flat surfaces, especially if you generalize it so that faces can be arbitrary polygons rather than just squares. But there are still other piecewise flat surfaces, and even piecewise square surfaces, that the program can't represent. In designing the program, we overlooked an important fact about edge identification: There are two different ways to identify a pair of edges, and our representation has ignored the second way. The first kind of identification, shown in figure 8.16a, is what we've been doing all along. This is called *orientation-preserving* identification. But figure 8.16b illustrates another possibility; the edges may be identified in an inverted manner. This is called *orientation-reversing* identification. In the general case you can recognize orientation-reversing identifications as follows: Draw arrows on the two identified edges in the atlas to indicate directions of identification; then orientation-reversing identifications have both arrows pointing with the same sense—either clockwise or counterclockwise— around their respective faces. If one arrow points clockwise and the other counterclockwise, the identification is orientation-preserving. Including orientation-reversing identifications in our atlases enables us to construct new surfaces, including some mathematical curiosities called *nonorientable surfaces*.

8.2.1 Nonorientable Surfaces

If you take a square and identify a pair of opposite sides in an orientation-preserving way you get a cylinder, just as we did in the first step of

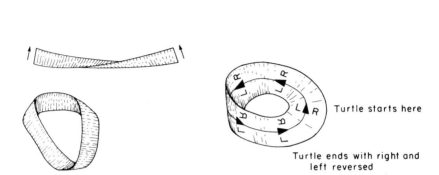

Figure 8.17
A Möbius strip, and a turtle path that confuses left and right.

constructing the flat torus. But suppose instead that you identify the edges with the orientation reversed. Try it with a strip of paper. The identification amounts to making a half-twist in the strip before gluing the edges together. The resulting (nonclosed) surface is called a *Möbius strip*.

Figure 8.17 shows the strange phenomenon observed by a turtle living in a Möbius strip. The turtle starts out at some point and takes a trip all the way around the strip. When it gets back to its initial position, it finds that left and right are reversed! Let's inspect this turtle trek in the atlas representation of the Möbius strip. The turtle crosses, say, edge number 3 with vertex V to its left. Having crossed the edge, the turtle still sees that its left side is the one closer to V, as shown in figure 8.18a. If you ask the turtle to turn left it will of course turn towards its left side. But that now appears as a *right* turn on the map (figure 8.18b). The turtle, having no external reference, won't have noticed that change. However, by walking down and across to the original position and checking the skid marks made in some previous left turn, even the turtle will be able to see that "left" is no longer the same direction as before (figure 8.18c).

The root of the problem is that right and left are not intrinsically defined. Start again with a turtle in the center of a square. A LEFT command results in a left turn from your point of view. But suppose you look at that same square from the other side. Now a LEFT command produces what looks like a right turn (figure 8.19). Whether a turn looks left or looks right depends on which side you are looking from—it is

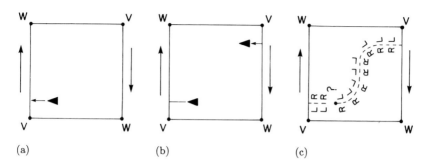

(a)   (b)   (c)

Figure 8.18
Confusing right and left on a Möbius strip, shown in the atlas representation. (a)
Turtle crosses edge with V to its left. (b) V remains to its "left," which now appears
as "right" on the map. (c) Returning to the original position, turtle discovers that
right and left have been reversed.

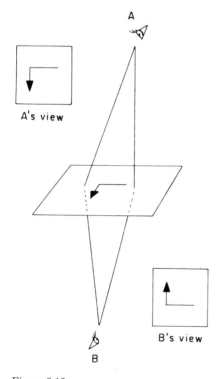

Figure 8.19
Whether the turtle is turning right or left depends on which side you look from.

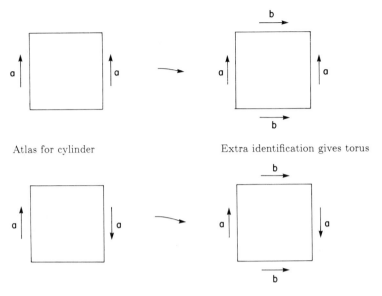

Atlas for cylinder   Extra identification gives torus

Atlas for Möbius strip   Extra identification gives Klein bottle

Figure 8.20
Comparing a torus and a Klein bottle.

an extrinsic property of the surface. It depends on setting up an external reference—are you looking from the top side or the bottom side? (Remember, the turtle is a two-dimensional creature who lives *in* the Möbius strip rather than "on top of" or "underneath" it. The turtle has no preference about whether you look at the strip from the top or bottom.)

So, properly speaking, right and left are only characteristics of the turtle's motions, not characteristics of the surface. We can define right and left on the surface with respect to a turtle that knows its left from its right. But this definition works only locally. You cannot look at some point of the surface and decide *a priori* that one direction is either right or left. You must first move the turtle there. And there is nothing to guarantee that, as the turtle moves around the surface, the commands LEFT and RIGHT will pick the same directions each time the turtle returns to a given point. This potential confusion is precisely what happened on the Möbius strip.

Of course, it may just happen that you have a surface on which left and right never get mixed up in this way. In that case, the surface is said to be *orientable,* and we could set up a consistent left and right

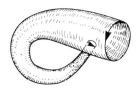
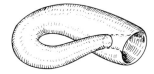

Figure 8.21
Folding a cylinder into a Klein bottle. Matching the directions on the arrows requires
sticking the bottle through itself.

definition on the surface by watching the turtle. In a case where the
turtle can take a trip that confuses left and right, the surface is called
nonorientable.

All of the closed surfaces we've run across so far have been orientable.
That's hardly surprising, since the classification theorem we mentioned
at the end of chapter 5 guarantees that any closed surface that fits
into three-dimensional space must be a sphere with handles, which is
orientable. (A sphere is orientable, and it is not hard to show that
adding a handle cannot change that.) The Möbius strip does fit into
three-dimensional space, but it is not closed. To transform it into a
closed surface, we can make an orientation-preserving identification of
the top and bottom edges on the atlas, in exactly the same way as
produces a torus from a cylinder (see figure 8.20). The resulting surface
is called a *Klein bottle*. Like the Möbius strip, it is nonorientable.

Can you make a topological Klein bottle out of this atlas by actually
bending and gluing a piece of rubber the way we did for a torus? What
we said above implies that you can't, in three-dimensional space. Let's
try to see why not. Gluing the horizontal edges is no problem. But if we
continue as with the torus the directions for the edge identifications will
not be correct. Instead, we must get one of the edges turned around as
shown in figure 8.21. That involves sticking the bottle through itself—a
rather unseemly thing to do, but the best that can be done in three
dimensions. The Klein bottle will not fit without self-intersections into
a three-dimensional space (even topologically; that is, even if we allow
bending and denting to distort distances on the surface). Contrast that
with the flat torus of subsection 8.1.4, which won't fit into three dimen-

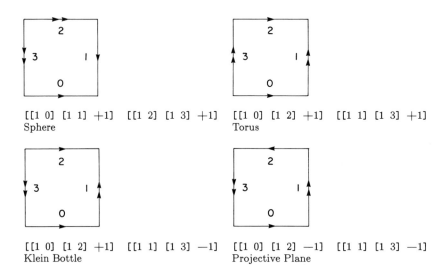

[[1 0] [1 1] +1]   [[1 2] [1 3] +1]   [[1 0] [1 2] +1]   [[1 1] [1 3] +1]
Sphere   Torus

[[1 0] [1 2] +1]   [[1 1] [1 3] −1]   [[1 0] [1 2] −1]   [[1 1] [1 3] −1]
Klein Bottle   Projective Plane

Figure 8.22
Atlases for four one-faced closed surfaces.

sions either, but will fit after being distorted into an ordinary "inner tube" torus.

If we start with a Möbius strip and close it up by making a second orientation-reversing identification, we get still another surface, called the *projective plane*. The projective plane, it turns out, is nonorientable and topologically distinct from the Klein bottle. Can you convince yourself of this?

8.2.2 A Program for Nonorientable Surfaces

It is not hard to extend the program sketch of section 8.1 to handle nonorientable surfaces. As before, we'll keep things simple by considering square faces only. The difference between this program and the one in 8.1 is that we must account for the possibility of edges identified in an orientation-reversing way. So our atlas must specify not only which edges are identified, but also whether the orientation is reversed. We'll indicate this by including a +1 or a −1, which we'll call the *transition parity,* in each atlas entry. A typical entry might look like [[2 1] [4 2] −1], which specifies that face 2, edge 1 is identified with face 4, edge 2 with the orientation reversed. Figure 8.22 illustrates the atlases for the four one-faced closed surfaces we've met so far: sphere, torus, Klein bottle, and projective plane.

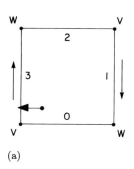

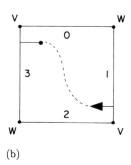

(a)   (b)

Figure 8.23
Crossing the edge of a Möbius strip as displayed by the program. (a) View "from
above"; (b) View "from below." Note that edge crossing always moves the turtle by
an ordinary wrap on the screen.

To generalize the program of section 8.1, we need to describe what
to do when the turtle crosses an edge with negative transition parity.
We will still handle the display so that the turtle's new position on the
display screen is obtained by an ordinary wrap. (This is dictated by the
design philosophy of "as the turtle sees it"; it ensures that we do not
suddenly see LEFT become a right turn.) Thus, when parity is reversed
we should display the face with the edge numbers increasing clockwise
rather than counterclockwise. (That is, when orientation is reversed,
continuity of turtle's viewpoint requires us to regard the new face "from
below" rather than from the standard atlas view "from above.") Figure
8.23 shows how the turtle trek on the Möbius strip would appear in this
representation.

So, in addition to CURRENT.FACE and ZERO.EDGE.SLOT, the program
needs to keep track of the parity $(P = \pm 1)$, which tells the orientation
for displaying the current face. Other than that, the program is the
same as before, except that parity considerations change the formulas
of 8.1.3 as follows: When a screen boundary is crossed, the edge hit is
given by

EDGE.HIT $= (P \times$ SLOT.HIT$) -$ ZERO.EDGE.SLOT (mod 4).

The new parity and ZERO.EDGE.SLOT are given by

$\langle$new $P\rangle = \langle$old $P\rangle \times \langle$transition parity, from atlas$\rangle$,
$\langle$new ZERO.EDGE.SLOT$\rangle$
    $=$ NSLOT $- P \times \langle$new edge as found in the atlas$\rangle$ (mod 4).

The correspondence between face coordinates and window coordinates becomes

```
TO DISPLAY.COORDS.OF [X Y]
    RETURN [(P*X*COS(A) - Y*SIN(A)) (Y*COS(A) + P*X*SIN(A))]

TO FACE.COORDS.OF [X Y]
    RETURN [P*(X*COS(A) + Y*SIN(A)) (Y*COS(A) - X*SIN(A))]
```

Exercises for Section 8.2

1. [D] List all possible atlases that give closed surfaces with one square face. Sort them according to topological type. How many of each type are there? [A]

2. Show that the Klein bottle we constructed in the text has zero curvature density at every point, just like the flat torus. [HA]

3. How many vertices does the projective plane we made out of one square have? What is the total curvature? Demonstrate that the projective plane is nonorientable by finding a closed turtle path that confuses left and right. [A]

4. Convince yourself that the "bottle" shown in figure 8.21 really can be cut open to give the Klein bottle atlas. Identify where the cuts are on the figure.

5. Suppose we have an atlas that includes only orientation-preserving identifications. Prove that the resulting surface actually is orientable by constructing a global definition for right and left that is consistent over the whole surface. [HA]

6. The fact that an atlas for a surface contains orientation-reversing identifications does not necessarily imply that the surface is nonorientable. Consider the atlas with two square faces:

```
[[1 0] [1 2] +1]    [[2 0] [2 2] +1]
[[1 3] [2 1] -1]    [[1 1] [2 3] -1]
```

What surface (topological type) does this describe? [A]

7. Pretend that the Klein bottle pictured in figure 8.21 is a real bottle (that is, ignore self-intersections). Observe that has no inside or outside. Just as with orientation, you can declare one side to be the "inside" in some locality and propagate that from place to place. But you will find

that the propagation eventually comes back to contradict itself, just like orientation. Describe in detail a propagation of "inside" and show how it comes to contradict itself. (In other words, if you set out to paint the entire "inside" of a Klein bottle, you'll end up painting the "outside" as well.) Note that if a surface does have an inside and an outside, you can find a consistent orientation by specifying left to be "left as viewed from the outside." Convince yourself that this extrinsic criterion, "having an inside and an outside," does imply orientability.

8. [D] What topological closed surfaces can be made with two square faces but not with one? [HA]

9. [P] What would it mean to say that the universe we live in is nonorientable? What are some of the phenomena you might observe in a three-dimensional nonorientable universe? [H]

10. [PD] Generalize your piecewise flat space simulation (exercise 17 of the preceding section) to include nonorientable spaces, and explore these.

8.3 Curvature and Euler Characteristic

Our investigation of surfaces, begun in chapter 5, has been rooted in a theory of curvature. In this section we examine the curvature of piecewise flat surfaces. In doing so we shall uncover a new topological invariant called the Euler characteristic, which is expressed in terms of the number of vertices, edges, and faces of a surface, and which turns out to be a disguised form of our old friend the total curvature.

8.3.1 Curvature of Piecewise Flat Surfaces

As we noted at the outset of this chapter, all the curvature in a piecewise flat surface is concentrated at the vertices. This makes the total curvature easy to compute. We need only to sum up the excesses of small turtle paths around each of the vertices:

$$K = \sum_{\text{vertices}} \langle \text{excess of a small path around the vertex} \rangle.$$

(Σ is the mathematical sign for summation; $\sum_{\text{vertices}}$ means to sum the specified quantity over all the vertices.)

Let's try to transform this formula into the simplest, most meaningful terms. Remembering that excess is equal to 2π minus the total turning,

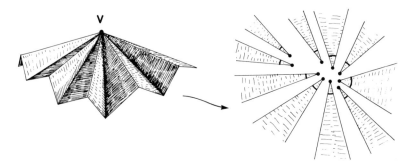

Figure 8.24
Total turning around a vertex is equal to the sum of the interior angles of the faces
meeting at the vertex.

we can rewrite the equation as

$$K = \sum_{\text{vertices}} \langle 2\pi - \text{total turning around the vertex} \rangle,$$

and separating out the 2π terms (one for each vertex) gives the formula

$$K = 2\pi V - \sum_{\text{vertices}} \langle \text{total turning around vertex} \rangle$$

where V is the number of vertices in the surface. This is better; the first
term is simple enough. Can we do something better with the second
term? We can, if we rewrite this formula using the fact that the total
turning around a vertex is equal to the sum of all the interior angles
meeting at that vertex (figure 8.24). Summing now over all the vertices
gives us all the interior angles of all the faces in the surface. If we
regroup these angles according to the faces they lie in, we can compute
total curvature as

$$K = 2\pi V - \sum_{\text{faces}} \langle \text{sum of the interior angles of the face} \rangle.$$

This is a somewhat surprising result, because we can compute the second
term without knowing how the edges are glued together. So if you have
all the individual faces of a piecewise flat surface, and somebody tells
you V, you can compute the total curvature without figuring out or
being told anything more about the atlas.

For piecewise square surfaces the formula is even easier, since the sum
of interior angles of any face is 2π. Hence, $K = 2\pi V - 2\pi F = 2\pi(V -
F)$. Here we have a formula for total curvature that doesn't mention
angles at all! But we can do even better. Remarkably enough, it turns

out that we can compute the total curvature of any closed piecewise flat surface without knowing any angles. We need only know the total number of faces and vertices and the number of edges.

Theorem For a closed piecewise flat surface with V vertices, E edges and F faces, the total curvature is

$$K = 2\pi(V - E + F).$$

Proof Since we already know that

$$K = 2\pi V - \sum_{\text{faces}} \langle \text{sum of the interior angles of the face} \rangle,$$

the point of the proof is to show that the sum

$$\sum_{\text{faces}} \langle \text{sum of the interior angles of the face} \rangle$$

can be expressed independent of the particular values of the angles. Now we don't know much in general about the sum of the interior angles of a face, but we do know a closely related quantity: the sum of the exterior angles. Since the boundary of each face is a simple planar closed path, we know that the sum of the exterior angles is 2π. To relate the exterior angles to the interior angles, notice that each exterior angle pairs off with an interior angle to sum to $\pi = 180°$ and there are as many of these pairs as there are edges to a face. Therefore,

$$\langle \text{sum of the interior angles of a face} \rangle$$
$$= \langle \text{sum of } (\pi - \text{exterior angle}) \rangle$$
$$= \pi \times \langle \text{number of edges of the face} \rangle$$
$$\quad - \langle \text{sum of the exterior angles of the face} \rangle$$
$$= \pi \times \langle \text{number of edges of the face} \rangle - 2\pi,$$

and so summing this quantity over all the faces gives

$$\sum_{\text{faces}} \langle \text{sum of the interior angles of the face} \rangle$$
$$= \pi \sum_{\text{faces}} \langle \text{number of edges in the face} \rangle - 2\pi F.$$

Now we must simplify the sum

$$\sum_{\text{faces}} \langle \text{number of edges in the face} \rangle.$$

The trick is to notice that, in a closed surface (once it is glued together), each edge is shared by precisely two faces, and so summing the number of edges in a face over all the separate faces counts each edge precisely twice, and therefore

$$\sum_{\text{faces}} \langle \text{number of edges in the face} \rangle = 2E.$$

Combining this with the preceding equation yields

$$\sum_{\text{faces}} \langle \text{sum of the interior angles of the face} \rangle = 2\pi(E - F),$$

and putting this into our formula for K gives the result

$$K = 2\pi V - \sum_{\text{faces}} \langle \text{sum of the interior angles of the face} \rangle$$

$$= 2\pi(V - E + F).$$

8.3.2 Euler Characteristic

The quantity $V - E + F$ is called the *Euler characteristic* of a surface and is usually denoted by the Greek letter χ (chi). Using this notation we rewrite our curvature formula as

$$K = 2\pi(V - E + F) = 2\pi\chi.$$

You can think of this equation as a convenient way of calculating the total curvature of a piecewise flat surface, but it is suggestive of much more than that. After all, K is not just any number associated to a piecewise flat surface; it has some special properties. First of all, K is defined for all surfaces, not only piecewise flat ones. Moreover, as we saw in section 5.3, K is a topological invariant. So our formula should lead us to suspect that there must be some way to see that the Euler characteristic also has these properties. That is, it is natural to ask the following questions: Is there some direct way to see that $V - E + F$ is a topological invariant? Is there some way to define $V - E + F$ for all surfaces, not just piecewise flat ones?

Let's look at topological invariance first. What happens to $V - E + F$ when we start bending, denting, stretching, and generally bashing up a piecewise flat surface? (To be fair, until we deal with the second question we should limit our zeal in deforming to leave the surface piecewise flat.) The answer is: absolutely nothing! After all, $V - E + F$ is just a counting job, and unless we cut a face in two, remove an edge, or perform

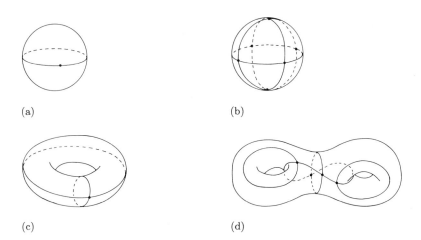

(a)   (b)

(c)   (d)

Figure 8.25
Nets on (a) a sphere with $V = 1$, $E = 1$, $F = 2$, and $\chi = 2$; (b) a sphere with $V = 6$, $E = 12$, $F = 8$, and $\chi = 2$; (c) a torus with $V = 1$, $E = 2$, $F = 1$, and $\chi = 0$; (d) a two-holed torus with $V = 4$, $E = 8$, $F = 2$, and $\chi = -2$.

some other such nontopological transformation, none of the numbers can change. That answers the first question.

Now let's turn to the problem of defining $V - E + F$ for an arbitrary surface. The image of a distorted piecewise flat surface makes a solid suggestion as to what we should mean by vertices, edges, and faces on a general surface: "Faces" on the surface will in general not be flat polygons but should be topological disks. "Edges" need not be straight lines, but should be simple arcs with a vertex at either end. More precisely, we define a *net:*

A *net* on a general surface is an arbitrary collection of simple arcs (terminated at each end by a vertex) that divide the surface into topological disks.

Figure 8.25 illustrates some nets on surfaces. We will continue to call the constituents of a net edges, vertices, and faces, so that, given a net, we can define the Euler characteristic χ by the same formula, $\chi = V - E + F$.

The definition of Euler characteristic presents a problem: One can draw infinitely many different nets on a given surface. How do we decide which net to use in computing the Euler characteristic? The answer is: It doesn't matter which one we choose! This is because of the following:

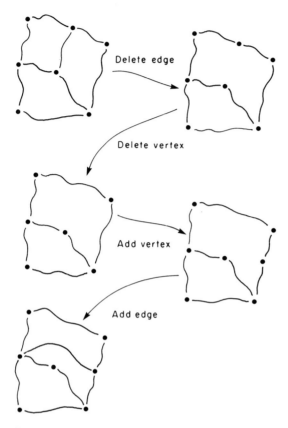

Figure 8.26
Elementary net transformations.

Theorem All nets on the same closed surface have the same Euler characteristic.

Proof One way to prove this theorem is to imagine starting with a particular net on a surface and transforming the net into a different net by adding or deleting vertices or edges. Of the various ways we might go about changing a net, we single out two *elementary net transformations:* (1) Add (or delete) a face by drawing in (or erasing) an edge between existing vertices. (2) Add (or delete) a vertex. These operations are illustrated in figure 8.26. Let's see how these transformations effect the value of χ. Suppose we add an edge (a type 1 transformation). Then E, the number of edges, certainly increases by 1. But the important thing to notice is that F, the number of faces, also increases by 1. Hence, $F - E$ is unchanged. And since V is unchanged, we see that $\chi = V - E + F$

is unchanged by type 1 transformations. What happens if we add a new vertex (a type 2 transformation)? This produces not only a new vertex, but also a new edge. So under a type 2 transformation V and E each increase by 1, and F is unchanged; hence, $V - E + F$ is again unchanged. In conclusion, we find that χ is invariant under net transformations of type 1 and 2. To complete the proof that any two nets on the same surface will give the same value of χ, we claim that, given any two nets, you can always get from one to the other by a sequence of transformations of types 1 and 2. The proof of this fact is not hard, and the details are left as an exercise (exercise 3).

So $\chi = V - E + F$ can be defined for any surface and is a topological invariant. This means we have two topological invariants for surfaces—Euler characteristic and total curvature—and we know that $K = 2\pi\chi$ for piecewise flat surfaces. It seems natural, then, to conjecture that $K = 2\pi\chi$ for any surface. This is indeed the case, as expressed by the following theorem:

Gauss-Bonnet Theorem For any closed surface, total curvature and Euler characteristic are related by $K = 2\pi\chi$.

Proof We'll sketch two different proofs of this theorem. The first is based on the fact that K and χ are both topological invariants. Suppose that we start with an arbitrary surface and deform it into a piecewise flat surface. Since K and χ are both topological invariants, the deformation leaves them unchanged. But we know from subsection 8.3.1 that $K = 2\pi\chi$ for the piecewise flat surface. Therefore, this is true for the original surface as well. The only catch in this proof is that we must show that any surface can be deformed into a piecewise flat surface. Intuitively, that seems very plausible; the idea is to flatten the surface piece by piece, pushing all the curvature into the edges between the pieces, then flatten the edges piece by piece, pushing all the curvature into the vertices. But the details of this are hard to write out rigorously. Exercise 5 gives pointers on how to do this. A second proof that $K = 2\pi\chi$ is based on a direct computation of K for any surface and is similar to the way we proved the theorem for piecewise flat surfaces. This is outlined in exercise 10.

The Gauss-Bonnet theorem is one of the key results in the geometry of surfaces because it forms a bridge between quantities defined purely

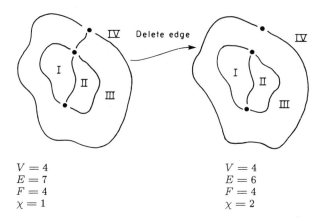

$V = 4$ $V = 4$
$E = 7$ $E = 6$
$F = 4$ $F = 4$
$\chi = 1$ $\chi = 2$

Figure 8.27
How can deleting an edge increase the Euler characteristic?

in terms of topology (such as Euler characteristic) and quantities defined purely in terms of distances and angles (such as total curvature).

Exercises for Section 8.3

1. Calculate the Euler characteristics of the sphere, torus, Klein bottle, projective plane, and two-holed torus. For each of these surfaces, draw a net and compute V, E, and F. Remember the restrictions on what can be a net. You might try to draw the simplest possible net that does the job.

2. How does adding a handle to a surface (subsection 5.3.3) change the Euler characteristic? Demonstrate explicitly how a net on the surface can be modified to give a new net on the surface with handle attached. [HA]

3. Complete the proof in 8.3.2 that Euler characteristic is a topological invariant by showing that any two nets on a surface can be transformed from one to the other by a sequence of elementary net-changing operations of types 1 and 2. [H]

4. Consider the planar net shown in figure 8.27. If we remove the edge marked A, the Euler characteristic increases by 1. Doesn't that contradict what we said about removing edges not changing the Euler characteristic? [A]

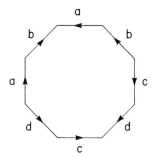

Figure 8.28
Identifying the edges of an octagon to produce a closed surface.

5. [DD] In the first proof of the Gauss-Bonnet theorem sketched above, we assumed that any surface can be deformed into a piecewise flat surface. Show that this is true, at least for surfaces in three-dimensional space. [H]

6. Show from $\chi = V - E + F$ that for a piecewise square surface we have $\chi = V - F$, and hence that $K = 2\pi(V - F)$. Generalize this to express χ in terms of V and F for closed piecewise flat surfaces in which all faces are n-gons. [A]

7. [D] Notice that $K = 2\pi(V - F)$ gives bounds on the amount of curvature in a piecewise square surface in terms of the number of faces in the surface. For example, if there are two faces, $F = 2$, then V must be at least 1 and at most $4F = 8$. That puts K between -2π and 12π. What is the actual range of values of possible K? Give answers here both if you allow surfaces with more than one component (for example, two separate spheres) and also if you require all surfaces to be in one piece. [A]

8. [D] Rather than obtaining different values for K by increasing F and keeping the faces all square, it is interesting to increase the number of sides of a single-faced surface. Use the Euler characteristic to give bounds on K for surfaces that can be made by identifying faces of a single n-gon. [A]

9. [D] Show that the single-faced surface shown in figure 8.28 has exactly one vertex and has the smallest possible total curvature among all surfaces that can be made by identifying edges of a single octagon, as established in exercise 8. In general, a single-faced surface with $4n$ edges can be made into an n-holed torus. Show how, and verify that the resulting figure is orientable and has the correct total curvature.

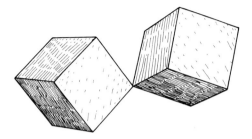

Figure 8.29
Double cube.

10. Prove directly (by computing K as a sum) that $K = 2\pi\chi$ for any surface, provided the edges of the net are turtle lines. [H]

11. [D] Consider the "double cube" shown in figure 8.29, which consists of two cubes with a vertex in common. How would you define total curvature here? One might view the surface topologically as a sphere with the equator pinched to a point, and so get $K = 4\pi$. Alternatively, one might take as curvature the sum for the two cubes, and so get $K = 8\pi$. Show, on the other hand, that $\chi = 3$ for this surface and therefore the Gauss-Bonnet theorem is contradicted whichever of these values we take for K. Mathematicians have gotten out of this bind by defining the term "surface" to exclude objects like this. Can you come up with a definition of the term "surface" that will include spheres, tori, cubes, cones, and even Klein bottles and projective planes, but not this double cube? [HA]

12. [D] We've already mentioned handle attaching as a general way of modifying surfaces. Now we'll introduce another modification technique, called *adding a crosscap*. Start with any surface and cut a square hole in it as shown in figure 8.30. Now close up the hole by making orientation-reversing identifications of the opposite edges. ("Adding" a crosscap is really deleting part of the surface followed by identifying). What does adding a crosscap to a surface do to the total curvature? What does it do to the orientability of a surface? What surface (topological type) do we get by adding a crosscap to a sphere? How about adding two crosscaps to a sphere? [A]

13. [DD] Here's a problem to test your powers of visualization: Show that starting with a surface, adding a handle, and then adding a crosscap produces the same result (topologically) as starting with the original surface and adding three crosscaps.

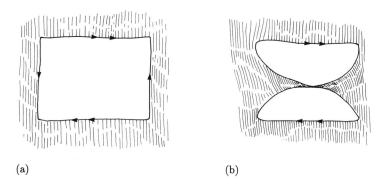

(a)   (b)

Figure 8.30
Adding a crosscap to a surface. (a) Cutting a hole; (b) The surface after the first
identification. The second identification cannot be realized in three dimensions
without self-intersections.

14. [D] A *regular net* is a collection of faces, edges, and vertices that
is "everywhere the same"—each face has the same number of arcs, S,
along its periphery and each vertex has the same number of arcs, T,
leading away from it. Find all possible regular nets on a sphere. Draw
pictures of them. Compare these with the five Platonic solids (section
5.3, exercise 14), which, by nature of their definitions, define regular nets
on the sphere. You should find that there are more than five regular
nets. Why can't those other regular nets correspond to Platonic solids?
[HA]

15. [D] Show that there are an infinite number of regular nets (see above
problem) on a torus, but that there are only three allowable values for
S. [HA]

16. [D] Study regular nets in the plane. Let S = number of edges to a
face and T = number of edges coming together at a vertex. Show that
there are regular nets with $S = 3$, 4, and 6. Show $S = 8$, $T = 3$ is
possible if you don't insist that the regions are congruent. Show that
$S = 5$, $T = 3$ is impossible in any case. Can you list all possible regular
nets? [HA]

17. [D] A *regular tesselation* (tiling) of a surface is a division of the
surface into a collection of congruent pieces. Therefore, any regular
tesselation defines a regular net. Show that in any regular tesselation of
the plane S must be 3, 4 or 6. [H]

9

Curved Space and General Relativity

> Things should be made as simple as possible, but
> not simpler.
> Albert Einstein

Chapter 8 used atlases to investigate piecewise flat surfaces, both in
designing computer simulations and in theorizing about geometry. This
chapter begins by discussing a similar technique for handling surfaces
that are curved everywhere. We then undertake a brief exploration of
higher-dimensional curved spaces. To emphasize an intrinsic point of
view, we'll speculate about the phenomena you might observe if the
three-dimensional space you live in were curved, and then if both space
and time were curved. Such speculation is not pure fantasy—according
to Einstein's General Theory of Relativity, we do live in a universe
where space and time are curved. We discuss the basic, striking claim of
Einstein's theory: that the force of gravity is in reality no force at all, but
rather a manifestation of the curvature of space and time. In addition,
we describe some of the more subtle effects predicted by relativity, such
as the gravitational red shift and the "bending" of light. Finally, we
show how to implement a computer program that uses turtle methods
to simulate motion in a relativistic universe.

9.1 Wedge Representations

The technique we will use for exploring curvature, called *wedge representation,* is a method for representing symmetric worlds. In most
cases the symmetry will be radial; that is, everything will "look the
same" along each line leading outward from some fixed "center" point.
Fortunately, this is sufficient for the General Relativity simulation we
will design later. But before venturing into curved space and time, we'll
discuss wedges in a more familiar setting by taking yet another look at
geometry on the surface of a sphere.

9.1.1 A Parable: At the Edge of a Wedge

A turtle once lived on a sphere. You and I can imagine the turtle's
world quite well. It is like the surface of a very round planet. But the

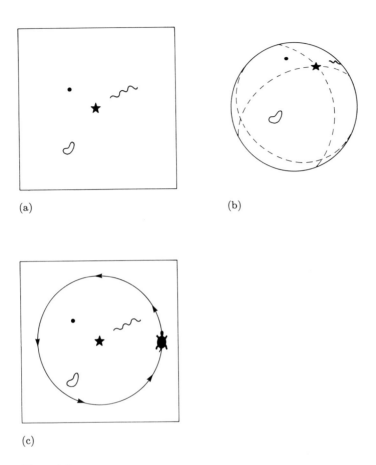

Figure 9.1
A "straight line" orbit on the turtle's flat map of its spherical world. (a) Turtle's
map. (b) Actual world. (c) Turtle map with "orbit."

turtle's view of its world was purely intrinsic; it knew nothing outside
of this two-dimensional surface—only where it walked and how much it
turned. For most of its life the turtle experienced only local geometry,
for it lived very near the north pole and did not venture more than a
tiny fraction of the sphere's circumference away from home. The turtle
was a clever mathematician and had discovered many regularities about
walking and turning, which it called Euclidean geometry. It discovered
the Pythagorean theorem for right triangles. It knew that the total
turning around any polygon was 360°. None of the parallel lines it had
constructed ever met. Of course, none of these things could have been

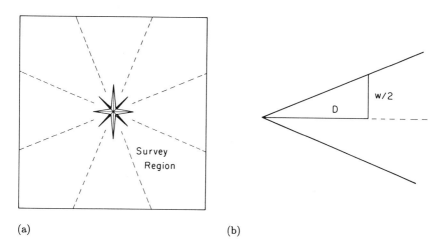

(a)   (b)

Figure 9.2
The turtle surveys its world. (a) Dividing the map into regions. (b) Finding the
width of a region at a given distance from home.

exactly true, but the turtle's measuring instruments were not so precise
that it could detect any discrepancy.

One day the turtle decided to explore farther and farther away from
home. To keep records it sketched a rough map of its wanderings (figure
9.1a). For a long time everything was just fine. But then the turtle went
so far as to reach the equator of the sphere and started walking along
it on a straight line. Lo and behold, the "straight line" led in a closed
path! What a perplexity!

The turtle stared at a sketch of this path on the map (figure 9.1c).
"How can this be?" it wondered. "It's as if some mysterious force were
pushing me and making me turn even though I was trying to walk in a
straight line. The force has made me orbit the north pole."

The mysterious force made the turtle nervous. It decided that it would
need a better map of these lands before venturing farther. So it divided
its current map into eight regions surrounding each of the eight compass
points pointing away from the north pole, and took to surveying each
wedge carefully (figure 9.2). The survey method was quite simple. First
the turtle marked the boundaries between the regions all the way out
to beyond the mysterious "orbit." Then it measured the width of each
region at various distances from home. The data were collected into
charts like this:

Distance from home	Width of region	Distance from home	Width of region
5	3.9	55	36.8
10	7.8	60	38.9
15	11.6	65	40.7
20	15.3	70	42.2
25	19.0	75	43.4
30	22.5	80	44.3
35	25.8	85	44.8
40	28.9	90	45.0
45	31.8	95	44.8
50	34.4	100	44.3

Unit distance = 100 turtle steps

Using the charts, the turtle constructed a small scale-model map of each region. When the maps were finished, the turtle moved them together to assemble a complete and detailed map of the whole known world. But to its great surprise, the pieces of the map did not fit together without leaving huge gaps (figure 9.3a). How could there be gaps when the turtle had seen the regions connected?

"Let me look at what happens upon crossing an edge of one piece on my map," said the turtle. "I didn't see any gaps, so these pieces must touch out there." Pushing the pieces together, the turtle drew a straight turtle walk as in figure 9.3b. But now the region near home, which it knew so well, was split apart. This was even worse than the first try.

The turtle mused as it rearranged the pieces as in figure 9.3a so that its home once more fit together properly. This made its "straight line" path look like an orbit. "What if the world were really like this. What's in those gaps? Who lives there? Someone, perhaps a demon. A demon! That's it! There must be a demon there. A demon who hides in the gaps and doesn't want anybody to know he's there. Perhaps he's responsible for the force that turns me when I walk and try not to turn." The turtle's mind ran quickly. "Yes, it must be a demon who wants no company in the gaps of the world. What a clever demon! He always picks me up as I reach the edge of a wedge, and moves me to the next wedge so quickly that I never see it. And he turns me, too, so I never suspect that the gaps are there. But I know better, thanks to my careful survey. The mysterious turning force is the work of the demon."

The story is not quite at an end. The turtle carefully resurveyed each wedge and found that it, too, must be made of wedges. All in all, the turtle decided, the world is composed of many, many narrow

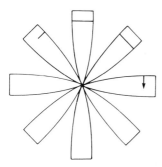

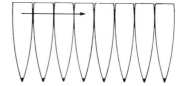

Wedges don't fit together.   Trying another fit.

Figure 9.3
Musing with map pieces.

wedges, with the demon acting almost constantly as the turtle walks. The turtle thought and measured, but never found an inconsistency in this belief. Distances measured on long walks were not Euclidean, but the discrepancy could be accounted for by the demon's gaps. "Parallel" lines became unparallel and met, but the amount of turning away from parallel was always exactly demon turning. A demon acting as the turtle theorized explained every feature of the geometry.

9.1.2 Symmetric Wedge Maps

You should recognize the turtle's map as an atlas similar to the atlases for the piecewise flat surfaces of chapter 8. Actually gluing those wedges together would give quite a good model of the sphere's geometry. Had the turtle merely invented rules for the map that said "treat the pieces as glued together, even though you don't see how they can be," then we could hardly quarrel with this representation. But because the turtle does not know about curved worlds, it is faced with a conflict between maintaining its familiar flat geometry and maintaining the connectedness of its experienced world. The response is to invent a demon. And one can well understand how the idea of a demon reinforced the turtle's initial interpretation that some "force" was making it turn in curved paths even when it tried to walk straight.

The demon seems superfluous in mapmaking, but we will soon see that it is easy to embody the demon as a "corrective process" that is the difference between walking on a plane and walking on a curved surface. Moreover, the idea of modeling a curved world as a flat one plus a very dependable "force" is, as we hinted, the essence of the General Theory of Relativity.

As the turtle discovered, the use of a flat map to picture the geometry of a nonflat surface becomes more and more satisfactory as the number of wedges increases. The reason is that a very narrow wedge of the actual surface needs to be distorted only slightly in order to fit onto a planar map. In fact, we could imagine a completely accurate planar map as consisting of an infinite number of infinitely thin wedges interspersed with an infinite number of infinitely thin gaps. Looking at paths on such a map, you would see no difference from a more ordinary map which merely deforms some distances and angles when it depicts curved surfaces.

This is the representation we shall use in our computer simulation. The display screen will serve as the planar map, and we'll use this map to watch the path of a turtle walking on the surface. We will observe that the path of a turtle walking straight will not look straight on the display screen (owing to the distortion in the mapping from surface to plane, or, in other words, the workings of the demon).

If we were using a rough map with only a few wedges, then computing the display image of the turtle's walk would be no problem. The turtle would walk in a flat, Euclidean world so long as it did not cross the edge of a wedge. When it did come to an edge, we could have the computer simulate the "demon" by picking up the turtle and moving it from one wedge to the next and turning it appropriately. This process would be cumbersome for accurate maps with large numbers of thin wedges (not to mention maps with an infinite number of infinitely thin wedges), so we shall have modify the technique, but only slightly.

From the way the turtle made its map you can see that the map would appear the same as an ordinary map that deforms the sphere into a plane by stretching distances along latitudes but not along longitudes. Thus, in going from sphere to map, circles drawn at various radii from the north pole gain extra circumference but keep the same radius from the north pole. For the time being we will consider only radially symmetric surfaces like the sphere, and will always lay out wedges evenly so as to preserve that symmetry on the map. That way radial distances will never need any distortion, but distances on circles around the center will be uniformly (at a given radius) stretched or shrunk. Figure 9.4 shows another radially symmetric surface—a plane with a "hill" on it— and the corresponding wedge map.

The demon's corrective process (like all things turtle) has two parts: moving and turning. Correspondingly, in simulating a radially sym-

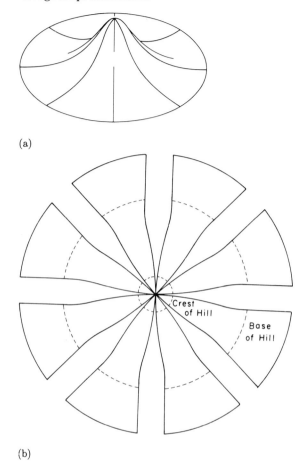

(a)

(b)

Figure 9.4
(a) A plane with a symmetrical hill in it. (b) Corresponding wedge map.

metric world we will have two functions that determine the distortion of the circles around the central point: the ratio of the gap between wedges to the thickness of a wedge and the amount of demon turning from wedge to wedge. Both of these are given as functions of radius. Alternatively, we can specify equivalent information by giving the circumference and total turning, $C(r)$ and $TT(r)$ respectively, of circles of radius r as measured on the surface. The equivalence between these two ways of giving the information is expressed by the relation

quantity on the map = quantity on the surface + demon quantity

where quantity is either turning or distance.

As an example, you may recall that we computed C and TT for a sphere in subsection 7.3.5:

$$C(r) = 2\pi R \sin \frac{r}{R},$$

$$TT(r) = 2\pi \cos \frac{r}{R}$$

where R is the radius of the sphere and r is the radius of the circle as measured on the sphere. If the map is scaled so that r is also equal to the distance from the turtle to the central point as measured on the map, then the corresponding circumference and total turning for circles on the map are $2\pi r$ and 2π. That leaves the differences, namely $2\pi[r - R\sin(r/R)]$ and $2\pi[1 - \cos(r/R)]$, respectively, for total gap distance and demon turning in going around a circle.

We can use this corrective process to develop a computer program for displaying the map image of a turtle walking on the surface. The procedure is this: Move the turtle a little bit at a time. Each little piece of walk will consist of a short straight segment that represents the actual walking on the wedges, plus two correction factors. If we represent the turtle's heading (on the map) as a unit vector $\mathbf{H}$, then the actual walking that the turtle does in going a distance D can be represented as a vector $\mathbf{Realwalk} = D \times \mathbf{H}$. The first correction (a move) we will call "leaping." It adds in the total amount of moving done by the demon. The second correction (a turn) rotates the heading by the total amount of "demon turning" done along the short path. We treat these two effects separately.

Leaping

Figure 9.5a depicts a highly magnified view of a walk on a map made up of many thin wedges. Observe that the walk is composed of two different types of pieces: the real walking done on the wedges and the demon's leaping done in the cracks. If we represent each piece as a vector, we can take advantage of the commutativity of vector addition to reassemble the pieces into a single "real walk" part and a single "leaping" part (figure 9.5b). Thus we have the vector equation

Walk = Realwalk + Leap

where **Walk** is the turtle's total change in position on the map.

Now, the **Leap** vector can be constructed from the real walk as follows. First project **Realwalk** onto the line perpendicular to the gaps (that is, along the leaping direction, which is perpendicular to the radial

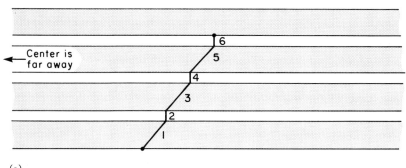

(a)

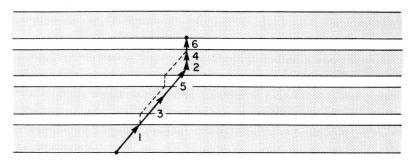

(b)

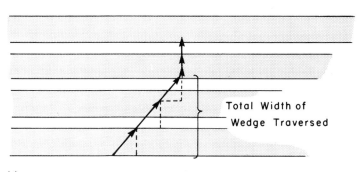

(c)

Figure 9.5
(a) Wedge map path traversing three wedges and three gaps. (b) Uniting real walks
(1, 3, 5) and leaps (2, 4, 6). (c) Projecting to find the width of the wedges traversed.

line from the map's center to the turtle) to find the total width of the
wedges traversed (figure 9.5c). Then just multiply by the ratio of gap to
wedge, which we call GAPRATIO. If you remember from chapter 3 how
to project vectors using dot products, you can easily derive the vector
equation

$$\textbf{Leap} = \text{GAPRATIO} \times (\textbf{S} \cdot \textbf{Realwalk}) \times \textbf{S} \tag{1}$$

where **S** is a unit vector in the tangential direction (that is, pointing
perpendicular to the radial line). **S** gives the appropriate direction
for projection, and supplies the **Leap** vector with its direction as well.
GAPRATIO can be simply computed as the ratio of that part of the map
circle that is not wedges to the wedge part:

$$\text{GAPRATIO} = \frac{2\pi r - C(r)}{C(r)} = \frac{2\pi r}{C(r)} - 1. \tag{2}$$

Demon Turning
The turtle of our parable in 9.1.1 found that, even when it was walking straight, it accumulated some extra "demon turning" each time it
crossed a wedge. The total demon turning over a short walk is proportional to the number of wedges crossed. If the wedges are infinitely thin
and uniformly spread out, then the number of wedges crossed in a short
turtle walk is in turn proportional to the central angle swept out by the
radial line to the turtle as it moves on the map. Thus we have

$$\text{DEMON.TURNING} = \text{CENTRAL.ANGLE} \times \text{TURNING.PER.ANGLE}. \tag{3}$$

The TURNING.PER.ANGLE will, like the GAPRATIO, depend on the turtle's
distance r from the central point. We can compute TURNING.PER.ANGLE
if we know the total demon turning done on a circle, which has a central
angle of 2π:

$$\text{TURNING.PER.ANGLE} = \frac{2\pi - TT(r)}{2\pi} = 1 - \frac{TT(n)}{2\pi}. \tag{4}$$

(This formula, like all formulas in this chapter, has angles expressed
in radians. You may want to convert to degrees for the computer
simulation.)

We can compute the central angle by using the unit tangential vector
S again. With what we learned about dot products and projections in
chapter 3 it should not be difficult to verify that the central angle for a
short turtle walk is approximately equal (see exercise 5) to

$(1/r) \times (\textbf{Walk} \cdot \textbf{S})$.

9.1.3 A Computer Simulation

The above computations can be readily expressed in program form. As
with the turtle simulations we have already discussed, the turtle's motion
is kept track of by a position vector **P** and a heading vector **H**. The
basic command is WEDGEFORWARD, which moves the turtle on the map
corresponding to a "real" FORWARD on the surface:

```
TO WEDGEFORWARD D
    REPEAT UNTIL D < SMALLDISTANCE
        WALKSTEP SMALLDISTANCE
        D ← D - SMALLDISTANCE
    WALKSTEP D
```

The program walks a fixed small distance at a time until the amount
remaining to be walked is also small, then just walks that remaining
distance.

Walking a small distance entails the following steps:

• Do a normal FORWARD on the map (and compute **Realwalk**, the vector
that describes this displacement).

• Compute the parameters r and S. Leap according to equations 1 and
2 of 9.1.2 (and compute total map displacement, **Walk = Realwalk +
Leap**).

• Rotate the turtle according to the demon turn computed using equations 3 and 4.

• Finally, show the turtle at the resulting position on the display screen.

Here is the procedure:

```
TO WALKSTEP D
    REALWALKSTEP D
    COMPUTE.PARAMETERS
    DEMONLEAP
    DEMONTURN
    DISPLAY
```

Filling in the details in the subprocedures is simple:

```
TO REALWALKSTEP D
    REALWALK ← D * H
    P ← P + REALWALK
```

```
TO DEMONLEAP
   LEAP ← GAPRATIO * DOT(S, REALWALK) * S
   WALK ← REALWALK + LEAP
   P ← P + LEAP

TO DEMONTURN
   TURNING ← CENTRAL.ANGLE * TURNING.PER.ANGLE
   H ← ROTATE(H, TURNING)
```

The `COMPUTE.PARAMETERS` procedure computes the turtle's distance r from the origin and the tangential vector **S**, and uses these to determine `GAPRATIO` and `TURNING.PER.ANGLE`. `CENTRAL.ANGLE` should be computed after **Leap**. (See exercise 5 concerning **S** and `CENTRAL.ANGLE`.) Observe that ordinary turtle (nondemon) LEFT and RIGHT turning is implemented just as in the planar case, except that we must explicitly update the heading vector **H**.

The surface itself is determined by specifying the functions $TT(r)$ and $C(r)$, which will be used in the above computations. To do a sphere simulation use the formulas given in subsection 9.1.2. Other surfaces are discussed in the exercises.

Incidentally, `DEMONTURN` is really the more important of the two corrections to `REALWALK`. A worthwhile first step is to write the program without `DEMONLEAP`. Experiment with that geometry to see what it looks like and how it differs from the fully corrected version.

In writing the program, beware of the following bugs:

• Don't start your simulation precisely at $r = 0$ without considering what happens to your formulas.

• The overall accuracy of the simulation suffers if you use large increments. (This is in contrast with the sphere simulation of chapter 7, which suffers only in picture displayed if you choose large increments for the steps in FORWARD.) You will probably have to choose `SMALLDISTANCE` such that `CENTRAL.ANGLE` is a few degrees at most.

• As given, the program gets much less accurate near the south pole of the sphere. To fix this you may want to insert a step at the beginning of the loop in `WEDGEFORWARD` that selects `SMALLDISTANCE` according to where the turtle is. (How about taking `SMALLDISTANCE` to be `CONSTANT÷ GAPRATIO`, which ensures that LEAP does not get large as `GAPRATIO` does?)

Exercises for Section 9.1

1. Write down equations 1–4 of subsection 9.1.2 for the special case of a sphere. [A]

2. Convert your answers to exercise 1 and the formula given in the text for CENTRAL.ANGLE to measure angles in degrees rather than radians. Recall that the sphere simulation in chapter 7 was arranged so that the input to FORWARD was an angle in degrees. What value should you use for R so that the input to the WEDGEFORWARD procedure will likewise be an angle in degrees? [HA]

3. [P] What are $TT(r)$, $C(r)$, and equations 1–4 for a cone, expressed in terms of the cone's "pie angle" θ? Make a computer wedge map program for a cone and explore its geometry. In particular, check that away from the center the surface is flat. How is this flatness reflected in the equations? Circles, not necessarily around the center, make a particularly interesting topic of study. [H]

4. For a cone with negative curvature, you should find that $TT(r)$ is greater than 2π. What does this mean about demon turning? How about leaping? Can we still interpret the map as consisting of wedges with gaps in between? Does the program still work? [A]

5. The problem of computing the central angle corresponding to a given **Walk** has a simple answer if the length of **Walk** is much smaller than the distance from home. Project **Walk** onto a line perpendicular to the position vector. That projection is very nearly an arc of length d on a circle of radius r around home; hence the central angle is nearly d/r (in radians). Use this method to verify the approximation given in 9.1.2. Note that the unit vector **S** can be easily expressed in terms of the unit radial vector **U** as $\mathbf{S} = \mathrm{Perp}(\mathbf{U})$. **U**, in turn, is easy to express in Cartesian coordinates. If $(0,0)$ is the center, $\mathbf{U} = (x/r, y/r)$.

6. [P] Figure 9.4 shows the wedge map of a plane with a symmetric bump in it. For developing a computer simulation you can use the following formulas:

$$C(r) = 2\pi[r + BQ(r)]$$

$$Q(r) = \begin{cases} \cos \dfrac{r}{s} - 1 & \text{if } r \leq \pi s \\ -2 & \text{if } r > \pi s \end{cases}$$

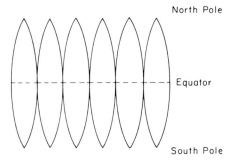

North Pole

Equator

South Pole

Figure 9.6
Another wedge layout for the sphere.

$$\text{TURNING.PER.ANGLE} = \begin{cases} \dfrac{B}{s}\sin\dfrac{r}{s} & \text{if } r \le \pi s \\[2mm] 0 & \text{if } r > \pi s \end{cases}$$

Here πs is the size of the bump, and the number B determines its
steepness. $B = s$ means that the bump has vertical sides (an equator) at
one point, $B < s$ means a flatter bump (no equator), and $B > s$ means
a bulbous bump (two equators). What are the corresponding formulas
for GAPRATIO and $TT(r)$? Verify that these formulas give the qualitative
features of the bump. Draw a map path of a straight turtle line that
starts on the flat part of the surface and goes over the bump (but not
directly over the center of the bump). Make a computer simulation and
check your guess.

7. [P] Make a simulator of a terrain with several bumps. This is no longer
radially symmetric, but you can still use the implementation outlined in
9.1.3 if you divide the map into several regions, each containing a single,
symmetric bump. Use your simulator to invent a computer game, say,
based upon trying to shoot a target across the bumpy terrain. For this
purpose, demon leaping is probably not needed.

8. The wedge map for the plane with a bump differs from undistorted
flat maps, even in the regions away from the bump where the surface is
flat. Explain the nature of the distortion. [A]

9. [D] Our program is based upon specifying the surface using the two
fundamental parameters $C(r)$ and $TT(r)$. But in fact it is sufficient to
give only one of these. If you know calculus, show that $TT(r)$ is equal
to dC/dr, the derivative of $C(r)$. [HA]

10. [D] The sphere map in figure 9.6 illustrates a layout of the wedges
that is not radially symmetric. With infinitely thin wedges, this makes

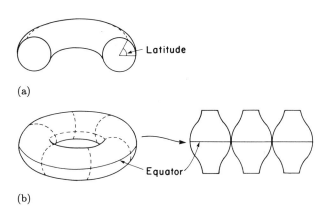

(a)

(b)

Figure 9.7
(a) Torus and latitude on it. (b) Corresponding wedge layout.

latitude circles on the surface correspond to lines $y = $ constant on the map. We can still use the basic simulation scheme of 9.1.2 and 9.1.3 if we give new formulas for demon turning and GAPRATIO on this kind of map. What are these formulas in terms of C and TT? In which direction is the leap correction? [HA]

11. [P] Investigate the layout described in exercise 10 for a wedge map of a sphere. This layout has the advantage that lines of latitude and longitude are lines of constant y or constant x. Thus, it may be good for simulating navigation problems. Show that the demon turning for a short walk is $(\Delta x/R) \times \sin(y/R)$ where y is the y coordinate on the map and Δx is the change in x coordinate. Find GAPRATIO as well. Use this information to make a simulation.

12. [P] Improve your simulation of exercise 11 so that it knows what to do when the turtle walks off the edge of the map. Improve it again so that is does not get much less accurate near the poles.

13. [PD] The kind of layout discussed in exercise 10 is particularly convenient for making a wedge map of a torus. To figure out the appropriate parameters we can return to the "cone method" analysis we used to derive the parameters for a sphere in subsection 7.3.5. The result of the cone method may be succinctly stated as follows: The total turning in going around a circular track banked at θ from flat is $2\pi \cos\theta$. Consider a torus with latitudes labeled by angle LAT as shown in figure 9.7a. Walking around such a latitude appears to a turtle to be just like

following a circular track banked at 90 — LAT. Hence, total turning around it is

$$2\pi \cos(90 - \text{LAT}) = 2\pi \sin(\text{LAT}).$$

On a wedge map of the torus, as in figure 9.7b, those latitudes appear on the map as straight lines; thus, the turtle's real turning is exactly canceled by demon turning. So the demon turning over a complete latitude is $2\pi \sin(\text{LAT})$. Write a program to simulate the wedged version of a torus. If the map is rectangular, with width w and height h, show that the demon turning along a straight turtle walk is

$$2\pi \frac{\Delta x}{w} \sin \frac{2\pi y}{h}.$$

14. What should one mean by an "equator" of the torus? How many equators does a torus have? Prove using the wedge method of analysis that a turtle line that repeatedly intersects an equator always intersects it at the same angle. [A]

15. Do exercise 9 for the rectangular layout shown in figure 9.6. That is, let $W(y)$ be the total (real) width of the surface as a function of distance up from the middle line, and show that TT along a line of constant y is dW/dy.

16. [P] In traveling over a hill on a plane, a turtle must go farther than in making the same trip if the hill were not there. In contrast, make a simulation of a plane with a "hill" where the distance through the "hill" is less than the planar distance. Such a surface cannot fit in three-dimensional space.

17. [P] Make a simplified simulator with no leaping. Play with different TT functions and correlate bending toward or away from the center, circular "orbits," etc. with properties of the TT function.

18. When the edges of adjacent wedges are parallel there is no demon turning. The world there is locally flat and would fit into a planar map. Conversely, if the edges are not parallel there is demon turning. The sense of demon turning, toward or away from the center, is determined by whether the edges get closer together or farther apart as you move toward the center. Go back and analyze the umbrella of exercise 16 of section 5.2 as a wedge map of a curved surface according to the above considerations. Correlate positive and negative curvature, if possible, to bending toward or away from the center.

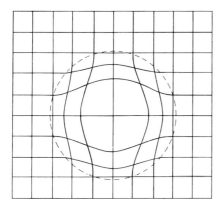

Figure 9.8
Rectangular grid viewed through spherical bent-space region.

9.2 Phenomena of Curved Space and Time

It is easy to feel smug about the turtle's interpretation of curvature as mysterious gaps in the world occupied by a demon. As three-dimensional creatures, we have a privileged exterior view of spherical geometry which the turtle does not have. On the other hand, when it comes to visualizing what curved space can mean, we find ourselves in a position more like the turtle's. We are no longer able to step outside the world we live in and "see" it as a curved part of a higher-dimensional world. (Luckily, we have since chapter 5 put aside such extrinsic notions of curvature in favor of a more general, intrinsic sense of what it means to be curved.) More than that, our everyday experience is purely flat, like the turtle's. Very few people have ever questioned whether the geometry of the universe could be other than flat Euclidean. Fewer still have a coherent idea of what it might be like were it not flat.

9.2.1 Curved Space

What would it be like to live in a curved world? Rather than dilute the experience by talking about long walks in space, careful measuring, and mapmaking, imagine that a piece of your living room (say, a sphere about a foot in diameter) contains space that is curved. Your situation would be analogous to that of a turtle faced with a hill in an otherwise flat plane, as depicted in figure 9.4.

The first thing you notice as you enter the room is that objects appear distorted when viewed through the spherical region. Figure 9.8 shows

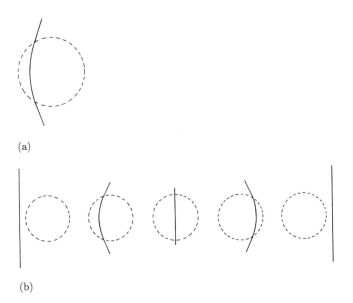

(a)

(b)

Figure 9.9
(a) Wire "bends" when poked through region. (b) Sequence of views as wire is drawn
through region.

what a rectangular grid looks like. Next, you poke the region with a
piece of stiff wire. The wire goes effortlessly in and out, but appears to
bend as you push it in. The bend is more than a distorted image, since if
you poke the wire all the way through it comes out the other side at an
angle to its original direction (figure 9.9a). You try the same experiment
with a thin glass rod, which is too rigid to bend without breaking. But
the same thing happens—the rod comes out of the region at an angle
to its original direction. Passing rods and wires through the sphere a
few more times draws attention to another phenomenon: When they
are poked straight through the center of the sphere, they do not appear
bent at all but seem shorter than when they started. Figure 9.9b shows
a sequence of views as a wire is drawn through the sphere.

A bee makes a sudden appearance and flies at great speed on a beeline
toward and into the region. None the worse for wear, it comes out the
other side at the same speed, but its trajectory is reaimed exactly as if
it had flown along your bent wire. Intrigued by this coincidence of bee
trajectory and wire bending, you shine a penlight beam along the wire
into the region. Sure enough, the beam emerges deflected exactly as the
wire was bent.

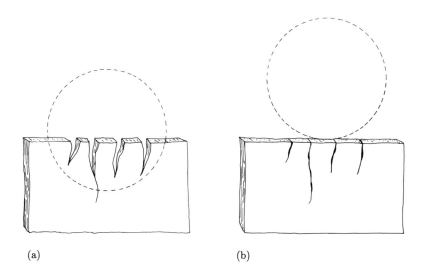

(a)   (b)

Figure 9.10
(a) Board cracks apart as it is pushed into the region. (b) Gaps close after board is removed.

Getting more aggressive, you take a thin but rather wide (wider than the region) board and push it sideways towards the center of the region as if trying to slice the region in half. In sharp contrast to the wire, the board resists. Pushing harder and harder, you eventually succeed in getting it in, but the board splits in several places (figure 9.10a). Withdrawing the board, you find that the gaps are gone but the splits have not healed (figure 9.10b).

As a final experiment, you fill a large aquarium with water and place it below the region. Now you raise the aquarium until the region is submerged. The water level drops!

Let's summarize the phenomena seen so far. They can be organized into two camps: moves and turns.

Distance distortion Distances through the curved region differ from seemingly parallel distances not through it. This accounts for the board breaking. As figure 9.11 shows, a flat board embodies the constraint that parallel segments have the same length. If the region of space (shaded) requires extra distance to traverse it, there will not be enough board to bridge the gap and the board must break. Containing more distance, the region also contains more volume than you would expect—hence the water effect.

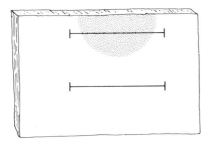

Figure 9.11
Two parallel segments of a flat board must have the same length.

Bending Lines (wires, light rays, beelines) all bend globally, but there is ample evidence that they are not experiencing any bending locally. This should remind you not only of the demon turning in our turtle parable, but also of the first time the turtle set foot on the sphere in chapter 5 and found that things can get turned without turning locally.

It is time for a bit more precision in investigating this curved-space region. You decide to make a map, as the turtle did. So you coat a rubber sheet with epoxy and hold it centered in the region. After the epoxy dries you cut the sheet into wedges. The wedges fit together perfectly until you remove them from the region. When you do that, you perceive some stress and maybe a bit of buckling. But if the pieces are small enough, they will survive and still nearly fit flat in a plane. The result is just the wedged "hill" map of figure 9.4. You could now predict bending of wires and beelines from this map by just drawing straight segments within each wedge and "demon leaping and turning" when necessary to get to a new wedge. Of course, there would be some error, since the individual wedges needed some distortion in order to fit into a plane. But if you had the patience, you could make maps with narrower and narrower wedges until the distortion in any single wedge was negligibly small. This would yield a very accurate wedge map.

Notice that, even in flat (three-dimensional) space, you could glue together all the wedges without any gaps at all if you allowed the resulting surface to bulge out of the plane to produce the hill of figure 9.4. Such a map would be a perfect map of a two-dimensional slice of the region of curved space. But it suffers two defects. First, it is embedded unsymmetrically in three-dimensional space, with a hill on one side and a dent on the other—whereas the slice it maps is actually a perfectly symmetrical slice through the curved-space region. (This is another example of the nonintrinsic characteristics a surface can pick up by being embedded in a higher-dimensional space. Recall the "curvature" of a cylinder, or the fact that edges of a cube look distinguished from but are really intrinsically the same as points interior to faces.) More important, there is no guarantee that a general wedge map can be glued together in three-dimensional space. If, for example, the curved-space region had less space than it appeared to have from outside, you should be able to convince yourself that the wedge map could not be glued together at all in flat three-dimensional space.

9.2.2 Curved Spacetime

Suppose you discover that your watch loses time whenever you put it into your jewelry box. The watch is guaranteed accurate and you've had it checked. If you leave the watch on the table just a few inches away from the box it doesn't lose time. There simply is something about that box. Repeating the curved-space experiments of the previous section with the box shows nothing unusual. Wires poked into the box seem perfectly normal, and the beam from your penlight doesn't bend. But while experimenting with the light you notice one other peculiarity: Dust particles are deflected as they fall past the box. Aside from that and the time loss, everything seems normal.

Those deflected particles should make you suspicious. More than that, your adventures with curved space might have already led you to think of a way to describe the time-loss phenomenon. One could say that the region in the box contains "less time" than nearby regions, just as the curved region contained "more space." And perhaps this "less time" accounts for the deflection of the dust particles in the same way that the curved space bent the bee's path. But this is a very fuzzy theory. The fact that dust-particle paths bend but light rays and wires don't is particularly puzzling.

Let's explore the geometric possibilities. We can represent time as an extra dimension in addition to the usual spatial ones. In terms of vectors, adding dimensions is not much trouble. We just add a fourth coordinate, t, to the triple x, y, and z. Thus, a point in *spacetime* specifies a particular place at a particular time. To link with your experience, we'll call such a thing an *event* to imply that a particular time characterizes it as well as a particular place.

But this is too formal. Is there some way to see spacetime and get some feeling for it? Think of a situation with motion in it—say, some white billiard balls moving on a black billiards table. A snapshot from

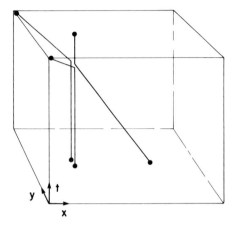

Figure 9.12
A billiards shot in spacetime with initial and final ball positions shown in the bottom and top slices.

above gives a nice scale-model "map" of the balls' positions at an instant. Now think of piling the negatives from a whole sequence of pictures, one on top of another, into a thick pile. Through the clear celluloid you see black lines representing the paths of the balls. Each slice shows the positions of the balls at an instant. But in addition to positions, changes in time are represented in this "map" as well, by moving up or down in the pile. What we have is a spacetime map of the billiards table and balls. Notice how this model has used the third dimension, otherwise unused in this case, to represent time. We can use this technique, drawing three-dimensional pictures, whenever the motion we are interested in is restricted to two spatial dimensions.

The path of a particle in spacetime (that is, the collection of events that gives the particle's position at different times) is called the *world line* of the particle. For a ball at rest on the table, its image in sequential negatives is directly over itself; the world line is vertical. If the ball is moving, the image is slightly displaced from one negative to the next and the world line will be tilted away from vertical. Figure 9.12 shows a billiards shot down the middle of the table toward two stopped balls. Upon striking, the ball stops but propels the two other balls into the corners of the table. Figure 9.13 shows a circular "earth orbit," which in a spacetime map becomes a helix winding its way around the vertical world line that represents the stationary sun. Notice that a particle's velocity is represented by its heading in spacetime. In particular, a

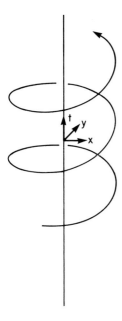

Figure 9.13
The earth orbiting the sun traces out a helix in spacetime.

heading parallel to the time axis means zero velocity. As the particle picks up speed its heading tilts farther and farther away from the time axis. The spatial component of the heading points out where in space the particle will be after the passage of some time—that is, it gives the direction of spatial motion.

Let's take a planar slice of our jewelry box and call it the x,y plane. Piling up slices, we get a three-dimensional model of the region of spacetime that contains all events, no matter when they occur, as long as they occur in the chosen slice. For a moment let's specialize to one spatial dimension, the x axis, that can represent the line along which you insert and remove your watch. That way we can draw our spacetime map in two dimensions.

Suppose that this region of spacetime is curved, and in particular that there is "less time" at the center of the box ($x = 0$). We can represent this as a "wedged" two-dimensional spacetime with the wedges thinner toward the center as in figure 9.14a. Figure 9.14b shows the world line of a watch inserted in the box at $t = 0$ (bedtime) and removed at $t = 9$ hours (breakfast time). The watch has traversed less time (because

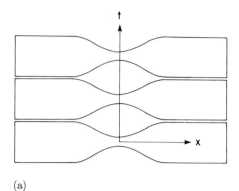

(a)

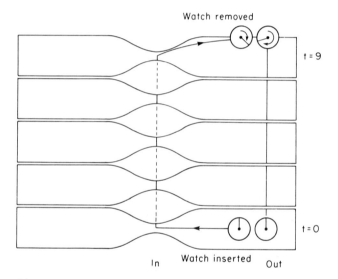

(b)

Figure 9.14
(a) Wedge map of spacetime; "less time" near the center. (b) Watch inserted at $t = 0$
and removed at $t = 9$ traverses less time than watch that remains outside the box.

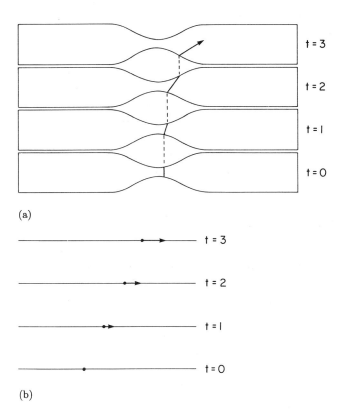

(a)

(b)

Figure 9.15
(a) Particle starts at rest at $t = 0$, deflects and picks up greater and greater velocity.
(b) Spatial view (x axis) at various times shows the particle moving and accelerating.

of "demon leaps," if you like that terminology) than watches outside the distorted region of spacetime, so it appears to be running slow even though it has ticked off the locally appropriate amount of time. You should recognize this time-interval distortion as the exact analog of distance distortion in space alone.

How about those deflected dust particles? Take a look at figure 9.15a, which shows the world line, for one spatial dimension, of a particle that starts from rest. You can see how the "demon turning" from wedge to wedge causes the world line of the particle to "bend." This is precisely analogous to spatial bending, but to distinguish the two we will use the term *deflection* to denote bending due to spacetime curvature.

Consider how an observer watching the spatial part of the world line (the particle's path in space) will interpret deflection. First of all, the

initially vertical heading will tilt and acquire a spatial projection, that
is, a nonzero velocity. The accumulated effect of the acquired velocity
will be motion along the x axis. As the heading tilts more and more, the
observer sees more and more velocity, that is, acceleration (figure 9.15b).
The natural interpretation of seeing an object at rest gradually pick up
velocity and move off in some direction is that some force is making it
do that. But now that we know about curvature, we can see that this
"force" is no more real than the turtle's demon. In three-dimensional
spacetime, this demon turning can change the direction of the spatial
projection of heading—that is, the direction of motion—as well as the
speed.

9.2.3 The Four Curvature Effects

Let's summarize our position. We have investigated with two thought
experiments the observed phenomena associated with curved space and
curved spacetime. We can organize these into four major effects, corresponding to the "move" and "turn" parts of each kind of curvature:

Distance distortion Spatial lengths of seemingly parallel paths may differ.
This effect depends in no way on what kind of ruler you use.

Bending Curved space causes straight paths to appear to bend when
measured against "straight" as determined by other paths outside the
curved region. All objects—wires, beelines, light rays, and so on—
exhibit exactly the same bending in curved space.

Time-interval distortion When viewed from outside a region of curved
spacetime, the "passage of time" within the region may proceed at a
different rate. All phenomena occurring within the region experience
the identical slowing down or speeding up.

Deflection To an observer situated in space (as opposed to one who
"sees" spacetime), the paths of moving particles appear to be deflected
by a region of curved spacetime. The quality of the deflection (changing
direction of motion, or merely speeding up or slowing down) may depend
on the particle's velocity, but all objects with the same initial position
and velocity experience the same deflection.

In these descriptions we have emphasized the universality of the effects
of a curved geometry. All clocks, regardless of construction, appear to

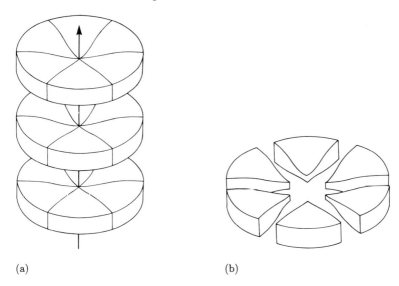

(a)   (b)

Figure 9.16
(a) Spacetime wedge map showing a two-dimensional space with curvature in the
time dimension. (b) If the space itself is curved, each disk must be wedged.

slow down the same amount. All beelines, light rays, and wires bend
the same. All particles, regardless of composition, will follow the same
trajectory if set up with the same velocity (heading in spacetime). We
call this fact—that paths or world lines can depend only on position
and heading—the *principle of geometric indifference*, to remind you that
these curvature effects are purely geometric in origin and thus indifferent
to the type of "ruler" used to measure the effects.

   In conclusion, let us observe all these effects operating together in a
region of curved space and time. For definiteness, imagine a hill in a
flat plane (as in figure 9.4) that is also curved to contain "less time."
The resulting spacetime map, shown in figure 9.16a, can be viewed
as a collection of disks piled up and centered along the t axis. The
disks are all thinner toward the middle, and far away from the curved
region they approach a uniform thickness. As a check, we can cut
these disks with any plane containing the t axis and obtain the previous
diagram for one spatial dimension (figure 9.14). Slicing one of these
disks perpendicular to the t axis should produce the spatial plane at
some fixed time. We know that that this "plane" is not flat but should
be viewed a collection of wedges as in figure 9.4. Thus, each disk must
really be a circular arrangement of peculiarly shaped three-dimensional
pie wedges, as shown in figure 9.16b.

An observer probing the region would see all four of the curvature effects. Rulers and clocks would sense distance and time-interval distortion. An object initially at rest would cross only spacetime gaps, not purely spatial ones, and hence would sense only spacetime deflection. A stiff wire held firmly could resist spacetime deflection (the tendency to acquire velocity), but would be powerless to resist bending due to spatial curvature. A beeline would be both bent and deflected.

Exercises for Section 9.2

1. What does the "speed" at which a turtle treks out a spacetime path mean? Remember that the change in position per change in time (real speed) is shown as heading on the diagram. [A]

2. The world line of a particle has heading vector $\mathbf{H} = (H_x, H_y, H_t)$ at some point. What is the particle's speed? What is the velocity vector (v_x, v_y) of the particle's motion in space? [A]

3. [P] Consider the optical properties of a region of curved space; for example, verify that bending of light rays will cause a grid to appear as in figure 9.8. If you build a "hill" simulation (exercise 6, section 9.1), look for true lenslike behavior. In particular, if the hill is not too steep and you consider only rays passing near the center, can you find anything like a focal point? (A focal point is where parallel rays going into a lens converge.)

4. How will a soap bubble behave upon approaching and entering a region of curved space? Will it be attracted or repelled? [A]

5. [D] An effect almost like that associated with curved space can be achieved if objects are heated or cooled unevenly. Pouring a hot liquid into a glass heats the inside faster, makes it expand, and violates the constraints in the solid structure of the glass, causing it to break. This is much like the case of our board in curved space. Compare the effects of heating and cooling with the effects of curved space. Here are some questions to consider: Suppose objects instantly took on the temperature of the surrounding region of space. Is there some spatial distribution of temperature that would mimic our curved-space hill? If so, how could you distinguish it from curved space? Notice that an object will not break if it is heated uniformly (at least if the object is made of uniformly expanding material). How is this reflected in the curved-space analogy? [A]

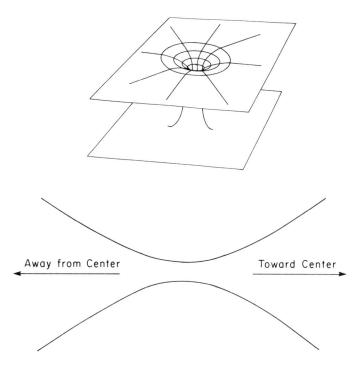

Away from Center   Toward Center

Figure 9.17
Two planes with a handle between and a wedge.

6. [PD] Imagine that you fill a cubical mold centered on a curved-space region such as described in subsection 9.2.1 with plaster of Paris and let it harden. Now cut it apart into six pyramids whose bases are the cube's faces and whose peaks meet at the center of the cube. Withdraw the pieces from the region (assuming that there is enough flexibility to do this without breaking) and describe their shape. You can make a more accurate wedge map if you use a dodecahedron or icosahedron rather than a cube. Can you embody this technique in a computer program that is the three-dimensional analog of the one in section 9.1?

7. Describe the problems of pushing a board broadside into a curved-space region. [A]

8. [P] Figure 9.17a shows a surface that looks like two planes hooked together by a handle. Figure 9.17b gives the shape of the wedge in a wedge map for such a surface. Can you describe the phenomenology of a spherically symmetric three-dimensional space that has this as a

cross section (just as the hill was the cross section of the curved-space region in subsection 9.2.1)? Answer as we did in 9.2.1 in terms of wires, beelines, etc. [H]

9. An apple is hanging in a tree. What is the heading of its world line? Suppose you throw an apple in a (parabolic) trajectory due north. What is the heading now? Draw spacetime diagrams showing the apple's heading and world line in both cases. Suppose you make a continuous stream of water arch just like the apple's trajectory. Draw a three-dimensional spacetime diagram of the stream, and indicate the headings of a few sample drops of water. [H]

9.3 The General Theory of Relativity

We have described the phenomena associated with curved space and time purely as a mathematical fantasy. But Einstein's General Theory of Relativity says that the universe really is curved in this way. In fact, the theory asserts that the spacetime around a mass is curved approximately as depicted in figure 9.16. Small objects (like people) make very small distortions, which are hardly noticed, but massive objects like the sun make distortions spreading across millions of miles, "bending" the straight paths of objects. One can only marvel at Einstein's insight in putting forth this theory, for he did not conjecture that spacetime is curved on the basis of observations of all the curvature phenomena, as we imagined doing in the previous section; rather, he guessed on the basis of facts known since Newton, together with some general theoretical considerations, that spacetime should be curved. Moreover, he developed equations that predict the nature of the curvature from certain facts about the universe, in particular the distribution of mass in it.

These predictions have been experimentally confirmed in the case of a large enough mass, such as the sun. For example, during a solar eclipse, one can see stars that we know to be actually behind the sun. This can be interpreted as a consequence of the curvature of space—the spatial bending of the light rays from the stars, as in figure 9.18. Even with a mass the size of the sun, however, the light is deflected only a tiny fraction of a degree. Time-interval distortion is also observable. Looking at light from the sun, scientists have found that spectra emitted by atoms in the sun are shifted "towards the red"—everything is of slightly lower frequency than in spectra of atoms of the same chemical elements on earth or in free space. This indicates an apparent slowing down of atoms (which are very accurate clocks) in the vicinity of the sun.

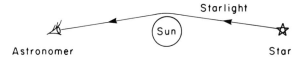

Figure 9.18
Bending of starlight.

9.3.1 Gravity as Curvature

It requires precise measurement to observe the spatial-bending and time-interval-distortion effects of curved spacetime, even in the case of a huge mass like the sun. And scientists have only recently been able to measure the long distances across the region of space occupied by the sun accurately enough to verify distance distortion. But there is nothing at all subtle about the fourth of the curvature effects predicted by General Relativity. Perhaps you have guessed already: Deflection, the mysterious "force" that deflects the paths of objects moving through curved spacetime, is readily observable as the familiar "force" of gravity. Gravity is thus not a real force at all; it is the "demon turning" associated with locally straight motion through curved spacetime!

The hypothesis that gravity is a purely geometric phenomenon leads to strong predictions. The principle of geometric indifference implies that any particle should follow the same trajectory under gravity's influence, as long as it starts at the same place with the same velocity (spacetime heading). Galileo is said to have dropped two different weights and found that they fell identically. Over the past 20 years careful experiments have validated this to high accuracy with objects of widely differing makeup. Another strong prediction is that gravitational "acceleration," for example, falling towards a planet, is really no acceleration at all but rather locally straight motion in spacetime. Thus, particles deflected or falling because of gravity should not feel any force. Astronauts in orbit do not experience any force; they are weightless. Finally, the hypothesis predicts a correlation between two seemingly disparate effects, the red shift and gravitational force. One could in principle measure relative thickness of wedges from red-shift data, and, from the shape of the wedges thus determined, compute the demon turning (the force of gravity). Insofar as this experiment can be performed, it has validated the correlation.

9.3.2 Rotating World Lines

Identifying gravity as the deflection due to curved spacetime is a powerful and beautiful idea. But there is a serious bug in the theory as we have explained it so far. Take another look at figure 9.15, which shows the deflection corresponding to a region of "less time." Indeed, the path of a moving particle is deflected—but it is deflected away from the curved region rather than towards it. The theory as presented so far would predict that gravity repels rather than attracts!

The bug in our theory is a profound one. The root of the problem lies in our representation of spacetime as simply space with an extra time dimension. Let's take a more careful look. For simplicity, we'll look at two-dimensional spacetime (that is, motion along one spatial dimension), and we'll suppose that everything is flat so there are no wedges to worry about. Figure 9.19a shows such a diagram. The straight lines represent the world lines of particles moving at constant velocity. The different slopes of the lines represent different velocities.

We've already said that the vertical t axis represents zero velocity—moving through time without changing position in space. If you like, you can regard the horizontal x axis as "infinite velocity"—changing spatial position without moving through time. Beyond that, spacetime diagrams are usually "calibrated" by stipulating that an angle of 45° corresponds to the speed of light. Directions above the 45° line are usually referred to as *timelike directions* because they lie close to the time axis. Directions below the 45° line are referred to as *spacelike directions*.

So far, things are perfectly straightforward. Our spacetime diagram seems no different from a normal Euclidean plane with some straight lines drawn on it. But now comes a crucial difference, and that difference has to do with *rotations*. Is there some meaningful geometric "rotation" operation one can perform on a spacetime diagram that is consistent with the interpretation of the diagram as depicting world lines in space and time, and is consistent with what one actually observes when looking at motion in the real universe?

Einstein discovered that there is indeed such an operation. But the operation is not the usual kind of rotation shown in figure 9.19b. Rather, it is the geometric operation shown in figure 9.19c. This operation is called a *Lorentz rotation*. As the figure shows, a Lorentz rotation, in contrast to a normal rotation, has the following properties: Timelike directions move in the opposite direction from spacelike ones, and lines at a 45° angle do not move at all.

In the following section we'll discuss the physical meaning of Lorentz rotations and why this is the "correct" rotation operation for spacetime diagrams. For now, let's just verify that the interpretation of gravity as the deflection due to spacetime curvature really does produce an attrac-

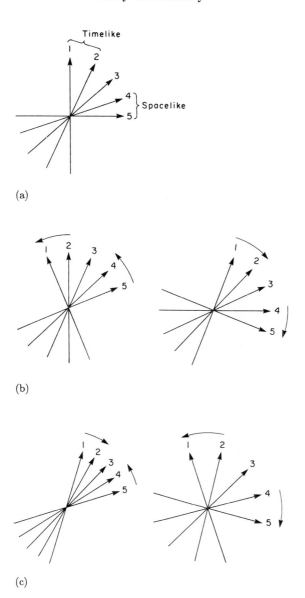

Figure 9.19
(a) World lines of constant velocity; line 3 represents the speed of light. (b) Regular rotations. (c) Lorentz rotations.

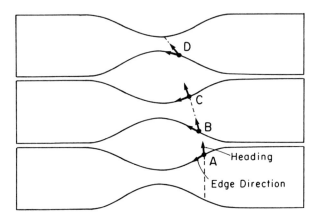

Figure 9.20
Lorentz rotation causes heading to turn opposite to edge rotation.

tive force so long as we assume that the "demon turning" from one
time-slice wedge to the next goes by the Lorentz rotation rule. Figure
9.20 shows once more a particle in a region of curved spacetime that
is about to be "demon turned" while moving from one wedge to the
next at the point marked A. Notice that the edge of the wedge lies in a
spacelike direction and the particle's heading lies in a timelike direction
so long as we assume that the particle is moving at less than the speed
of light (see exercise 7). According to the Lorentz rule, the particle's
heading and the edge of the wedge will move in opposite directions in
going from one wedge to the next. Figure 9.20 at B shows the edge must
rotate clockwise and the heading must therefore rotate counterclockwise
across the gap. The resulting velocity deflection will be toward the mass
rather than away from it. The same thing happens from C to D.

When we implement a General Relativity simulator later in this chapter, we will need to be able to compute Lorentz rotations. Since the
"demon turning" in our simulation occurs only in small increments, it
will be sufficient to have a formula that tells how to Lorentz-rotate
through a small angle. For comparison, let's look at the analogous formula for ordinary rotations. If we knew nothing about sines and cosines,
we could not make use of the rotation formula of chapter 3 to find how
to rotate vectors. But if we're only interested in rotating a vector $\mathbf{v}$
through small angles, we can make do (exercise 4 below) by adding to $\mathbf{v}$
a small vector perpendicular to $\mathbf{v}$ (that is, tangent to the circle in which
$\mathbf{v}$ moves under the rotation):

$\text{Rotate}(\mathbf{v}, A) \approx \mathbf{v} + A \times \text{Perp}(\mathbf{v}).$

The formula is quite accurate if the rotation angle A is small (and measured in radians). Recall that the Perp operation is given in coordinates by

$$\text{Perp}(x, y) = (-y, x).$$

The corresponding formula for Lorentz rotations is the same, except we use a different Perp operation:

$$\text{LRotate}(\mathbf{v}, A) \approx \mathbf{v} + A \times \text{LPerp}(\mathbf{v})$$

where LPerp (the "Lorentz perpendicular") is defined by

$$\text{LPerp}(x, t) = (t, x).$$

Verify that this rotation satisfies the two qualitative properties of Lorentz rotations described (exercise 5).

9.3.3 Understanding Lorentz Rotations

We debugged the curvature interpretation of gravity by pulling out of a hat the assertion that spacetime rotations follow the Lorentz rule, but we gave no indication as to why this should be so. In fact, we never even said what rotating a spacetime diagram should mean. One way to think about a rotation is that it is a way of associating to each line through the origin a new line through the origin—it is a correspondence between headings and headings. In a spacetime diagram the headings indicate velocities of particles moving in space. So the rotation of a spacetime diagram can be viewed as an operation that takes a velocity as input and outputs a new velocity.

The theory of relativity hypothesizes a natural physical interpretation for this operation on velocities: Rotating a world line corresponds to looking at that same world line from a new frame of reference. Of course, normal rotations can be looked at in this way as well, but there is one crucial difference. The change in frame of reference must be one that changes velocities. Thus, Lorentz rotation is like hopping a freight train and seeing the letters on the side of a boxcar, initially a blur of speed, become stationary and readable, rather than like turning your head to see the world from a rotated perspective.

Returning to spacetime diagrams, suppose we have a particle whose world line depicts motion at some constant velocity. Now we apply a Lorentz rotation that makes the particle's world line appear vertical (that is, makes it represent zero velocity). Relativity interprets this zero-velocity rotated world line as the same motion of the same particle, only this time as seen from the viewpoint of an observer who is moving at the same velocity as the particle.

If we accept this interpretation, questions about how rotations should behave are transformed into experimentally decidable questions about motion in the real world. Suppose we make a rotation that transforms to vertical a world line representing constant velocity v. We would like to know how this same rotation should transform some other world line, say, one representing constant velocity w. The corresponding experimental question is this: Suppose we observe two particles, one with velocity v and one with velocity w. Now we shift to a frame of reference that is moving along with the first particle. How fast is the second particle moving as observed from the new frame of reference?

You may think that the answer is obvious: An observer moving along with the first particle should see the second particle moving with velocity $w - v$. But that is not what happens. In fact, at the core of the theory of relativity lies the following fundamental and extremely counterintuitive postulate: The speed of light will be observed to be the same in any frame of reference. This implies, for example, that if you measure the speed of a light ray emitted from earth while you are riding in a rocket moving away from the earth at high speed, then you will obtain the same answer as if you had made the measurement while you were standing on the earth. And this should be the case even if the rocket, as seen from earth, is itself moving at 99 percent of the speed of light! That is certainly not obvious, nor even intuitively plausible. And yet as far as anyone has been able to measure, it is true.

In terms of rotating spacetime diagrams, this invariance of the speed of light means that any Lorentz rotation should leave 45° lines unchanged, since these correspond to the speed of light. From a physical point of view, this is the most salient feature of Lorentz rotations. Spacelike and timelike directions pivot in opposite directions like the two ends of a teeter-totter balanced on the fixed hinge, the speed of light.

The theory of Lorentz rotations and spacetime diagrams is called the Special Theory of Relativity, and we have hardly been able to hint at the scope of this theory here. We hope we have at least suggested that there are experimental grounds for believing that the Lorentz rule gives the "correct" way of rotating spacetime diagrams.

Exercises for Section 9.3

1. The convention that the speed of light is 45° on spacetime diagrams is almost universally held, since it gives space and time equal billing.

This calibrates these diagrams in a peculiar way. Show that if you use a unit of one second on the time axis, an equal spatial distance must be 186,000 miles. What heading (angle from vertical) represents 100 miles per hour on such a diagram? [A]

2. John and Sam are identical twins. John goes to live at the center of the sun for a while, then returns to Sam on the earth. Who is now older and by how much? (Answer in terms of the thickness of wedge strips.) Can one "time travel" this way? [A]

3. Spatial curvature, even around the massive sun, is so small that it is hard to measure in terms of either distance or bending. On the other hand, of the two effects of spacetime curvature, one—gravitational red shift—takes careful instrumentation to observe, while the other—the "falling" influence of gravity—is obvious. Why are these two effects of such apparently different magnitudes? [HA]

4. [P] In subsection 9.3.2 we gave approximate formulas for small rotations, both the normal and the Lorentz kind. One can perform large rotations by repeating these small rotations over and over. Write programs to carry this out. Plot the trajectories of the tips of spacelike and timelike vectors as they are Lorentz-rotated. For the usual kind of rotation, compare your results to the exact answer as computed by the rotation formula of chapter 3. How small an angle must you take for the small rotations if you want the large rotation to be accurate to within 10 percent? To within 0.1 percent?

5. Verify that the formula for small Lorentz rotations does indeed leave 45° lines invariant, and causes spacelike lines to move in the opposite direction from timelike ones. [A]

6. Show that no sequence of small Lorentz rotations can change a timelike direction to a spacelike one. This can be interpreted as follows: If you see a particle moving at less than the speed of light, then you cannot shift to a frame of reference (for example, by moving faster and faster in the opposite direction) from which you will observe the particle to be traveling at light speed or greater. [A]

7. A particle that moves faster than the speed of light is called a *tachyon*. According to exercise 6, you cannot speed up a normal particle to produce a tachyon, so tachyons, if they exist, must have been created as such. (No one knows whether or not tachyons exist.) In analogy to exercise 6, show that if you do have a tachyon you cannot slow it down

to below light speed by shifting to a new reference frame. Predict how tachyons behave in a gravitational field. [A]

8. Imagine three turtles going straight off in different directions on a sphere. When they meet, each accuses the other two of having turned while out of sight. And what's more, two turtles who agree that the third has secretly turned cannot agree on how much it has turned by. How, then, can we ever settle on a definite number (total "demon turning") for the bending of starlight? [HA]

9. We know that gravity can make things travel in (almost) closed orbits, as planets travel around the sun. It turns out that velocity deflection is crucial to this effect; spatial bending alone could not make a "turtle line" become a closed orbit. What geometric property of the spatial curvature due to gravity ensures that this is true? [A]

10. In chapter 5 we settled on a definition of "straight line" as an equal-strided turtle walk. Can you give an analogous definition of "straight line" in three dimensions? Show that a "straight" wire will always lie along such a line. Can you give any justification for expecting a light ray to follow such a path? [A]

11. In subsection 9.2.2 we imagined observing time distortion by putting a watch in a box and later removing it. Alternatively, we could have observed the watch ticking while it was in the box, or listened to the ticks. More generally, we could have arranged for the watch to send us some kind of "tick messages" to indicate how fast time was passing in the box. Show on a spacetime diagram that tick messages received from a clock in a region of curved spacetime will reveal the same slowing down as would be observed by inserting a watch and later removing it to check its time. Show that this fact is independent of the message mechanism. This justifies our claim that red-shift data from the sun measure wedge thickness. [HA]

12. [D] We said in 9.3.3 that we could reduce the question of how world lines should rotate to experimental questions by seeing how the velocity of a particle changes when the observer shifts frame of reference. On the other hand, we can't observe anything moving faster than the speed of light, so we can't find out how spacelike world lines are rotated by measuring velocities of particles traveling at these speeds. Describe an experiment that will give information about how spacelike headings are rotated. [HA]

13. [D] It turns out that half the bending of starlight is due to spatial bending and half is due to spacetime deflection. But we said that Lorentz rotations leave 45° (speed of light) lines invariant. How is it, then, that velocity deflection can contribute anything at all to the bending of starlight? [HA]

14. You may need to recalibrate your intuitions a bit in order to really think of gravity as geometry. In particular, answer the following question: If gravity is not a force, why do you have to push up on everything (like an apple in your hand) to counteract gravity and keep the apple from falling? [HA]

9.4 A Simulator for General Relativity

It is not too difficult to embody the previous discussion in a program that allows you to observe the paths of particles moving in curved spacetime. If the spatial part of the motion lies in a plane, then we can display the spatial motion on the screen and keep track separately of a "clock" that gives the time coordinate. (If you get more ambitious you might consider implementing a program showing the three-dimensional world lines in perspective.) The program is essentially the same as the curved-surface simulation of subsection 9.1.3, with an extra dimension added. Curved spacetime is represented as in figure 9.16: a stack of disks, each made up of wedges. The curvature is determined by four fundamental parameters, which play the role of $C(r)$ and $TT(r)$, or equivalently GAPRATIO and TURNING.PER.ANGLE from the simulation in section 9.1:

TIME.GAPRATIO, the ratio of gap between disks, to disk thickness encountered in moving in the time direction,

TURNING.PER.TIME, the corresponding amount that a world line must be Lorentz-rotated per unit change in time (t coordinate) on the map,

SPACE.GAPRATIO, the ratio of gap to disk distance encountered in moving in a spatial circle within one disk, and

TURNING.PER.ANGLE, the corresponding (spatial) demon turning per central angle .

There is one way in which our program is simpler than the one in 9.1.1: We don't care how long a world line is, and we don't have to worry about stopping the simulation after a certain distance. (Time marches on.) So we needn't take **H** to be of unit length. We might as well just take it to be an appropriately small increment to position (the equivalent of SMALLDISTANCE $\times$ **H**). In addition, we'll simplify the program by not including provisions for turning other than that caused by curvature. You can add these features if you wish, but what we give here will be sufficient to allow you to observe trajectories of any particle moving solely under the influence of gravity.

9.4.1 The Coordinate Systems

Two things make the relativity simulation more complex than the one for curved surfaces. First, we must keep track of two kinds of demon turning and leaping, those associated with spatial rotations (bending) and those associated with Lorentz rotations (deflection). This is not much of a problem, since we can do each part of the correction separately. The second problem is that we must now rotate the turtle's heading as a vector in three dimensions rather than two. We have rotated vectors in three dimensions before, but only vectors perpendicular to the axis of rotation. The heading vector will not in general satisfy this property for the rotations we need to accomplish.

This problem can be overcome by taking advantage of an old friend from chapter 3, the linearity principle. Decompose the vector we want to rotate into its component along the axis of the rotation plus what is left over (which lies in the plane perpendicular to the axis). Since rotating (even Lorentz-rotating) is a linear operation, we can rotate these two components separately and then add them to get the result. Rotating the parts separately is easy; the component along the axis doesn't change, and the rotation of the leftover part is a rotation in a plane, which we know how to do already. The decomposition and subsequent rotation will be simple if we choose a coordinate system that has an axis coinciding with the axis of rotation.

Let's implement this plan for the rotations needed in the simulation. For spatial rotations the axis is parallel to the time axis, and the x, y plane is where the action is. Spacetime rotations take place within the plane that includes the turtle and the t axis (the sun). So both kinds of rotations can be easily accomplished if we express the heading vector in the so-called r, s, t coordinate system, which is specified by components in the time direction **t**, in the spatial direction **r** directly away from the sun (the radial direction), and in the direction **s**, which is perpendicular to the above two (figure 9.21). These coordinates allow us to take ad-

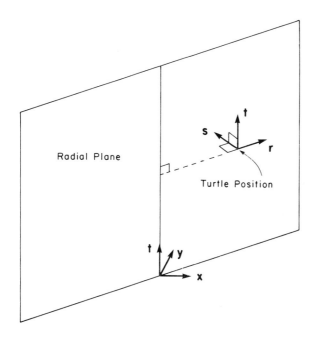

Figure 9.21
The r, s, t coordinate system. Spatial rotations rotate around the t axis, Lorentz rotations around the s axis.

vantage of the fact that the spatial rotations occur purely in the spatial plane (the plane containing **r** and **s**), while the spacetime rotations occur purely in the radial plane (the plane containing **r** and **t**). (Note that the spatial plane is always parallel to the x, y plane of the x, y, t coordinate system.)

Although the r, s, t coordinate system is good for doing the rotations, it changes each time the turtle changes position. So we shall keep position and heading in x, y, t coordinates, converting the heading to r, s, t coordinates when we need to rotate. Fortunately, the relation between the heading expressed in x, y, t coordinates (H_x, H_y, H_t) and the heading expressed in r, s, t coordinates (H_r, H_s, H_t) is simple:

H_t is the same in both sets of coordinates,

$H_r = (H_x, H_y) \cdot \mathbf{U}$,

$H_s = (H_x, H_y) \cdot \mathbf{S}$

where **U** is the unit vector in the spatial plane which points from the sun to the turtle's position, expressed in x, y coordinates. **U** is the same as the basis vector **r** above, but we use the notation from our sphere simulation to avoid confusion with r, the distance from the sun. As mentioned in exercise 5 of section 9.1, **U** is the vector $(x/r, y, r)$, and **S** = Perp(**U**).

The reverse transformation, from r, s, t coordinates to x, y, t coordinates, is obtained by writing for the spatial part of the vector

$$(H_x, H_y) = H_r \mathbf{U} + H_s \mathbf{S}$$

with **U** given, as above, in x, y coordinates. The t coordinates are the same in both systems.

9.4.2 Turning and Leaping

Once we have the heading vector expressed in r, s, t coordinates, it is easy to implement the demon turning as a rotation in the spatial plane followed by a Lorentz rotation in the radial plane. The amount of the first rotation is determined by the amount of rotation between the wedges of a spatial disk—it is equal to some factor (TURNING.PER.ANGLE) times the central angle traversed in the spatial plane. The amount of the second rotation is determined by the amount of rotation between the disks—it is equal to some other factor (TURNING.PER.TIME) times the change in the time coordinate.

The leap correction also comes in two parts, one across the gap from disk to disk (in the time direction) and one across the gaps within the disks (in the **S** direction). The equations are essentially identical to equation 1 of 9.1.2, except that projection in the appropriate direction is trivial to compute in r, s, t coordinates:

Spaceleap ← SPACE.GAPRATIO × $(0, H_s, 0)$,
Timeleap ← TIME.GAPRATIO × $(0, 0, H_t)$.

Note that these leap vectors must be converted from r, s, t coordinates to x, y, t coordinates before being added to the position.

9.4.3 The Program

The final program is much like the one given in 9.1.3. To start the program choose initial values for the turtle's position $\mathbf{P} = (P_x, P_y, P_t)$ and heading $\mathbf{H} = (H_x, H_y, H_t)$ given as vectors in x, y, t coordinates.

```
TO CURVED.SPACE.WALK
    REPEAT FOREVER
        REALWALK
        COMPUTE.PARAMETERS
        DEMONLEAP
        DEMONTURN
        DISPLAY
```

REALWALK simply modifies the position according to **H**:

```
TO REALWALK
    [PX PY PT] ← [PX PY PT] + [HX HY HT]
```

The COMPUTE.PARAMETERS procedure computes quantities used in transforming between x, y, z and r, s, t coordinates. These must be recomputed each time the turtle's position changes. The procedure also computes the heading in r, s, t coordinates.

```
TO COMPUTE.PARAMETERS
    R ← SQRT(PX↑2 + PY↑2)
    U ← (1/R) * [PX PY]
    S ← (1/R) * [PY -PX]
    [HR HS HT] ← CONVERT.TO.RST([HX HY HT])
```

DEMONLEAP computes the leap correction as given in 9.4.2 and modifies the position accordingly, computing the total **Walk** vector as well:

```
TO DEMONLEAP
    SPACELEAP ← SPACE.GAPRATIO * [0 HS 0]
    TIMELEAP ← TIME.GAPRATIO * [0 0 HT]
    LEAP ← TIMELEAP + SPACELEAP
    [WALKR WALKS WALKT] ← LEAP + [HR HS HT]
    [PX PY PT] ← [PX PY PT] + CONVERT.TO.XYT (LEAP)
```

DEMONTURN modifies the heading as discussed in 9.4.2 and recomputes the x, y, z heading vector:

```
TO DEMONTURN
    CENTRAL.ANGLE ← (1/R) * WALKS
    SPATIAL.TURNING ← CENTRAL.ANGLE * TURNING.PER.ANGLE
    [HR HS HT] ← ROTATE([HR HS HT], SPATIAL.TURNING)
    SPACE.TIME.TURNING ← WALKT * TURNING.PER.TIME
    [HR HS HT] ← LORENTZ.ROTATE ([HR HS HT], SPACE.TIME.TURNING)
    [HX HY HT] ← CONVERT.TO.XYT([HR HS HT])
```

Finally, the display of position and time can be handled by

```
TO DISPLAY
  MOVE.TO [PX PY]
  PRINT PT
```

The programs for converting between the two coordinate systems implement the formulas given in 9.4.1:

```
TO CONVERT.TO.RST [VX VY VT]
  VR ← DOT ([VX VY], U)
  VS ← DOT ([VX VY], S)
  RETURN [VR VS VT]
```

```
TO CONVERT.TO.XYT [VR VS VT]
  [VX VY] ← VR*U + VS*S
  RETURN [VX VY VT]
```

The next procedure is used by DEMONTURN to rotate a vector in the r, s spatial plane. Rather than using sines and cosines, we use the approximation for small angles given in 9.3.2:

```
TO ROTATE (V, A)
  RETURN V + A * SPERP (V)
```

The appropriate perpendicular to use here is really the spatial perpendicular of the spatial part of the vector. (The spatial part is the only part that participates in the rotation; the time component is invariant.) This perpendicular contains nonzero components only in the plane of the rotation.

```
TO SPERP [VR VS VT]
  RETURN [VS -VR 0]
```

A similar pair of procedures accomplishes the Lorentz rotation:

```
TO LORENTZ.ROTATE (V, A)
  RETURN V + A * LPERP (V)
```

```
TO LPERP [VR VS VT]
  RETURN [VT 0 VR]
```

9.4.4 Help with Units

For experimentation you may select the four fundamental functions that determine the shape of this curved universe. The following values correspond quite closely to the spacetime curvature around a mass, as predicted by Einstein. For TIME.GAPRATIO you can use m/r. Here r is, as always, the spatial distance to center, and m is determined by the mass of the attracting center (see exercise 4). This only approximates the actual value of TIME.GAPRATIO, but it is quite good if m is small compared with r (say, $r > 50m$) (see exercise 12). A corresponding approximation for TURNING.PER.TIME is m/r^2. Notice that this is precisely the Newtonian formula for gravitational acceleration. A realistic function for SPACE.GAPRATIO is hard to write down in simple form, but $m(\ln r)/r$ is a good approximation as long as it is small. The corresponding TURNING.PER.ANGLE is m/r. (The symbol $\ln r$ donates the natural logarithm of r.)

You may wish to start out with simpler functions than these, or to experiment with different functions for comparison. Another simplification, which will not do much harm to the simulation, is to use these functions but leave out leaping. This obviates the TIME.GAPRATIO and SPACE.GAPRATIO functions, so you won't have to compute logarithms.

To start your simulation you need to know ballpark figures for m, r, and v (the particle's velocity). To do this you may proceed as follows. Settle on a number, c, for the speed of light. If v/c is small and the spatial orbit is nearly circular, the radius of the orbit is determined by $m = (v/c)^2 r$ (see exercise 2). If you take $r \approx 100$, $v \approx 100$, and $c \approx 10,000$, then $m = \frac{1}{100}$ is a reasonable value.

To relate distances and times to what you see on the screen, remember that a 45° world line represents the speed of light. So if c is 10,000 turtle units per second, then the units for the time axis are 1/10,000 second. With this unit of time on the t axis, a spacetime heading of (v_x, v_y, c) represents a velocity of $v = \sqrt{v_x{}^2 + v_y{}^2}$. Finally, remember that heading is added to position in each step of the simulation. Hence, using a heading vector (v_x, v_y, c) makes each simulation step correspond to one second of elapsed time. If you want one-minute simulation steps, the appropriate heading vector to use is $(60v_x, 60v_y, 60c)$, which is a vector in the same direction.

Exercises for Section 9.4

1. Error in the approximations and computer roundoff error may accumulate in the length of the spacetime heading. Introduce in your simulation a step to make sure the time increment (time component of heading) stays constant. Make sure any correction you make doesn't change velocity. [A]

2. [D] If an orbit is to be circular, then the rotation of the spatial part of the heading must be the same as the CENTRAL.ANGLE in order to ensure that velocity will always be perpendicular to the radius. When v/c is small, show that this means $m = (v/c)^2 r$. [HA]

3. [P] Do elliptical orbits in your simulator close exactly, or do they precess? (Precession means the ellipse as a whole rotates slowly.) Can you do the simulation accurately enough so that you are sure any precession you might see is not error in the simulation? Assume for this purpose that the formulas for demon turning and GAPRATIO are exact. [H]

4. [P] Convert your simulator to use physical units—for example, distance in meters, mass in kilograms, time in seconds. In this case m is given by GM/c^2 where $G = 6.7 \times 10^{-11}$ is the universal gravitational constant and M is the gravitating mass. The speed of light, c, is $300,000,000$ meters per second. You will need to scale your vectors to fit the screen. Use the sun as a test case and see if your simulator gets the right period for planetary orbits. (The mass of the sun is $M = 2 \times 10^{30}$ kg.) How about using the earth as the central mass: Do earth satellites exhibit the right velocities and periods for circular orbits? (The mass of the earth is 6×10^{24} kg and its radius is 6.4×10^6 meters.)

5. [P] Experiment with the bending of starlight, $v = c$. For a real light ray just grazing the surface of the sun, the actual bending is only about 1.75 seconds of arc (5×10^{-4} degrees). Try setting this up on your simulator, using the units given in exercise 4. (The radius of the sun is 7×10^8 meters.) Do you think you have any hope of observing such a small effect on the simulator? How much must you increase the mass of the sun before the effect is easily observable?

6. [P] Implement the simulation both with and without demon leaping. How much difference does it make to your simulation, for example, with closed orbits?

7. Verify the formulas for the leap corrections given in subsection 9.4.2. [H]

8. [D] The time coordinate printed by the program allows us to compute time intervals in the simulation. These time intervals correspond to intervals measured by which clock—a clock on the moving planet? a clock on the sun? some other clock? [A]

9. [D] The so-called Lorentz length of a vector **v** is given by

$$\sqrt{v_t{}^2 - v_x{}^2 - v_y{}^2}.$$

Lorentz length is unchanged by Lorentz rotations, just as normal length is unchanged by normal rotations. The Lorentz length of a piece of world line **v** has an important interpretation: It is the time as experienced by the particle in making that little walk along **v**. Add a part to your simulator that accumulates this time—that is, accumulates $\sqrt{HT^2 - HX^2 - HY^2}$—and compares it with the coordinate elapsed time. Can you reason qualitatively to predict the difference between the two times in an orbit? How does the difference in times change from one orbit to another? Under what circumstances is the difference large? [A]

10. [D] Make a very rough estimate of the amount of acceleration (velocity acquired per second) due to deflection if a spacetime region in a jewelry box 8 inches across causes a 50 percent time distortion and really is curved as indicated in figure 9.15. Compare this with gravity (32 feet per second per second). Using the "Einstein" formulas that correlate mass with curvature, given at the end of section 9.4, compute very roughly the mass needed to provide this curvature. See the physical-unit discussion in exercise 4 above. [A]

11. [D] A gyroscope makes a good pointer for computing demon turning in curved space. How many revolutions of the earth will a gyroscope in a satellite need to show a demon turning of 1°? (Use the "Einstein" formulas at the end of 9.4 and the physical-unit correlation from exercise 4.) [HA]

12. [P] As we said in 9.4.4, our approximations to the actual curvature break down when one gets very close to very massive objects. In reality, if the object is massive enough and close enough, nothing can escape from its gravitational attraction, not even light rays. This phenomenon is called a *black hole*. Push your General Relativity simulator to its extreme near the center. Does it exhibit any black-hole behavior before it goes completely haywire? (Actually, the space around black holes, if such exist, is curved approximately as described in exercise 8 of section 9.2.)

Appendixes

Appendix A
Turtle Procedure Notation

This appendix provides a cursory description of the Turtle Procedure Notation used in this book. Turtle Procedure Notation is meant to be a consistent and readable way to describe turtle programs independent of the quirks, details, and limitations of common computer languages, yet in such a way that the programs can be readily translated into whatever computer language is available. (Some sample translations are given in appendix B.) In relation to available languages, Turtle Procedure Notation is closest to Logo, a language developed at MIT for educational uses. Almost all of the computer work for developing the material in this book was done in Logo.

Basic Operations and Data Types

Turtle Procedure Notation includes the basic arithmetic operations—addition, subtraction, multiplication, division (denoted /), and exponentiation (denoted ↑). These obey the usual precedence conventions; for example, in a string of operations, multiplication and division are performed before addition and subtraction. Thus, 5+2*3-7 is equal to 4. The order of operations can be modified or clarified by using parentheses. For example, (5+2)*(3-7) is equal to -28.

In addition to the basic arithmetic operations, there are numerous other operations that take numbers as inputs. The SQRT operation, for example, returns as its value the positive square root of its input (which must be a non-negative number). By "returns as its value" we mean that the result of the operation is available to be used as the input to succeeding operations. For example, the command

```
PRINT (SQRT 144) + (SQRT 144)
```

will print the number 24.

Not all operations return values. The FORWARD operation, for instance, which tells the turtle to go forward the number of units specified by its input, does not return a value. (Such operations are frequently referred to by the more general term *command*.) There are also operations that do not take inputs. One such is HEADING, which returns the turtle's current heading.

As with almost all computer languages, we actually use two types of numbers: integers and real (or "floating point") numbers. Turtle Procedure Notation distinguishes real numbers from integers by includ-

ing a decimal point in their printed representation. Arithmetic operations may combine integers and real numbers (for example, 3.45 + 2).
The kind of number returned is determined by the rule that the result
of a division is always a real number, whereas the result of an addition, a subtraction, or a multiplication will be real if any of its inputs
are real. For turtle programing it is desirable to maintain the position
of the turtle in real-number coordinates, but to allow the state-change
operators FORWARD, LEFT, etc., to accept either real or integer inputs. It
is convenient to keep the turtle's heading as an integer until a RIGHT, a
LEFT, or a SETHEADING is executed with a noninteger input.

In addition to numeric data, Turtle Procedure Notation also makes
use of character strings. When specifying a literal character string, you
must enclose it in quotes to avoid confusing it with commands in the
language. For example,

```
PRINT SQRT 144
```

will print 12, whereas

```
PRINT "SQRT 144"
```

will print a string of eight characters: S, Q, R, T, space, 1, 4, 4.

Variables

The assignment operator ← is used to assign names to data objects. A
name can be any non-numeric character string that does not contain a
space. For example,

```
BIG ← 10000
SMALL ← .005
CHEER ← "TURTLE, TURTLE, RAH RAH RAH"
```

followed by

```
PRINT BIG * SMALL
PRINT CHEER
```

prints 50 and the cheer, respectively.

Procedures

Procedures provide a way to build complex operations by combining

simpler ones. A procedure is simply a list of commands, which are
executed in sequence whenever the procedure is invoked. For example,
the following procedure will make the turtle draw a line 20 units long
and then return to its starting place:

```
TO DASH
    FORWARD 20
    BACK 20
```

Note that the procedure is defined by providing a title line consisting
of the word TO followed by the name of the procedure. The body of
the procedure is then listed under this, indented. (Actual computer
languages commonly use some means besides indentation to mark the
end of the defining process. Many languages use the special marker END.)

To invoke (or "call") a procedure, one simply uses the name of the
procedure as a command in the language, either by typing it directly
into the computer (at "top level") or by using it as one of the commands
in another procedure. There is no difference between the way one calls
a procedure and the way one calls an operation that is built into the
language. A procedure definition should therefore be thought of as a
way of extending the set of operations in the language.

Procedures may also be defined to take inputs. These are specified
by providing names for the inputs on the procedure's title line. (These
names are often called "parameters" or "dummy variables.") For example, the following procedure is just like the above DASH, except that
it allows the length of the line to be specified as an input:

```
TO VARY.DASH DISTANCE
    FORWARD DISTANCE
    BACK DISTANCE
```

When a procedure is called, such as by typing VARY.DASH 100, the actual values of the parameters are substituted for the parameters' names
throughout the procedure body. A procedure may be defined to accept any number of inputs. Inputs can be of any data type—numbers,
character strings, and others which will be described below.

In addition to accepting inputs, procedures may also return a value,
or "output." This is accomplished by using the RETURN command, as in

```
TO AVERAGE X Y
    RETURN (X + Y) / 2
```

The procedure can now be used as a value in other statements. For example,

```
PRINT AVERAGE 5 7
AV ← (AVERAGE 5 7) - 6
```

will print 6 and set the variable AV to 0, respectively.

When the RETURN command is executed, the procedure will terminate directly and not execute any further commands within it. It is also possible to use this effect of RETURN without returning a value. This will simply stop the procedure. For example,

```
TO LAZY.FORWARD DISTANCE
   IF DISTANCE > 50 THEN RETURN
   FORWARD DISTANCE
```

will not move the turtle if the input is greater than 50.

Turtle Procedure Notation assumes that a procedure can return only a single entity (which, however, may be a compound data object, as described below in the section on lists). Some other languages distinguish "functions" from "subroutines." In Turtle Procedure Notation there is no distinction; procedures play both roles.

Parentheses, Commas, and Comments

Complex expressions can often be made more legible through judicious use of parentheses. For example,

```
AVERAGE X + 3 AVERAGE 3 * Y SQRT 5
```

is not as intelligible as

```
AVERAGE (X + 3, AVERAGE (3 * Y, SQRT 5))
```

—especially if we don't remember that the AVERAGE procedure takes two inputs. In general, readability can be increased in a procedure call by enclosing the inputs to the procedure in parentheses, separated by commas. One can do the same in the title line of a procedure that takes several inputs. In contrast with many languages, this use of parentheses and commas is optional.

Another way to increase program readability is to use comments. Anything that appears after a semicolon on a line will be ignored when the procedure is executed, and hence can be used as commentary.

Conditional Expressions

As in most languages, our notation for turtle programs makes use of an
"if ... then ... else ..." construction. For example,

```
TO GREATER X Y
   IF X > Y THEN RETURN X ELSE RETURN Y
```

returns the greater of two numbers. As in many computer languages,
the "else" part is optional.

The clauses governed by THEN and ELSE can consist of more than one
command. If so, the clause is delimited by indenting as in the following
example:

```
TO SOLVE.QUADRATIC.EQUATION (A, B, C)
      ; this procedure prints the real-number solutions to
      ; a quadratic equation, given the coefficients
      ; as inputs
   DISC ← SQRT ( B ↑ 2 - 4 * A * C)
   IF DISC < 0
      THEN
         PRINT "NO REAL SOLUTIONS"
      ELSE
         PRINT (- B + DISC) / (2 * A)
         PRINT (- B - DISC) / (2 * A)
```

(Other languages use line numbers or "begin ... end" blocks to specify
the scope of conditional clauses.)

The item that is tested by the IF, as in "DISC < 0" above, should be
either true or false. An operation that outputs "true" or "false" is called
a *predicate*. Turtle Procedure Notation uses the predicates >, <, and =.
(= works for testing equality of all other data types as well as numbers.)
In addition, one can define new predicates simply as procedures that
return the character strings TRUE or FALSE. For example, the following
procedure tests whether its first input is within the range specified by
its second and third:

```
TO BETWEEN (A, B, C)
   IF BOTH ( A > B, A < C)
      THEN RETURN "TRUE"
      ELSE RETURN "FALSE"
```

(The BOTH operation outputs TRUE only if both its inputs are true. There is a corresponding EITHER operation.) The BETWEEN procedure could also be written as

```
TO BETWEEN (A, B, C)
   RETURN (BOTH (A > B, A < C))
```

Iteration Commands

Another element of Turtle Procedure Notation is given by the iteration (or looping) constructs, signaled by the word REPEAT. For example, the form "REPEAT ⟨number⟩ ⟨commands⟩" repeats the designated commands the specified number of times, as in

```
TO SQUARE SIZE
   REPEAT 4
      FORWARD SIZE
      LEFT 90
```

The set of commands to be repeated is indicated by indenting, just as with the conditional expressions.

Besides using REPEAT with a numeric input, one can also use the construct "REPEAT FOREVER," which will cause the designated section to be repeated until the user pushes the "stop" button (some special key on the keyboard).

Another form of REPEAT is "REPEAT UNTIL ⟨condition⟩ ⟨commands⟩," which keeps repeating the designated commands so long as the condition is false. This is used in the following procedure, which can be a handy way to find square roots when this capability is not built in:

```
TO SQRT X
   GUESS ← 1
   REPEAT UNTIL ABS(X - GUESS ↑ 2) < .001
      GUESS ← (GUESS + (X / GUESS)) / 2
   RETURN GUESS
```

A variant of this is "REPEAT ⟨commands⟩ UNTIL ⟨condition⟩," which is almost the same except that it tests the condition *after* doing the commands, rather than before:

```
TO POLYSTOP SIDE ANGLE
   TURN ← 0
   REPEAT
      FORWARD SIDE
      LEFT ANGLE
      TURN ← TURN + ANGLE
   UNTIL REMAINDER (TURN, 360) = 0
```

This is useful in circumstances when the condition for termination is initially true. For instance, note that the following procedure will not perform any turtle moves at all:

```
TO POLYSTOP SIDE ANGLE
   TURN ← 0
   REPEAT UNTIL REMAINDER (TURN, 360) = 0
      FORWARD SIDE
      LEFT ANGLE
      TURN ← TURN + ANGLE
```

A final version of REPEAT is "REPEAT FOR ⟨range⟩ ⟨commands⟩," as in the following procedure, which prints all the integers between its two inputs:

```
TO PRINT.SEQUENCE X Y
   REPEAT FOR I = X TO Y
      PRINT I
```

It is also possible to use REPEAT FOR in a slightly more general form in which the range is specified explicitly as a list of values. This form is "REPEAT FOR ⟨variable⟩ IN ⟨list of values⟩," as in

```
REPEAT FOR I IN [1 2 3 7 12]
```

Recursion

Although it is implicit in the description of procedures, we should point out explicitly that a procedure can include calls to any procedure, including itself. Here, for example, is a simple program from chapter 1:

```
TO POLYSPIRAL (SIDE, ANGLE)
   FORWARD SIDE
   LEFT ANGLE
   POLYSPIRAL (SIDE + 1, ANGLE)
```

This kind of program structure, in which a procedure calls itself, is known as *recursion*. One can have more complex recursive structures, such as when procedure 1 calls procedure 2 which calls procedure 1. This structure is used in the following alternative version of the DUOPOLY procedure (subsection 3.1.4):

```
TO DUOPOLY (SIDE1, ANGLE1, SIDE2, ANGLE2)
   POLY1 (SIDE1, ANGLE1, SIDE2, ANGLE2, 0, 0)

TO POLY1 (SIDE1, ANGLE1, SIDE2, ANGLE2, H1, H2)
   SETHEADING H1
   FORWARD SIDE1
   LEFT ANGLE1
   POLY2 (SIDE1, ANGLE1, SIDE2, ANGLE2, HEADING, H2)

TO POLY2 (SIDE1, ANGLE1, SIDE2, ANGLE2, H1, H2)
   SETHEADING H2
   FORWARD SIDE2
   LEFT ANGLE2
   POLY2 (SIDE1, ANGLE1, SIDE2, ANGLE2, H1, HEADING)
```

The process is started with DUOPOLY, and thereafter POLY1 and POLY2 execute alternately. The H variables are used by POLY1 and POLY2 to keep track of the headings with which they should start drawing the next time they are called.

Lists

One very important feature of Turtle Procedure Notation is the ability to combine the basic data objects—numbers and character strings— to form compound data objects. Various computer languages allow different compound data objects. In this book we've used only one kind of compound data object, the *list*. A list is simply a sequence of data objects. To specify a list in Turtle Procedure Notation, one lists the objects in sequence, surrounded by brackets. For example, [1 (3+5) 7] is a list of three numbers: 1, 8, and 7. Lists may contain character strings as well as numbers.

More significantly, lists may contain items that are themselves lists. For instance, [1 2 [3 4 5]] is a list of three items, the third of which is itself a list of three items. Consequently, lists can readily be used to represent *hierarchical structures*, that is, structures consisting of parts which themselves consist of parts. We used this capability in chapter 8, when we constructed the atlas representation for piecewise flat surfaces.

The ITEM operation is used to extract the elements of a list. ITEM(L,N) returns the Nth item from the list L. So

```
ITEM ([1 2 [3 4 5]], 3)
```

returns [3 4 5], and

```
ITEM (ITEM ([1 2 [3 4 5]], 3), 2)
```

returns 4. There are two other useful operations for taking lists apart: The operation FIRST returns the first item of a list (thus, FIRST is the same as ITEM with a second argument of 1). The operation REST returns the list with the first element removed (thus, REST[1 2 3] returns [2 3] and REST[2 3] returns [3]).

One very important property of lists in Turtle Procedure Notation is the fact that they can be manipulated as *first-class data objects,* which is to say that they can be assigned names using variables, passed as inputs to procedures, returned as outputs from procedures, and so on. We made crucial use of this property in chapter 3 when we implemented vectors as lists of numbers and wrote procedures that had vectors as inputs and outputs. For example, here is a procedure that takes as inputs two vectors, each represented as a list of two numbers, and outputs their vector sum:

```
TO SUM (V, W)
   RETURN [ITEM(V,1)+ITEM(W,1)  ITEM(V,2)+ITEM(W,2)]
```

So if we set

```
A ← [1 3]
B ← [5 -1]
```

then SUM(A, B) will return [6 2].

Structure-Directed Operations

Writing programs that deal with lists often entails unpacking items from a list, performing some computation, and repacking the results into a new list. This kind of operation is facilitated by a technique known as *structure-directed assignment.* An example will illustrate how this works: If L is a list of three items, then the single assignment statement

```
[A B C] ← L
```

will set A to the first item of L, B to the second item of L, and C to the third item of L. A similar technique enables procedures to specify *structure-directed inputs* in the title line. For example, the vector-sum procedure above could also be written as

```
TO SUM ([V1 V2], [W1 W2])
   RETURN [(V1 + V2) (W1 + W2)]
```

Local Variables

In dealing with large programs consisting of many interacting procedures, it is important to have techniques for making the program *modular* by controlling the interactions between different parts of the program. One valuable modularity mechanism that can be provided by a computer language is to make it possible for the programer to assign variable names independently in different parts of a program, without worrying about conflicts of names or about one part of the program accidentally destroying the variables of another part. The general problem of how to do this, and exactly what constitutes "different parts of a program," is referred to in computer-language design as the issue of "scope of variables." Different languages have different conventions for dealing with this issue.

One point on which most of these conventions agree is that the names of inputs to procedures should be made totally internal, or *local*, to the procedure call. For example, a programer should be able to use the absolute-value procedure

```
TO ABS X
   IF X > 0 THEN RETURN X ELSE RETURN -X
```

without worrying that the input is called X. In particular, one should be able to write

```
X ← 10
PRINT ABS (X + 3)
```

without any conflict between the variable X outside the procedure (which is equal to 10) and the variable X inside the procedure (which is equal to 13).

This mechanism for local variables is especially useful in recursive procedures, since it ensures that each call to the procedure will have its own private set of inputs. Consider, for example, the following procedure from subsection 2.4.1:

```
TO NESTED.TRIANGLE SIZE
   IF SIZE < 10 STOP
   REPEAT 3
      NESTED.TRIANGLE SIZE/2
      FORWARD SIZE
      RIGHT 120
```

Each instance of the procedure has its own variable SIZE, and the different SIZEs do not conflict.

Most computer languages also have ways of declaring variables to be local without having them be procedure parameters, but the examples in this book have not used this capability.

The EXECUTE Command

A final feature of Turtle Procedure Notation is the ability to execute character strings as commands in the language. This is accomplished by the EXECUTE command. For example,

```
EXECUTE "PRINT 3 + 5"
```

will print 8. A less silly example is the following procedure, which takes two commands as character-string inputs and alternates them over and over:

```
TO ALTERNATE (COMMAND1, COMMAND2)
   REPEAT FOREVER
      EXECUTE COMMAND1
      EXECUTE COMMAND2
```

EXECUTE is useful in writing programs to manipulate other programs, for example the "parallel-processing monitor" of subsection 2.1.2.

This appendix is an aid to adapting the programs in this book for work with computer systems and languages that are widely available. It should also be useful as a guide to selecting a computer system suitable for work with this book. Personal computers are changing rapidly for the better as regards advanced languages and high-resolution graphics, and readers should take this into account.

General Considerations

Display

In addition to a computer equipped with a suitable language, work with turtle geometry requires a graphic-output device capable of producing line drawings. One possibility is a computer-controlled plotter using paper and ink, although a display screen is superior for most purposes. Fortunately, inexpensive graphic displays based on television technology— some with built-in monitors and some designed for use with ordinary televisions—are rapidly becoming standard for personal computers.

Programing Language

Given enough memory, essentially any programing language can do the same things as any other. Thus, selecting a computer language is to some extent a question of style and personal preference. But a language that forces you to worry about details that have nothing to do with the process you are trying to implement, or does not mesh with good methods of problem solving and algorithm specification, can make using a computer tedious and burdensome. On the other hand, a computer language similar to the Turtle Procedure Notation used in this book can simplify the programing and allow you to concentrate on the mathematics, on inventing and exploring. It can even serve as a language to help you think about issues and solve problems.

We list here some issues of computer-language design and say what we think are desirable ways to deal with them from the point of view of turtle geometry.

Procedures, Inputs, and Outputs (Extensibility)

Dividing a problem into meaningful and relatively independent subparts is a vital step to solving any complex problem. A programing language should recognize this by allowing you to define your own procedures at will and use them whenever you want with no fuss. For purposes of exploration it is especially useful to be able to create a complete environment of procedures, such as FORWARD, RIGHT, and LEFT, and to not only use them as steps in other procedures, but to also select and execute them at will in controlling an ongoing process (such as a picture coming into being).

Allowing procedures to have inputs vastly increases the flexibility of such an environment of procedures. The names of procedure inputs should be local to the procedure, so that the user need not worry about the internals of a procedure when using it (see the section on local variables in appendix A). The ability of procedures to output is also important, because it enables the programer to extend the language by adding new functions.

Repetition and Recursion (Flow of Control)
Repetition is such a useful computational structure that every language has constructs for carrying it out. The question is whether these constructs are natural and easy to use. For example, a "REPEAT...UNTIL..." construct can always be implemented in terms of GOTO's, but this often leads to careless errors. Recursion is nearly as useful, but unfortunately it is not implemented in primitive languages such as FORTRAN and BASIC since it requires the computer to keep track of different instances of the same procedure (in a recursive hierarchy).

Data Types
For the purposes of this book we focus on one important feature: the ability to create data types with several parts (*compound* data types) and to be able to deal flexibly with the whole or the parts. The case in point is the way we use lists to represent vectors. In Turtle Procedure Notation these can be passed as units into and out of a procedure (with inputs and outputs). But it is just as important to be able to easily assemble and dissassemble such units for internal computation. Unfortunately, mechanisms like Turtle Procedure Notation's structure-directed operations are not at all common, and various special tricks must usually be used, depending on the computer language. The only other data-type issue we will be concerned with is distinction between integers and real numbers. Real numbers are crucial for doing geometric calculations such as vector rotations, intersections, and so on. On the other hand, the display routines of many computer systems can handle only integer inputs, in which case the result of the geometric calculations must be converted to integers before being shown on the display.

Consideration of Specific Languages

BASIC

BASIC is by far the most widely available language on inexpensive microcomputers at the present time (1981). Unfortunately, it is deficient by several of the criteria listed above. BASIC also comes in many incompatible versions. We have selected one of these—APPLESOFT II BASIC (TM)—to use in examples, because it comes on a popular, inexpensive machine (the Apple II with high-resolution graphics) that has adequate graphics capability for turtle geometry.

Procedures Inputs and Outputs

BASIC lets you define only one program at a time. The RUN command, which executes the program currently in memory, is essentially the only way to make any user-definable thing happen. RUN may, however, take an optional input that specifies the number of the program line at which to start. In that case you can get the effect of selecting different programs in response to direct user commands by starting the program at one of a number of sections of code, each of which ends with END.

Most BASICs have another mechanism, which gives the effect of having separate procedures *within* a program: You can treat portions of your program as subprocedures, or "subroutines" as they are called, by using the GOSUB command (although you cannot name these procedures or insulate their effects with local variables, inputs, and outputs). GOSUB takes an input specifying the line number at which the subroutine starts. (The subroutine ends with a RETURN.) It is sometimes possible to use a variable to specify the line number so that programs will be a bit easier to read. If this is the case, then you can invoke a "FORWARD" subroutine by saying GOSUB FORWARD, where FORWARD is a variable that has been set to 10000 or whatever line number begins the "FORWARD" subroutine. In this appendix we will use this feature for its readability, although you may have to actually use literal numbers with GOSUB.

Passing "inputs" to subroutines must be handled as global variables, so you are always liable to find some subroutine destroying some other subroutine's inputs. You can minimize this problem by establishing an appropriate convention for choosing variable names, such as letting input variables consist of two characters: the first letter of the subroutine name and a number used to distinguish among possible multiple inputs. Thus you will find yourself regularly writing code such as

```
F1 = 10: GOSUB FORWARD
```

or

P1 = 90 : P2 = 100 : GOSUB POLY

Outputs must be handled in a similar way, using, say, RF1, RF2,... for
the returned values of a FUNCTION subroutine.

  Below is an APPLESOFT II BASIC implementation of turtle commands that works on Apple's high-resolution graphics system. It differs
from the full vector version given in chapter 3 principally by keeping
heading as an angle rather than as a vector. "POSITION VECTOR" is in
PX, PY; "HEADING" is H; "PEN STATE" is in PS (pen is down when PS=1).

```
10 FORWARD = 10000 : REM the following index subroutines
11 LEFT = 10100
12 RIGHT = 10200
13 CLEARSCREEN = 10300
14 DRAWLINE = 10400

10000 REM *** FORWARD distance F1 subroutine ***
10010 HX = COS(H*3.14159/180) : REM heading vector components
10020 HY = SIN(H*3.14159/180)
10030 NX = PX + HX * F1 : REM add [HX HY]*F1 to position vector
10040 NY = PY + HY * F1 : REM save "new-position" vector [NX NY]
10050 IF PS <> 1 GOTO 10070 : REM if the pen is up, don't draw
10060 D1 = PX : D2 = PY : D3 = NX : D4 = NY : GOSUB DRAWLINE
10070 PX = NX : PY = NY : REM update position vector
10090 RETURN

10100 REM *** LEFT angle L1 (in degrees) subroutine ***
10110 H = H + L1
10120 RETURN

10200 REM *** RIGHT angle R1 (in degrees) subroutine ***
10210 H = H - R1
10220 RETURN

10300 REM *** CLEARSCREEN subroutine ***
10310 HGR : HCOLOR = 7 : REM clear the screen
10320 PX = 0 : PY = 0 : REM initialize position vector
10330 H = 0 : REM initialize heading
10340 PS = 1 : REM start with pen down
10350 RETURN
```

```
10400 REM *** DRAWLINE from [D1 D2] to [D3 D4] subroutine ***
10401 REM The inputs to HPLOT center [0 0] and make increasing
10402 REM y and x correspond to "up" and "to the right."
10410 HPLOT 140 + D1 , 80 - D2 TO 140 + D3 , 80 - D4
10420 RETURN
```

Here is a POLY program that uses these routines:

```
100 REM *** POLY program ***
110 INPUT "ANGLE?"; A
120 INPUT "DISTANCE?"; D
130 GOSUB CLEARSCREEN
140 F1 = D : GOSUB FORWARD
150 L1 = A : GOSUB LEFT
160 GOTO 140
```

Notice the practice of having a program such as this—which is meant to be RUN, that is, called from top level rather than called as a subprocedure—explicitly *ask* for its inputs by using the INPUT command.

Repetition and Recursion
Repetition can usually be handled reasonably in BASIC with GOTO statements and stop rules, as in the following sequence to compute the square root of a number A (compare the example in appendix A):

```
100 G = 1.0 : REM initialize guess
110 G = (G + A/G) / 2 : REM update guess
120 E = ABS(A - G*G) : REM error in guess squared
130 IF E > .001 GOTO 110 : REM stoprule is error no more than .001
```

Alternatively, one can use BASIC's do-loop mechanism as in the following sequence to accumulate in T the sum of the first 50 integers:

```
100 T = 0 : REM initialize accumulator
110 FOR N = 1 TO 50 DO
120 T = T + N
130 NEXT N : REM increment N and GOTO the line after FOR
```

Recursion in BASIC is so inconvenient in the general case as to be almost hopeless. (One would have to implement at the user level nearly the whole mechanism for keeping track of local variables that is built into more sophisticated languages.) Fortunately, many of the uses to which we put recursion can be handled by iterative processes. For example, any "tail recursion," where the recursive call is just the last line of the procedure, is at most just a matter of using a GOTO after changing the value of a variable whose old value is never used again. POLYSPI and INSPI could well be written as repetitive loops with an inserted command to change SIZE or ANGLE variables each time through the loop.

Even in cases where true recursion seems to be required, as in the recursive designs of chapter 2, there are a few tricks that often work. If the number of levels is small you may be able to get away with using the subroutine mechanism. The chief problem is how to keep subroutines from destroying their own (recursively called) inputs. This is manageable in cases where the process of computing the inputs to the next level down is a reversible process. That way each subroutine can maintain a sort of "state transparency" (see subsection 2.3.2) by changing the value of its "inputs" when it starts and undoing the change just before it returns. For example, here is a BASIC implementation of the recursive binary tree of 2.3.2:

```
15 BRANCH = 2000 : REM so we can say GOSUB BRANCH


200 GOSUB CLEARSCREEN
210 INPUT "SIZE?"; SIZE
220 INPUT "LEVEL?"; LEV
230 GOSUB BRANCH
240 END

2000 IF LEV = 0 GOTO 2100 : REM stoprule
2010 SIZE = SIZE/2 : LEV = LEV - 1 : REM change parameters
2020 F1 = SIZE : GOSUB FORWARD
2030 L1 = 45 : GOSUB LEFT
2040 GOSUB BRANCH
2050 R1 = 90 : GOSUB RIGHT
2060 GOSUB BRANCH
2070 L1 = 45 : GOSUB LEFT
2080 F1 = -SIZE : GOSUB FORWARD
2090 LEV = LEV + 1 : SIZE = SIZE * 2 : REM undo change
2100 RETURN
```

Note how the main program merely sets up for the subroutine, and the subroutine's second and last steps are inverses. It may be valuable to have the main program set a more appropriate starting point on the screen.

A slight variation on this (check how parity is handled in line 3030) allows the HILBERT curve of section 2.4.3 to be written as follows:

```
16 HIL = 3000 : REM index subroutine

300 GOSUB CLEARSCREEN
310 INPUT "SIZE?"; F1
320 INPUT "LEVEL?"; L
330 P = 1
340 GOSUB HIL
350 END

3000 IF L = 0 GOTO 3140 : REM stoprule
3010 L = L - 1
3020 L1 = P * 90 : GOSUB LEFT
3030 P = (-P) : GOSUB HIL : P = (-P)
3040 GOSUB FORWARD
3050 R1 = P * 90 : GOSUB RIGHT
3060 GOSUB HIL
3070 GOSUB FORWARD
3080 GOSUB HIL
3090 R1 = P * 90 : GOSUB RIGHT
3100 GOSUB FORWARD
3110 P = (-P) : GOSUB HIL : P = (-P)
3120 L1 = P * 90 : GOSUB LEFT
3130 L = L + 1
3140 RETURN
```

Data Types

BASIC's compound-data-type capability is so weak that is is almost always best to deal with compound things in terms of the separate parts. Thus, vectors will be handled as separate variables for components, VX, VY, VZ, etc. Given this, it makes less sense to subroutinize vector addition and scalar multiplication, since setting up multiple inputs and outputs is so clumsy. You will find yourself writing more and thinking more in terms of components when you program in BASIC, but try to resist at least the thinking part. Here is a subroutine to rotate a two-dimensional vector (R1 and R2 are the input coordinates and R3 the angle of rotation; RR1 and RR2 are the rotated coordinates; we suppress line numbers). Compare this with the rotation procedure of subsection 3.2.2:

```
S = SIN(3.14159*R3/180)
C = COS(3.14159*R3/180)
RR1 = R1 * C - R2 * S
RR2 = R2 * C + R1 * S
RETURN
```

Notice we have not explicitly used PERP, but only its components.

A three-dimensional YAW subroutine (see subsection 3.4.3) operating directly on the components of heading and left vectors would look as follows:

```
S = SIN(3.14159*Y1/180)
C = COS(3.14159*Y1/180)
THX = C * HX + S * LX : REM "T" FOR TEMPORARY
THY = C * HY + S * LY
THZ = C * HZ + S * LZ
LX = C * LX - S * HX
LY = C * LY - S * HY
LZ = C * LZ - S * HZ
HX = THX : HY = THY : HZ = THZ
RETURN
```

If your display requires integer inputs, make sure to convert with an INTEGER function.

Logo

Logo is the name for a philosophy of education and for a continually evolving family of computer languages that aid its realization. The Logo computer language has been used over the past ten years at MIT and elsewhere as the basis for many innovative experiments in harnessing computer technology to enhance education, including the experiments that led to the writing of this book. Because Logo is such a sophisticated and powerful language, it was for many years not feasible to design Logo implementations for computers inexpensive enough to be used in homes and schools, and the use of Logo was restricted mainly to research centers. Recently, the tremendous decline in the cost of computers has changed this state of affairs. At least two Logo implementations for personal computers—the Apple II and the Texas Instruments 99/4— are commercially available. (Interested people should contact the Logo Project at MIT for further information.)

Except for minor variations of syntax, Logo is substantially the same as the Turtle Procedure Notation used in this book. In particular, Logo is highly interactive, organizes programs as collections of procedures, includes lists as "first-class" data objects, and has built-in turtle graphics. For comparison with Turtle Procedure Notation, here is a Hilbert curve program (see subsection 2.4.3) in Logo. (To save us from utter boredom, we have introduced a slight variation that draws the curve on a diagonal.)

```
TO HILBERT :SIDE :LEVEL :P
H (-:P)
RFR :P
H :P
RFR (-:P)
H :P
RFR :P
H (-:P)
END

TO RFR :P
RIGHT :P * 45
FORWARD :SIDE
RIGHT :P * 45
END

TO H :P
IF :LEVEL = 0 RIGHT :P * 90 STOP
HILBERT :SIDE :LEVEL - 1 :P
END
```

Notice that the program is basically a collection of recursive calls to itself (H) interspersed with a "corner turn" primitive motion (RFR). The major difference between the above code and the Turtle Procedure Notation used in this book is that the variable names are preceded by colons.

Pascal

Pascal has recently become widely available in a standardized version developed at the University of California at San Diego. UCSD Pascal (TM) has been implemented on a number of inexpensive machines in a form suitable for turtle geometry. We mention in particular the APPLE II (with Pascal package) and the Terak 8510A. (The programs below use the Apple version where there is a difference.) In addition to Pascal's advantages of being a rather well-developed language by the criteria we outlined, this particular version includes built-in turtle commands MOVE, TURN, PENCOLOR(WHITE), PENCOLOR(BLACK), MOVETO, and TURNTO, which correspond, respectively, to Turtle Procedure Notation's FORWARD, LEFT, PENDOWN, PENUP, SETXY, and SETHEADING. There are also TURTLEX, TURTLEY, and TURTLEANG, which correspond to XCOR, YCOR, and HEADING.

Pascal's principal disadvantages are three: Its highly structured form requires the programer to pay attention to certain details of form which we have deliberately omitted from Turtle Procedure Notation. For example, one must always declare variables and their types (integer, real, array, etc.) before using them. Moreover, one cannot use the same variable for different types of data. These constraints not only lead to extra typing, but interfere with convenience and flexibility. Second, although Pascal does have facilities for handling compound data objects such as lists, the programer must deal with these structures in terms of special so-called "pointer variables" rather than as first-class data objects. The third disadvantage is that Pascal is a compiled language (in contrast to Logo and BASIC), which means there must be an extra compilation step between writing a program and running it. The way this is generally handled makes it difficult to generate environments of many independent, user-defined programs, such as one would do to create any of the various turtle geometries in this book (cube, three-dimensions, and so on). As a result, the image of creating and using a single program (as opposed to a continuously evolving cluster of procedures) dominates Pascal as it does BASIC.

Procedure Inputs and Outputs

Within a program, Pascal has extensive capabilities to have separate subparts (called procedures) which can take inputs and return values in a number of ways. Inputs specified by the user at run time, however, are usually handled, as in BASIC, by a separate INPUT command within the program. Below is a sketch of a program, TURTLE, which sets up a environment that allows a user to interactively choose commands according to what is seen developing on the screen. The main part of the program is a monitor loop (at the end of the program) that repeatedly allows the user to type in a command, which the monitor then executes as a procedure. We use a separate procedure ASK to ask the user for an input if that is necessary. In this way, procedures such as FD (FORWARD is reserved for a built-in command) can be used not only as direct user commands (in the monitor), but also in other procedures that do not ask the user for inputs.

```
PROGRAM TURTLE;
USES TURTLEGRAPHICS, APPLESTUFF;
VAR COMMAND: STRING; A, D: INTEGER;

    PROCEDURE ASK(QUESTION: STRING; VAR ANSWER: INTEGER);
    BEGIN
        WRITE(QUESTION);
        READLN(ANSWER)
    END;
```

```
    PROCEDURE GETCOMMAND;
    BEGIN
        REPEAT GRAFMODE UNTIL KEYPRESS;
        TEXTMODE;
        READLN(COMMAND)
        (*THIS ALLOWS GRAPHICS DISPLAY TO BE MAINTAINED UNTIL
          A COMMAND IS TYPED. THE METHOD OF HANDLING MIXED
          TEXT AND GRAPHICS WILL IN GENERAL DEPEND ON YOUR
          SYSTEM AND INGENUITY.*)
    END;

    PROCEDURE FD(D: INTEGER);
    BEGIN
        MOVE(D)
    END;

    PROCEDURE LT(A: INTEGER);
    BEGIN
        TURN(A)
    END;

BEGIN (*MONITOR LOOP*)
    INITTURTLE;
    PENCOLOR(WHITE);
    REPEAT
        GETCOMMAND;
        IF COMMAND='FD' THEN BEGIN
            ASK('HOW FAR? ', D); FD(D) END;
        IF COMMAND='LT' THEN
            BEGIN ASK('HOW MUCH? ', A); LT(A) END;
        IF COMMAND='CS' THEN
            BEGIN INITTURTLE; PENCOLOR(WHITE) END;
        IF COMMAND='PU' THEN PENCOLOR(NONE);
        IF COMMAND='PD' THEN PENCOLOR(WHITE);
    UNTIL COMMAND='DONE';
END.
```

Of course, this can serve as a model for setting up other environments
for exploration. Unfortunately, this system-type organization does not
allow the user to write even elementary experimental programs without
recompiling.

Repetition and Recursion

Pascal has a wide variety of REPEAT UNTIL, WHILE, FOR constructs similar to those in Turtle Procedure Notation. Here are two samples, a POLY procedure (to be used as an extension of the TURTLE environment above) and a SQRT function (to be used as part of some main program). See also the use of FOR in TURTLE3D below.

```
PROCEDURE POLY(A, D:INTEGER);
VAR HEAD, INITHEAD: INTEGER;
BEGIN
   INITHEAD := TURTLEANG;
   REPEAT
     FD(D);
     LT(A);
     HEAD := TURTLEANG;
   UNTIL HEAD = INITHEAD;
END;

FUNCTION SQRT(A, B:REAL):REAL;
VAR GUESS: REAL;
BEGIN
   GUESS := 1.0;
   WHILE ABS(A - GUESS*GUESS) > 0.001 DO
     GUESS := (GUESS + A/GUESS)/2;
   SQRT := GUESS
END;
```

Recursion is also neat in Pascal. Here is HILBERT again:

```
PROGRAM HILBERT;
USES TURTLEGRAPHICS, APPLESTUFF;
VAR L, P, S: INTEGER;

   PROCEDURE HIL(L, P:INTEGER);
   BEGIN
     IF NOT (L = 0) THEN
        BEGIN
           TURN(P*90);
           HIL(L-1, -P);
           MOVE(S);
           TURN(-P*90);
```

```
                HIL(L-1, P);
                MOVE(S);
                HIL(L-1, P);
                TURN (-P*90);
                MOVE(S);
                HIL(L-1, -P);
                TURN(P*90)
            END
    END;

BEGIN
    WRITE('SIZE? '); READLN(S);
    WRITE('LEVEL? '); READLN(L);
    INITTURTLE;
    PENCOLOR(WHITE);
    HIL(L, 1);
    REPEAT UNTIL KEYPRESS; TEXTMODE
END.
```

Data Types

Pascal's compound-data types are adequate for turtle-geometry work.
For vectors one will probably want to use arrays. Here are some service
procedures in the context a sketch of a three-dimensional turtle program (see subsection 3.4.3). Unfortunately, Pascal doesn't allow functions to output compound-data types, so subroutine vector arithmetic
is not worth the effort. On the other hand, call-by-name parameters (see
ROTATE below) make some types of vector operations transparent.

```
PROGRAM TURTLE3D;
USES TURTLEGRAPHICS, TRANSCEND, APPLESTUFF;
TYPE VECTOR = ARRAY[1..3] OF REAL;
    VAR I: INTEGER;
    A, D, LDIST: REAL;
    COMMAND: STRING;
    P, H, L, U, TEMP: VECTOR;

    PROCEDURE INIT;
    (*THIS PROCEDURE SHOULD SET INITIAL VALUES FOR LDIST, P, H, L
      U, AND PERFORM OTHER INITIALIZING ACTIVITIES*)

    PROCEDURE ASK; (*AS IN TURTLE PROGRAM ABOVE*)
```

```
PROCEDURE ROTATE(VAR V, PERPV: VECTOR; A: INTEGER);
VAR AR: REAL;
BEGIN
   AR := A * 3.14159/180.0;
   FOR I := 1 TO 3 DO
      TEMP[I] := COS(AR)*V[I] + SIN(AR)*PERPV[I];
   FOR I := 1 TO 3 DO
      PERPV[I] := COS(AR)*PERPV[I] - SIN(AR)*V[I];
   V := TEMP
END;

PROCEDURE PROJECT(V: VECTOR; VAR X,Y: INTEGER);
BEGIN
   X := ROUND(LDIST*P[1]/P[3]);
   Y := ROUND(LDIST*P[2]/P[3]);
   (*NOTE ROUNDING (CONVERTING TO INTEGER FOR MOVETO).
     APPLE DOES AUTOMATIC CLIPPING; OTHER SYSTEMS MAY
     REQUIRE SOME WORK TO MAKE SURE X AND Y ARE WITHIN
     RANGE REQUIRED BY MOVETO.*)
END;

PROCEDURE YAW(A: INTEGER);
BEGIN
   ROTATE(H, L, A)
      (*PITCH OR ROLL ARE SIMILAR, USING H AND U OR
        U AND L AS INPUTS TO ROTATE*)
END;

PROCEDURE FD(D: INTEGER);
VAR X, Y: INTEGER;
BEGIN
   FOR I := 1 TO 3 DO
      P[I] := P[I] + D*H[I];
   PROJECT(P, X, Y);
   MOVETO(X+140, Y+95)
END;

BEGIN
   (*MAIN LOOP HERE SIMILAR TO THAT OF THE PREVIOUS TURTLE
     PROGRAM. IT SHOULD INCLUDE INIT PROCEDURE.*)
END.
```

The program is intended to use the built-in penup and pendown mechanism (PENCOLOR) rather than keeping its own pen-state variable.

UCSD Pascal assumes that inputs to turtle (and other graphics) commands are integers, and you must make sure of this either by computing with integers or by converting to integers before calling them. You can use the built-in ROUND function as we did in PROJECT.

Other Languages

APL is quite suitable for turtle geometry. It is procedure-oriented, with inputs and outputs. It allows "environment building" in the way Logo does. Furthermore, it is recursive and handles compound data, such as vectors, in the cleanest fashion of any language mentioned here. APL has not yet been picked up by any of the major producers of inexpensive home computers. We do, however, know of at least one major installation that has turtle commands built into APL.

Lisp is another language that is structurally very compatible with our criteria. In fact, Logo is a direct descendant of Lisp. But so far Lisp has not been much associated with inexpensive, graphics-oriented hardware.

Smalltalk is a language that, like Logo, was developed explicitly for educational purposes. Not surprisingly, it fares well by our criteria, especially since it was designed to take advantage of the capabilities of high-resolution graphics and to be an extensible, interactive medium. Though it has not been publicly released by its developers at Xerox Corporation, there are plans to make the latest version, Smalltalk 80, available in the near future. Smalltalk programs are organized in a manner very different from the step-by-step procedure model that typifies the languages discussed above. Instead, the "knowledge" in a Smalltalk program is distributed among a number of "objects" which communicate among themselves by means of "messages." For example, a turtle might be a kind of object that knows how to respond to messages FORWARD, RIGHT, and so on. This so-called "object-oriented programing" has many advantages in dealing with graphics and simulations, and in particular with the kind of multiple turtle projects discussed in section 2.2. Although Smalltalk's fundamental constructs are very different from those of Turtle Procedure Notation, the translation of any of the above programs into Smalltalk is easy and elegant, with none of the difficulties of modularity and environment building encountered with Basic and Pascal. One can also expect Smalltalk implementations to include built-in turtle graphics.

Hints and Answers

Hints for Selected Exercises

Chapter 1

Section 1.1

2. Before worrying about the radius, try finding the circumference of the circle.

8. The answer depends on whether or not the ANGLE is divisible by 8. You should be able to guess the answer through experimentation, but you probably won't be able to give a proof until you've looked ahead to subsection 1.4.1.

9. In general, of two regular polygons with the same circumference, the one with more sides has a greater area. (This is not simple to prove. A neat proof without calculus was given by Galileo in his *Dialogues on the Two New Sciences*.) Or do a direct calculation.

11. One interesting effect is that programs always close when they would have closed if run on an infinite plane. Can you prove this?

12. Describe the geometric transformations as reflections in certain lines through the turtle's initial position.

13. One result is that eventually, at a small enough scale, all you ever see are straight lines.

Section 1.2

2. The first three vertices the turtle draws determine a circle. Now use congruent triangles to show that the rest of the vertices also lie on this circle.

6. How does the sum of the interior angles relate to the sum of the exterior angles?

7. Consider the closed turtle path formed by the arc and the line. What is the turtle's total turning while traversing this path?

9. Use the result of exercise 8 to relate the other two arcs of the circle to the two angles formed by the arcs and their respective chords. Now use the relation between A and these two angles.

10. Relate the angle turned by the turtle to the angle between the arc and the chord formed by a side of the POLY. Now use exercise 8.

11. Use the result of exercise 10 (although, since the method of proof suggested in exercise 10 is to use the simple-closed-path theorem, you'll have to find another proof in order to avoid a circular argument).

12. Compare with exercise 3 of section 1.1.

Section 1.3

5. Generalize the analysis for $A = 2$, INCREMENT $= 20 = 360/18$ given in subsection 1.3.2. To give a formula, use the fact that the sum of the first $n - 1$ integers is equal to $n(n - 1)/2$.

6. In keeping track of the total turning, divide the basic loop into two parts: one where the angle increases and one where the angle decreases. Then add the corresponding angles in pairs. Alternatively, use the following formula, which generalizes the one given in the hint above: If S and T are integers with $T > S$, then the sum of the integers from S through T (inclusive) is equal to $(S + T)(T - S + 1)/2$.

8. This can be done with vectors. See section 3.1, exercise 3. We'll leave it to you to find another method of proof.

Section 1.4

2. Use the following fact: If we can draw an n-pointed POLY using an integer angle, then we can also find some integer angle that draws an n-pointed POLY with rotation number 1.

3. The $180 - A$ answer depends on the value of A modulo 4. You should be able to guess the answer by experimenting. To prove it is harder. Try using the symmetry formula $n = \text{LCM}(A, 360)/A$ and comparing this with $\text{LCM}(180 - A)/(180 - A)$. The analysis may be easier if you take advantage of the fact (see exercise 16) that for any integers x and y, $\text{LCM}(x, y) \times \text{GCD}(x, y) = xy$. This reduces the problem to finding the relation between $\text{GCD}(A, 360)$ and $\text{GCD}(180 - A, 360)$.

7. What is the product modulo p of R, $2R, \ldots$, $(p - 1)R$?

11. To show that d can be represented as $\langle \text{integer} \rangle R + \langle \text{integer} \rangle n$, use the fact that R/d and n/d are relatively prime and hence that 1 can be represented as $\langle \text{integer} \rangle R/d + \langle \text{integer} \rangle n/d$. Also, show that d must divide any integer which can be represented as $\langle \text{integer} \rangle R + \langle \text{integer} \rangle n$, which implies both that d must be the smallest such integer and that the integers which can be represented this way are precisely the multiples of

d. Reducing the the numbers of the form ⟨integer⟩R+⟨integer⟩n modulo n gives the multiples of R modulo n.

14. If each of two variables is expressible in the form $aR + bn$, the difference is also expressible in that form. Show that this means the variables in the Euclid process are always of this form, including the final step when the two are both equal to d.

18. Apply the same "reduction rule" EUCLID uses to find the GCD: Imagine that we are in the case where $R < n$, so that we are about to reduce the problem of finding $\mathrm{GCD}(n, R)$ to that of finding $\mathrm{GCD}(n - R, R)$. Then suppose we already know how to find p and q such that $p(n - R) + qR = d$. Then, for that pair p and q, we have $pn + (q - p)R = d$. In other words, if $R < n$ and we know $\mathrm{DIO}(n - R, R) = (p, q, d)$, then we should return $\mathrm{DIO}(n, R) = (p, q - p, d)$. This leads to the computer procedure

```
TO DIO N R
   IF N > R THEN
      [P Q D] ← DIO (N-R, R)
      RETURN [P Q-P D]
```

Fill in the rest of the DIO procedure to handle the cases $N < R$ and $N = R$. (The statement "[P Q D] ← DIO (N-R, R)" sets the three variables P, Q, and D to the three respective pieces of DIO(N-R, R). This is an example of "structure-directed assignment," which is a useful although uncommon feature for a programing language. See appendix A for more information.)

19. Rather than reducing the problem for (n, R) to $(n, n - R)$, try reducing it to (R, rem), where rem is the remainder when n is divided by R. Suppose that the quotient when n is divided by R is quo and the remainder is rem. If $p \times R + q \times \mathrm{rem} = d$, show how to express the solution (x, y) to $xn + yR = d$ in terms of p, q, and quo. Use this to construct FASTDIO as a recursive procedure.

23. If you try some examples, you should notice that $\mathrm{GCD}(F(a), F(b))$ is itself a Fibonacci number. Now, which one is it?

24. Try examples and you will find that x and y are themselves Fibonacci numbers. Which ones are they?

Chapter 2

Section 2.1

2. One of the important results of statistics is that the average value for the square of the distance from home after s steps in a random walk is proportional to s (for s large). This means, roughly, that distance from home increases as $\sqrt{s}$.

9. If the turtle does draw a closed path, compute the total turning over the path and apply the simple closed-path theorem.

Section 2.2

9. Look at the situation from the point of view of the chaser. At each step it moves CHASE.SPEED closer to the evader. But also at each step, the evader moves "outward" from the chaser. Calculate the amount of this outward motion. Suppose that EVADE.SPEED is greater than CHASE.SPEED. Show that if the evader is far from the chaser the outward motion is less than the chaser motion, so the two creatures move closer together; and when the chaser is close to the evader the outward motion is greater than the chaser motion, so the two creatures move further apart. At what point do the two motions balance?

11. You can use analytic geometry and (x, y) coordinates. But once you become familiar with the vector methods in the chapter 3, you should try the following vector approach for finding the point on a given line that is closest to a given point: If the line is represented as $\mathbf{s} + \lambda \mathbf{v}$ (that is, the line parallel to a vector $\mathbf{v}$ and passing through the point $\mathbf{s}$) and the point is $\mathbf{p}$, then the point on the line closest to $\mathbf{p}$ is the point $\mathbf{r} = \mathbf{s} + \lambda_0 \mathbf{v}$ for which the line from $\mathbf{r}$ to $\mathbf{p}$ is perpendicular to $\mathbf{v}$—that is, the point for which

$$(\mathbf{p} - \mathbf{s} - \lambda_0 \mathbf{v}) \cdot \mathbf{v} = 0.$$

Solving this for λ_0 gives

$$\lambda_0 = \frac{(\mathbf{p} - \mathbf{s}) \cdot \mathbf{v}}{\mathbf{v} \cdot \mathbf{v}}.$$

Hence, the required point is $\mathbf{s} + \lambda \mathbf{v}$, where λ has this value.

12. Suppose that the defender has speed k times that of the attacker, and starts out less than k times as far from the target. (Otherwise, the attacker could actually reach the target.) Consider this description of

the optimal point to head for when $k = 1$—it is the closest point to the target, which is equally far from both players.

Section 2.3

4. Let the length of the branch drawn at the highest level be L. What is the sum of the lengths of the two branches drawn at the next level? What is the sum of the lengths of the four branches drawn at the next level (and so on)?

6. To find the total length, consider that each level has three times as many branches as the preceding one. Use the formula for the sum of a geometric series:

$$x^n + x^{n-1} + \ldots + x^2 + x + 1 = \frac{x^{n+1} - 1}{x - 1}.$$

9. Consider only complete spirals, which result from running EQSPI infinitely forward and backward in time. Then there can be no such thing as a size parameter, because just rotating the spiral does the same thing as increasing or decreasing size.

10. Show that each pass through the loop draws a scale model of the previous pass. Now focus on the net state change achieved in each pass in terms of that of the first pass.

Section 2.4

1. Draw half the side of the largest outer POLY, turn and do the process recursively with a smaller side, and complete the outer POLY without interruption. The trick is to find the factor that gives the reduction in size from one POLY to the next. You will have to use trigonometry.

2. For the length: What is the ratio of the length for level n to the length for level $n+1$? For the area: Decompose into a sum of equilateral triangles. What is the ratio of the total area of the level-n triangles to the area of one of the level-$(n + 1)$ triangles?

4. The Hilbert program at level n contains three FORWARD instructions plus four recursive calls. If $f(n)$ is the length of the level-n curve, write an equation for $f(n)$ in terms of $f(n - 1)$.

8. If you remove the four outer diagonal lines (darkened in the figure), the curve breaks into four pieces. Try giving a recursive description of each of the pieces.

Chapter 3

Section 3.1

3. Let S be the length of the first side. From each side of the POLYSPI, subtract a vector of length S parallel to the side. What is the sum of the pieces subtracted? What is left? (If the figure closes, then the turtle ends up in the initial heading, so the number of steps taken to close is a multiple of the number of steps in a POLY with the same angle.)

5. In terms of the spirograph analysis, suppose one arm moves in increments of ANGLE1 and the other in increments of ANGLE2. When do the two arms line up?

13. There is a different sense of "approximately symmetric," which becomes better as the difference between the displacements VECTOR(A1,S1) followed by VECTOR(A2,S2) as opposed to VECTOR(A2,S2) followed by VECTOR(A1,S1) becomes visually negligible.

18. Consider the distribution of numbers in the slot process.

19. Look at the assignment of the numbers in the slot process. Show that if the number 1 gets assigned to an odd-numbered slot then all odd numbers get assigned to odd-numbered slots and all even numbers get assigned to even-numbered slots; and conversely if 1 is assigned to an even-numbered slot. Now consider the sums of the numbers in the odd and even slots.

25. Show that there exist integers m and n with $2^m = 2^n \pmod{q}$. Then show that we must also have $2^{m-1} = 2^{n-1} \pmod{q}$ and so on.

26. Use the formula

$$1 + x + x^2 + \ldots + x^{r-1} = \frac{x^r - 1}{x - 1},$$

which gives the sum of a geometric series.

27. Rotate the sum by A and apply the vector form of the POLY closing theorem, or else rotate by $3A$ and look at the result.

28. Use Fermat's Little Theorem (see exercises for section 1.4) and the fact stated in exercise 17.

Section 3.2

5. Try to solve for a and b. What is the necessary condition for writing down a solution?

7. As a vector equation this condition is

$$\text{Perp}(a\mathbf{v}_1 + b\mathbf{v}_2) = -b\mathbf{v}_1 + a\mathbf{v}_2,$$

which must hold for any a and b.

8. Use the net displacement formula for DUOPOLY, neglecting the constant center vector.

Section 3.3

2. The points are given by the vector equations

$\text{NOSE} = \mathbf{P} + \text{TURTLE.HEIGHT} \times \mathbf{H},$

$\text{LEFT.LEG} = \mathbf{P} + \dfrac{1}{2}\text{TURTLE.WIDTH} \times \text{Perp}(\mathbf{H}),$

$\text{RIGHT.LEG} = \mathbf{P} - \dfrac{1}{2}\text{TURTLE.WIDTH} \times \text{Perp}(\mathbf{H}).$

Section 3.5

2. Use dot product.

3. You could work this out in coordinates, but a neater way is to make use of the definition of dot product in terms of projection. Use the facts that the projection of $\mathbf{v}$ onto $\mathbf{w}$ is 0 if $\mathbf{v}$ and $\mathbf{w}$ are perpendicular, and that the projection of $\mathbf{v}$ onto $\mathbf{v}$ is $|\mathbf{v}|$.

4. Relate $|\mathbf{v}|$, $|\mathbf{w}|$, $\mathbf{v} \cdot \mathbf{w}$ and A to $\text{Proj}(\mathbf{v}, \mathbf{w})$.

5. If the vectors form the sides of a triangle, then $\mathbf{t} + \mathbf{v} + \mathbf{w} = 0$. Notice that the angle opposite $\mathbf{t}$ is 180 minus the angle referred to in the preceding exercise.

6. You should discover that these three-dimensional looping programs close only in the degenerate case when the figure lies in a plane. Non-planar figures lie along a helix, just as POLYs lie along a circle in two dimensions.

7. We gave two proofs of the POLY closing theorem in subsection 1.2.2. The first proof, that the vertices of POLY lie on a circle, clearly uses the fact that the motion is in a plane. But how about the second proof? That one, remember, showed that assuming that the path doesn't close leads to a contradiction. What is this contradiction, exactly? How does it rely on the fact that the motion is in a plane?

9. ROLL until **ex** is in the plane of **ez**, **p**. Now rotate in the **ex**, **ez** plane (YAW) until **ez** is pointing toward **p**. Finally, ROLL opposite to undo your first ROLL and leave the angle between **ey** and the **ez**, **p** plane the same as when you started. The sine and cosine needed for the first ROLL are **p**·**ey**$/s$ and **p**·**ex**$/s$, where s is the square root of $(\mathbf{p}\cdot\mathbf{ex})^2 + (\mathbf{p}\cdot\mathbf{ey})^2$. The cosines and sines for the second rotation are then **ez**·**p**$/|\mathbf{p}|$ and **ex**·**p**$/|\mathbf{p}|$.

13. A four-dimensional cube is a three-dimensional cube at $t = 0$, consisting of the points $(0,0,0,0)$, $(0,0,1,0)$, $(0,1,0,0)$, $(0,1,1,0)$, $(1,0,0,0)$, $(1,0,1,0)$, $(1,1,0,0)$, $(1,1,1,0)$ connected in the appropriate way, plus one at $t = 1$ with corresponding vertices connected. A turtle procedure to draw this can be generalized from drawing a cube with the following procedure: Draw a square (FORWARD 1, LEFT 90 done four times), FORWARD 1, PITCH 90, and repeat this whole sequence four times. As far as rotating in four dimensions, you can check that rotating x, y coordinates and leaving z and t alone is a rotation; that is, it leaves all distances the same. In general, there will be one plane where the action is (like x, y here) and an invariant plane (the analog to a fixed axis). That means there are six fundamental rotations.

Chapter 4

Section 4.1

2. The program is equivalent to a repeating fixed instruction sequence that will complete one basic loop when LOCAL.PHASE returns to 0 modulo 360. Thus, it will close when both LOCAL.PHASE and the total turning are 0 modulo 360.

14. Consider some of the techniques used in the interpolation program of exercises 6–13. When exactly is a scissors a nondeformation? What exactly are the conditions under which a SHRINKSEG (exercise 5) causes a change in topological type? Are there other kinds of kinking or unkinking? Look at the criteria for pruned programs (exercise 1 of section 1.2), and make sure you rule out changes that unprune in such a way as to change total turning.

17. To find the extra piece of information, consider the case of no crossing points, then one crossing point.

Section 4.3

1. Imagine the turtle walking along the curve. Is the turtle's left foreleg or right foreleg the one that lies in the inside region?

3. Consider figure 4.16 together with the phenomenon illustrated in figure 4.11b.

5. Consider the set of minimum distances between nonadjoining segments.

Section 4.4

1. Use the ideas in subsection 4.4.3.

2. Spirals may or may not have infinite length or infinite total turning. The EQSPI spiral of section 2.3 has infinite total turning but finite length (from any point inward). If a turtle can travel at a constant speed and can turn as fast as necessary to follow any curve, an EQSPI maze does not spell doom unless it extends infinitely outward as well as inward.

Chapter 5

Section 5.1

1. How does the question of which side of the curve the turtle considers the "inside" relate to the question of which turning the turtle considers to be positive and which turning it considers to be negative? Compare exercise 1 of section 4.3.

4. Focus on the process of walking. If the turtle's right and left legs are doing the same thing, that adds an additional symmetry constraint beyond each leg independently marching off equal-distance steps.

5. The path can depend on size of the turtle, but not if you use smaller and smaller turtles until the turtle is much smaller than any features of the surface. This is the essence of calculus, and it requires surfaces that do not have arbitrarily small features ("smooth" surfaces).

6. Suppose we decide to compute the excess around a closed path as the net change in pointer heading. Then a trip around the sphere's equator and a trip around a circle in the plane both seem to cause no net change in pointer heading. But look more carefully—what is the difference between what a pointer does on the equator as compared to the planar circle where Excess = 0?

8. Consider the answer for exercise 7, where a turtle has one side in the middle of one lane and its other side in the middle of the adjacent lane.

Section 5.2

1. What is the region whose curvature the excess of the path is measuring?

4. Given two subdivisions of the surface, find an even finer subdivision that includes them both.

7. Find a subdivision of a football into polygons for which you know the excesses.

11. A small model of a cone is part of a larger one.

13. For global π look at the "real" radius of the circle. (The "real" center of the circle is not in the surface.) Answers to many of these question will be found in chapters 6 and 7.

15. Fill in the holes. Now how much curvature does the surface have? Cut them out. How much curvature did you remove?

16. Think about the finished umbrella. You can tell its total curvature from a turtle path around the edge. If you start cutting away ribbon after ribbon from the edge, does the total curvature ever increase, indicating that you cut away a strip of negative curvature? Now go back and relate this to things you could measure on the piece.

Section 5.3

2. Cut and paste.

5. This is a simple generalization of the "rectangle" argument for the curvature of the tin can given in the text.

6. The crucial part of the proof is on the turtle path common to both areas. Look back at exercise 5.

10. The result is topologically equivalent to one handle.

12. Choose any point p not on the surface, and let q be the farthest point on the surface from p. What must the surface look like near p? Compare exercise 9 of section 5.2.

13. Since the surface lies in three-dimensional space, it must be equivalent to a sphere with a bunch of handles attached. Now, what can

you say about the total curvature? Could it be zero? Use the previous exercise.

14. Since the surface is closed, exercise 12 implies it must have a point of positive curvature, which can only be a vertex. (No curvature is concentrated along any edge.) But all vertices are the same, so all vertices must have postive curvature. By exercise 13, therefore, the surface must be topologically equivalent to a sphere and hence have total curvature 4π. This total curvature is distributed among v vertices, all containing the same amount of curvature, c. Therefore, $vc = 4\pi$. Each vertex, on the other hand, is made up of a vertex from each of f faces coming together there. If the vertex of the regular polygon has interior angle i, then the curvature at the vertex is given by $c = 2\pi - fi$. (If you don't understand this, go over the section on curvature of cones.) In addition, for a regular polygon with s sides, $i = \pi - 2\pi/s$. Finally, it is clear that f, the number of faces meeting at a vertex, must be at least 3. Now, using all of this, show that i must be less than $2\pi/3$ and therefore s must less than 6; that is, there are no Platonic solids made from polygons with six or more sides. Finally, by analyzing the cases for $s = 3, 4, 5$ show that the only possible Platonic solids are the ones listed. What are v, f, i, and s in each case?

15. The definitions of face, vertex, and edge are at issue.

Chapter 7

10. Use the fact that the length of a chord that subtends an arc of measure θ is $2r \sin \frac{\theta}{2}$, where r is the radius of the circle. Apply this to the chord common to the two arcs that make up the path of the fixed point. Show that the radius of one of these is $\sin r$ and the other is

$$\sqrt{1 - \sin^2 r \cos^2 \tfrac{\beta}{2}}.$$

11. The proof that a fixed point exists follows the same outline as the proof in the text for the special case of perpendicular axes, except that the great circle going through both poles replaces the Greenwich longitude. The lemma in the text showing that a fixed point implies a rotation completes the proof that any two rotations combine to give a net rotation. For any sequence, the above result can combine the first two into a single rotation, and then that can be combined with the next, and so on.

12. Set up coordinates with $\mathbf{z}$ and $\mathbf{x}$ as before and $\mathbf{y}$ perpendicular to them. Now introduce $\mathbf{t}$ perpendicular to $\mathbf{z}$ but in the plane of arc B.

Show that $\mathbf{t} = (\sin \gamma)\mathbf{y} - (\cos \gamma)\mathbf{x}$. Finally, rotate $\mathbf{z}$ toward $\mathbf{t}$ to produce $\mathbf{b}$ and take the dot product with $\mathbf{a}$.

13. Use the approximations $\sin x \approx x$ and $\cos x \approx 1 - x^2/2$ and drop very small terms (more than degree 2 in α and β).

17. Check that, for each side of measure α of the original triangle, one will find an angle of α in the polar triangle.

Chapter 8

Section 8.1

2. Use an array (or a list), and store the answer to the ith question in the ith entry of the array. One way to number questions "which face and edge connect to edge e of face f?" is $i = 4f + e$.

8. What is the total curvature of the n-holed torus? If you identify edges in the atlas so that there is only one vertex on the surface, how much curvature will that produce?

15. Think about a turtle carrying a flag around a strip enclosing part of the edge. Better yet, use the recipe for concentrated curvature given in exercise 5 of section 5.3.

16. Qualitative features of this kind of gluing can be seen by viewing it on a special "map" of the surface as follows. Consider the map to be a plane with a line (the glue) drawn on it. Everything is as usual except that the scale of the map changes as you cross the line. As a turtle walks at a constant speed on the surface, it appears to speed up or slow down in crossing the glue line on the map. Now model the turtle as a two-wheeled creature (wheels turning equally fast) and take a look at crossing that line at an angle. One of the turtle's wheels will cross before the other, and its speeding up (or slowing) will cause it to gain (or lose) ground on the other wheel—that is, the turtle will turn. This deflection will not happen if the crossing is made perpendicular to the edge. That dependence on angle of intersection causes it to appear that the curvature concentrated along the edge depends on the measuring process and is not well-defined: A square with edges crossing perpendicular to the line will not have the same total turning as a triangle that crosses the line at the same points.

Section 8.2

2. Remember that curvature can only appear at the vertices.

5. Establish an orientation on each face and check that no contradiction can be found.

8. There are some easy answers: two spheres, two tori, ... But how about surfaces that come in one piece? Think about total curvature.

9. Simply "reversing right and left" is not enough—you can do that by standing on your head. You need an effect that cannot be gotten by any local, continuous operation. How about being able to put your right hand in your left glove? Suppose you took a trip (leaving you gloves at home) that allowed that trick when you got back. Would you be able to read a book you took with you? Would a friend who stayed with your gloves be able to read that book?

Section 8.3

2. Compute using a net which is set up so that ends of the handle match with edges of the net.

3. Given nets N_1 and N_2, show how to produce a "combined" net N_{12} that "contains" both N_1 and N_2 by essentially laying one on top of the other and adding vertices as necessary. Be careful to show that N_{12} can be constructed in all cases to satisfy the requirements of being a net. Show that N_1 and N_2 can each be transformed to N_{12} by elementary operations.

5. Show that such a surface can be "closely approximated" by a piecewise flat surface. To get started, consider how to approximate any simple closed curve in the plane by a polygonal path and look at a continuous deformation from one to the other.

10. Assume that the net does not have any concentrated curvature along its arcs. Then justify the assumption later if you can. You can use the net itself to define pieces of surface and paths around which to compute curvature. The trick is to relate angles turned by the turtle to interior corner angles again, and to note that the sum of corner angles at a vertex is always 2π.

11. What does the "local terrain" look like to a turtle standing at the "bad" vertex? Where does the proof of $K = 2\pi\chi$ for piecewise flat surfaces break down for the double cube?

14. A useful parameter for a regular net is $\chi_{\text{local}} = V - E + F$ per face. If S = number of sides to a face and T = number of arcs from a vertex, show that $\chi_{\text{local}} = 1 - S/2 + S/T$. Then try $S = 3, 4, 5, \ldots$ in sequence, checking for solutions to $\chi = F\chi_{\text{local}}$.

15. Use the hint to exercise 14.

16. $\chi_{\text{local}} = 0$ is sufficient to ensure a regular net. This gives $S = 3, 4, 6$ (see exercise 15). These are easy to draw. Try drawing $S = 5$, $T = 3$ or $S = 8$, $T = 3$.

17. Consider tiling an ever larger piece of the plane. As an example take a square consisting of n^2 smaller squares. At any stage we have three types of squares: those on the interior of the tesselation, those on the edge, and those in the corner. We also know that the Euler characteristic of the entire net must be equal to 1. If one takes χ_I, χ_E and χ_C to be the local Euler characteristics for each of these types, then $(n - 2)^2\chi_I + 4(n - 2)\chi_E + 4\chi_C = 1$. In order for this to hold at large n, the coefficient of n^2 (χ_I) must certainly be zero. This argument generalizes to show $\chi_I = 0$ for any infinite-plane tesselation.

Chapter 9

Section 9.1

2. Only (3) and (4) will be affected. Assume that sin and cos now take degrees as inputs, not radians, and you want to convert to degrees before returning DEMON.TURNING.

3. $TT(r) = 2\pi - \theta$; $C(r) = (2\pi - \theta)r$ with θ the constant pie angle.

9. Look back to exercise 7 of section 5.1.

10. Straight-line latitudes replace the circular latitudes of the old scheme. Leaping is in the **x** direction.

Section 9.2

8. Looking into the region would be something like looking at a reflection of the world around you in a spherical mirror, except it would be an entirely different, infinite world *inside* the sphere you would be seeing! If you were small and flexible enough to squeeze through the spherical opening (the neck of the slice in the figure), you would find yourself in a

different flat region of space. In science fiction terms, the spherical neck is a "wormhole" connection between two otherwise normal universes.

9. To point out heading, you will need to choose a spatial dimension and use it to represent time. For the parabolic trajectory use the dimension perpendicular to the plane containing it. The stream will be a parabolic arch in spacetime (like a sheet of paper bent so that its cross-section is a parabola), and droplets will be headed diagonally "up and over" within it.

Section 9.3

3. The largeness of the "falling" effect of gravity is due to the large speed of light.

8. Take a vote.

11. The key to the independence of method of sensing ticks is that the message mechanism doesn't change in time.

12. Construct two events that are spacelike with respect to one another, and observe them from a moving frame of reference.

13. Lorentz rotations leave 45° lines *in the plane of rotation* invariant. If a light ray has a heading not in that plane (not going directly toward or away from the sun), it will not project into that plane as a 45° line.

14. Your hand is actually accelerating the apple, which only appears "at rest" in your hand.

Section 9.4

2. Use the formula in the text, TURNING.PER.TIME $= m/r^2$. Ignore any other small effects, such as leaping.

3. Very eccentric orbits near the sun give the most precession. Generally speaking, you know that your simulation is getting near perfect accuracy when reducing the step size does not change the result much. You can estimate error by assuming it to be proportional to step size: If you reduce step size from STEPSIZE to F $\times$ STEPSIZE, the error in the result will be about F $\times$ ⟨change in result⟩.

7. The vector projection $(\mathbf{v} \cdot \mathbf{S}) \times \mathbf{S}$ is, in coordinates, just setting the non-S coordinates to zero.

11. Align the gyroscope in the plane of the orbit for maximum visible effect, and take the orbit near the surface of the earth. Use the formulas `TURNING.PER.ANGLE` $= m/r$ (see subsection 9.4.4), and $m = GM/c^2$ in physical units (see exercise 4).

Chapter 1

Section 1.1

2. All of the POLYs in the sequence have the same circumference: 360 turtle units. Thus, the limiting circle has a radius of $360/2\pi \approx 57$ turtle units.

3. According to the previous exercise, POLY(1, 1) should have a radius of $360/2\pi$ turtle units. So to make a circle of radius r in steps of $1°$ turning each would require a FORWARD step of $2\pi r/360 \approx 0.0175r$. Thus, an arc procedure can be defined by

```
TO ARC (RADIUS, DEGREES)
    FORWARD.STEP ← RADIUS * .0175
    REPEAT DEGREES
        FORWARD FORWARD.STEP
        LEFT 1
```

(This assumes that the number of degrees in the arc is an integer.)

4. We know from exercise 2 that POLY(D, A) draws a circle of radius $r = 360D/2\pi A$. Hence, the radius of curvature, D/A, is equal to $360r/2\pi$. If A is measured in radians, then r is equal to the radius of curvature.

7. There are three different nine-sided figures, produced by angles $40°$, $80°$, and $160°$, and two different ten-sided figures with angles $36°$ and $108°$. See section 1.4 for a way to determine the number of different n-sided POLYs in general.

8. For POLY vs. DOUBLEPOLY with the same ANGLE, if the ANGLE is divisible by 8, the two figures have the same n-fold symmetry. Otherwise DOUBLEPOLY has $n/2$-fold symmetry to POLY's n-fold symmetry. After reading subsection 1.4.1 you should be able to prove this, using the symmetry formula given in that section together with the fact that LCM$(A, 360) =$ LCM$(2A, 360)$ unless A is divisible by 8.

9. POLY(5, 5) has the larger area, since it is closer to a circle.

10. One example is an increment of 20 and an angle equal to 10 times an odd number. An analysis of the symmetry of INSPI is given in subsection 1.3.2.

12. Interchanging RIGHT and LEFT reflects the picture in the line along
the turtle's initial heading. Interchanging FORWARD and BACK can be
described as reflecting in this line followed by reflecting in the perpendicular line. (This can also be described as 180° rotation.) Reversing the
order of the program reflects only in the perpendicular line (assuming
that the program ends with the turtle in the initial position and heading). If we call these operations A, B, and C respectively, then A and C
make B; A and B make C; B and C make A; and A, B, and C together
make no change.

15. The following program draws an ellipse with size parameter S and
eccentricity $(1 + E)/(1 - E)$. It uses a variable, N, to keep track of
when to draw with high and when with low curvature. Techniques to
prove this will be developed in chapter 3.

```
TO ELLIPSE S E
   N ← 0
   REPEAT 360
      RIGHT N FORWARD S LEFT N
      LEFT N FORWARD S*E RIGHT N
      N ← N+1
```

Section 1.2

1. The pruned program should alternate FORWARD and turn (RIGHT and
LEFT) commands and should not have any FORWARD 0 commands nor
any turns greater than 180°.

3. The finiteness part follows from the fact that the vertices lie on a
circle. (This is true for any angle, rational or not, as you discovered if
you did exercise 2.) But the path can never close. If it did, the total
turning would have to be an integer multiple of 360°. But no integer
multiple of the irrational angle can be an integer multiple of 360°, or
that angle could be expressed as a ratio.

5. You need a third input to accumulate total turning:

```
TO POLYSTOP (SIDE, ANGLE, TURN)
   FORWARD SIDE
   RIGHT ANGLE
   IF REMAINDER (TURN, 360) = 0 THEN RETURN
   POLYSTOP (SIDE, ANGLE, TURN + ANGLE)
```

The program is called with the third input equal to the second.

6. Each interior angle is equal to $180°$ minus the corresponding exterior angle. Thus, the sum of the n interior angles is equal to $180n$ minus the sum of the exterior angles, or $180n - 360$; that is, $180(n-2)$. For a regular n-gon, all interior angles are equal, so each one is equal to $180(n-2)/n$.

7. For the closed path consisting of arc and line, the total turning is $180 - A$ plus $180 - B$ plus the turning over the arc. Since this must sum to 360, we have that the turning over the arc is equal to $A + B$.

8. Take A equal to B in exercise 7 to get $\theta = 2A$.

9. Let θ_1 and θ_2 be the other two arcs of the circle, and let A_1 and A_2 be the angles formed by the arcs and their respective chords. By the result of exercise 8, $\theta_1 = 2A_1$ and $\theta_2 = 2A_2$. But $A_1 + A_2 + A = 180$ (look at the three angles formed at the apex of the inscribed angle) and $\theta_1 + \theta_2 + \theta = 360$. Therefore, $A = \theta/2$.

12. If L is the distance between the wheels, then the bicycle is basically performing a POLY with side L and angle θ. As discussed in the answer to exercise 4 of section 1.1, the resulting circle has radius $360L/2\pi\theta$ if θ is measured in degrees, or L/θ if θ is measured in radians. Note that L/θ is the radius of curvature of the path.

Section 1.3

4. $36A + 180 \pmod{360}$.

5. $nA + \text{INC} \times n(n-1)/2$, or, equivalently, $nA + (n-1)180$.

6. Let $B = \text{BOTTOM}$ and $T = \text{TOP}$. Over one cycle of the basic loop, the successive angles turned are

$$B, B+1, \ldots, T-1$$

as the angle increases and

$$T, T-1, T-2, \ldots, B+1$$

as the angle decreases. Adding these pairwise,

$$B + T, (B+1) + (T-1), \ldots,$$

gives $T - B$ terms of $T + B$ each, or $(T-B)(T+B) = T^2 - B^2$ for the entire loop. For example, taking $T = 9$ and $B = 3$ gives a total turning of $81 - 9 = 72$; this is fivefold symmetry.

11. These are just POLYs, or decorated versions thereof!

Section 1.4

1. 350 is -10 (mod 360): $p = -1$, $q = 36$, so 36 points with rotation number -1. 35: $p = 7$, $q = 72$. 37: $p = 37$, $q = 360$. $12\frac{1}{2}$: $p = 5$, $q = 144$. $26\frac{2}{3}$: $p = 2$, $q = 27$.

2. If $nA = 360R$, where A is an integer and n and R have no common factors, then n must divide 360. Thus, the POLYs that can be drawn with integer angles are precisely the ones for which the number of points divides 360.

3. In going from A to $180 - A$ the number of points stays the same if A is odd, doubles if A is divisible by 4, and gets cut in half if A is congruent to 2 modulo 4. To prove this, use the symmetry formula $n = \text{LCM}(A, 360)/A$. Together with the relation $\text{LCM}(360, A) \times \text{GCD}(360, A) = 360A$, the symmetry formula can be written $n = 360/\text{GCD}(360, A)$. The symmetry for $180 - A$ is $360/\text{GCD}(360, 180 - A)$. So the problem reduces to comparing $\text{GCD}(360, A)$ with $\text{GCD}(360, 180 - A)$. It's not too hard to check that these are equal if A is odd, that $\text{GCD}(360, A) = 2 \times \text{GCD}(360, 180 - A)$ if A is divisible by 4, and that $\text{GCD}(360, A) = (1/2)\text{GCD}(360, 180 - A)$ if A is congruent to 2 modulo 4.

4. If nxA is a multiple of xB, then A is the same multiple of B; if nA is a multiple of B, then xA is the same multiple of xB. So the brute-force method will stop with the same n whether we use A and B or xA and xB. Therefore, $\text{LCM}(xA, xB) = x\text{LCM}(A, B)$. For the last part, simply pick x equal $\text{LCM}(q, s)$, use the prime-factorization method on xp/q and xr/s, then divide by x.

5. A and $360 - A$ will produce figures that look the same, so the number of different-looking n-pointed POLYs will be half the number of integers less than and relatively prime to n. For $n = 10$ there are two different ones, for $n = 36$ there are six, and for $n = 37$ there are eighteen.

6. $\phi(1000000) = 1000000(1/2)(4/5) = 400000$.

7. Since the multiples of R run through all the integers modulo p, we have, modulo p

$$R \times 2R \times 3R \times \cdots \times (p-1)R = 1 \times 2 \times 3 \times \cdots \times (p-1),$$

or

$$R^{p-1} \times 1 \times 2 \times 3 \times \cdots \times (p-1) = 1 \times 2 \times 3 \times \cdots \times (p-1).$$

Since $2, 3, \ldots$ have no factors in common with p, we can divide both sides of the congruence by each of these successively to obtain the result.

10. If we can solve $p_sR - q_sn = s$ for any s then let $p = p_1$ and $q = -q_1$ to get $pR + qn = 1$. Conversely, given p and q such that $pR + qn = 1$, set $p_s = sp$ and $q_s = -sq$ to get $p_sR - q_sn = s$.

15. The "GCD" of $\frac{1}{2}$ and $\frac{2}{3}$ is $\frac{1}{6}$. In general, if a/b and c/d are fractions reduced to lowest terms, then the program outputs $\mathrm{GCD}(a, b)/\mathrm{LCM}(c, d)$ (see exercise 4). If the two inputs are not rational multiples of each other, the program never terminates.

18. The complete procedure is

```
TO DIO N R
   IF R = 0
      RETURN [1 0 N]
   IF N > R
      THEN
         [P Q D] ← DIO (N-R, R)
         RETURN [P Q-P D]
      ELSE
         [P Q D] ← DIO (R-N, N)
         RETURN [Q-P P D]
```

The first clause works because DIO is doing the same reduction as Euclid's algorithm, so if R gets down to zero, N must equal the GCD.

19. With rem and quo defined as in the hint to this problem, we have $p \times R + q \times \mathrm{rem} = d$, which implies that $q \times n + (p - q \times \mathrm{quo}) \times R = d$. The corresponding recursive procedure is

```
TO FASTDIO (N, R, REM, QUO)
   IF R=0 THEN RETURN [1 0 N]
   [REM QUO] ← [REMAINDER(N, R) QUOTIENT(N, R)]
   [P Q D] ← FASTDIO (R, REM)
   RETURN [Q P-Q*QUO D]
```

The QUOTIENT function returns the integer quotient of its arguments. The function is called with two auxiliary inputs REM and QUO. (The initial values for REM and QUO are irrelevant. You may as well use 0 for the inputs.) These inputs are needed to ensure that REM and QUO are local to the procedure call. Otherwise the value of QUO would be changed during the recursive call. (Technically, we only needed to make QUO a local variable, since REM is not needed after the recursive call.) See appendix A for explanation of local variables.

20. $17 \times 62 + 117(-9) = 1$; $1234567 \times (-3553793) + 7654321 \times 573192 = 1$.

21. The fact that the EUCLID process is inverse to the FIBONACCI process means that, if you call EUCLID with $F(n)$ and $F(n-1)$ as inputs, EUCLID will reduce that to a recursive call with $F(n-1)$ and $F(n-2)$ as inputs, which reduces to $F(n-2)$ and $F(n-3)$, and so on, until we get to $(1,1)$. This shows that $F(n)$ and $F(n-1)$ are relatively prime.

22. The procedure runs so slowly because, for M $<$ N-2, FIB(M) is computed many times. For example, FIB(N-2) is run as a subprocedure to FIB(N), but also as a subprocedure to the other subprocedure of FIB(N), namely FIB(N-1). You can speed things up by using the following alternative method for computing F. (Can you see why this gives the same result?)

```
TO FIB N
    S ← 1
    T ← 0
    REPEAT N
        NEW.S ← S+T
        T ← S
        S ← NEW.S
    RETURN S
```

23. Did you guess that $\text{GCD}(F(a), F(b)) = F(\text{GCD}(a, b))$? It's not easy to prove. (This result, known as Lucas's theorem, was discovered in 1876.) If you're interested in seeing the proof, take a look at D.E. Knuth's *Art of Computer Programming*, vol. 1 (Reading, Mass.: Addison-Wesley, 1968).

24. You should discover that $F(n-3)F(n)-F(n-2)F(n-1) = (-1)^n$. It's not hard to give a proof using induction and the relation $F(n) = F(n-1)+F(n-2)$.

25. By examining successive pairs in the sequence

$$(p, q) \to (p+q, p) \to (2p+q, p+q) \to (3p+2q, 2p+q) \to \cdots$$

you should be able to deduce the formula $F(p, q; n) = pF(n)+qF(n-1)$.

Chapter 2

Section 2.1

1. RAND(-50,50) and RAND(0,50)-RAND(0,50) both produce numbers in the range -50 to 50, but the distribution is different. In the

first case, the numbers are selected with equal probability. In the second case, the numbers tend to bunch up around 0. For example, the only way that the second method can produce 50 is if the first RAND(0,50) is 50 and the second RAND(0,50) is 0. On the other hand, the second method will produce 0 whenever the two random numbers selected are equal. In fact, with the second method, the odds of producing zero are 51 times the odds of producing 50. A turtle using the second method would tend to turn smaller angles than one using the first.

9. Suppose the turtle starts out at distance D_0 and follows the procedure for n steps to end up at distance D_n. Since the turning at each step is DISTANCE - DISTANCE.LAST.TIME, the total turning over the entire path is $D_n - D_0$. If the path is closed, then $D_n = D_0$, so the total turning must be zero. But the simple-closed-path theorem says that the total turning over a simple closed path cannot be zero.

10. Let DX be the difference between the x coordinates of point and turtle, and let DY be the difference between the y coordinates. Then the DY/DX is the tangent of the angle TOWARDS, assuming that an angle of 90° means straight up. Assume that XCOR and YCOR output the x and y coordinates of the turtle, and that ARCTAN computes arc tangents in degrees. Then TOWARDS can be implemented as

```
TO TOWARDS [PX PY]
    [DX DY] ← [PX-XCOR PY-YCOR]
    IF DX > 0 THEN RETURN ARCTAN (DY/DX)
    IF DX < 0 THEN RETURN 180 + ARCTAN (DY/DX)
    RETURN 90 * SIGN DY
```

This assumes that ARCTAN returns angles between −90° and +90°, and that SIGN returns +1 or −1 depending on the sign of its input. The program gives the correct answer modulo 360, but in the range from −90° to +270°. (You decide what to do if both DY and DX are zero.) If HEADING returns the turtle's heading, then BEARING(P) is just TOWARDS(P)-HEADING.

Section 2.2

6. For three bugs, each bug travels two-thirds the side of the original triangle. For n bugs, let $A = 360/n$; then the distance traveled by each bug is equal to the side of the original polygon divided by $1 - \cos A$.

9. Let E be EVADE.SPEED and C be CHASE.SPEED. If the evader is distance D from the chaser and moves distance E at a bearing of 90°, then

the new distance from the chaser is $\sqrt{D^2 + E^2}$. Thus, at each point the evader is moving outward from the chaser a distance of $\sqrt{D^2 + E^2} - D$. When D is small this is approximately equal to E, which is larger than the amount C that the chaser moves toward the evader, so the net result is that the evader ends up further away. When D is much larger than E the outward motion is approximately $E^2/2D$, which is small, so the chaser motion dominates and the net result is that the chaser moves closer. The stable distance is the one at which these two effects balance; that is, where

$$C = \sqrt{D^2 + E^2} - D$$

or

$$D = \frac{E^2 - C^2}{2C}.$$

11. If $\mathbf{A}$ is the attacker's position, $\mathbf{D}$ is the defender's position, and $\mathbf{T}$ is the target's position, then we are looking for the point on the perpendicular bisector of the line from $\mathbf{A}$ to $\mathbf{D}$ which is closest to $\mathbf{T}$. Using the vector method outlined in the hint, we can represent the perpendicular bisector as $\mathbf{s} + \lambda \mathbf{v}$ where $\mathbf{s} = (\mathbf{A} + \mathbf{D})/2$ and $\mathbf{v} = \text{Perp}(\mathbf{D} - \mathbf{A})$. Then, as given in the hint, the point is $\mathbf{s} + \lambda \mathbf{v}$ where

$$\lambda = \frac{(\mathbf{T} - \mathbf{s}) \cdot \mathbf{v}}{\mathbf{v} \cdot \mathbf{v}}.$$

We translate this into Cartesian coordinates so you can check your answer if you didn't use vector methods:

$$(x, y) = (s_x + \lambda v_x, s_y + \lambda v_y),$$

where

$$(s_x, s_y) = \left(\frac{A_x + D_x}{2}, \frac{A_y + D_y}{2} \right),$$

$$(v_x, v_y) = (-D_y + A_y, D_x - A_x),$$

$$\lambda = \frac{v_x(T_x - s_x) + v_y(T_y - s_y)}{v_x^2 + v_y^2}.$$

12. The optimal strategy for each player is to head for the point closest to the target both can reach in the same time (assuming the initial posi-

tions and speeds are not such that the attacker can actually reach the target before the defender). Using analytic geometry, you can determine that this point is the closest point to the target which lies on a certain ellipse, that is determined by the initial positions and speeds of the players.

Section 2.3

4. LEVEL × LENGTH.

6. Total length of branches for LENGTH $= L$ and LEVEL $= n$ is $3 \times L \times (3^n - 1)/2$.

8. EQSPI(n, n, n) does not approach a limiting curve. However, if the growth factor is $1 + n$ or k^n, it does.

9. Size is irrelevant, and angle and growth factor can compensate for one another in the same way that angle and sidelength compensate in drawing circles. Thus, the appropriate parameter is something like growth per angle. But since growth factors multiply, rather than adding as distance does, the answer is the ath root of f, where a is angle and f is growth factor. (Making a GROWs of that amount is the same as one GROW of f.)

Section 2.4

1. The sidelength of the inscribed POLY is $\cos(A/2)$ times that of the outer POLY.

```
TO POLYNEST (SIZE, ANGLE, LEVEL, TOTALTURN)
    IF LEVEL = 0 THEN RETURN
    FORWARD SIZE/2
    SUBPOLYNEST (SIZE, ANGLE, LEVEL)
    FORWARD SIZE/2
    RIGHT ANGLE
    TOTALTURN ← ANGLE
    REPEAT
        FORWARD SIZE
        RIGHT ANGLE
        TOTALTURN ← TOTALTURN + ANGLE
    UNTIL REMAINDER(TOTALTURN, 360) = 0
```

```
TO SUBPOLYNEST (SIZE, ANGLE, LEVEL)
   RIGHT ANGLE/2
   POLYNEST (SIZE * COS(ANGLE/2), ANGLE, LEVEL - 1, 0)
   LEFT ANGLE/2
```

2. Each level curve has $\frac{4}{3}$ the length of the previous level, so total length for level n is $3 \times \text{SIZE} \times (\frac{4}{3})^n$. For area, at each level we add the area of three new triangles, each $\frac{1}{9}$ the area of a previous bigger triangle. Hence, if A is the area of an equilateral triangle of side s, the new area added at each level is $A/3^k$. So the total area is

$$A \times [1 + \tfrac{1}{3} + \tfrac{1}{9} + \cdots + (\tfrac{1}{3})^{n-1}] = 3A \times \frac{1 - (\tfrac{1}{3})^n}{2}.$$

Observe that, as the number of levels increases, the total length of the curve tends toward infinity, while the area of the curve approaches $3A/2$.

4. If $f(n)$ is the length of the level-n curve ($\text{SIDE} = 1$), then $f(n) = 3 + 4f(n-1)$. Thus,

$$f(n) = 3 \times (1 + 4 + 16 + \cdots + 4^{n-1}) = 4^n - 1.$$

8. The following procedure draws the recursive "one-fourth" of the curve. There are two different line lengths: S and $\text{DIAG} = \text{S}/\sqrt{2}$.

```
TO ONE.SIDE (S, DIAG, LEVEL)
   IF LEVEL = 0 THEN RETURN
   ONE.SIDE (LEVEL - 1)
   RIGHT 45
   FORWARD DIAG
   RIGHT 45
   ONE.SIDE (LEVEL - 1)
   LEFT 90
   FORWARD S
   LEFT 90
   ONE.SIDE (LEVEL - 1)
   RIGHT 45
   FORWARD DIAG
   RIGHT 45
   ONE.SIDE (LEVEL - 1)
```

Then the curve is made of four pieces, each piece is given as above, together with an extra DIAG piece:

```
TO SIERP (S, LEVEL)
   DIAG ← S/SQRT(2)
   REPEAT 4
      ONE.SIDE (S, DIAG, LEVEL)
      RIGHT 45
      FORWARD DIAG
      RIGHT 45
```

Chapter 3

Section 3.1

2. Starting from the same spot for a $\mathbf{v}$ and $\mathbf{w}$ displacement, $\mathbf{v} - \mathbf{w}$ is the displacement that takes you from (the tip of) $\mathbf{w}$ to (the tip of) $\mathbf{v}$.

3. Consider the vector statement of closure, $\mathbf{v}_0 + 2\mathbf{v}_1 + \cdots + n\mathbf{v}_{n-1} = \mathbf{0}$, where $\mathbf{v}_i$ are rotated versions of $\mathbf{v}_0$. Subtracting $\mathbf{v}_0 + \mathbf{v}_1 + \cdots + \mathbf{v}_{n-1} = \mathbf{0}$ gives $\mathbf{v}_1 + 2\mathbf{v}_2 + \cdots + (n-1)\mathbf{v}_{n-1}$. Now rotate the result, $\mathbf{v}_i \to \mathbf{v}_{i-1}$, and subtract from the original to give $n\mathbf{v}_{n-1} = \mathbf{0}$, which is impossible unless $\mathbf{v}_0 = \mathbf{0}$.

4. The theorem is the same, with q terms in the sum.

6. ANGLE1=17, ANGLE2=1 gives $45°$ (eightfold) symmetry; ANGLE1=18, ANGLE2=2 gives $90°$ (fourfold) symmetry; ANGLE1=28, ANGLE2=3 gives $216°$ (fivefold) symmetry; ANGLE1=101, ANGLE2=1 gives $18°$ (twentyfold) symmetry; ANGLE1=102, ANGLE2=2 gives $36°$ (tenfold) symmetry.

9. If the angles of the MULTIPOLY are $A_1, A_2, A_3, \ldots, A_k$, and A_1 is the smallest of them, then the symmetry angle of the spirograph is the least common multiple of the set

$$\frac{360}{\frac{A_2}{A_1} - 1}, \frac{360}{\frac{A_3}{A_1} - 1}, \ldots, \frac{360}{\frac{A_k}{A_1} - 1}.$$

The least common multiple of a set $a_1, a_2, a_3, \ldots, a_k$ can be found using the LCM of pairs of numbers as

$$\text{LCM}(a_1, \text{LCM}(a_2, \text{LCM}(a_3, \ldots, \text{LCM}(a_{k-1}, a_k)))).$$

10. Taking the $1, n, n^2, \ldots$ case and using the answer to exercise 9 above gives the least common multiple of $360/(n-1), 360/(n^2-1), \ldots$, which

is $360/(n-1)$. A clock has two hands, one of which moves 12 times as fast as the other. By the above analysis this gives elevenfold symmetry (since the hands move continuously, it is exact symmetry). This means that there are only eleven possible orientations for inserting a working mechanism into a clockface; that is, for which it is possible to set the clock with both hands pointing together at 12.

13. DUOPOLYs are always approximately bilaterally symmetric, in the sense that the associated spirograph is always bilaterally symmetric. But visually, approximate bilateral symmetry happens under different circumstances than approximate rotational symmetry. One situation that ensures exact bilateral symmetry is when the angles are negatives of each other and the sidelengths are the same. In this case, the axis of symmetry is perpendicular to the initial heading.

17. Since the spirolateral is closed, the sides form a collection of vectors $\mathbf{v}_i$ that sums to zero. By the theorem cited this must be a multiple of $\mathbf{V}$; that is, each $\mathbf{v}_i$ appears the same number of times. But that's precisely what it means to be regular.

18. The slot process will distribute the numbers 1 thru MAX among n slots so that the numbers in each slot sum to the same amount. Therefore, the sum of all the numbers from 1 through MAX must be divisible by n. And the sum of the numbers from 1 through MAX is MAX $\times$ (MAX $+$ 1)/2.

19. In the slot process, if a number k is assigned to slot i, then $k+1$ gets assigned to either $i+1$ or $i-1$ (mod n). Therefore, the claim made in the hint is true: Either all odd numbers get assigned to odd numbered slots and all even numbers to even numbered slots, or vice versa. But all slots must have the same sum, and there are the same number of odd and even slots. So the sum of the odd numbers from 1 to n would have to equal the sum of the even numbers from 1 to n, which it does not.

24. Rewrite the congruence as

$$2^k \times (360p/q) = 360p/q + \langle\text{integer}\rangle \times 360.$$

Now divide both sides of the equation by 360 and multiply by q.

28. By Fermat's Little Theorem (section 1.4, exercise 7), we have $2^{p-1} = 1$ (mod p). Hence, the order of 2 modulo p is at most $p-1$. That means that there are at most $p-1$ vectors in the Gospel basic loop. But according to the theorem cited in exercise 17 you must use all p vectors $\mathbf{v}_i$ in order to achieve a sum of $\mathbf{0}$.

Section 3.2

2. If x and y are the coordinates of $\mathbf{V}$, then the vector equation $R_A(\mathbf{V}) = \mathbf{V}$ can be be rewritten in coordinates as the pair of equations

$$x = x \cos A - y \sin A,$$
$$y = x \sin A + y \cos A.$$

Multiplying the first equation by $\cos A$ and the second by $\sin A$, adding, and using the fact that $\sin^2 + \cos^2 = 1$ gives

$$x \cos A + y \sin A = x.$$

Together with the first equation, this implies that $y \sin A = 0$, and hence $x \cos A = x$. So either x and y are both 0 or else $\sin A = 0$ and $\cos A = 1$; that is, either $\mathbf{V} = \mathbf{0}$ or $A = 0 \pmod{360}$.

3. This is just the coordinate form of the vector equation given by the POLY closing theorem, where $A = 360/n$ and $\mathbf{v}$ is the vector $[1\ 0]$.

4. If A is the heading of $\mathbf{v}$ and L is the length, then

$$L = \sqrt{v_x{}^2 + v_y{}^2},$$
$$H = \mathtt{TOWARDS}(v_y, v_x).$$

(See exercise 10 of section 2.1 for the TOWARDS function.) Conversely,

$$v_x = L \cos H,$$
$$v_y = L \sin H.$$

5. The condition is $v_{1x}v_{2y} \neq v_{1y}v_{2x}$.

6. Let $D = v_{1x}v_{2y} - v_{1y}v_{2x}$. Then $a = v_{2y}/D$, $b = -v_{1y}/D$, $c = -v_{2x}/D$, and $d = v_{1x}/D$.

7. The geometric condition is that $\mathbf{v}_1$ and $\mathbf{v}_2$ must be perpendicular and of the same length. The algebraic condition is

$$v_{1x} = -v_{2y},$$
$$v_{1y} = v_{2x}.$$

8. The net displacement from the constant center is $R_{kB}(\mathbf{r}_u) + R_{-kB}(\mathbf{r}_v)$. Since these vectors are rotating in opposite directions, we can always choose to start looking at them when they are lined up. If $t = 0$ corresponds to the lined-up position, the subsequent displacements are given

by $R_{tB}(\mathbf{r}) + R_{-tB}(E\mathbf{r})$, where $\mathbf{r}$ has their common lined-up direction and the length of $\mathbf{r}_u$. E is the ratio of the length of $\mathbf{r}_v$ to $\mathbf{r}_u$, namely C/A. Now choose coordinates so that $\mathbf{x}$ points along $\mathbf{r}$, and the DUOPOLY becomes the set of Cartesian points

$$(r\cos Bt + rE\cos Bt, r\sin Bt + rE\sin(-Bt))$$
$$= r((1+E)\cos Bt, (1-E)\sin Bt).$$

This set of points satisfies the equation

$$\frac{x^2}{(1+E)^2} + \frac{y^2}{(1-E)^2} = r^2,$$

and therefore is an ellipse as advertised. Note how choosing the $t = 0$ time and the coordinate system with origin at $\mathbf{c}$ with $\mathbf{x}$ pointing toward $\mathbf{r}$ simplifies calculation and puts the answer in easily recognizable form.

Section 3.5

2. $\mathrm{Proj}(\mathbf{v}, \mathbf{w}) = \mathbf{v} \cdot \mathbf{w}/|\mathbf{w}|$. In coordinates, this is A divided by B where

$$A = \mathbf{v} \cdot \mathbf{w} = v_x w_x + v_y w_y + v_z w_z,$$
$$B = \sqrt{w_x{}^2 + w_y{}^2 + w_z{}^2}.$$

4. $\mathrm{Proj}(\mathbf{v}, \mathbf{w}) = |\mathbf{v}| \cos A$. But $\mathrm{Proj}(\mathbf{v}, \mathbf{w}) = \mathbf{v} \cdot \mathbf{w}/|\mathbf{w}|$ also; thus the result follows.

5. Simply compute the length of $\mathbf{t}$ as

$$|\mathbf{t}| = |-\mathbf{t}| = |\mathbf{v} + \mathbf{w}| = (\mathbf{v} + \mathbf{w}) \cdot (\mathbf{v} + \mathbf{w}) = |\mathbf{v}|^2 + |\mathbf{w}|^2 + 2\mathbf{v} \cdot \mathbf{w}.$$

Now use the formula for dot product given in the preceding problem, together with the fact that the angle A is $180°$ minus the angle used in that problem.

7. The proof of the POLY closing theorem in subsection 1.2.2 boils down to the fact that if the turtle's path were not closed the turtle would wander off to infinity in two directions simultaneously, which is impossible. More precisely, we found that the turtle would have to wander off to infinity along some line L, and then that it would have to wander off to infinity along a rotated version of L. But, in three dimensions, L and L rotated can be the same line! In fact, while a nonzero rotation in the plane cannot leave any line invariant, any nonzero rotation in three dimensions will *always* leave some line invariant (namely, the axis

of the rotation). So there is no contradiction. Moreover, this tells us how to find the line L: It is the axis of the "net rotation" of the three-dimensional POLY step. In fact, all the points of the POLY lie on a helix that winds around L.

Chapter 4

Section 4.1

15. For one crossing point the possible values are $0, \pm 720$; for two crossing points, $\pm 360, \pm 1080$; for three crossing points, $\pm 1440, \pm 720, 0$.

16. The direction in which the turtle travels defines a "positive" direction along the curve. At the crossing point we can single out two directions: Let D_1 be the positive direction through the crossing point of the piece of arc the turtle traveled first, and let D_2 be the positive direction of the piece of arc traveled second. Think about rotating D_1 until it lines up with D_2. Define the crossing point to be left-handed or right-handed, depending on whether the rotation from D_1 to D_2 is counterclockwise or clockwise. (In rotating from D_1 to D_2 we take the "short way around": We rotate so that D_1 does not cross over the other two arcs coming in to the crossing point.) To make this unambiguous you can, for example, start tracing around the curve from a section of the curve that is reachable from the outside (that is, not on an inside loop).

17. With crossing direction defined as above, each right-handed crossing will contribute $360°$ to total turning and each left-handed crossing will contribute $-360°$. The extra piece of information is the direction the turtle travels around the "whole curve." It can be determined, for example, by looking at the leftmost point on the curve and seeing whether positive direction on the curve is pointing up or down at that point. So let LH be the number of left-hand crossings and let RH be the number of right-hand crossings. Let X equal 1 if the positive direction at the leftmost point on the curve is down and -1 if the direction is up. Then the total turning is $360(RH - LH + X)$.

Section 4.3

1. Count turning left as positive and turning right as negative. If the total turning around the curve is $360°$, then the turtle's left leg lies in the inner region. If the total turning is $-360°$, the turtle's right leg lies in the inner region.

2. If there are crossing points, then there are more "local configurations" than the ones shown in figure 4.20. For example, the northeast corner could be a crossing point and the collapsing process would get stuck.

3. On the plane, any succession of northeast corners, each one blocking the previous one, must terminate because the curve only has a finite number of vertices. But on a surface like the torus, a finite sequence of corners could loop around the torus to come back on itself. For a loop like this, the collapsing process would get stuck.

5. The set of numbers specified in the hint is finite (fewer than n^2, where n is the number of segments) and does not contain zero, so it must have a minimum member which can be used for D. (If you want extra safety, you can always divide by, say, 3.)

6. The secret is to invent a process that can be carried out locally (within a grid square) yet does not violate any global constraints:

• Take a square grid of sidelength equal to the safety zone in exercise 5. Call this the *gross grid*.

• Now move the grid a bit if necessary to make sure that no line has a heading that is a multiple of 45°, that no edge in the grid is divided exactly in half by a segment of the path, and that no vertex lies on the grid. (These conditions ensure no ambiguity in what follows.)

• Consider the two points on the boundary of each square where the path enters and exits and find the smallest distance, s, between these (along the periphery). Add lines to the gross grid to make a finer grid of size less than s.

• Repeat the second step as necessary.

• Except in regions of the grid within vertex-containing gross squares, deform the path to the boundary of the grid squares so that the path enters and leaves the square at the corner of the square closest to its undeformed entry or leaving point and so that the path follows the shortest path along the boundary of the square from entry corner to exit corner.

• Within the remaining gross-grid squares that contain only one vertex and two segments of path (there is now at least one complete grid-square edge between entry and exit points), use any deforming process that links up properly to the entry and exit points. (For example, simply connect the point of entry to the point of exit along the shortest path along the boundary of the gross grid.)

Section 4.4

1. On any run along a particular northward section, the turtle's state must be the same. That means it has a unique future path from there that cannot separate (and come back together).

Chapter 5

Section 5.1

1. We can establish a convention: If the turtle counts left turns as positive, then the inside of the region is the region to the turtle's left; if the turtle counts right turning as positive, then the inside is the region to the right. Observe how this works out consistently with the formula relating excess to area. If the total turning (left turns counted positive) around a curve is T, then the excess will be $2\pi - T$ and the area of the region must be $(2\pi - T)r^2$. If right-hand turning is counted as positive, then the total turning of the same walk will be measured as $-T$, and hence the excess will be $2\pi + T$ and the area $r^2(2\pi + T)$. Thus, the two areas sum to $4\pi r^2$, which is the area of the whole sphere. This is consistent because, by the convention above, we were considering in the two cases areas of the two complementary regions of the sphere which the path creates.

2. Each interior angle is π minus the corresponding exterior angle, so the sum of the interior angles for the triangle is 3π minus the total turning. Putting this together with the area formula implies that the sum of the interior angles is equal to π plus A/r^2, where A is the area of the triangle and r is the radius of the sphere.

6. The problem is that the "change of heading" of anything, such as the "net change of pointer heading" which might be used to determine excess, is only defined modulo 360. However, "total turning" watches the whole process rather than net change of state and can distinguish multiples of 360. That is why the ⟨2π − total turning⟩ form of excess is unambiguous. In the same way, watching the turtle-carrying-pointer process can avoid the ambiguity. One can see the difference between circle and equator (0 and 2π excess) in that during the latter the turtle's line of sight never crosses over the pointer's direction. In general, the particular multiple of 360 can be determined from the number of times the turtle's sight crosses over pointer direction from left to right minus the number of right-to-left crossings.

7. This important relationship reduces turning to a question of distances. Consider a two-wheeled turtle that turns by holding one wheel still while continuing forward on the other. During such a pivot, the extra distance traveled by the moving wheel is just the arc of a circle of radius d ($=$ distance between wheels) having measure θ ($=$ turning of turtle); the extra distance is $d \times \theta$. For a bunch of turns the total extra distance of one wheel over the other will be $d \times \theta_1 + d \times \theta_2 + \cdots = d(\theta_1 + \theta_2 + \cdots) = d \times$ (total turning). The answer to the final question is yes.

8. Using the hint, the excess distance of one lane over the other is (width of track) $\times$ (total turning). For a simple closed track $TT = 2\pi$; for a figure-eight $TT = 0$. These are false in general for a banked track.

Section 5.2

1. The path on the cylinder does not bound a topological disk, so there is no reason for the excess around the path to be the total curvature of the interior.

2. Locally, all such surfaces are rolled sheets of paper. Now a roll can be thought of as a bunch of small-angled folds along lines (or line segments, if the line goes off the sheet), and this preserves the nonintersecting property of parallel lines or segments immediately on either side of the fold. In general this suggests that any surface that can be decomposed into a (necessarily infinite) collection of straight lines or segments that don't meet (these are the fold lines) is flat. Such a surface is called a *ruled surface*. If you don't allow kinks such as would arise if two folds meet at a point, any flat surface is ruled.

3. The outside (longest) path and the inside (shortest) path are both turtle lines. The path along the top is not. You can see this by using the same reasoning we used to decide that the equator of a sphere is the only line of latitude that can be a turtle line: Compare the length of the paths trod by the turtle's left and right legs.

4. Suppose that P and Q are two different subdivisions of the surface into topological disks. We have to prove that the sum of the excesses over the boundaries of P is equal to the corresponding sum for Q. So make an even finer subdivision R of the surface into topological disks such that each piece in P is a sum of pieces in R, so that each piece of Q is a sum of pieces in R, and so that in forming pieces of P or Q out of pieces of R we can use the "join two pieces at a time along a single

arc" method (which is what is needed to make the additivity theorem true). All of this can be done if we are willing to make the pieces of R small enough. Now we can apply the additivity theorem to conclude that, for each piece of P, the excess around the boundary is equal to the sum of the excess of the pieces of R that make up that piece of P. Therefore, the total sum of *all* the excesses of all the pieces of P is equal to the total sum of all the excesses of all the pieces of R. By the same reasoning, the sum of the excesses of the pieces of Q is also equal to the sum of the excesses of the pieces of R, and hence equal to the sum for P.

5. A tin can has curvature along its rim (see subsection 5.3.2).

6. A radial circle about a general point on a cone (not the tip) is not a turtle circle if the tip of the cone is interior to it. On spheres, radial circles are the same as turtle circles.

7. A football has an equator (equidistant from the football's "points") which divides it into two topological disks of excess 2π each.

8. The total curvature of the cube is 4π. The curvature density is zero everywhere except at the vertices. There is $\pi/2$ curvature concentrated at each vertex.

10. Scaling the surface doesn't change any angles, and so doesn't change the excess of any path. Therefore, the total curvature K is unchanged, since this can be computed using excess. The area of the surface changes by s^2, and, since curvature density k is equal to excess per unit area, k must be multiplied by $1/s^2$.

11. A smaller scale model cone can be thought of as just part of the original cone. But since it contains all the curvature of the original, the remaining part of the cone is left with no curvature. Continuing the shrinkage, no part of the cone, except the tip, can have any curvature.

12. From exercise 6 of section 5.1,

$$TT = \frac{\text{Excess distance}}{\text{Width of turtle}}$$
$$= (2/100) \times (\text{length of walk}).$$

Walking a circle on a plane has $TT = 2\pi$; length of walk $= 100\pi$. A 25-turtle-step walk makes 1/2 radian turning; Excess $= 2\pi - \frac{1}{2}$. For a 400-step walk the excess is negative, $-(8 - 2\pi)$.

15. If you fill in the holes you have a topological disk whose total curvature is the excess around its boundary, $E(B)$. Cutting out the holes removes topological disks with total curvature given by the excesses around their boundaries, $E(H_1), E(H_2), \ldots$, leaving $E(B) - E(H_1) - E(H_2) - \cdots$ as the total curvature of the surface with holes.

16. Except for the tip, which has concentrated positive curvature, all curvature is concentrated along sews. Moving along the edge of one of the pieces, a turtle can tell positive curvature from negative according to whether it has to turn toward or away from the interior of the piece. Accordingly, there is positive curvature where an edge is locally convex and negative where an edge is locally concave.

18. Ω is precisely the angle excess around the boundary of A.

Section 5.3

1. Make a cut that goes through the tip.

2. The surface has the same total curvature as it would if the handle were not knotted. You can see this by chopping the knotted handle in two, untying the knot without deforming near the chop, and regluing.

3. If we allow extrinsic information, a simple answer can be given as follows: Consider a turtle walking along a line of symmetry of the dent (radially). The change in steepness of the grade the turtle is walking along correlates directly with curvature. Getting steeper means negative curvature, constant steepness is zero, and getting less steep means positive.

4. Certainly. Take a cylinder and bend it around on itself without deforming near the boundary, then glue the two boundary circles together to make a torus.

5. The measures are subtracted since in the rectangle argument the turtle would be traversing the arc in opposite directions on opposite sides. If two turtles traverse the arc in the same direction on opposite sides, one of them will get the negative of the amount of turning which needs to be added. To avoid deciding which to subtract from which, add the measures, but take turning to be positive if it is toward the arc (that is, if the arc is on the turtle's left, left turns count positive) and negative otherwise.

6. The proof assumed that the turtle can trek the same path (or an equivalent one) in traversing the common arc for measuring each path.

Thus, the excess-additivity theorem will work provided the turning along the common arc is well-defined; that is, provided it is the same immediately on either side of the arc (where the turtles must tread when measuring the pieces individually).

7. The surface is topologically a sphere, and hence it has total curvature 4π. There are twelve cubelike vertices, each with concentrated curvature $\pi/2$. The remaining four vertices, where the two cubes are joined, each have concentrated curvature $-\pi/2$.

8. If we require the torus to be "smooth" (having no abrupt changes in curvature), then the answer is yes. Since the torus has zero total curvature, if there is a region of positive curvature density there must also be a region of negative curvature density to balance this out. And if the curvature varies smoothly, there must be a place of zero curvature density on any path between the regions. But if we allow the curvature to vary abruptly (for example, if we make a torus out of pieces which are joined together so as to produce concentrated curvature), then this is no longer true. For example, rather than forming a torus by pasting together two cylinders as in figure 5.24, form the torus out of two flanged handles. We can choose each handle to have negative curvature density everywhere. So the resulting torus will have negative curvature density everywhere except along the arcs where the handles meet, which will have concentrated (positive) curvature. See exercise 10.

9. Remove a flat disk from each sphere and connect the holes with a handle. The result is topologically equivalent to a single sphere. Equating total curvature and using the fact that the disks are flat shows that the total curvature of a handle must be minus the total curvature of a sphere.

10. The resulting surface is topologically equivalent to a single handle, and hence it has total curvature -4π. Therefore, there must be 4π of curvature concentrated along the circle.

12. We give a proof which follows the outline in the hint: Choose any point p that does not lie on the surface. Since the surface does not run off to infinity, there is some point on the surface that is farthest from p. Call this point q. We claim that the surface has positive curvature density at q. To see this, imagine rotating both p and the surface so that q lies directly above p. Then, near q, the surface must look like a hill with q as the highest point. According to the prescription given in exercise 9 of section 5.2, hills indicate positive curvature density.

13. We know from the previous exercise that there is some point on the surface where the curvature density is positive. But there are no points of negative curvature density to cancel this positive contribution. Therefore, the total curvature must be strictly positive. At the same time, we know that the surface must be topologically equivalent to a sphere with some number of handles attached. But even one handle would be enough to cancel out the total curvature of the sphere, and more than one handle would give negative total curvature. So the only possibility is that the surface is a sphere with zero handles attached.

15. Examples like this violate the intuitive sense of what faces, edges, and vertices should be. They also cause problems in stating certain theorems (see the discussion of Euler characteristic in chapter 8). If you insist that faces be topological disks bounded by simple topological arcs (no intersections) which are in turn bounded by points (vertices), and faces only meet along a series of arcs, that excludes viewing this object as a Platonic solid.

17. -4π. The proof that adding a handle reduces curvature by 4π works whenever you can add the handle without deforming any part of the original surface near a boundary. This is a plane with a handle attached.

Chapter 6

Section 6.1

1. The vanishing of the denominator means that the two line segments are parallel. Thus, CHECK.EDGE should look at the denominator before computing MU and return "NO INTERSECTION" if it is zero. Observe that the denominators in the expressions for LAMBDA and MU are the same except for sign; one will vanish if and only if the other one does too. So only one zero check is necessary.

5. Each of the two line segments is contained in an infinite line. Values of λ and μ outside of the 0–1 range mean that the lines intersect at points outside of the designated segments. Negative values correspond to points on the line before the initial point of the segment. Values greater than 1 correspond to points on the line after the endpoint of the segment.

Chapter 7

2. Because of the symmetry in the arguments, POLY (α, β) cannot have more vertices than POLY (β, α), just as the reverse cannot be so. The only remaining possibility is equal number of vertices.

4. They have the same θ but not the same axis of rotation. Note that the time-reversed action, RIGHT β, BACK α, has the same axis as FORWARD α, LEFT β. Now perform the following operation on the entire sphere-plus-axes system: Rotate the FORWARD axis 90° until it coincides with the original LEFT axis. Now reflect the whole thing in the plane of the original FORWARD and LEFT axes. This action has the net effect of turning RIGHT β, BACK α into FORWARD β, LEFT α and carrying the axis of the former (also the axis of FORWARD α, LEFT β) into the axis of FORWARD β, LEFT α.

5. For stars the formula should be $n \times 2\pi - \text{Area}/R^2$, where n is the rotation number and the area is given as follows: Imagine tying a rubber band to the turtle and to a pivot at the center of the POLY figure. The appropriate area is what is swept out by this rubber band as the turtle draws the POLY. Thus, for a 5-pointed star the area of the central pentagon is counted twice.

7. Radius of curvature $= (1/R) \times \cot(r/R)$; $TT = \sqrt{(2\pi)^2 - (c/R)^2}$.

9. After deriving the formula in radians, just change units by multiplying every angle in the formula by the appropriate conversion factor. But then you can cancel that conversion factor out of the formula. (This is because all terms in the formula are angles raised to the same power. You could not cancel the factors if the formula included other terms, say, angles cubed or constants.)

16. $n = 2\pi/\theta = 2\pi/\sqrt{a^2 + b^2}$; $TT = n\beta = 2\pi\beta/\sqrt{a^2 + b^2}$; $c = n\alpha R = 2\pi\alpha R/\sqrt{a^2 + b^2}$. To show consistency, check $(TT)^2 + (c/R)^2 = (2\pi)^2$ and compare with exercise 7.

17. Consider two vertices coinciding at the north pole and their corresponding equators. We are going to move one vertex away from the other to make them the ends of one side of the original triangle. As one vertex moves away from the north pole a distance α, its corresponding equator tilts an angle α from its initial plane, and hence the tilting equator makes an angle α with the equator of the other vertex. That angle between tilting equators is one angle in the polar triangle. The

other two angles of the polar triangle match the measures of the other two sides of the original triangle in the same way.

Chapter 8

Section 8.1

8. You need n squares to make an n-holed torus. If you have S squares and identify edges so that there is only one distinct vertex on the surface, then that vertex will have total turning $2\pi S$ and hence excess $2\pi(1-S)$. This is the most negative curvature you can produce with S squares. (Verify that.) But an n-holed torus has total curvature $2\pi(1-n)$, so S must be at least n. Conversely, if you do identify the edges of n squares so that there is only one vertex, you will get an n-holed torus. (This assumes that the identifications preserve orientation; see section 8.2.)

9. Consider a polygon with sides labeled counterclockwise consecutively $1, 2, 3, \ldots, 4n$ and identified 1 to 3, 2 to 4, 5 to 7, 6 to 8, and so on. (The most counterclockwise end of 1 is identified with the most clockwise end of 3, etc.) By following a path around "vertices" you will find one real vertex with a total turning of $2\pi(2n-1)$, for an excess of $4\pi(1-n)$.

11. Surprisingly, the answer is no. Near a vertex of negative curvature, the "shortest distance" may force the turtle to walk through a vertex. The resulting path is not a turtle line. (It is, however, two turtle lines joined.)

15. If we use the second method suggested in the hint on any part of the glued segment, except one including an endpoint, there will be no turning on either side (since the sides are straight); hence, $0 - 0 = 0$ curvature.

16. The line between the pieces can be modeled as follows: It really consists of two parallel lines infinitesimally separated, with each have the same (infinite) curvature concentrated on them, but of opposite sign. Thus, if you measure curvature of the "edge" by paths crossing perpendicular to the edge, the $+$ and the $-$ curvature cancel. If you cut at an angle you will include different lengths of $+$ and $-$ and wind up seeing a net curvature. This problem taxed our ingenuity at understanding it in terms of curvature. We developed the above model by first sticking a trapezoid between long and short identified segments (to match each), then making a wedge map (chapter 9) of this, and imagining shrinking the height of the trapezoid to zero.

Section 8.2

1. We use a more compact notation for identifications; abc denotes that side a is glued to side b with transition parity having sign c. Spheres: $[12 + 34 +]$, $[14 + 23 +]$. Projective planes: $[12 - 34 +]$, $[12 + 34 -]$, $[14 - 23 +]$, $[14 + 23 -]$, $[13 - 24 -]$. Klein bottles: $[12 - 34 -]$, $[14 - 23 -]$, $[13 + 24 -]$, $[13 - 24 +]$. Torus: $[13 + 24 +]$. Some of these, while topologically the same, are geometrically distinguishable (for example, the first and last projective planes).

2. Simply count total turning around the vertices as in subsection 8.1.4. You'll find that the Klein bottle has only one vertex, with total turning 2π, and hence excess 0. Thus, the bottle is flat at the vertex as well as everywhere else.

3. The projective plane has two vertices, each with total turning π, and hence excess π. Thus, the total curvature is 2π. You should verify that any straight line through the center of the square in figure 8.22 represents a closed path on the projective plane which confuses left and right.

5. Let "left" mean counterclockwise as viewed from above in the standard atlas layout of separate faces. Within each face the turtle can never suddenly change orientation. Can crossing an edge confuse the global definition? Consider a turtle leaving a face (its left foreleg will be pointing counterclockwise around the boundary). An orientation-preserving gluing finds the turtle coming onto a (possibly) new face with its left foreleg pointing clockwise around the boundary. But since the turtle is now facing toward the center rather than away, this is no contradiction of the global definition.

6. A torus.

8. Only one closed connected surface can be made with two squares but not with one—it is nonorientable, with total curvature -2π.

Section 8.3

2. A net on a handle has $\chi = 0$, but removing two holes from the surface in order to glue the handle in place reduces F by 2. Thus adding a handle decreases the Euler characteristic by 2.

4. The problem is that removing the edge destroys the property of being a net; it is not an elementary operation. In the second net, region III is no longer a topological disk.

6. Since the edges of the faces are identified in pairs, the total number of edges in the surface will be $nF/2$. Hence, the Euler characteristic $V - E + F$ will be equal to $V + F(1 - n/2)$.

7. $V = 1$ is possible, giving a minimum of $2\pi(1 - F)$. If only connected surfaces are allowed, the maximum is 4π. Otherwise, $4\pi F$ is possible.

8. A face with $2n$ sides has a maximum of 4π and minimum of $4\pi - 2\pi n$.

11. Any proof that $K = 2\pi\chi$ will need to use the fact that a small neighborhood of any point on the surface is a topological disk. (Otherwise, curvature will not even be well defined.) Any neighborhood of the common vertex in the double cube looks like two cones glued at their vertices—which is not a topological disk.

12. Adding a crosscap decreases the total curvature by 2π and always makes the surface unorientable. A sphere with a crosscap added is a projective plane. Adding two crosscaps gives a Klein bottle.

14. $\chi = F(1 - S(\frac{1}{2} - \frac{1}{T}))$. You will find a solution for each Platonic solid plus a class of solutions $T = 2$, $F = 2$, $S =$ anything. These last correspond to two identical polygons glued along their boundary, and contain no volume. In ordinary three-dimensional space the glued faces must coincide entirely when the gluing is performed.

15. $\chi_{\text{local}} = 0$ implies $S(\frac{1}{2} - \frac{1}{T}) = 1$. Solutions are $T = 3$, $S = 6$; $T = 4$, $S = 4$; and $T = 6$, $S = 3$.

16. To see that $S = 5$ is impossible, note that in trying to draw it you always wind up with a "complete" net which cannot be added to in any way. This particular "complete" net can be formed by stretching open one face of a dodecahedron so that you can lay down the whole net on a plane. To see that $T = 3$, $S = 8$ is possible, see p.235 of *The World of M. C. Escher* (New York: Abrams, 1972). (Look at the picture and imagine stretching the edges of the disk out to cover the whole plane.)

Chapter 9

Section 9.1

1. If s and c denote the sine and cosine of r/R, GAPRATIO $= r/Rs - 1$ and TURNING.PER.ANGLE $= 1 - c$.

2. Equation (3) remains true, but with CENTRAL.ANGLE computed in degrees. TURNING.PER.ANGLE is given by $1 - \cos(180r/\pi R)$, and one

possible formula for CENTRAL.ANGLE is $180/\pi$ times that given in the text. Take $R = 180/\pi$ to get distance to be the same as angle in degrees.

4. Demon turning and leaping are opposite to the direction they were in before. Now wedges overlap, but the simulation will still work if you make the necessary backward leaps and negative demon turning.

8. Because of leaping, the turtle's heading doesn't point tangent to the path. As the gap ratio changes, this difference in angle between heading and tangent to path changes; paths still look somewhat bent on the map.

9. Imagine a turtle with one wheel at r and one at $r + \Delta r$. The formula pointed out in the hint gives $(C(r + \Delta r) - C(r))/\Delta r$ for total turning. In the limit of small turtle this is dC/dr.

10. **LEAP** = GAPRATIO $\times$ ($\mathbf{x} \cdot$ **REALWALK**) $\times$ $\mathbf{x}$. In x,y coordinates, **LEAP** = (GAPRATIO $\times$ REALWALKX, 0). GAPRATIO = $(2\pi R - C(r))/C(r)$; DEMON.TURNING = $\Delta x \times$ TURNING.PER.MAPX, where Δx is the change in map x coordinate in the walk. TURNING.PER.MAPX = $(1/R)\sin(y/R)$, where y is the y coordinate on the map.

14. Any reasonable definition for an equator will provide for two of them which are the inside and outside boundary circles if you cut a torus like a bagel. (In addition, you might allow an infinite class which are slices in a perpendicular plane; however, that claim made in the problem is false for that class.) To prove the claim, run two turtles forward and backward simultaneously from the center equator of figure 9.7 until they get to the other equator, which is the edge of the map. The two pieces together are a map image of a complete walk from the second equator back to itself. Because of the symmetry of the wedge map, demon turning above and below the central equator must be the same in magnitude but opposite in sign, thus canceling out on the whole path.

Section 9.2

1. It means nothing at all. How fast you draw a map changes nothing about the world.

2. The speed is the ratio of distance traveled per time,

$$v = \sqrt{H_x{}^2 + H_y{}^2}/H_t.$$

In components, $\mathbf{v} = (H_x/H_t, H_y/H_t)$.

4. A soap bubble "wants to shrink" to the minimum surface area subject to the constraint of containing its fixed volume of air. A large bubble

will find it attractive to enclose the whole region, as it can hold all its air, but with a reduced surface area. Thus it will be "pulled into the region" by its own surface tension. Small bubbles will generally be attracted toward regions of highest positive curvature, where more volume will be contained with a given surface area. You can think about this correlation of curvature with the relation of surface area and volume by analogy with two dimensions. There, the area (analog of volume) contained within a circle of a given circumference (analog of surface) around the tip of a cone gets bigger as the curvature of the cone increases.

5. You can distinguish the "temperature world" from curved geometry *only* because different materials generally expand unequally in response to heat. The wedge map of the hill could not be simulated by a temperature world, as the local stretch depends on direction. Circles are stretched, but radial lines are not, and temperature doesn't have such directionality. On the other hand, there is a plane-like temperature world that is a perfect sphere (except for one point). This is the stereographic projection (figure 7.14), which, it turns out, does locally expand the same in any direction as in any other. The uniform-heating story (that if everything expands uniformly, rulers included, the world is totally indistinguishable from what it was before) has important implications: Intrinsic geometry is the effect of *inhomogeneity* of "lengths," changes from one region to a neighboring one. Absolute length, like absolute temperature, is not determinable in any geometric way. Only relative expansion produces intrinsically observable effects.

7. Even before the board gets a significant area inside the region (and suffers problems like the side-on attack), the first part of the board that enters the region will be "bent" concave inward. This will conflict with the flat configuration maintained by the rest of the board.

Section 9.3

1. 100 miles per hour corresponds to 1.5×10^{-7} radians away from vertical on the map.

2. Sam is older by GAPRATIO times John's aging. If the world were such that GAPRATIO were huge (it isn't), you could visit the distant future. But you couldn't return to the present.

3. A small red shift (or, more accurately, a small change in red shift) means a small deflection angle per map time unit. But even a small deflection angle β rotates a vector representing a time change of t (on a

clock) to have a spatial component βct. This follows from the convention that $45°$ is the speed of light and from our description of Lorentz rotations using that convention. The moral is that a small bit of time is worth a whole lot of space.

5. LROTATE$_\beta(x, t) = (x + \beta t, t + \beta x)$. If $x = \pm t$ (the speed of light) it is easy to check that the rotated vector is just a scaled version of the original and hence is invariant in direction. In the first quadrant and time-like—$t, x > 0$ and $t > x$—the above formula shows that the x component increases more than the t; that is, the vector is rotated clockwise. If $x > t$ (spacelike), the t component increases more than x (counterclockwise rotation). Other cases follow similar analyses.

6. Take the case $t > x > 0$, as above. The difference in the t and x components of the rotated vector is $(t - x)(1 - \beta)$, which is greater than zero provided $\beta < 1$. Thus, this timelike vector remains timelike, $t > x$, for any small rotation and sequence of rotations. Other cases follow with similar analyses.

7. Tachyons' paths will still be bent by spatial curvature the same as anything else. But since their heading is spacelike, they get velocity deflected away (repelled) by spacetime curvature. Which effect (attraction or repulsion) predominates is a matter for calculation in particular circumstances. Could it be that the second effect explains why no tachyons have been observed on earth (they've all been blown away by gravity)?

8. On a sphere, there is no way of justifying one turtle's point of view over another. But in a curved world in which geometry is flat far away from the gravitating center, all turtles that stay far from the curved region will agree on who is deflected how much.

9. Gravity (including spatial bending) gets weaker the farther out you go. But any orbit has *increased* spatial curvature as the orbiting object approaches its farthest point and starts "falling back" toward the sun. Thus, if an orbit is the least bit noncircular, spatial bending could not make it come closer to the sun again after starting to move away.

10. One can construct a straight line by piling up a stack of flat poker chips. Constant thickness at the edge of the disk replaces the two-dimensional criterion of constant step length at the edges of the turtle. A straight wire is one that can be decomposed into such flat disks. Most physicists believe that all the laws of nature, like those governing the propagation of light, are local in nature. Anything can respond only to what is nearby. If this is true (all current theories of light are local) and

the experimental observation that light goes locally straight is precise, then we would be certain that light anywhere (globally) follows turtle lines.

11. Look at the world line of a message from origin to receipt on a wedge map. As long as the geometry and the message mechanism don't change in time (it would be silly to watch for the first tick and listen for the next), the delay is some constant map time interval. Thus, the receipts of messages are just shifted up the map by a constant delay from transmissions, and the interval between receipts is independent of delay. This provides a red-shift measurement identical to that of the insert-and-remove-watch experiment.

12. Send two laser pulses out simultaneously from the center of a board toward each end. The pulses reaching receivers at the ends of the board are two simultaneous events; that is, they are purely spacelike. Observed from a moving frame of reference, Lorentz rotations predict a rotation in spacetime (of the vector pointing from one event to the other) which will pick up a time component. Thus, one of the events (the one at the end in the direction of observer motion) will have been observed *later*. This change in simultaneity is an important effect of Special Relativity.

13. In x, y, t coordinates consider a lightlike vector $(0, 1, 1)$. Now make a Lorentz rotation in the x, t plane (which leaves the y coordinate invariant); x becomes $x + \beta t$ and t becomes $t + \beta x$. The resulting heading $(\beta, 1, 1 + \beta)$ has a different spatial direction $(\beta, 1)$ from the original $(0, 1)$. It has deflected.

14. You can always make particles travel in nonstraight lines by applying forces, just as a normal turtle's turn commands make it travel in nonstraight lines. In particular, a particle at rest with respect to the global criterion of distance from the center of the earth is actually being deflected away from its natural, locally straight path (natural path = falling). In demon terms, your hand is supplying a force (turning) which is canceling out demon turning to produce a map-straight line. In fact, the curvature of the deflected path you are causing (turning / length of world line) is proportional to the force you need apply. The proportionality constant turns out to be the mass of the particle, and thus we see that Newton's law $F = ma$ is replaced by $F = mk$, where k is the spacetime curvature of the path. Einstein's metaphor for this situation was that inside an accelerating elevator you accuse an object in your hand of pushing on you, whereas in actuality you are pushing on it to make it accelerate with the elevator. The analogy is precise,

because standing on the surface of the earth, you *are* accelerating (being deflected from your natural path).

Section 9.4

1. The step should scale the vector so that the t component is a constant. [HX HY HT] ← (constant/HT) × [HX HY HT].

2. Consider a circular orbit, and set up coordinates so position is $(r, 0, t)$ and heading is $(0, v, c)$. We are going to make sure the spatial projection of the heading vector remains perpendicular to the position vector, a condition which will ensure circularity. Step one unit of time, which adds heading to position and Lorentz-rotates heading in the x, t plane by $\text{HEADING}_T \times (-m/r^2) = -mc/r^2$. This gives a new position $(r, v, t+c)$ and new heading $(-mc^2/r^2, v, c)$. The pure spatial parts of these are (r, v) and $(-mc^2/r^2, v)$. To be perpendicular the dot product of these must be 0: $-mc^2/r + v^2 = 0$. Thus, $m = (v/c)^2 r$.

8. It is as read on the clock of any observer far from the center, where the gaps are tiny and spacetime is flat.

9. The experienced elapsed time becomes small as the velocity approaches the speed of light. This adds to the time-interval distortion to make a fast, close-to-the-sun orbiter experience very little time compared with a slow, faraway observer.

10. We use MKS units, so the radius of the region is about 0.1 meter. The time unit on the map corresponding to a spatial unit of 1 meter is in clock time: $1/c \approx 3 \times 10^{-9}$ seconds (see subsection 9.4.4). Now if a thin wedge of thickness T time units thins to $T/2$ (roughly as shown in the figure 9.14) in 0.1 meter, then it must have a maximum slope angle of at least $T/0.1 = 10T$. That's roughly the turning needed from wedge to wedge, so TURNING.PER.TIME is equal to turning/wedgethickness, which is rougly equal to 10. That means a rotation of one radian in 0.1 time units. Since 1 radian means a change in speed from rest to a significant fraction of the speed of light, we get an acceleration roughly equal to ⟨speed acquired⟩/time, or $10c$ meters per second per map time unit. Converting to velocity per second (rather than per map unit) gives numerically $10c^2 \approx 10^{18}$ m/sec², which is 10^{17} times the acceleration of gravity.

11. In n revolutions we want a demon turning of 1°, $360GMn/rc^2 = 1$. n is about 4 million orbits, roughly 680 years of orbiting near the surface of the earth.

Index